SPECULUM VITAE: A READING EDITION

EARLY ENGLISH TEXT SOCIETY
No. 331
2008

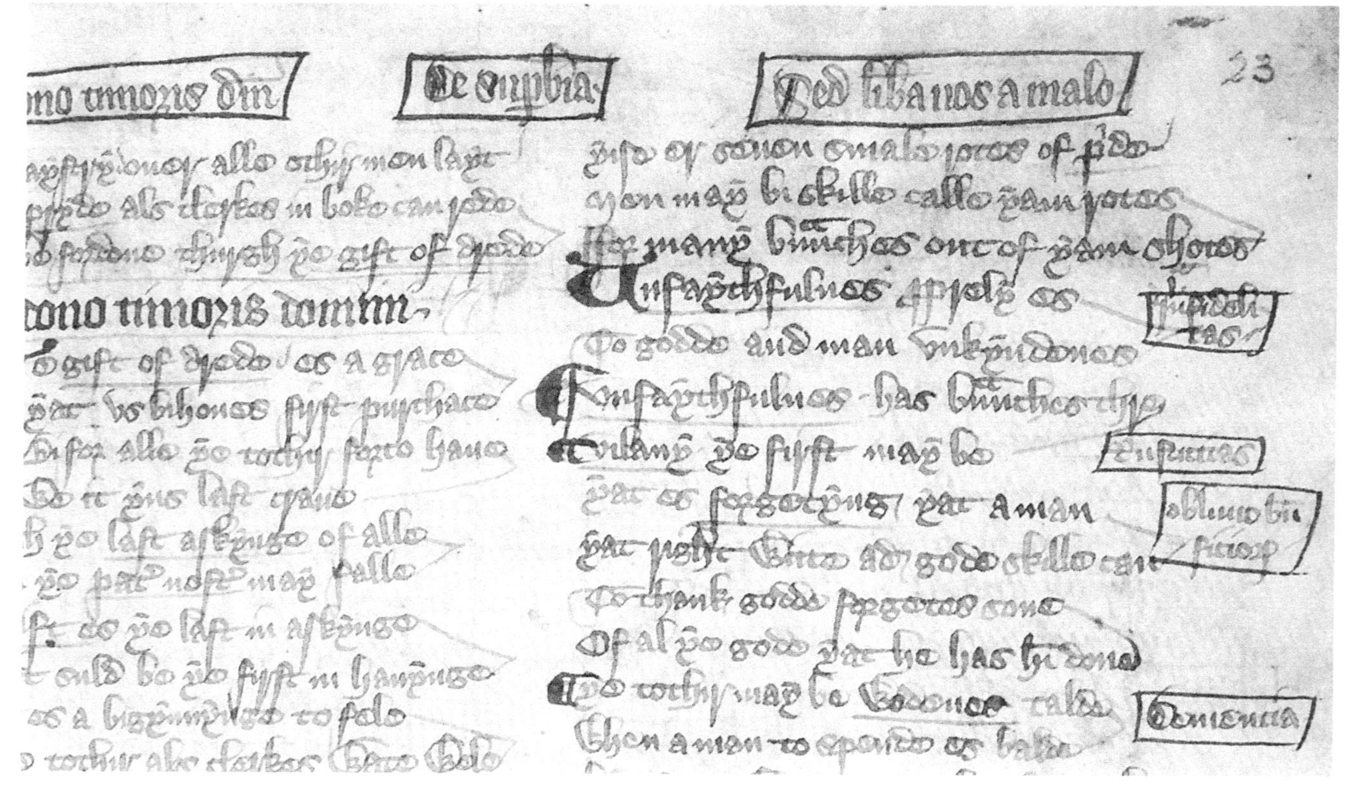

British Library, MS Additional 33995, fo. 23r (top).
Reproduced by permission of the British Library

SPECULUM VITAE:
A READING EDITION

EDITED BY

RALPH HANNA
using materials assembled by Venetia Somerset

VOLUME I

Published for
THE EARLY ENGLISH TEXT SOCIETY
by the
OXFORD UNIVERSITY PRESS

Great Clarendon Street, Oxford OX2 6DP
United Kingdom

Oxford University Press is a department of the University of Oxford. It furthers the University's objective of excellence in research, scholarship, and education by publishing worldwide. Oxford is a registered trade mark of Oxford University Press in the UK and in certain other countries

First Edition published in 2008

Published in the United States of America by Oxford University Press
198 Madison Avenue, New York, NY 10016, United States of America

British Library Cataloguing in Publication Data
Data available

Library of Congress Cataloging in Publication Data
Data available

Original Series, 331

Set ISBN 978-0-19-956401-9

Vol. 1 ISBN 978-0-19-956399-9
Vol. 2 ISBN 978-0-19-956400-2

PREFACE

This is a thoroughly collaborative effort, one I should never have undertaken without the contributions of a great many people. I have had a fascination with this poem for more than twenty years, one certainly piqued by protracted experiences, in the services of another Society edition, with one of the manuscripts central here, that at Princeton. But only a happy coincidence of circumstances finally led me to believe that I could approach editing it in any form.

My principal debt (and inspiration) is to the poem's longest and most careful student, Venetia Somerset (who published on *Speculum Vitae* as Venetia Nelson). Although having long given up these interests for alpaca farming in the bush of New South Wales, she has been unfailingly generous to her followers in the project, and I have ultimately reaped the benefit of her learning and enthusiasm. Some years ago, Somerset passed on her materials—including a nearly full collection of microfilms and a copy of her Sydney Ph.D. dissertation—to Matthew Sullivan, then at Aberystwyth and subsequently head of English at Marlborough College. Through his generosity, I have, in my turn, inherited the benefits of Somerset's devotion to the poem (including the loan of the dissertation copy, now Anne Hudson's). Since, as will emerge, this edition will scarcely provide a definitive study of the text of *Speculum Vitae*, I have emulated Somerset in leaving all her materials to future researchers; they are on deposit in the English Faculty Library, University of Oxford.

Secondly, I owe an immense debt to Dr Christine Robinson, Department of English Language, University of Edinburgh. Robinson, who prepared the file as part of her Ph.D. work, gave me access to her unusually accurate transcription of British Library, MS Additional 33995. This valuable electronic resource, available on the Oxford Text Archive, saved me a vast amount of effort at transcription (always a major excuse not to attempt this volume). Robinson's work, corrected and expanded to include the Latin materials of the manuscript, forms the basis for the edition that follows. In addition, I am grateful to her for drawing my attention to the Scots fragment of the poem in Bodleian Library, MS Rawlinson Q.b.4.

I owe a further central debt to the deeply missed Pamela Gradon and to her friend and executor Anne Hudson. Pamela, in the process of annotating Dan Michel of Northgate's *Ayenbite of Inwyt*, the oldest Middle English translation of the French text underlying *Speculum Vitae*, work that appeared as the splendid Early English Text Society 278 (1979), amassed a vast amount of material on the French text. Anne passed this archive on to me, including photographic facsimiles of the copy of Lorens's *Somme* to which I make frequent reference.

There are a further series of smaller, but important, indebtednesses to record. Ian Doyle, with his usual generosity, provided me with photocopies of James D. Gordon's correspondence on the descent of the text. That indefatigable troller of local record offices, Thorlac Turville-Petre, found the Stafford fragments of the poem and told me about them. Prof. Toshiyuki Takamiya lent me a facsimile of his manuscript of the poem. Linne Mooney, engaged in a meticulous electronic *Index of Middle English Verse* based on examination of the manuscripts, shared references to copies. Siegfried Wenzel offered advice on the fate of Gordon's work with the poem (which seems to have been incomplete and certainly to have disappeared totally). Leo Carruthers gave me a copy of his inaccessible monograph on *The Book of Vices and Virtues*, probably the best-known Middle English Lorens translation. Jill Havens tracked down and sent another inaccessible study of the poem for me. I also owe thanks to the organizers of two conferences who forced me to formulate for oral presentation what have become portions of the introduction: to Sally Mapstone and Alasdair MacDonald (the conference 'Religion in England and the Low Countries in the Late Middle Ages', St Hilda's College, Oxford, March 2003) and to Robin Gilbank (the conference 'Northern English Religious Writers', Gregynog, July 2006). In addition, Sally pointed out to me Rod Lyall's discussion of a second Scots fragment of the poem, at Edinburgh University Library, and reminded me of Thomas Ireland's indebtedness to *Somme le roi*. I acknowledge with pleasure the English Faculty, University of Oxford, and my colleagues at Keble College, whose grants of study leave have enabled me to bring this partial edition to conclusion.

Finally, submission to and publication by the Early English Text Society has produced further indebtednesses. Derek Pearsall has been a good-tempered, provocative, and careful reader of the script; in addition, at an early point in my researches, he passed on to me a copy of Nelson's Sydney thesis, which he had from Elizabeth Salter.

Helen Spencer and Bonnie Blackburn have subjected the script to their unusually helpful ministrations; their painstaking interest in format and consistency has made the volume a great deal better than the script EETS originally received. And Anne Joshua, as she has twice before, demonstrated her customary cheerful perseverence in dealing with messy files in antiquated computer language.

R.H.
St Mark's Day, 2007

CONTENTS OF VOLUME I

ABBREVIATIONS

I. WORKS FREQUENTLY CITED

Bestiary — *Bestiarium: Fac-simile du manuscrit du bestiaire Ashmole 1511 . . .*, ed. Xenia Muratova et al., 2 vols. (Paris, 1984)

BL — The British Library, London

Bloomfield — Morton W. Bloomfield et al., *Incipits of Latin Works on the Virtues and Vices, 1100–1500 A.D.* (Cambridge, Mass., 1979)

BodL — The Bodleian Library, Oxford

Briquet — C.-M. Briquet, *Les Filigranes: Dictionnaire historique des marques du papier des leur apparition vers 1292 jusqu'en 1600. A Facsimile of the 1907 Edition with Supplementary Material Contributed by a Number of Scholars*, ed. Allan Stevenson, 4 vols. (Amsterdam, 1968)

BVV — *The Book of Vices and Virtues*, ed. W. Nelson Francis, EETS 217 (London, 1942)

CUL — Cambridge, University Library

Cursor — *Cursor Mundi: A Northumbrian Poem of the XIVth Century*, ed. Richard Morris, 7 vols., EETS OS 57, 59, 62, 66, 68, 99, 101 (London, 1874–93)

Gradon — *Dan Michel's Ayenbite of Inwyt*, ii: *Introduction, Notes and Glossary*, ed. Pamela Gradon, EETS 278 (Oxford, 1979)

IMEV — Carleton Brown and Rossell Hope Robbins, *The Index of Middle English Verse* (New York, 1943), with Robbins and John L. Cutler, *Supplement to IMEV* (Lexington, Ky., 1965)

IPMEP — R. E. Lewis, N. F. Blake, and A. S. G. Edwards, *Index of Printed Middle English Prose* (New York, 1985)

Jolliffe — P. S. Jolliffe, *A Check-List of Middle English Prose Writings of Spiritual Guidance* (Toronto, 1974)

Ker, *MLGB* — N. R. Ker, *Medieval Libraries of Great Britain: A List of Surviving Books*, RHS Guides and Hand-

	books, 3 (2nd edn., London, 1964), with Andrew G. Watson, *MLGB Supplement*, RHS Guides and Handbooks, 15 (London, 1987)
Ker, *MMBL*	N. R. Ker (vol. 4 with A. J. Piper), *Medieval Manuscripts in British Libraries*, 4 vols. (Oxford, 1969–92)
LALME	Angus McIntosh, M. L. Samuels, and Michael Benskin, *A Linguistic Atlas of Late Mediaeval English*, 4 vols. (Aberdeen, 1986)
Legenda	Iacopo da Varezze, *Legenda Aurea*, ed. Giovanni P. Maggioni, 2 vols. (2nd edn., Tavarnuzze [Florence], 1998)
Lewis–McIntosh	Robert E. Lewis and Angus McIntosh, *A Descriptive Guide to the Manuscripts of the* Prick of Conscience, Medium Ævum Monographs, NS 12 (Oxford, 1982)
Piccard	Gerhard Piccard, *Die Wasserzeichenkartei Piccard im Hauptstadtsarchiv Stuttgart: Findbuch*, 17 vols. to date (Stuttgart, 1961–)
Piers B	William Langland, *Piers Plowman: The B Version . . .*, ed. George Kane and E. Talbot Donaldson (London, 1975)
PL	Patrologia Latina
Prick	*The Pricke of Conscience (Stimulus Conscientiae): A Northumbrian Poem . . .*, ed. Richard Morris (Berlin, 1863)
SC	Falconer Madan et al., *A Summary Catalogue of Western Manuscripts in the Bodleian Library at Oxford*, 7 vols. in 8 (Oxford, 1895–1953)
Walther	Hans Walther, *Proverbia sententiaeque Latinitatis Medii Ævi: Lateinische Sprichwörter . . .*, 5 vols. (Göttingen, 1963–7)
Whiting	Bartlett J. Whiting, *Proverbs, Sentences, and Proverbial Phrases from English Writings Mainly before 1500* (Cambridge, Mass., 1968)

On 15 July 2008, while these volumes were in proof-sheets, La Société des anciens textes français announced the publication of Frère Laurent, *Somme le roi*, ed. Édith Brayer and Anne Françoise Leurquin-Labie (Abbeville, 2008).

2. MANUSCRIPT SIGLA

A	British Library, MS Additional 33995
B^1	Bodleian Library, MS Bodley 48
B^2	Bodleian Library, MS Bodley 446
B^3	Bodleian Library, MS Eng. poet. a.1 ('the Vernon Manuscript')
B^4	Bodleian Library, MS Greaves 43
B^5	Bodleian Library, MS Hatton 18
B^6	Bodleian Library, MS Hatton 19
B^7	Bodleian Library, MS Lyell 28
B^8	Bodleian Library, MS Rawlinson C.884
B^9	Bodleian Library, MS Rawlinson C.890
BSG	Paris, Bibliothèque Ste-Geneviève MS 2899
C	British Library, MS Cotton Cleopatra A.v
E	Bodleian Library, MS Eng. poet. d.5
L	Liverpool University Library, MS F.4.9
P	Princeton University Library, MS Taylor Medieval 11
R	British Library, MS Royal 17 C.viii
S	British Library, MS Stowe 951
W	Aberystwyth, National Library of Wales, MS Peniarth 395

INTRODUCTION

1. *SPECULUM VITAE*

The great unedited piece of Middle English verse is the Yorkshire translation of the *Somme le roi* by Lorens of Orleans, OP, called *Speculum Vitae* (*IMEV* 245). The work, 16,100 lines in four-stress couplets, is extant in more than forty copies; the great majority of these provides reasonably full renditions of the text. But unlike the even more widely promulgated *Prick of Conscience*, available in Richard Morris's 'best text' edition, only small bits of the *Speculum* have ever seen print, most notably Ullman's transcription of the opening 370 lines,[1] several reproductions of the ascription of the work to William of Nassington, and lines 6353–402 from Avarice.[2]

This silence is unfortunate. First of all, the *Speculum* represents an important centre of a generally ignored regional literary culture. In part because of the age of the editions, in part because of editorial difficulties, scholars have overlooked the generative force of Yorkshire verse *c.*1280–1380.[3] The *Speculum* should be available, if only for comparison with other monuments of this tradition, *Cursor Mundi*, *The Prick*, and the (again, largely unedited) *Northern Homily Cycle*.

Second, the work is important as a versification of a too little known[4] medieval instructional classic, Lorens's *Somme*. This lengthy formulation of septenary catechesis was a ceaseless inspiration for Middle English translators.[5] Yet even in this context, the *Speculum*

[1] Ullman, 'Studien zu Richard Rolle de Hampole', 468–72.

[2] *Reliquiae*, ii. 38–9.

[3] To these motives for ignoring this literary culture, one could also add (1) that the poems universally appear to be versified 'papistic' theology of an uninteresting sort, usually (like *Speculum Vitae*), translated, not 'imaginative' and (2) that they do not fit within that London–south-eastern bias that shapes the received national literary tradition.

[4] Although see Tuve, *Allegorical Imagery*, *in extenso*.

[5] See the diagram illustrating the *Speculum* in 'the Vernon MS', fol. 231^{v} (also in colour in the facsimile, pl. xiii); the discussions of Aarts, 'The Pater Noster'; Henry, '"The Pater Noster in a table ypeynted"'; Hussey, 'The Petitions of the Pater Noster'; the facsimile of an earlier, widespread septenary diagram in Sandler, *The Psalter of Robert de Lisle*, 54–5; and n. 42 below.

remains unique: it is the only known translation into verse, and the only known Northern example.[6]

Finally, to an extent unusual with comparable works, the poem was widely influential. There are two fairly complete dérimages, both composed at the edges of the work's circulation, those places where it contacted other local literary cultures. The Suffolk sermon cycle *Jacob's Well* remains only partly edited, but there is, somewhat incongruously, in the absence of any edition of *Speculum Vitae*, a full edition of the derivative *A Myrour to Lewde Men and Wymmen*, a text that appears to have been constructed in northern Gloucestershire.[7] The poem was also recycled in various forms near the area of its Yorkshire composition, as has long been recognized. It inspired 'The Desert of Religion'; the redacted version of Richard Rolle's 'The Ten Commandments' in BodL, MS Hatton 12; and probably the lost York and Beverley 'Pater Noster Plays'.[8]

2. THE MANUSCRIPTS

On the whole, it is time for an edition. This must begin with a presentation of the manuscript evidence for the poem, never thoroughly reported. Given the substantial number of copies, I provide at the head a summary list. Copies here noted without comment are 'substantially complete'; that is, they reproduce more than 12,000 lines of the poem.

[6] As Doyle, 'A Survey of the Origins and Circulation', i. 83, notes, forestalling any other efforts in this region.

[7] On *Jacob's Well* (Salisbury Cathedral, MS 103), in addition to Carruthers variously, see Doyle, 'A Survey of the Origins and Circulation', i. 64 n. 1. The unique manuscript of the work was copied by the same scribe 'Rose' as Cambridge, St John's College, MS B.6 (*The South English Legendary*) and Dulwich College, MS 24 (Robert Manning's *Handling Sin*); for him, see Beadle, 'Prolegomena to a Literary Geography', 104 (nos. 44, 68). Rose provides *LALME* LP 4646 (extreme south-east Norfolk, just north of Bungay). Like scribes of *A Myrour*, Rose carried over a smattering of Northern forms from the Yorkshire *Speculum* MS used as a source by his author. On *A Myrour*, in addition to Nelson's edition, see Stover, 'A Myrour to Lewde Men and Wymmen'.

[8] 'The Desert' (*IMEV* 672) was edited in Hübner, 'The Desert of Religion'; Allen, 'The Desert of Religion: Addendum' first pointed out its dependence upon *Speculum Vitae* (compare ead., *Writings Ascribed to Richard Rolle*, 309). For MS Hatton 12, see EETS 329, pp. lix–lx, 16–18, 136–40. On the lost York and Beverley plays, see Johnston, 'The Plays of the Religious Guilds of York', esp. 70–80; Anderson, *Drama and Imagery*, 60–71; and Wyatt, 'The English Pater Noster Play'.

1. Aberystwyth, National Library of Wales, MS Peniarth 395
2. Cambridge, University Library, MS Ff.iv.9
3. Cambridge, University Library, MS Gg.i.7
4. Cambridge, University Library, MS Gg.i.14
5. Cambridge, University Library, MS Ii.i.36
6. Cambridge, University Library, MS Ll.i.8
7. Cambridge, University Library, MS Additional 2823 (substantial fragment)
8. Cambridge, Fitzwilliam Museum, MS McClean 130
9. Cambridge, Gonville and Caius College, MS 160/81
10. Cambridge, Trinity College, MS R.3.13, fos. i–ii (one folio of text)
11. Cambridge, Trinity College, MS R.3.13
12. Cambridge, Trinity College, MS R.3.23
13. Dublin, Trinity College, MS 76 (four folios)
14. Dublin, Trinity College, MS 423
15. Edinburgh, University Library, MS Laing II.318 (two folios)
16. Glasgow, University Library, MS Hunter 89 (substantial fragment)
17. Liverpool, University Library, MS F.4.9
18. London, British Library, MS Additional 8151
19. London, British Library, MS Additional 22283 ('The Simeon Manuscript')
20. London, British Library, MS Additional 22558
21. London, British Library, MS Additional 33995
22. London, British Library, MS Cotton Tiberius E.vii (badly damaged)
23. London, British Library, MS Harley 435
24. London, British Library, MS Harley 2260
25. London, British Library, MS Harley 6718 (eighteen folios)
26. London, British Library, MS Royal 17 C.viii
27. London, British Library, MS Sloane 1785 (substantial fragment)
28. London, British Library, MS Stowe 951
29. Sion College, MS Arch. L.40.2/E.25, currently a Lambeth Palace Library deposit (twelve folios of excerpts)
30. Marlborough (Wilts.), St Mary's, Vicar's Library, currently a Bodleian Library deposit, Marl. C 31 (one folio)
31. Nottingham, University Library, MS Mi(ddleton) LM 9
32. Oxford, Bodleian Library, MS Bodley 48
33. Oxford, Bodleian Library, MS Bodley 446

34. Oxford, Bodleian Library, MS Eng. poet. a.1 ('The Vernon Manuscript')
35. Oxford, Bodleian Library, MS Eng. poet. d.5
36. Oxford, Bodleian Library, MS Greaves 43 (substantial fragment)
37. Oxford, Bodleian Library, MS Hatton 18
38. Oxford, Bodleian Library, MS Hatton 19
39. Oxford, Bodleian Library, MS Lyell 28
40. Oxford, Bodleian Library, MS Rawlinson C.884
41. Oxford, Bodleian Library, MS Rawlinson C.890
42. Oxford, Bodleian Library, MS Rawlinson Q.b.4 (two folios)
43. Princeton, University Library, MS Taylor Med. 11
44. Stafford, Staffordshire Record Office, MSS D (W) 1734/4/1/6–8 (ten folios and two strips)
45. Tokyo, Prof. Toshiyuki Takamiya, MS 15

In the following descriptions, all dimensions are presented in millimetres (height preceding width) and writing areas measured to the bounding lines, not the ends of the verses. I have ignored most post-medieval indications of provenance and all post-1700 bindings (including their associated flyleaves), except in exceptional instances, and I cite only reasonably full modern descriptions.

1. Aberystwyth, National Library of Wales, MS Peniarth 395 (W)

Vellum. s. xiv/xv. Fos. 175 (perhaps 173 + ii, the final two leaves numbered fos. 174–5; most older accounts follow a previous pagination). Overall 265 × 140 (writing area 215–20 × 95; up to 110 wide in the prose). 48 lines to the page (49–50 lines in the prose). Written in anglicana.

CONTENTS

1. Fos. 1^{r}–164^{v}: *Speculum Vitae*, lacking lines 12507–698 (on two leaves missing after fo. 130).

2. Fos. 165^{r}–73^{v}: the Middle English *Mirror of St Edmund*, a translation of Edmund Rich (*IPMEP* 796, 800), including the lyric *IMEV* 2320 (fo. 171^{v}). Material equivalent to the content of two folios is missing after fo. 166.

3. Fo. 174^{rv}: the refrain poem 'Sufferance is best' (*IMEV* 4121). The final three texts are all later hand additions, in four different

hands (the third writing two of the recipes in item 5, the fourth the remaining three).

4. Fos. 174^{v}–75^{r}: the Vernon–Simeon refrain poem on the earthquake of 1382 (*IMEV* 4268).

5. Fo. 175^{rv}: five Middle English medical recipes, all later additions on a blank leaf, printed in full in Marx, *Index of Middle English Prose*, 62.

COLLATION. $1–10^{12}$ 11^{12} (−11, −12) $12–13^{12}$ 14^{12} (−11, −12, probably both blank) [fo. 164, a production boundary] | $15^{12+1?}$ (−3, −4; +13, fo. 175; but 9 to 11, fos. 171–3, are now mounted singles, and the binding is too tight to ascertain whether fos. 174 and 175 are conjoint with earlier leaves or with one another: in the latter case, 15^{12} [−3, −4, −12] + ii). Catchwords near the inner bounding line, boxed or in half-boxes with grotesque heads, that at 84^{v} with red; no signatures.

TEXTUAL PRESENTATION. Relatively plain: a four-line unflourished red lombard at the opening; the text occasionally divided by similar two-line examples. No running titles, but vestiges of the marginal annotation programme, diminishing through the volume.

LANGUAGE. *LALME* LP 319 (coordinates 396/341, north-central Staffordshire); see iii. 461–2.[9]

PROVENANCE. At the end of item 2 (fo. 173^{v} foot), the scribal signature 'Dammary'; 'Iohn ap Ryl ap Peued ap Roger ap Ieuan ap Kuyryg ap Wyllyam o Aberchwllarh' (s. xvi in., fo. 175^{v}); the book was given to John Prichard (who signs as 'de Prion' (?), with date 1648, upside down in the lower margin, fo. 145^{v}) by Robert Wynne of Dyffryn Aled (fo. 175^{v}).

DESCRIPTIONS. The best available provided Marx, *Index of Middle English Prose*, 61–2.

2. Cambridge, University Library, MS Ff.iv.9, part 1

Paper, folded in folio, each quire six full sheets, on a single stock, the type Anchor, one from Piccard 6, nos. 231–73 (Franco-Burgundian papers, 1461 × 1480). There are 39 full sheets and most of three others, with the mark. s. xv med. or $xv^{3/4}$. Fos. 80 (the library foliation to fo. 83 includes lost leaves). Overall 290 × 215 (writing area 245 × 165 in the first quire, thereafter 235–7 × 165–70). 38

[9] For a mapping of the overall dialect distribution of the text, see Beadle, 'Middle English Texts and their Transmission', 83–5. Two manuscripts Beadle includes, CUL, MS Additional 6686; and Dublin, Trinity College, MS 155, include texts with titles similar to the text here edited but are actually Nicholas Love's *Mirror* (*IPMEP* 553) and a *Prick of Conscience* derivative (*IMEV* 484) respectively.

lines to the page in quire 1, 44–56 thereafter. Written in secretary bookhand.

CONTENTS

Fos. 1ra–83va: *Speculum Vitae*, lacking lines 9443–9860, 12554–669, owing to missing leaves. Only twenty-one lines on the last side, the remainder blank.

Fos. 85–107, with poems of Scogan, Lydgate, and Burgh, are a separate manuscript, on different papers (marked Bull's head with cross, Blazon) and by a different scribe.

COLLATION. 1–4^{12} 5^{12} (–4, –5) 6^{12} (–7) 7^{12} (–12, a thick stub, probably blank). Catchwords; a couple of partial signatures.

TEXTUAL PRESENTATION. Annotations in column in red. Occasional running titles in textura, and the text divided by two- or three-line red lombards with flourishing in the text ink. Both these latter features generally cease at fo. 40.

LANGUAGE. *LALME* LP 527 (coordinates 470/308, east-central Leicestershire); see iii. 243.

BINDING. Brown calf over millboards, s. xvii ex. Pastedowns from a quarto *A Revelation Touching Antichrist*, s. xvii.

PROVENANCE. Thomas Right (vertically in the margin, fo. 18); 'Dominus de M–' (fo. 74^{v}, upper margin).

3. Cambridge, University Library, MS Gg.i.7

Vellum and paper. To fo. 122, the end of quire 12, each quire a single paper sheet folded in quarto within a vellum sheet and an additional vellum half-sheet inserted between the paper leaves (thus VPVPV/). Thereafter, of similar construction, but with an added paper half-sheet, either as the second outmost bifolium (so quire 16), or as the second or third inmost bifolium, before the vellum at the quire centre (so quire 19—thus VPVPPV/). There are three stocks:

A Letter P: one from among Piccard 4/i, nos. 412–85 (Troyes papers of 1384 × 1401, with scattered later examples): the sole stock of quires 2–12 (so far as can be determined, given losses—six more or less intact full sheets survive)

B Letter P: as the previous, or perhaps Piccard 4/i, nos. 501–3 (Troyes papers of 1394 × 1400): the sole stock of quires 14–18 (five full sheets and two half-sheets with watermark)

C Bird: Briquet 12095 (Paris, 1395; a type in use, mostly in France, 1384 × 1413, mainly in the 1390s): the sole stock of quires 19–25 (seven full sheets and three half-sheets with watermark)

s. xiv/xv or s. xv in. Fos. 223 (the library foliation 12–277 includes lost leaves). Overall 210 × 140 (writing area 165–70 × 85–90). 26–30 lines to the page. Written in anglicana with secretary *a*.

CONTENTS. Fos. 12^{r}–277^{v}: *Speculum Vitae*, lacking lines 1–648, 2301–59, 2415–75, 3254–306, 3421–74, 4099–158, 4273–330, 4569–626, 4685–744, 4861–918, 4973–5030, 5145–200, 5258–316, 5377–947, 6881–938, 7113–674, 9736–88, 10209–61, 12499–602, 12874–982, 13309–64, 14747–857, 15583–end, owing to missing leaves.

COLLATION. $1^{12?}$ (lacks all but the last, fo. 12) 2^{10} (–5, a cancel, with no text loss) $3^{10}4^{10}$ (–7, –9) $5^{10}6^{10}$ (–4, –7) 7^{10} (–9) 8^{10} (–2, –7, –9) 9^{10} (–2, –4, –7, –9) [quire 10 lost] $11^{10}12^{10}$ (–7) [quire 13 lost] 14–$16^{12}17^{12}$ (–2, –11) 18–$20^{12}21^{12}$ (–6, –7) 22^{12} (–1, –2, –9) $23^{12}24^{12}$ (–11, –12) 25^{12} $26^{?}$ (only the first, fo. 277, survives). No catchwords or signatures.

TEXTUAL PRESENTATION. Headings in a more formal version of the hand, red-boxed. Two- and three-line red lombards, a few filled in in red. Extensive sidenotes and regular running titles red-boxed, often with red paraphs. Red-slashed capitals at line openings. Numerous red pointing hands in the margins.

LANGUAGE. *LALME* LP 487 (coordinates 423/481, the Masham area, North Riding, Yorkshire); see iii. 586–7.

BINDING. Affixed 1960, replacing an early modern one.

4. Cambridge, University Library, MS Gg.i.14

Vellum. s. xiv ex. Fos. 202 (the library foliation 1–242 includes lost leaves; a medieval foliation covers fos. 5–242, running iij–[239], no number assigned the cancelled fo. 116). The first six leaves have lost their edges and are mounted, but with minimal text loss; the vellum generally poor, many leaves patched before writing (e.g. fo. 151). Overall 225–30 × 155 (writing area 165–70 × 95). 33–5 lines to the page to fo. 116, thereafter usually 30–2 lines (some patches up to 34 lines). Written in anglicana formata.

CONTENTS. Fos. 2^{r}–242^{v}: *Speculum Vitae*, lacking lines 1–68, 856–3315, 3719–88, 6111–69, 15427–end, owing to missing leaves. Omitted couplets frequently added in the lower margins (not the scribe's hand). On fo. 130^{v}, lines 8495–500 (on burial in a religious house) erased.

COLLATION. 1^{12} (–1) [quires 2–4 lost] 5^{12} (–7) 6–$7^{12}8^{12}$ (–7) 9^{12} 10^{8} (–8, a cancel, without text loss) 11^{12} 12^{6} 13–21^{12}. Catchwords centred and boxed; all leaves in the first half of each quire signed with roman numerals, added quire letters on the first leaves (quires 5–15, 18, 20–1 = *e–p*, *s*, *x–y*).

TEXTUAL PRESENTATION. Headings and in-text Latin in display anglicana of the type customary in *Statute* manuscripts, boxed in red. Extensive marginalia boxed in red. To fo. 49, running titles in the same display script as the headings, thereafter supplied, sometimes only at openings of sections, in anglicana, s. xiv/xv. Red paraphs and line openings with red-slashed capitals. Rhymes joined by angle brackets in the text ink.

LANGUAGE. *LALME* LP 486 (coordinates 407/488, the area of West Witton, North Riding, Yorkshire); see iii. 585–6.

PROVENANCE. 'Ex dono Edwardi G⟨ ⟩' (fo. 2 upper margin, s. xv); 'Robert W⟨ ⟩' (fo. 2 foot, s. xv ex.); the (?) John Moore shelfmark '493'.

5. Cambridge, University Library, MS Ii.i.36

Vellum. s. $xv^{1/4}$ (1422–3; see below). Fos. 231 (foliated to 230, but includes both fos. 150 and 150*). Overall 230 × 158 (writing area 180 × 80–2). 36 lines to the page. Written in anglicana formata (avoids anglicana *r*).

CONTENTS. Fos. 1^r–225^r: *Speculum Vitae*, complete, preceded by the certificate of the alleged 1384 Cambridge examination. Doyle, 'A Survey of the Origins and Circulation', i. 85 n.17 reports an erased colophon: 'Explicit compilacio compendiosa Ricardi Rolle heremite de hampole in barnesdale'. Fo. 150^v has only five lines, cancelled in red, with a following extra leaf, blank on the recto and continuing the text. At the end, fo. 225^v, with the two following leaves now mostly excised but counting in the foliation, is bounded and ruled, the remainder blank.

COLLATION. 1–14^{10} 15^{10+1} (+11, fo. 150*) 16–22^{10} 23^{10} (–6, –7, thick stubs, both counted in the foliation). Boxed catchwords; all leaves in the first half of each quire originally signed, with letter and roman numeral, the majority cut away (quires 1–18 = *a–s*).

TEXTUAL PRESENTATION. At the opening of the certificate, a two-line blue lombard with red flourishing and a five-line red and blue lombard with flourishing of both colours, joined by a red and blue bar border. The text is divided by red paraphs and two-line red lombards; some Latin underlined in red. An extensive marginal annotation programme, many running titles (most cut into by the binder).

LANGUAGE. *LALME* LP 79 (coordinates 542/315, the Ely–Lincolnshire border); see iii. 101–2.

PROVENANCE. 'In die sanctorum Crispini et Crispiani scribere incepi et 3°. die post festum annunciacionis beate Marie finem habui anno domini 1423°.' (fo. 230^{v}, top, i.e. 25 October 1422–28 March 1423). There is also an early note of donation: 'ȝe þat rede þis boke or here it redde I pray ȝow praith for sir Roberte soule and alle cristen soules þat gaf þis boke to þis place for woso praith for anoþer laburse for hymselfe and schal haue grete mede' (fo. 225^{v}, the conclusion echoing lines 16088–9 of the poem); Doyle, 'A Survey of the Origins and Circulation', i. 84–5 suggests 'þis place' may have been Wisbech.

DESCRIPTIONS. No. 53 (1:33) in P. R. Robinson, *Catalogue of Dated and Datable Manuscripts*, with reproduction of fo. 53 (plate 53).

6. Cambridge, University Library, MS Ll.i.8

Vellum. s. xiv/xv or xv in. Fos. 207. Overall 245 × 145 (writing area 185 × 90–5). 40–3 lines to the page. Written in anglicana.

CONTENTS

Booklet 1 = fos. 1–200

1. Fos. 1^{r}–200^{v}: *Speculum Vitae*, complete, the colophon 'Explicit quidam tractatus super pater noster secundum Ricardum Hampol qui obijt Anno domini millesimo ccc^{mo}. octogesimo quarto'. As Nelson demonstrates ('The Middle English *Speculum Vitae*', 74–8), this book, along with MS Harley 2260 (and in part, MS Bodley 446), includes a set of non-authorial interpolations.

COLLATION. 1–25^{8}. No catchwords; all leaves in the first half of each quire signed (quires 1–25 = *a–z*, *2a–2b*).

Booklet 2 = fos. 201–7

2. Fos. 201^{r}–7^{v}: Richard Rolle, 'Meditations on the passion' A (*IPMEP* 618). A sloppy patch of correction on fo. 206, with an omission supplied after erasure and rewriting, parts of the text in both margins.

COLLATION. 26^{8} (–8, probably a cancelled blank).

TEXTUAL PRESENTATION. At the opening, a four-line blue lombard with red flourishing. At inner divisions, similar two- and three-line examples. The line-initials slashed in ochre. Rhymes bracketed in red. Considerable marginal notation of topics, typically preceded by red paraphs, a few patches with ochre-slashed capitals. Item 2 divided by red paraphs with following ochre-slashed capitals; biblical lemmata in anglicana formata, many ochre-slashed.

LANGUAGE. *LALME* associates with west Norfolk (i. 223); see Beadle, "Prolegomena to a Literary Geography', 104 (no. 42).

BINDING. Brown calf over millboards, s. xvii, on five thongs.

PROVENANCE. The scribe signs on fo. 200^{v}, 'Reynoldus cognomen scriptoris possidet omen'. A monastic library pressmark 'K.14' (perhaps 'l.14', fo. 1).

7. Cambridge, University Library, MS Additional 2823

Vellum. s. xv in. Fos. 44 (the library foliation 1–48 includes lost leaves). Overall 205 × 150 (writing area 150 × 77). 44 lines to the page. Written in anglicana formata.

CONTENTS. Fos. 1^{r}–48^{v}: *Speculum Vitae*, a fragment ending at line 4214; in addition, lacks lines 881–1230, owing to missing leaves.

COLLATION. 1^{8} 2^{8} (–3 to –6) 3–6^{8}. Catchwords in the gutter; all leaves in the first half of each quire signed in arabic, the quires numbered *j–vj* in roman at the centre of the upper margin, first leaf.

TEXTUAL PRESENTATION. Fairly plain, with the text divided by paraphs in the scribe's ink, occasional three-line unfilled blanks for capitals. Frequent marginal annotations but no running titles.

LANGUAGE. 'Northern, possibly northwest Yorkshire, but may be mixed' (*LALME* i. 66).

PROVENANCE. 'This book belonged to ye Monastery of St Augustin at York—given by Catherion Turgeon at York to Dr White Decem. 25 1781. May 9 1794 Given to Jas. Atkinson by J. White' (the modern paper front flyleaf). The ascription to the York OESA convent noted with a query Ker, *MLGB* 218. Atkinson also donated to York Minster its MS XVI.I.9 (*Speculum spiritualium*), a Mount Grace book, in 1800.

8. Cambridge, Fitzwilliam Museum, MS McClean 130

Vellum. s. xv in. Fos. 199 (foliated 2–200, to account for the missing first leaf). Overall 215 × 115 (writing area 160 × 65–70, narrower later). Usually 40 or 41 lines to the page. Written in small neat anglicana formata, with secretary *r* and hybrid *g*.

CONTENTS. Fos. 2^{r}–200^{r}: *Speculum Vitae*, lacking lines 1–78, on the lost first leaf. Fo. 200^{v} is blank.

COLLATION. 1^{12} (–1) 2–15^{12} 16^{8} 17^{12}. Catchwords centred, a number cut away; all leaves in the first half of each quire signed with letters and roman numerals (two sets, neither in the text ink, one in red; quires 1–17 = *a–r*).

TEXTUAL PRESENTATION. Well turned out, with a full set of annotations in red. Occasional two-line blue lombards with red flourishing, as well as alternate red and blue paraphs.

LANGUAGE. 'Southwest Lincolnshire, mixed with a more northerly component' (*LALME* i. 63).

PROVENANCE. James reports that the volume formerly had a bookplate suggesting it may have been in the library of the late seventeenth-century collector Henry Fermor of Tusmore (Oxfordshire); he also owned BL, MS Additional 46919 (William Herebert, OFM's notebook).

DESCRIPTIONS. James, *A Descriptive Catalogue of the McClean Collection*, 277–8.

9. Cambridge, Gonville and Caius College, MS 160/81

Vellum. s. xv^{1}. Fos. iii + 208 (paginated, the text only, as pp. 1–416; a modern pencilled College foliation as fos. 1–3 [the flyleaves], 4–211) + iii (paginated 417–22). Overall 235 × 145 (writing area 177 × 85–90). 39 lines to the page. Written in anglicana.

CONTENTS

1. Pp. 1–412: *Speculum Vitae*, complete, preceded (fo. iii^{v}) by the certificate of the alleged 1384 Cambridge examination.

2. Pp. 413–15: Middle English prose on temptation, inc. 'Hit es inpossible þat þou be one of Goddes darlynges þat ert noght assaied' (Jolliffe J.6). With a brief Latin note at the end; on the originally blank p. 416, in the same hand as the flyleaf notes (see Binding below) an added Latin note, citing Gregory the Great's anecdote from *Dialogi* 3.7 (PL 77: 229–32).

COLLATION. $1–26^{8}$. Catchwords centred, usually boxed in red; no signatures.

TEXTUAL PRESENTATION. Rhymes bracketed in red. Two-line red or blue lombards, the latter sometimes with red flourishing. Blue paraphs, often with a red outline. A full annotational programme, marginalia often introduced with a red paraph and underlined in red (supplemented by frequent notes, s. xvii).

LANGUAGE. *LALME* LP 500 (coordinates 427/427, the Batley area, West Riding, Yorkshire); see iii. 645–6.

BINDING. Worn white skin over bevelled wood, s. xv, on six thongs (modern rebacking). Two sets of nail marks inside the upper board (and one repaired scar outside) from strap seatings; two sets of scars near the middle of the lower board from the pins to hold the clasps. At front and rear, three flyleaves (in both instances a conjoint bifolium followed by a leaf probably conjoint with the pastedown). Fo. i^rv has two lengthy Latin notes on Psalms appropriate for various occasions (the second discussion is that ascribed to Hilarius of Arles). At the rear, p. 421 has a few Latin proverbs and a trial alphabet (s. xv), but most of these leaves have been covered with medical notes and verse fragments in the hand of William Gonell, a London priest (s. xvi ex.).

PROVENANCE. 'Orate pro anima Magistri Iohannis Lyghton et pro benefactoribus domini Thome Chamber(s)' (s. xv med., p. 416 near the foot); the later signature 'Symon Watson' (s. xvi^1/2, p. 1 upper margin).

DESCRIPTIONS. James, *A Descriptive Catalogue . . . Gonville and Caius College*, i. 184–5.

10+11. Cambridge, Trinity College, MS R.3.13

The First Copy = fos. i–ii

Vellum. s. xv^2/4 or xv med. Fos. 2 (numbered fos. i–ii, the front flyleaves of the manuscript). Overall 290 × 220 (writing area 245 × 145). 47 and 48 lines to the column, in double columns. Written in anglicana, with limited secretary forms (-*s*, mixed usage with *r*, a tendency to use sigmoid *s* in initial position).

CONTENTS. Fos. i^ra–i^vb: *Speculum Vitae*, a fragment with lines 1–188 only. Although fo. ii is blank, its verso shows the same frame-rules as the conjoint fo. i^r. Fo. i appears to have been once pasted down.

COLLATION. A bifolium, presumably the first and last leaves, from the first quire of an apparently abandoned text.

TEXTUAL PRESENTATION. Two-line (three-line at the opening) unfilled blanks for initials; one marginal note from the usual annotation programme.

LANGUAGE. Brief, and possibly mixed, but probably West Riding, Yorkshire, from Wakefield or slightly south, e.g. OE *ā* universally retained as *a*, but schal/schul/schulde (sulde 1x), both hyr' and þair, al(l)-yf, through/þrough/þrugh.

The Second Copy

Vellum. s. xv^1. Fos. 85. Overall 290 × 220 (writing area usually 245 × 145–50; near the end up to 255 × 155–60). 44–5 lines to the column, in double columns; in the last quire, up to 51 lines. Written in mixed anglicana/secretary, the first quire, with more emphatic secretary features (including secretary/textura *d*), conceivably a different hand.

CONTENTS. Fos. 1ra–85vb: *Speculum Vitae*, complete.

COLLATION. 1–5^{12} 6^{14} 7^{14} (–12 to –14, presumably blank and at least two of them stubs). Catchwords on scrolls, underlined, or bracketed; all leaves in the first half of each quire signed, originally with roman or arabic numerals, added red examples with quire letters and roman numerals (quires 1–7 = *a–g*).

TEXTUAL PRESENTATION. At the opening, a red and blue bar demivinet with sprays. The text is divided by two-line blue lombards with red flourishing and modest sprays (only assiduous through quire 4). Headings placed in-column and ochre-slashed, as are the initials at line-openings. A reasonably full annotational system through the fourth quire (running titles usually only on opening page of a discussion). Near the end, a few red or blue paraphs to separate runover between the columns.

LANGUAGE. 'Appears to be slightly mixed, [but] substantially West Riding, Yorkshire, of the Harrowgate area or somewhat north of there' (*LALME* i. 65).

BINDING. Brown calf over millboards, with gold-stamped achievement of arms and motto 'Expertus credo', s. xvii, perhaps those of the donor George Wilmer (d. 1626).

PROVENANCE. The spine-binding has been strengthened with a wrapper, from a roll of presentments in the manorial court of Horsham (Sussex), 8 Henry VIII (1517).

DESCRIPTIONS. James, *The Western Manuscripts*, ii. 63–4.

12. Cambridge, Trinity College, MS R.3.23

Vellum. s. xiv ex. or xiv/xv. Fos. 180 (foliated 1–179, but includes both fos. 146 and 146a). Overall 280 × 180 (writing area 205 × 100). 38 lines to the page. Written in anglicana formata.

CONTENTS. Fos. 1^r–179^v: *Speculum Vitae*, lacking lines 1–606, 3957–4108, 5787–5940, 11475–628, 11781–856, 12313–33, 12351–72, 14941–end, owing to lost and torn leaves. Fo. 123^v is blank, save for five cancelled lines at the head (they appear also at the top of fo. 124); fo. 150 about half a leaf with only 38 lines total.

COLLATION. [quire 1 lost] 2–6^8 7^8 (–4 to –6, the last a stub and one probably a cancel, without text loss) 8^6 9^8 10^8 (–7) 11^8 (–1, a cancel, without text loss?) 12–19^{8} 20^{8} (–2, –3, –6) 21^{8} (most of 5, fo. 146a, torn away) 22^{8} (1, fo. 150, a partial leaf, perhaps not conjoint with 8) 23–24^{8} 25^{8} (–7, –8, both stubs). Catchwords centred; from quire 20, sporadic letters (*a–d*) as leaf signatures in the first halves of quires.

TEXTUAL PRESENTATION. The text is divided by two-line blue lombards, unflourished, and alternate red and blue paraphs. A full annotational programme.

LANGUAGE. *LALME* LP 423 (coordinates 535/307, the Ely–Lincolnshire border); see iii. 104–5.

DESCRIPTIONS. James, *The Western Manuscripts*, ii. 96.

13. Dublin, Trinity College, MS 76 (A.4.7), fos. i–iv

Vellum. s. xv in. Fos. 4. Overall 235 × 155 (writing area 185–90 × 92–5). 36 lines to the page. Written in textura semiquadrata.

CONTENTS. Fos. i^{r}–iv^{r}: *Speculum Vitae*, a fragment with lines 137–382 only, fo. iv^{v} blank. Fos. i^{r}–ii^{r}, at least, have earlier been used as pastedowns and are generally illegible; all the leaves have been cancelled in red.

COLLATION. The 3rd to 6th leaves of the opening eight-leaf quire.

TEXTUAL PRESENTATION. Unfilled spaces for two-line initials at inner divisions. Parts of the annotational system, some running titles and marginal materials.

LANGUAGE. 'Too short to assess adequately, but the language may be of Derbyshire' (*LALME* i. 77).

BINDING. This discarded start on the poem has presumably been retained from an earlier binding where the leaves prefaced the following texts, a table of biblical lections and the Wycliffite gospels (preceded by two of the prefaces to *Oon of Foure*, the translation of Clement of Llanthony).

14. Dublin, Trinity College, MS 423 (D.4.3), fos. 1–103

Mixed vellum (10 surviving leaves only) and paper; except in the final quire, a vellum sheet folded around a large number of paper ones to form inner and outer bifolia. The paper, folded in folio, represents a single stock, Mountains, like the smaller examples Piccard 16/i, nos. 1151–69 (widely used 1439 × 1451; the general type nos. 1151–1253 extensively used *c.*1440–70). There are 44 full sheets, four unwatermarked half-sheets, and one watermarked half-sheet.

s. xv med. (the second scribe probably early s. $xv^{3/4}$). Fos. 103. Overall 265 × 215 (writing area 218–25 × 155–68). 36–40 lines to the column (36–8 in scribe 1 portions, 38–40 in scribe 2), in double columns. Written by two scribes, quires 1–2 in anglicana with secretary ductus (and secretary *r*, reduced *w*); quires 3–4 in a less formal anglicana (elaborate circled *w*, frequent anglicana *r*).

CONTENTS. Fos. 1ra–103ra: *Speculum Vitae*, lacking lines 145–438, 3313–462, and 8125–286, owing to missing leaves. Fo. 103 is a torn part leaf, its verso originally blank, with only six lines (recopied at the surviving foot, s. $xvi^{2/2}$) and a scribal colophon (*IMEV* 1197.4).

COLLATION. 1^{24} (–2, –3, –5, the last a cancel without text loss) 2^{32} (–1) 3^{30} (–1) 4^{24} (22 a partial leaf, –23, –24, both probably blanks). No catchwords; each quire signed on the final verso with a total of leaves, for example, 'Summa Foliorum istius quaterni xxxiij' (fo. 21^v, here an error for 'xxiij', the remainder accurate, except the 'Summa totalis . . . Cxvj. di.' on fo. 103 including the earlier error in its count).

TEXTUAL PRESENTATION. To fo. 3, line-initials red-slashed and red brackets to connect rhymes; thereafter, only ochre-slashed line-initials. At the opening (fo. 1), crude two- and four-line alternate red and blue lombards. In later portions, two-line spaces left for initials, filled in ink later; they diminish throughout the manuscript, the text fundamentally undivided near the end. Although running titles do not occur (the leaf is pared very close at the head), a number of shorter marginalia, esp. identifications of authorities, are present.

LANGUAGE. The first scribe's 'language has a Cambridgeshire element, but probably mixed'; the second scribe identified as also Cambridgeshire (*LALME* i. 77).

PROVENANCE. A good many marginalia, all of s. xvi med., typically on the edges of leaves and often cut into or off. Many of these indicate that the book was circulating in Coventry 1546 × 1565; at the latter date Richard Over mercer sold the book to Thomas Jackson (fo. 118^v). In addition, there are a decorative drawing of a vine and flower panel, of a sort typical in Horae (fo. 15 foot), a trial alphabet (fo. 43^v foot), and the rime royale stanza John Lydgate, *The Life of our Lady* (*IMEV* 2574) 3.1–7 (fo. 103^v).

DESCRIPTIONS. Colker, *Trinity College Dublin*, ii. 839–44; part 2 (fos. 104–23) is entirely Latin, and part 3 (fos. 124–49) includes a life of Christ, for which see Salter, 'The Manuscripts of Nicholas Love's *Myrrour*', 127.

15. Edinburgh University Library, MS Laing II.318

Paper (neither leaf appears to have a watermark). s. xv ex. (1490s?). Fos. 2. Overall 280 × 190 (writing area 195 × 88). 31–5 lines to the page. Written in Scottish secretary (anglicana *d*).

CONTENTS. *Speculum Vitae*, two leaves with lines 10812–78 and 11138–205.

COLLATION. Now two single leaves, but potentially originally a bifolium, and if so, the 2nd and 7th leaves of a quire.

TEXTUAL PRESENTATION. Two-line red lombards, unflourished, at divisions in the text, red-slashed capitals at the line-openings.

LANGUAGE. Scots; Lyall, 'The Lost Literature', 35–6, cites, from the verso of the second fragment, lines 11181–205, indicative of the language.

BINDING. Preserved loose in a folder, amidst documents collected by Andrew Laing.

DESCRIPTIONS. See Lyall, 'The Lost Literature', 35–6. I am grateful to Edinburgh University Library for photocopies.

16. Glasgow University Library, MS Hunter 89

Vellum. s. xv^{1}. Fos. 73. Overall 280 × 165 (writing area 225–35 × 107, the first quire significantly shorter, *c*.210–20). 44 lines to the page. Written in anglicana.

CONTENTS. Fos. 1^{r}–73^{v}: *Speculum Vitae*, a fragment, lacking lines 1–2679 and breaking off at 8896.

COLLATION. [four missing quires] 5–13^{8} 14$^{?}$ (the single leaf, fo. 73, and bit of stub from its conjugate). Catchwords at the inner bounding line, usually boxed; all leaves in the first half of each quire signed with a letter and roman numeral, many cut away (quires 7–13 = *f*–*m*, none extant in quire 9).

TEXTUAL PRESENTATION. At divisions, two-line unflourished red lombards. A fragmentary explanatory programme, only sporadic running titles and marginalia in early portions as in-column headings in red.

LANGUAGE. *LALME* LP 422 (coordinates 523/357, south-central Lincolnshire); see iii. 278–9.

PROVENANCE. Robard Haide (followed by 'abcenes'?, s. xv ex., fo. 61^{v}), Howmo Wise (s. xv/xvi, fo. 54), Richard Pidgeon (1683, fos. 51 and 53).

DESCRIPTIONS. Young and Aitken, *A Catalogue*, 96–7.

17. Liverpool University Library, MS F.4.9 (L)

Vellum. s. xiv/xv. Fos. i + 206 + i (foliated 1, 2–207, 208). Overall 203 × 137 (writing area 168 × 70–85). 40 lines to the page. Written in anglicana formata.

CONTENTS

1. Fos. 2^r–203^r: *Speculum Vitae*, complete.

2. Fos. 203^v–207^v: 'The Layfolk's Mass Book' (*IMEV* 3507), incomplete at the end; Ker associates this form of the text with that of CUL, MS Gg.v.31, a Northern book (with *Northern Passion* and *Northern Homily Cycle*).

COLLATION. 1–$5^{12}6^{12}$ (6 and 7, fos. 67–8, reversed in the binding) 7–$16^{12}\,17^{8}\,18^{8}$ (–7, –8). Boxed catchwords; all leaves in the first half of each quire signed with letter and roman numeral near the centre of the leaf, a number missing (quires 1–17 = *a–g*, *a–c*, *a–g*).

TEXTUAL PRESENTATION. Headings, when present, provided marginally in the text hand. At major divisions, three-line blue lombards with red flourishing and marginal extensions. The text also divided by occasional blue paraphs. Couplets bracketed in red; early on, line-initials ochre-slashed. No running titles, but a reasonably full marginal programme of annotations (including displaced headings), underlined in red. In item 2, blocks of the text written in red ink.

LANGUAGE. *LALME* LP 460, unmapped, but the description implies that the language is similar to BL, MS Stowe 951 (LP 526, described below); see iii. 636–7.

BINDING. Single medieval flyleaves, front and rear, retained in a binding of early s. xviii for the Earl Gowers, a Yorkshire family.

PROVENANCE. A few pen-trials on the rear flyleaf (fo. 208).

DESCRIPTIONS. Ker, *MMBL* iii. 308–9.

18. London, British Library, MS Additional 8151

Paper, folded in quarto, each quire usually three full sheets. There are three stocks:

A Unicorn's head: one of Piccard 10, nos. 1037–44, 1046, 1054–5 (central Italian papers of the later 1390s): the sole stock of quires 1–6 (11 full sheets, most of four more sheets with at least half the mark, and one unwatermarked quarter-sheet)

B Mountains: the type of Piccard 16/ii, nos. 486–635 (Italian, in wide use 1380 × 1425): the sole stock of quires 7–8, 10–15, and the middle sheet of quire 16 (22 full sheets, most of two more sheets with the mark, and one unwatermarked half-sheet)

C Horn: one of Piccard 7/vi, nos. 110–85 (central Italian, 1390 × 1407, with a few later examples): the sole stock of quires 17–20 and the central and outer sheets of quire 16 (11 full sheets, most of another sheet with half the mark, and a half-sheet with the mark). s. xv in. Fos. 201 (foliated 3–203; fos. 1–2 assigned to modern paper leaves at the front). Overall 225 × 150 (writing area 165–70 × 95–100). 30–6 lines to the page, progressively more packed and the script sprawling out horizontally. Written in anglicana.

CONTENTS

1. Fos. 3r–200v: *Speculum Vitae*, the main text ending fo. 199 and lacking lines 1603–2400, 3140–268, 6571–7606, 10742–814, and 15077–218, owing to missing leaves. Followed, fos. 199v–200v, by lines 137–208, materials to replace an omission, noted marginally on fo. 5, with folio reference to the supply and signe de renvoie.

2. Fo. 200v: *IMEV* 4006. The remainder was originally blank.

3. Fos. 201v–3v: 'The Little Children's Little Book' (*IMEV* 1920), added in mixed anglicana/secretary, s. xv².

COLLATION. 1^{12} (–1, no text loss and lost before the book's second set of signatures) 2^{12} (–11, –12) 3^{12} (–1 to –11; fo. 24 is 'c.xii' in the second set of signatures) 4^{12} (–11, –12) $5–8^{12}$ [quire 9 lost] 10^{12} (–1 to –3) $11–12^{12}$ 13^{12} (–12) $14–18^{12}$ 19^{12} (–1, –2) 20^{8} (–8). Catchwords, a little sporadic early on, in or near the gutter, some boxed and with grotesque heads and red. The scribe signed all leaves in the first half of each quire with letter and roman numeral, cut away early on (quires 2, 4–7, 10–20 = *a*, *d–g*, *k–t*). In addition, all leaves were signed at the centre, considerably later, in a similar system (quires 1–19 = *a–h*, *l–t*, *w*, *y*). The signatures are the only guide to the original construction; a careless Library rebinding has glued many leaves once single to the wrong quires.

TEXTUAL PRESENTATION. At the head and to divide the text, two-line red lombards, unflourished. Smaller divisions indicated by frequent red paraphs, line-initials red-slashed. A full annotational programme, both running titles and marginalia, in textura rotunda, usually set off with extended red paraphs.

LANGUAGE. *LALME* LP 56 (coordinates 475/309, eastern Leicestershire); see iii. 232.

19. British Library, MS Additional 22283 ('The Simeon Manuscript')

Vellum. s. xiv ex. Fos. 172 (a fragmentary 173rd a stub after fo. 167), of an original 382; the survivals are from among the original fos. 178–379. Overall 585 × 393 (writing area 460–8 × 281–8). 84–92 lines to the column, in the relevant portions in triple columns. Written in anglicana, by a scribe (A) slightly later than the principal hand of the volume (B), who is also the copyist of BodL, MS Eng. poet. a.i ('The Vernon Manuscript', described below) and who writes anglicana formata.

CONTENTS. Booklet 1 = fos. 1–61 (the original 178–242)

1. Fos. 1ra–30va: *The Northern Homily Cycle* (in *IMEV* as numerous separate poems), the so-called 'Midland Version', shared only with 'the Vernon manuscript' described below; see Nevanlinna in the edition, pp. 3–4.

2. Fos. 30va–32vb: 'How a man shall live perfectly' (*IMEV* 1512), a partial versified translation of Edmund Rich.

3. Fo. 32^{vbc}: 'The visions of St Paul' (*IMEV* 1898), a fragment, with the following leaf lost.

4. Fos. 33ra–61va: *Speculum Vitae*, beginning at line 1065, with earlier materials on leaves now lost.

5. Fo. 61^{vac}: A prose meditation on the Five Wounds (*IPMEP* 109), here as filler, most of the last column blank. Materials continuous in Vernon here appear in a separate booklet (fos. 62–91), mainly by Scribe B and opening with *The Prick of Conscience*.

COLLATION [three lost quires] 4^8 (−1, −3) 5–7^8 8^8 (−3 [now an unnumbered stub], −4, −5) 9–11^8 12^2. Catchwords usually under the final column; some signatures, a letter, and roman leaf number, within the lower bounding lines (quires 4–6, 9 = *g–I*, *m*).

TEXTUAL PRESENTATION. At the openings, seven- to nine-line champes and demivinets with floral sprays; similar openings for major divisions of the texts. The text is divided by champes, the gold leaf on alternate grounds of one colour only, either blue or violet. Occasional line-fillers in violet and blue. This scribe uses a large display anglicana for Latin lemmata.

LANGUAGE. Scribe B is identical with the hand of all of Vernon except its contents quire: *LALME* LP 7630 (coordinates 389/270, north-central Worcestershire near Bordesley); see iii. 553.

PROVENANCE. Fos. 38 and 121^v have notes in the same hand

indicating use of Simeon and Vernon as exemplars (a note corresponding to the first appears at Vernon, fo. 239^{v}). That on fo. 38 says that Johannes Scriveyn will copy for Dom. Thomas Heneley a part of *Speculum Vitae*. Scriveyn, who may be identical with the 'John' who copied the Vernon contents quire, or another of the name, appears in Lichfield deeds of the 1390s and 1409. Thomas Hanley (who died 1422) was a secular priest, associated with Lichfield cathedral from 1389 until his death, and holder of other ecclesiastical offices in the area (Hereford Cathedral, the chapel of Tettenhall, Staffs.) and elsewhere. Fo. 91^{v}, at the foot, had a signature once supposedly legible as 'Joan boun'. She was the daughter of Richard Fitzalan, earl of Arundel, sister of archbishop Thomas Arundel, and widow of Humphrey Bohun, earl of Hereford, Essex, and Northampton—he died 1373, she in 1419.

DESCRIPTIONS. Doyle, 'University College, Oxford, MS 97' and introduction in *The Vernon Manuscript*; the former considers connections between Simeon and Oxford, University College, MS 97, the source of the filler prose at the end of the section described here.

20. British Library, MS Additional 22558

Vellum. s. xv in. or xv^{1}. Fos. 194 (foliated 11–212, but fos. 40–1, 174, 176, 196, 198–9, 201 are modern tip-ins with notes or replacements of lost leaves, and 207 a stub with line-openings only). Overall 235 × 155 (writing area 145–50 × 77). 32 lines to the page. Written in anglicana formata.

CONTENTS. Fos. 11^{r}–212^{v}: *Speculum Vitae*, lacking lines 1–2050, 3197–448, 14921–84, 15049–176, 15241–304, 15625–87 (a few line-openings survive), and 16009–end, owing to missing leaves.

COLLATION. [four lost quires] 5^{8} (–3 to –6) 6–8^{8} 9^{8+2} (+2, +3, modern insertions) 10–24^{8} 25^{8+2} (+6, +8, modern insertions) 26–7^{8} 28^{8+4} (–2, –4, –5, –7; +2, +4, +5, +7, modern vellum blanks to replace the lost medieval leaves) 29^{8} (5 only a strip with line-openings on the recto, now mounted) 30$^{4?}$ (–3, –4). Centred catchwords; fragmentary signatures, especially early on, all leaves in the first half of each quire signed with roman numerals in red (the only full set intact in quire 6).

TEXTUAL PRESENTATION. At divisions, two-line unflourished red lombards. Line-initials ochre-slashed, as are the catchwords and, occasionally, the openings of sidenotes. A fairly full marginal explanatory programme (only sporadic running titles), all entries introduced by red paraphs.

LANGUAGE. *LALME* LP 590 (unmapped, described as Northern, with 'somewhat mixed language'); see iii. 674–5.

PROVENANCE. Substantial marginalia, s. xvi med., most in hands which identify themselves as Edward Glover and Nicholas Kychyn (e.g. fos. 23, 86^{v}, together fo. 97). Among the many names noted are 'Thomas Nedom of Plostton, sone to Robert Nedom' (fo. 23), 'Sir Edmund Molyneius' (one of the King's sergeants, fo. 129^{v}), and 'Thomas Parker of Claypoyll' (Lincs., SE of Newark on Trent?). One name is of a woman, 'Ezabell Bowlay' (fo. 165).

21. British Library, MS Additional 33995 (A)

Vellum. s. xiv$^{3/4}$. Fos. 156 (fo. 157 is an extraneous leaf from a book of s. xiii). Overall 305 × 205+ (writing area 235 × 150). Except for text 2, usually 40–2 lines (scribe 1) or 44–6 lines (scribe 2) to the column, in double columns. (Text 2 in 40 or so long lines to the page, writing area 255 × 150). Written in two anglicana bookhands (the stints divide at the folio boundary, 101^{v}/102).

CONTENTS

1. Fos. 1ra–96rb: *Speculum Vitae*, complete.

2. Fos. 96^{v}–101^{v}: 'Stimulus conscientie minor' (*IMEV* 244).

3. Fos. 102ra–155ra: *The Prick of Conscience*, a Type I (Yorkshire) text (*IMEV* 3428), identified Britton, 'Unknown Fragments', 328–9 as the best surviving copy of the poem.

4. Fos. 155rb–56vb: William of Nassington, 'The Band of Love', breaking off at line 329 (*IMEV* 11; the only other copy in Lincoln Cathedral, MS 91, fos. 189^{r}–91^{r}, copied by Robert Thornton of East Newton, North Riding, Yorkshire).

COLLATION. 1–8^{12} 9^{10} (–10) 10–12^{12} ?13^{16} (–16). Catchwords; from quire 2 and throughout scribe 1's stint, all leaves in the first half of each quire signed with letter and roman numeral (quires 2–9 = *b*–*i*). The two hands split in the odd 9th quire, probably a production break after *Speculum Vitae*, with the cancel presumably indicating they were working together with scribe B having already begun *The Prick* in following succession of quires and tailoring the opening.

TEXTUAL PRESENTATION. Headings in red, also used for boxes around running titles and marginalia. At textual divisions, two- and three-line red lombards, unflourished. The text is divided by both large extended and one-line red paraphs. In item 1, couplets bracketed in ink; in item 2, in red. A full explanatory programme, with both running titles and marginal notations.

LANGUAGE. The scribe of *Speculum Vitae* is not surveyed in *LALME* but identified with 'northwest Yorkshire' (i. 101). The second scribe is *LALME* LP 468 (coordinates 387/491, the Hawes area, North Riding, Yorkshire, an improbable placement, since at this time uninhabited); see iii. 583–4.

DESCRIPTIONS. Lewis-McIntosh, 77–8 (MV 44); this book and Wellesley, Mass., Wellesley College, MS 8, with erased Byland ex-libris and ownership at Skeeby (near Richmond), s. xv/xvi, form a textual pair.

22. British Library, MS Cotton Tiberius E.vii

Vellum. s. xiv ex. Fos. 281, currently in two volumes 127 + 154. Damaged in the fire of 1731, the upper and outer margins now lost, the outer columns typically in shrunken strips, although the full text often survives; all leaves have been individually mounted in paper. Currently 290 × 170 overall. 48 lines to the column, in double columns. Two scribes, whose stints split at the folio (and quire) bound fos. 81^{v}/82, the first in anglicana formata, the second textura quadrata.

CONTENTS

Booklet 1 = fos. 1–81

1. Fos. 1ra–81vb: *Speculum Vitae*, complete, although badly damaged, most of the final column blank. Heavily rewritten and probably conflated; see Nelson, 'Cot. Tiberius E.vii' (and 'The Middle English *Speculum Vitae*', 39, 63–6, 95).

COLLATION. 1^{12} (–1 to -3) $2–7^{12}$. The signatures, if any, have been lost owing to fire damage; the collation depends entirely on fairly regular catchwords under the inner columns.

Booklet 2 = fos. 82–281

2. Fos. 82ra–85va: a dialogue of St Bernard and the Virgin (*IMEV* 771, also in BodL, MS Rawlinson poet. 175, and the Sion College MS described below).

3. Fos. 85vb–90ra: Richard Rolle, 'The Form of Living', chs. 1–6 only, paraphrased in verse (*IMEV* 1442, unique); for discussion, see Blake, '*The Form of Living* in Verse and Prose'.

4. Fos. 90rb–101rb: The verse *Gast of Gy* (*IMEV* 3028, also in BodL, Rawlinson poet. 175).

5. Fos. 101rb–240rb: *The Northern Homily Cycle* temporale,

'expanded version', including an intercalated version of the 'expanded' Northern Passion (*IMEV* 170) at fos. 165rb–184ra. This item and the next are unique to this book and to BL, MS Harley 4196 (which forms the basis for Nevanlinna's edition).

6. Fos. 240va–281ra: *The Northern Homily Cycle* sanctorale, unique to the 'expanded version'.

7. Fo. 281^{rb-vb}: a largely illegible poem about the Magi, incomplete at the end.

COLLATION. 8–$22^{12}23^{10}24^{12}$ (–8 and –12, the latter probably blank).

TEXTUAL PRESENTATION. Headings and biblical lemmata in red, the former prefixed by a blue lombard, the latter by alternate red and blue lombards. At openings and major inner divisions, two-line alternate red lombards on violet flourishing and blue lombards on red flourishing. Similar initials preceding the large textura pericopes for the individual homilies. The second scribe often divides the text by two-line ochre-slashed lombards in the text ink.

LANGUAGE. *LALME* describes the two hands only as 'Northern' (i. 107). But the language of both is nearly identical with that of Rawlinson poet. 175, *LALME* LP 174 (coordinates 431/485, the Burneston area, North Riding, Yorkshire; see iii. 576–7), and these books, as well as BL, MSS Harley 4196 and Cotton Galba E.ix, were produced together. Indeed, the scribe who copies *Speculum Vitae* here probably also wrote the first four quires of the Galba manuscript (*Ywain and Gawain*, *The Seven Sages*), illustrated EETS 254 (1964), frontispiece. See Hanna, 'Yorkshire Writers', 92–100, and Hanna (2008).

DESCRIPTIONS. See Nevanlinna's edition, *The Northern Homily Cycle*, i. 11–17.

23. British Library, MS Harley 435

Vellum. s xv med. Fos. 100 (foliated 1–102, but including, as fos. 6, 50, and 59, paper replacement leaves of s. xvi ex., and fo. 47 repeated). A fair amount of damage from damp at both ends of the book. Overall 275 × 200 (writing area 195–215 × 140–50; the first quire and part of the second more generous, 240 × 145–50). 35–6 lines to the column (40–1 early on), in double columns. Written in anglicana (secretary *a* and a reduced *w* composed of three loops).

CONTENTS. Fos. 1ra–102ra: *Speculum Vitae*, lacking lines 978–1152, 8318–451, 8910–9053, and 9755–898, owing to lost leaves. All but the third of these omissions has been supplied on inserted paper leaves, s. xvi ex.; the same hand has added omitted lines and restored damaged text elsewhere (for example, fos. 94, 95, 97). The remainder of the book is blank, some pen-trials on fo. 102^{rv}.

COLLATION. 1^8 (–6, with modern replacement) $2–6^8$ 7^8 (–3, with modern replacement, –7) 8^8 (–5, with modern replacement) $9–13^8$. Catchwords; no signatures.

TEXTUAL PRESENTATION. Two-line unflourished red lombards at (relatively infrequent) major divisions, supplemented by red paraphs to divide the text. A fairly full explanatory programme, the side-notes introduced by red paraphs and Latin materials within the column in red. No running titles.

LANGUAGE. *LALME* LP 232 (coordinates 555/290, the Ely–Norfolk border); see iii. 103–4.

24. British Library, MS Harley 2260

Vellum. s. xiv/xv or s. xv in. Fos. 183. A fair number of lower edges and outer margins repaired. Overall 260 × 170 (writing area 200 [*c.*190 near the end] × 95–100). 37 lines to the page. Written in anglicana.

CONTENTS. Fos. 1^r–183^v: *Speculum Vitae*, lacking lines 1–2926 at the head. As Nelson demonstrates ('The Middle English *Speculum Vitae*', 74–8), this book, along with MS Ll.i.8 (and in part, MS Bodley 446), includes a set of nonauthorial interpolations.

COLLATION. [four lost quires] $5–8^{10}$ 9^{12} $10–11^{10}$ 12^{12} 13^{2+1} [fo. 87, the end of a production unit] | $14–19^{10}$ 20^{12} $21–2^{10}$ 23^4. Catchwords, sometimes centred or boxed; quires 5–12 signed, usually for the opening, with a leaf letter and roman quire number in brown crayon (*iiij–xj*), and a large X in the same crayon across the central opening of each quire. Given the four quires missing at the head (+, *j–iij*), the odd quire 13 facilitated a division into two roughly symmetrical pieces, conceivably for binding in two volumes (fo. 88 begins with the heading 'Adueniat regnum tuum Donus intellectus' and line 9081).

TEXTUAL PRESENTATION. Two- (very occasionally three-) line blue lombards with red flourishing. Smaller divisions by alternate red and blue paraphs. A full explanatory programme, the side-notes often with ochre-slashed initial capitals (as also some line-openings), running titles on the first leaves of sections.

LANGUAGE. *LALME* LP 198 (coordinates 521/335, southern Lincolnshire); see iii. 266–7.

25. British Library, MS Harley 6718, fos. 16–33

Paper, worn and mounted, folded in folio, each quire six full sheets. There are three stocks:

A Unidentified, perhaps Mountains: the two surviving outer sheets of quire 1

B Flower (and leaves): similar to Piccard 12, nos. 1495–1500 (northern and central Italy, 1388 × 1400) and Briquet nos. 6636–8 (1345 × 1372), but the leaf-stems independent of that of the flower: the three inner sheets of quire 1

C Bull's head: the general type of Piccard 2/ii, Type I, nos. 360–485 (northern Italy, mainly 1330 × 1351, but later examples to 1395): the sole stock of quire 2

s. xiv ex. Fos. 18. Overall 295–300 × 210–5 (writing area 265–75 × 175). 32–6 lines to the column, in double columns. Written in very rough anglicana.

CONTENTS. Fos. 16ra–33ra: The opening of a(n abandoned?) copy of *Speculum Vitae*, lines 156–1798, 1983–3130. Fo. 33^{v} was originally blank.

COLLATION. 1^{12} (–1, probably –8, –12) 2^{12} (–10 to –12). All leaves in the first half of each quire signed with roman numerals, fo. 25 signed 'ij^{us}. quaternus primi fol' [*sic*].

TEXTUAL PRESENTATION. Thoroughly unfinished.

LANGUAGE. *LALME*, identifying the text as perhaps a fragment of *The Prick of Conscience*, describes the language as 'Northern' (i. 113).

PROVENANCE: 'Thomas Farla⟨ne⟩' (s. xv ex.; fo. 33^{v}, an originally blank leaf now covered with pen-trials).

26. British Library, MS Royal 17 C.viii (R)

Paper, folded in quarto, each quire four full sheets. There are three stocks:

A Mermaid: close to Briquet nos. 13858–59, although with a flower as no. 13862 (northern France, 1458 × 1477): the sole stock of quires 1–4, the two inner sheets of quire 5 (18 full sheets)

B Bull's head: one of Piccard 2/ix, nos. 221–31, 233, 256–7 (northern French papers, 1443 × 1454; the analogous Briquet nos. 14223–4, 14227–9 in some cases slightly older): the sole stock of quires 6–19, the two outer sheets of quires 5 and 20 (60 full sheets)

C Star: probably Briquet no. 6053 (Italian, in use 1444 × 1472), but perhaps the later no. 6056 (Rhine and Low Countries, 1481 ×

1502, although a smaller sheet): the sole stock of quire 21, the two inner sheets of quire 20 (six full sheets)

s. xv med. (see further 'Provenance' below). Fos. i (numbered fo. 1) + 336 (foliated 2–337). A good deal of discolouration from damp in the lower third of the leaves (a few with mounts). Overall 213 × 145 (writing area 140–55 × 80–90). 23–6 lines to the page. Written in secretary with frequent anglicana *g*, secretary reduced *w* and *-s*.

CONTENTS. Fos. 2^r^–336^r^: *Speculum Vitae*, complete. Fos. 336^v^–337^v^ are blank.

COLLATION. 1–21^16^. Catchwords; all leaves in the first half of each quire signed, toward the inner bound and frequently just under the text, with letter and roman numeral (quires 1–21 = *a–v*, *x*).

LANGUAGE. *LALME* LP 392, described as 'Northern' but umapped; see iii. 664–5.

PROVENANCE. The scribe 'Richard Rokeby' signs the colophon, and then adds, in red, a note dating his work 1418. The book thus appears in Watson, *Catalogue of Dated and Datable Manuscripts*, i. 156 (no. 903) with a facsimile of part of fo. 98^v^ as plate 351. As my assessment of the hand and paper indicates, this notation has been supplied from elsewhere (probably Rokeby's exemplar), and the book is much later.

Fo. 1 is an old vellum flyleaf, formerly a pastedown; cut from a rent roll and bound in with the head in the gutter, it bears accounts, in anglicana, for 'Stansted' (probably the place in north-west Kent), 28–9 Edward III (1354–6). This leaf also has notes to a binder, written vertically: 'Sir William I lat you wyt þa⟨.⟩ stond ewen in ordour as you shall se in in [*sic*] þe buk etc. And sett þe two qweres of saynt Edmoundes lyff [no longer here, of course] in þe latter end of þe buk' (secretary, s. xv/xvi). There are further late fifteenth- and early sixteenth-century signatures of 'John Thomas trauis . . . of kyrdford' (Sussex) (fo. 337^v^, as owner), Thomas Treves (fo. 337), and John Thorne of Wrottam (Kent, as owner).

DESCRIPTIONS. Warner and Gilson, *Catalogue of Western Manuscripts*, ii. 240–1.

27. British Library, MS Sloane 1785, fos. 29–60

Vellum. s. xv med. Fos. 32. Overall 230 × 165 (writing area 187–95 × 130–6; fo. 36 in a smaller format, 182 × 130). 43–51 lines to the column, in double columns (typically more in scribe 2's portion (fo. 36, 45 lines). Written by three scribes: fos. 30ra–35vb, 37ra–39vb in textura rotunda, fos. 40ra–60rb in anglicana (avoiding below-line *r*), fo. 36^{rab} in a different anglicana with the final eighteen lines added in textura.

CONTENTS. Fos. 30ra–35vb, 37ra–60rb, 36^{rab}: *Speculum Vitae*, a fragment containing lines 360–6164, with some textual disruptions (e.g. a version of lines 1615–28 precedes 1455 at the head of fo. 37ra), 6334–402 (fo. 36, from 6383 the textura addition). Fos. 29^{rv} and 36^{v} (as well as about twenty lines on 36rb) are blank and probably appropriated from elsewhere, on heavy vellum.

COLLATION. i^2 (fos. 29+36, probably originally a wrapper) 1^8 (–1, –2) (fos. 30–5) 2–4^8 (fos. 37–60). No catchwords or signatures.

TEXTUAL PRESENTATION. Unfinished; two-line unfilled spaces for initials and unfilled blanks for headings. There is no annotational programme. On fo. 36^{r}, one heading filled in red (an in-column use of a marginal note), a few red brackets to join couplets.

LANGUAGE. *LALME* LP 505 (coordinates 457/317, north-central Leicestershire); see iii. 242.

28. British Library, MS Stowe 951 (S)

Mixed vellum and paper, both folded in quarto, each quire three paper sheets folded inside one of vellum, which then forms the inner and outer bifolia. The final quire is entirely vellum. There are at least two stocks, identifications often difficult because the mark falls in the gutter, but both appearing in both parts of the book (60 original full sheets):

A Ox: one of Piccard 15/iii, nos. 859–98 or 935–1039 (in common use 1426 × 1437 and 1433 × 1454 respectively)

B Ox: one of Piccard 15/iii, nos. 1096–7, 1099–1102, 1104 (all German, in use 1441 × 1444)

s. $xv^{2/4}$. Fos. 320 (foliated 4–322, but a stub with some writing after fo. 4 unnumbered). Overall 210 × 145 (in *Speculum Vitae*, writing area 155–60 × 85–95). 28–30 lines to the page. Written in anglicana (usually with short *r*); the hand of item 1 similar but not identical.

CONTENTS

Booklet 1 = fos. 4–31

1. Fos. 4^{r}–29^{r}: *The Three Kings of Cologne* (*IPMEP* 290). Fos. 29^{v}–31^{v} blank.

COLLATION. 1^{16} (2 an unnumbered stub) 2^{16} (–13 to –15). Catchwords; all leaves in the first half of each quire signed with letter and roman numeral (quire 2 = *I*, quires 3–20 = *a–s*).

Booklet 2 = fos. 32–322

2. Fos. 32r–312r: *Speculum Vitae*, complete.

3. Fos. 313r–322r: 'Quixley''s translation of Gower's Anglo-Norman balades on chaste love (*IMEV* 4105, unique; the translator identifies himself in line 7). Fo. 322v is blank.

COLLATION. $3\text{–}20^{16}\,21^{4}$ (–4).

LANGUAGE *LALME* LP 526 (coordinates 417/466, the Pateley Bridge area, West Riding, Yorkshire); see iii. 646–7.

BINDING. The bare medieval wooden boards, now reversed and rebacked. Grooves and nail holes from two original straps and their clasp-plates towards the spine on the original lower board.

PROVENANCE. On Quixley, probably John Quixley of Quixley (modern Whixley, near Knaresborough), see MacCracken, 'Quixley's Ballades Royal', 37–9, with due attention to John Gower's Yorkshire pedigree. Signatures of Thomas Hvkane (fo. 322, s. xv²); Richard Garthwait (fos. 318v in Greek letters, 320v; s. xvi/xvii); John Trollop of Thornley (fos. 312, 318v, s. xvii in., the first below Anthonye Trollop).

DESCRIPTIONS. *Catalogue of the Stowe Manuscripts*, 634–5.

29. London, Sion College, MS Arch. L.40.2/E.25, currently a Lambeth Palace Library deposit

Paper (except the vellum binding leaf, fo. 134). There are four stocks, all folded in quarto, each quire three full sheets (or three with a half-sheet), one stock distinctly predominant:

A Two circles: visible is Briquet 3194 (Brussels, 1392; although recorded from a considerably larger sheet than here). But marks of this type often have a cross, perhaps here obscured in the binding (compare Briquet 3160–3, or 3227, which appears in BL, MS Arundel 507, probably copied in Durham, s. xiv ex.): the sole stock of quires 1–3, 7–12 (24 full sheets, including two that have lost a leaf and another that has lost two leaves, two watermarked half sheets, and two unwatermarked half sheets [quire 3 also includes a sheet without watermark])

B (Bow and?) Arrow: resembles Piccard 9/ii, 1088 et seq.: the sole stock of quire 4 (one probable full sheet and five single leaves, two with halves of the mark)

C Wheel: not in Briquet: the sole stock of quire 5 (three full sheets)

D Pot ?: not in Briquet: the sole stock of quire 6 (three full sheets, including one that has lost a leaf with half the mark)

s. xiv/xv. Fos. 133 + i (fo. 134); fo. 31 has been mostly torn away and is now a large stub. Overall 220 × 150 (writing area 180 × 100–5 in *Speculum*, up to 190 × 110 in scribe 3 portions). Usually 30–7 lines to the page (scribe 3, 43–51 lines, partly continued as 40–4 in scribe 2's quire 10). Written by three scribes, all in anglicana, the first, quires 1, 5–6; the second, quires 2–4, 10–12; the third (anglicana formata), quires 7–9.

CONTENTS

Booklet 1 = fos. 1–12

1. Fos. 1^r–12^v: *Speculum Vitae*, brief and scattered excerpts only, beginning with a block from line 7799 on (fos. 1^r–3^r), 5595–6004 (with some interpolated material from the 7800s already presented on fo. 2, fos. 3^r–8^v), then progressively shorter excerpts, especially from the discussion of Chastity, breaking off with line 15042.

COLLATION. 1^{14} (–1, –2). A single formal catchword, centred in a red box, fo. 82^v, examples in informal hands, fos. 113^v and 123^v; scribes 1 and 2 sign all leaves in the first half of each quire with a roman leaf numeral.

Booklet 2 = fos. 13–38

2. Fos. 13^r–38^v: a verse 'gospel of Nicodemus' (*IMEV* 512), also in BL, MSS Cotton Galba E.ix and Harley 4196, books produced with Cotton Tiberius E.vii above.

COLLATION. 2^{12} 3^{14} (7, fo. 31, mostly torn away).

Booklet 3 = fos. 39–47

3. Fos. 39^r–47^r: a dialogue of St Bernard and the Virgin (*IMEV* 771), also in Cotton Tiberius E.vii.

COLLATION. 4^{14} (–10 to –14).

Booklet 4 = fos. 48–133

4. Fos. 48^r–133^v: *The Prick of Conscience* (*IMEV* 3428); although earlier booklets show connections with Tiberius and related books, with fine copies of this poem, Britton's stemma ('Unknown Fragments', 329) demonstrates that this version is significantly advanced in transmission.

COLLATION. 5^{12} 6^{12} (–1) 7–8^{12} 9^{12} (–1, –4, -6, –7, –12) 10^{12} 11^{12} (–1 to –3) 12^{12} (–12).

TEXTUAL PRESENTATION. Headings in text ink and more formal versions of the text hand, sometimes approaching textura quadrata. At openings, two- to four-line red lombards, unflourished (isolated blue examples with red flourishing, fos. 125, 128). Red boxes around biblical citations in item 4, as well as around marginalia; to fo. 7, rhymes bracketed in red. Line initials red-slashed, similar slashing on some decorative top-line ascenders in scribe 3's portions. Substantial remains of the explanatory programme for *Speculum Vitae*, marginal portions only.

LANGUAGE. *LALME* identifies only two hands. That in quire 1 is associated with the West Riding, Yorkshire (i. 137); that of quire 2 is LP 481 ('Northern' and unmapped; see iii. 670–1).

BINDING. Modern brown leather over millboards; fo. 134 is probably a pastedown from an earlier binding, taken from a noted missal.

PROVENANCE. 'Ryder' (fo. 38ᵛ, lower margin, s. xv); 'Iste liber pertinet Fratri Iohanni Holonde Monacho Westm'' (fo. 134), a Westminster monk who said his first mass 1472 and was subprior in 1500.

DESCRIPTIONS. Ker, *MMBL* i. 289, Lewis-McIntosh, 82–3 (MV 49). Richard Morris's identification of item 1 as *Speculum Vitae*, at EETS OS 23 (1866), pref. 2 n. 1, seems unaccountably to have been ignored (although see Allen, 'The Authorship of the *Prick of Conscience*', 169 n.1).

30. Marlborough (Wilts.), St Mary's, Vicar's Library, currently a Bodleian Library deposit, Marl. C 31

Vellum. s. xiv/xv or s. xv in. Fo. 1. Overall 200 × 144 (cut down into the writing area which is 110 mm wide). 41 lines to the page, of an original 42–3. Written in anglicana formata (frequent textura *d*, often with biting; textura *r* universal).

CONTENTS. *Speculum Vitae*, a single-leaf fragment with lines 5206–46, 5249–90. Not entirely legible, even with ultraviolet, especially on the original verso, the exposed side of the leaf.

TEXTUAL PRESENTATION. Two-line red lombards, unflourished, at divisions in the text, red-slashed line initials. Full marginalia in red.

LANGUAGE. *LALME* has two entries, associating the language with both East Riding, Yorkshire and Northumberland (i. 139), but the language, although a brief sample, appears to me West Riding, Yorkshire.

BINDING. The leaf, folded across its middle, formed the wrapper of C 31: Bernhard Textor, *Obseruationum practicarum ad ecclesiae aedificationem . . . adumbratio* (Herborn, 1598). Now removed, the leaf is preserved separately.

PROVENANCE. On the history of the library, bequeathed the vicars of St Mary's, Marlborough, in 1677 by William White, formerly Master of Magdalen College School and rector of Pusey (Berks.), see Kempson, 'The Vicar's Library'. The passage of the collection to the Bodleian is reported in *Bodleian Library Record*, 12/1 (1985), 76–7.

DESCRIPTIONS. See Fischer, 'Ein nordenglisches moralisch-religiöses Versfragment' and *Horae Eboracenses*, 165–7. Nelson, 'The Middle English *Speculum Vitae*', 657–61, provides a more accurate transcription.

31. Nottingham University Library, MS Mi(ddleton) LM 9

Vellum. s. xv in. Fos. ii + 260 (numbered 1–257, but unnumbered leaves after fos. 46, 121, 137, and 195; and 87 omitted in the sequence) + ii. Overall 245 × 140 (writing area 165–70 × 83–5). 32 lines to the page (item 2, 178 × 95 in 34 lines). Written in anglicana formata; booklet 2 a second contemporary scribe in similar script.

CONTENTS

Booklet 1 = fos. 1–247

1. Fos. 1^r–247^r: *Speculum Vitae*, complete, although lines 11181–212 (forbidding sex during menstruation) have been erased (fo. 172^{rv}). About half of fo. 247^r and the verso are blank, but bounded.

COLLATION. 1–25^{10}. Catchwords near the inner bounding line; all leaves in the first half of each quire signed with letter and roman numeral, the majority cut away (quires 3–25 = *c*–*y*, –, &, *z*).

Booklet 2 = fos. 248–57

2. Fos. 248^r–256^r: John Gaytryge's 'Lay Folks' Catechism' (*IPMEP* 71); see Hudson, 'A New Look', 246. The remainder is blank but bounded.

COLLATION. 26^{10}. Signed *b*–*e* on fos. 249–52, and a partially cut away signature in red *a ii*⟨ ⟩ on fo. 251.

TEXTUAL PRESENTATION. Headings in the margins, as if part of the annotational programme. At the opening, a four-line blue lombard with red foliate flourishing and marginal extensions. Two-line examples at major internal divisions. The text is also divided by alternate red and blue paraphs, line-initials red-slashed. A full marginal explanatory programme, entries underlined in red with red-slashed capitals. Running titles in bastard anglicana in red boxes, sporadic to fo. 54, thereafter regular.

LANGUAGE. 'Mixed, but apparently has a Leicestershire ingredient' (*LALME* i. 144).

BINDING. Brown leather over bevelled wooden boards, s. xv, sewn on six thongs, pegged two to a hole. Two thin leather straps with metal hooks, remains of the pins to which they attached near the centre of the lower board. The flyleaves are the raised pastedowns.

PROVENANCE. A variety of pen-trials, signatures, etc., mostly in the hand that signs 'William Fleccher' (s. xv^2 or xv ex.); one of these may imply a connection with the Fitzhughs (of Ravensworth, North Riding, Yorkshire). A Leicestershire provenance would be provocative, since the Willoughby family, who certainly owned locally acquired manuscripts in the fifteenth century, take their title from the family estate at Middleton, in eastern Warwickshire.

DESCRIPTIONS. Stevenson, *Report on the Manuscripts*, 237–9 (with extensive quotation); Turville-Petre and Johnson, *Image and Text*, 8 (with a reduced facsimile of fo. 17^r).

32. Oxford, Bodleian Library, MS Bodley 48 (B^1)

Vellum. s. xv^1 or s. $xv^{2/4}$. Fos. i (numbered fo. iii) + 334. Overall 180 × 130 (writing area in *Speculum Vitae*, 140–5 × 85–90). 28–31 lines to the page. Written in anglicana, with incipient forward lean in the Latin (a blockish secretary *a* universal, long *s* in all positions, and, in the English only, *g* formed from with anglicana upper stroke and the flat open lower loop, with curved finish, from secretary).

CONTENTS

Booklet 1 = fos. 1–46

1. Fos. 1^r–23^v: Richard Rolle, the Latin *Emendatio Vitae*.

2. Fos. 23^v–29^r: ps.-Rolle, the Latin 'Nouem virtutes'; see Allen, *Writings Ascribed to Richard Rolle*, 318.

3. Fos. 29^v–32^r: Rolle, the Latin 'Super orationem dominicam'.

4. Fos. 32^r–45^r: Rolle, the Latin 'Super symbolum apostolorum'.

5. Fos. 45^r–46^v: Lydgate, 'The Kings of England' (*IMEV* 3632), added on blank leaves in anglicana, s. xv med., as are items 8 and 9. below.

COLLATION. 1^{16} 2^{20} 3^8 4^2. As in the remainder of the book, no catchwords; quires signed with a letter in the top right corner of the first recto, a number missing (quires 1–4 = *a*, –, *c–d*).

Booklet 2 = fos. 47–331, with added 332–4

6. Fos. 47^{r}–325^{r}: *Speculum Vitae*, complete. All the missing leaves are cancels without text loss, but the scribe's behaviour is frequently erratic. On at least two occasions, he appears to have mishandled his copy or the in-progress quire and to have reversed folio-long blocks of material, and he lost at least one other folio's worth of material following fo. 279^{v}, where lines 13330–89 are not represented.

7. Fos. 325^{v}–331^{r}: 'Simony and Covetise' (*IMEV* 1992, unique), a three-leaf hiatus in mid-text.

8. Fos. 331^{v}–332^{r}: Lydgate, 'Stans puer ad mensam' (*IMEV* 2233).

9. Fos. 332^{v}–334^{v}: Lydgate, 'Dietary' (*IMEV* 824), not divided from the preceding text.

COLLATION. 5^{16} 6–7^{12} 8–12^{16} 13–14^{14} 15^{20} (–10) 16^{12} (–6) 17^{16} (–16) 18^{12} 19^{16} 20^{16} (–10) 21^{12} 22^{16} 23^{16} (–16) 24^{8} (–1, –2) 25^{4} (–4, probably blank). Quires 5–23 signed *a–T*, with substantial omissions; the unsigned quire 24 includes the main scribe's added item 7, and quire 25 was supplied by the later scribe to accommodate his added runover.

TEXTUAL PRESENTATION. At divisions, two-line unflourished red lombards. Line-initials are red-slashed. A fairly full marginal explanatory programme (only sporadic running titles), all entries introduced by red-slashed capitals.

LANGUAGE. Görlach, *The Textual Tradition*, 86 and 248 nn. 74–5 describes the mixture of south-west Midland and south-eastern forms in the scribe's other known manuscript, BL, MS Cotton Julius D.ix (*South English Legendary*). Embree and Urquhart, in *The Simonie*, 15, more narrowly identify the two strata as Essex/Suffolk and Gloucestershire. (In addition to linguistic similarities, Görlach notes features of book production in the Julius manuscript reminiscent of behaviours here.)

BINDING. Brown leather over millboards, s. xvii, disbound and rebacked 1983, on six thongs. Fo. iii is probably a pastedown from an earlier binding, also on six thongs.

PROVENANCE. Presented to the Bodleian, with twenty-six other manuscripts, by Sir George More, a prominent courtier and frequent Surrey official, in 1604; see *SC* i. 88–9. Two other books in the gift were Middle English, MSS Bodley 207 (Nicholas Love) and 277 (Wycliffite Bible).

DESCRIPTIONS. *SC* ii/1. 97–8 (no. 1885).

33. Bodleian Library, MS Bodley 446 (B^2)

Vellum. s. xv in. Fos. ii + 207 + ii (fos. 208–9). Overall 255 × 180 (writing area to fo. 70, 198 × 95–100, in later portions 210–25 × 95–100). 34–6 lines initially; after fo. 70, 38–43 lines to the page. Written in anglicana formata.

CONTENTS. Fos. 1–207^v: *Speculum Vitae*, complete, preceded by the certificate of the alleged 1384 Cambridge examination (in red ink). As Nelson demonstrates ('The Middle English *Speculum Vitae*', 74–8, 83–4), this book shares, probably by selective conflation, some added lines of MSS Ll.i.8 and Harley 2260.

COLLATION. $1–6^8$ 7^6 $8–21^8 22^6$ $23–5^8 26^{10+1}$ (+10). Catchwords usual but a few missing; all leaves in the first half of each quire probably signed with roman numeral, the majority cut away, almost universally so late in the book.

TEXTUAL PRESENTATION A six-line blank for an initial at the opening; all other spaces for initials similarly unfilled, two- and three-line blanks with guide letters. A full explanatory programme, with a ruled marginal column and running titles, materials provided in the text ink. The last line of marginal annotations underlined in red. In-column headings, in display anglicana, boxed in red (exceptionally, on fo. 123^v, in textura and in red).

LANGUAGE. *LALME* LP 196 (coordinates 527/317, the Lincolnshire–Ely border); see iii. 265–6.

BINDING. Whittawed leather, now browned on the covers, over wood in cushioned bevel, s. xv, rebacked, on five thongs. The stub of a central leather strap with three nails, the nail from the plate for clasping at the centre of the lower board. Pitting in the wood and nail holes from an institutional chain-staple (not Bodley's) in the upper board, lower leading edge. The flyleaves each form a bifolium, the outer of the pair previously pasted down.

PROVENANCE. 'Donum Roberti Treswel alias Somerset' (fo. 1, the hand of Thomas Bodley); the donation occurred 1605–11, and in 1612, Trewel, the king's woodward and Somerset Herald, gave a further manuscript (now MS Bodley 181, mostly Giles of Rome and the ps.-Aristotelian *Secreta*, s. xv).

DESCRIPTIONS. *SC* ii/2. 493 (no. 2685).

34. Bodleian Library, MS Eng. poet. a.1 ('The Vernon Manuscript') (B^3)

s. xiv ex. Vellum. Fos. 350 (of an original 422 or 426); the foliation cited is that of the facsimile, based on that affixed at the time quires were collected for indexing and binding; it includes missing leaves. 544 × 393 (writing area *c*.412–20 × 284–94). 80 lines to the column, in this portion in three columns. In anglicana formata (one scribe, except for fos. i–viii^{ra}, the quire of front matter).

CONTENTS. Booklet 3 = fos. 167–318

1. Fos. 167ra–227^{vc}: *The Northern Homily Cycle* (in *IMEV* as numerous separate poems), the so-called 'Midland Version', shared only with the 'The Simeon manuscript', described above; see Nevanlinna in the edition, 3–4.

2. Fos. 227^{vc}–230^{rc}: 'How a man shall live perfectly' (*IMEV* 1512), a partial versified translation of Edmund Rich.

3. Fos. 230^{rc}–231ra: 'The visions of St Paul' (*IMEV* 1898).

4. Fo. 231^{ra-vc}: 'Pope Gregory's Trental' (*IMEV* 1653), followed by a painted diagramme (reproduced in colour, facsimile plate xiii).

5. Fos. 231va–265^{rc}: *Speculum Vitae*. Lacks lines 7717–8197, owing to loss of the leaf assigned fo. 248.

6. Fos. 265ra–284ra: *The Prick of Conscience* (*IMEV* 3428), preceded by an illumination (reproduced in colour, facsimile plate xv).

This booklet, one of five in the whole, contains twenty-six further items; prominent among these are: 'The Prick of Love', a versification of Edmund Rich's *Speculum* (*IMEV* 974, fos. 284ra–86^{rc}), a translation of Grosseteste's Anglo-Norman 'The Castle of Love' (*IMEV* 3270, fos. 293^{rc}–296va), 'Ypotis' (*IMEV* 220, fos. 296va–297^{vc}), 'Robert of Sicily' (*IMEV* 2780, fos. 300^{rc}–301^{rc}), 'The King of Tars' (*IMEV* 1108, fos. 304vb–307ra); trilingual versified proverbs, the English translating Nicholas Bozon (*IMEV* 3501, fos. 307rb–309va); a trilingual Cato, the Anglo-Norman the common version of 'Evrart' (*IMEV* 247+820, fos. 309va–314rb), 'Susannah' (*IMEV* 3553, fo. 317^{ra-vb}), and 'the long charter of Christ' (*IMEV* 1718, fos. 317vb–318rb). At the end, fo. 318^{v} is blank, although bounded and ruled.

COLLATION (quires 23–41 of the whole) 1–10^{8} 11^{8} (–2) 12–19^{8}. Catchwords; in this portion, all leaves in the first half of most quires signed with letter and roman numeral (quires 23–41 = *r*–*v*, three unsigned quires, *a*–*c*, *k*–*n*, the last five quires unsigned).

TEXTUAL PRESENTATION (In this portion only:) Headings in red. At the openings, five- or six-line champes with floral demivinets. At inner divisions, the hierarchy varies slightly: sometimes two-or three-line champes, sometimes five-line examples, frequently with a painted bar extension (a 'tallia' or 'taille'), some with painted sprays. The text is divided by red and blue paraphs, usually alternate, or by gold-leaf lombards on brown or violet flourishing.

LANGUAGE. *LALME* LP 7630 (coordinates 389/270, north-central Worcestershire near Bordesley); see iii. 553.

BINDING. Recovered wooden boards, s. xv, traces of brown calf visible beneath the present covering, s. xix red leather, on six double thongs. Depressions in the upper board from the seatings for two straps.

PROVENANCE. Coincidence of many lyrics and of dialect features would associate the manuscript with British Library, MS Additional 37787, produced by or for John Northwood, a monk of Bordesley (OCist) in north Worcestershire; see Baugh, *A Worcestershire Miscellany*. The scribe of the front-matter quire, *LALME* LP 7670 (coordinates 378/262; see iii. 555), also copied legal records for Bordesley's daughter-house, Stoneleigh (in western Warwickshire), as well as portions of two related ('Lichfield subgroup') manuscripts of *The Prick of Conscience*, Holkham Hall, MS 668; and Oxford, Trinity College, MS 16B; see Lewis-McIntosh, 54–5, 121–2 (MV 23, 89). Vernon might be associated with that locale, with Bordesley's other two daughter establishments in Warwickshire, with some consortium of these, or with a large nunnery in the area (for example, Nuneaton, Warwickshire).

DESCRIPTIONS. Doyle, *The Vernon Manuscript* 1987 (both the introduction and the report of production features on the rear flyleaf); Pearsall, *Studies in the Vernon Manuscript*, *passim*.

35. Bodleian Library, MS Eng. poet. d.5 (E)

Vellum. s. xiv/xv. Fos. i + 218. Overall 255 × 175 (writing area 175–200 × 110–17). 33–40 long lines to the page, generally the hand increasing in size as the MS proceeds. Written in anglicana formata, mainly a single scribe, but a substantial change in at least duct, and probably hand, at fos. 170^v/6–79^r/2 (the last eight plus leaves of quire 15, lines 12680–13265).

CONTENTS. Fos. 1^r–218^r: *Speculum Vitae*, complete. Fo. 218^v is blank.

COLLATION. 1^{10} $2–10^{12}$ 11^{12} (5 and 8, fos. 123 and 126, reversed in binding) $12–18^{12}$ 19^{4}. Catchwords; all leaves in the first half of each quire signed with letter and roman numeral (quires 1–19 = *a–h*, *k–v*).

TEXTUAL PRESENTATION. At the opening, a six-line red lombard, unflourished, two- to four-line examples at textual divisions. Red paraphs, many red-slashed capitals (including examples of *w*- at midline), extended red lines to join couplets, red boxes around marginalia and running titles. A full explanatory programme.

LANGUAGE. 'Northern' (*LALME* i. 148).

BINDING. Brown leather over wooden boards, s. xv, on five thongs, rebacked. Grooves for two leather straps, one nailed stub intact; stubs of the nails from plates for pins at the centre of the lower board. At the front, a medieval vellum flyleaf (fo. ii).

PROVENANCE. The scribal signature 'Explicit liber de Paternoster per Iohannem Kylyngwyke'.

36. Bodleian Library, MS Greaves 43 (B^4)

Vellum. s. xv in. Fos. 47 (1, 38, and 47 fragments). There is a faulty early modern pagination. Overall 240 × 130 (writing area 185–205 × 90–5). 38 lines to the page. Written in bastard anglicana (textura *d*, ascenders of *b*, *h*, *k* not looped but with a flat top stroke).

CONTENTS. Fos. 1^r–37^v: *Speculum Vitae*, materials from lines 8292–365 (fo. 4) and 9531–14054. Lacks lines 9660–959 (after fo. 2), 10718–11016 (after fo. 13), and 12458–915 (after fo. 32), owing to lost leaves.

COLLATION. 1^{12+1} (= fos. 1–9; –3, –5 to –7; +4, a single from an earlier quire) 2^{12} (–5 to –8) 3^{12} 4^{12} (–4 to –9, a note 'desunt m⟨ulta⟩', s. xvi, in the gutter, fo. 32^v) 5^{12}. No catchwords; all leaves in the first half of each quire signed with roman numerals in brown crayon, fo. 10 with quire signature *m*.

TEXTUAL PRESENTATION. At major divisions, two-line blue lombards, unflourished. Scattered red paraphs to mark smaller divisions. An explanatory programme with red-boxed side-notes but no running titles; rhymes bracketed in red.

LANGUAGE. *LALME* LP 165 (coordinates 430/589, the Sheffield area); see iii. 616–17.

PROVENANCE. John and Edward (? or Edmund) Iset (the latter as owner, fos. 14, 17, respectively, s. xvi), the first with a reference to the 'parson of Pulton'; an extract from a deed or will concerning

John Parfit's debts (fo. 37, s. xvi²); Anthony Huish (as owner, fos. 12ᵛ, 17ᵛ, s. xvii).

DESCRIPTIONS. *SC* ii/2. 746 (no. 3815).

37. Bodleian Library, MS Hatton 18 (B⁵)

Paper; there are four stocks, all folded in folio:

A Chariot: probably Briquet no. 3528 (widely dispersed 1429 × 1453): the sole stock of quires 1–4, 6 and the three outer sheets of quire 5 (47 full sheets and one half-sheet with the mark)

B Ring: not in Briquet (the mark shaped like the much later no. 699): the inner six sheets of quire 5 and five sheets each in quires 7–8 (16 sheets)

C Crescent (?): not in Briquet, but the type of nos. 5215–18, 5220, 5222 (1346 × 1483 variously), but with more rays and no apparent cross: four sheets each in quires 7–8 (eight sheets)

D Crown: Piccard 1, type I, no. 325 (mainly German, 1454 × 1470): the sole stock of quires 9–12 (33 sheets)

s. $xv^{2/4}$. Fos. i (a modern flyleaf, numbered fo. 1) + 209 (fos. 2–210). Overall 303 × 215 (writing area 217–35 × 125, in later portions 208 × 95–110). 33–7 (later portions 41–3) lines to the page. Written in anglicana, with frequent secretary *a* and *r*, by two scribes; the second, who has an exaggerated left shoulder on his anglicana *r*, takes up at the last line of fo. 108 (a substantial change in the first scribe's ductus at fos. $52^{v}/53$).

CONTENTS. Fos. 2^{r}–210^{v}: *Speculum Vitae*. The MS lacks lines 1–65, owing to a lost leaf at the head.

COLLATION. 1^{16} (–1) 2–3^{18} 4^{20} 5–9^{18} 10–12^{16}. Virtually all production data appears to have been cut away in binding; exceptionally, fos. 53 and 109 have quire signatures '3^{a}.' (the top only, remainder cut away) and '7^{mus}. quaternus' respectively, and seven of the leaves in first half of quire 8 are signed with the appropriate arabic numerals.

TEXTUAL PRESENTATION. At the openings of sections, two- to four-line red lombards, unflourished, many spaces unfilled. The lombards occasionally have ochre flourishing, often with drawings of heads in green, ochre, and text ink (further examples in the margins, e.g. a head and a dog, fo. 91). Couplets bracketed in red to fo. 179, line initials red-slashed. A full explanatory programme, with running titles; early on, the marginalia are ochre-slashed, later occasionally underlined in red.

LANGUAGE. *LALME* LP 4231 (coordinates 575/279, north-west Suffolk); see iii. 475–6.

BINDING. Brown leather over millboards, with a fillet in blind, on five thongs, probably s. xvii ex.

PROVENANCE. 'Hic fuit frater Iohannes Fakun', 'Iste liber est venerabilis domine dompne Elesabeth Throckmorten abbetisse de denney Teste Thoma Sywerd in eodem monasterio olim manenti' (both s. xvi in., fo. 210^{v}). Doyle, 'A Survey of the Origins', i. 86, identifies Fakun as the last vice-warden of the Cambridge Franciscans and Throckmorton as the last abbess of Denny (Cambridgeshire, Franciscan nuns); only the latter appears in Ker, *MLGB* 57, 251. In addition, Bartholomew Swalow (fos. 40^{v} and 210^{v}, on the latter occasion as owner), s. xvii in.

DESCRIPTIONS. *SC* ii/2. 844 (no. 4111).

38. Bodleian Library, MS Hatton 19 (B^6)

Vellum. s. xv^{1}. Fos. ii (numbered fos. 1–2) + 94 (fos. 3–96). Overall 308 × 223 (writing area 225 × 170). 45 lines to the column, in double columns. Written in an erect secretary (anglicana *w*).

CONTENTS. Fos. 3ra–94vb: *Speculum Vitae*, complete. Fo. 95 blank but bounded and ruled.

COLLATION. $1–11^{8}\ 12^{8}$ (–7, –8, both blanks). Catchwords (sometimes boxed); all leaves in the first half of each quire signed, usually with letter and roman numeral, many cut away (quires 1–12 = +, *a–c*, *d* [altered from *c*] *d–e*, –, *I*, *l*, *I*, *l*). At the head of fo. 59, the instruction 'Incipe correct'.

TEXTUAL PRESENTATION. At the opening, a four-line champe, with a two-line example at line 19, both joined in a bar border with leaf and flower sprays in blue, violet, and green. A full explanatory programme in red, with running titles and with the customary marginalia often written as in-column headings. Line-initials ochre-slashed. Infrequently (fos. 54va, 55ra) ornamental ascenders on the first initials on a page.

LANGUAGE. *LALME* LP 7610 (coordinates 382/278, Worcestershire, near the county's juncture with Shropshire and Staffordshire); see iii. 552.

BINDING. Whittawed leather over cushioned bevel boards, s. xv, on six thongs. Stubs of two leather straps on the upper board, holes and one intact nail from the pin seatings near the centre of the lower board. The nails from these seatings have penetrated the last two leaves. Fos. 1 and 96 are former pastedowns.

PROVENANCE. A scribal colophon 'Nomen scriptoris Thomas Doule plenus amoris'; on the upper part of the outer lower board, a partially defaced inscription, read (when probably more legible than now) by *SC* as '-deryngton'; by Doyle ('A Survey of the Origins', i. 86 n. 18) as 'monasterio'.

DESCRIPTIONS. *SC* ii/2. 844 (no. 4110).

39. Bodleian Library, MS Lyell 28 (B^7)

Vellum. s. xiv ex. Fos. 79 (with a fair amount of water damage, especially at tops of leaves near both ends of the book). Overall 340 × 240 (a few leaves broader, and quire 5 about 25 mm shorter) (writing area 265–70 × 158). 45 or 46 lines to the column, in double columns. Written in anglicana.

CONTENTS. Fos. 1ra–79vb: *Speculum Vitae*, lacking lines 1–179 at the head, 1395–569 (after fo. 7), 4046–399 (after fo. 21), 4581–756 (after fo. 22), 11391–12108 (after fo. 59), 14985–15344 (after fo. 75), and 16064–96 at the end, owing to missing leaves.

COLLATION. 1^{12} (–1, –9, both stubs) 2^{12} (–12, a stub) 3^{12} (–1, –3, the latter a stub) 4–5^{12} 6^{12} (–5 to –8) 7^{12} 8^{8} (–1, –2, –7, –8, the last surely blank). Catchwords in red-slashed boxes; occasional signatures for leaves only (e.g. fos. 33, 46–9), in roman numerals.

TEXTUAL PRESENTATION. Headings written in textura quadrata in text ink and red-boxed. A full explanatory programme, with both running titles and side-notes, also red-boxed. At textual divisions, two-line red lombards, unflourished. Line-initials red-slashed. Paraphs in the text ink, as are the brackets joining couplets, the paraphs red-slashed.

LANGUAGE. Not in *LALME* but identified Beadle, 'Middle English Texts', 84 as 'Northern'; probably, more narrowly placeable in north-western Yorkshire.

BINDING. Limp vellum, s. xvi/xvii, the wrapper remounted recently over cardboard, on four thongs (probably modern replacements).

PROVENANCE. Signatures of Ewen Browne of Ringisbory, Thomas Byelbye, Thomas Thynning(es?) (all s. xvii in., inside the lower wrapper).

DESCRIPTIONS. de la Mare, *Catalogue*, 59.

40. Bodleian Library, MS Rawlinson C.884 (B^8)

Paper, folded in quarto, each quire originally six full sheets. There are three paper stocks:

A Circle: closest to Briquet no. 3134 (1408 × 1439, France and Italy): the sole stock of quires 1 (where two sheets are indeterminate), 2–5, 9–10, and the two outer sheets of quire 6, the outer sheet of quire 11, and the five inner sheets of quire 8 (48–50 original full sheets)

B Dog: not in Piccard 15, but very like Briquet no. 3643 (? 1400 × 1415, Italian): the sole stock of quire 7 (one sheet indeterminate), the four inner sheets of quire 6, and the outer sheet of quire 8 (10–11 original full sheets)

C Scales: one of Piccard 5/i, nos. 11–209 (in widespread use, most prevalently 1400 × 1440): the sole stock of quires 12–13 and the five inner sheets of quire 11 (17 original full sheets)

s. xv^{I} or $xv^{2/4}$. Fos. i + 288 (I follow an original foliation, centred at the page top [from fo. 233 in the upper corners], in roman numerals, 8–310, including losses). Overall 225 × 150 (writing area 155–70 × 80–5). 23–7 lines to the page, diminishing through the book. Written in anglicana (secretary and anglicana *a* alternate, a distinctive anglicana *g* with two open loops, the lower written to the right of the upper).

CONTENTS. Fos. 8^r–310^v: *Speculum Vitae*. Lacks lines 1–383 at the head, 1041–93 (fo. 20), 1255–1307 (fo. 24), 3799–851 (fo. 73), 4317–68 (fo. 83), 4930–79 (fo. 95), 5033–85 (fo. 97), 7539–645 (fos. 145–6), 8689–792 (fos. 167–8), 8844–94 (fo. 170), 9903–52 (fo. 191), 11698–744 (fo. 227), 13021–67 (fo. 255), 13672–716 (fo. 269) and 15558–end (after fo. 310).

COLLATION. 1^{24} (−1 to −7, −20, −24) 2–$3^{24}4^{24}$ (−1, −11, −23) 5^{24} (−1) $6^{24}7^{24}$ (−1, −2, −23, −24) 8^{24} (−2, −23) $9^{24}10^{24}$ (−11) 11^{24} (−15) 12^{24} (−5) 13^{24} (−23, −24). Catchwords near the gutter; all leaves in the first half of each quire signed with letter and roman numeral (quires 1–13 = *a*–*N*).

TEXTUAL PRESENTATION. At the opening, a two-line blue lombard with a red ground and crude flower and leaf border, including a brightly painted bird. Elsewhere, unfilled two-line blanks for capitals at divisions, and generally without finishing. A full explanatory programme, both marginally and running titles, including a subsidiary foliation in roman to indicate the sections signalled by the running titles (just above the upper bound in the margin).

LANGUAGE. Not in *LALME* and certainly a mixture, with a heavy carry-over of forms from a Northern exemplar. However, a substantial level of the language appears placeable in north-western Leicestershire, near that county's juncture with Derbyshire and Warwickshire.

BINDING. Brown leather over millboards, s. xix, on five thongs. The front flyleaf (fo. i), now partially mounted, is from a medieval binding, perhaps originally a pastedown.

PROVENANCE. 'I L', a monogramme among various pen-trials (fo. 211).

41. Bodleian Library, MS Rawlinson C.890 (B^9)

Vellum. s. $xv^{2/4}$. Fos. iii + 146. Overall 250 × 150 (writing area 200–5 × 100–5). 50–2 lines to the page. Written in anglicana formata.

CONTENTS. Fos. 1^r–146^v: *Speculum Vitae*, breaking off, with a catchword, at a quire end, with line 14992. Lacks lines 5332–547 after fo. 53, either through archetypal damage or through turning two pages in the archetype.[10]

COLLATION. $1–4^{10}\ 5^{12}\ 6^{10}\ 7–13^{12}$. Catchwords towards the inner bounding line; nearly all signatures cut away (exceptionally, in quires 12–13, all leaves in the first half were probably signed with letter [*m*, *n*] and roman numeral, most still cut away).

TEXTUAL PRESENTATION. At the opening, a five-line blue lombard with red flourishing, forming a full bar border. At internal divisions, two- to four-line lombards, most typically alternate red with blue and blue with red flourishing, the flourishing typically foliate and within the initial (a few unfinished, e.g. fo. 42). At smaller divisions, alternate red and blue paraphs. A full explanatory programme with marginalia and running titles (some of the latter added later).

LANGUAGE. *LALME* LP 382 (coordinates 455/374, Nottingham-

[10] The scribe was not always careful. Textual disruptions imply that he was transcribing from an exemplar with forty-two lines to the single-column page, quired in eights. At the boundary between fos. 14 and 15, the scribe apparently disordered his copy. From this point (line 1454), he copies lines 1540–1618, 1455–1539, 1619–1786, 1871–1954, 1787–1870, 1955 on, with no signes de renvoie. With the exception of the initial disruption, which probably occurred after he had copied a few lines from the original second leaf of the exemplar quire (its fo. 18), all breaks in the material occur at mid-page in Rawlinson. The scribe had reversed the second and third bifolia of the quire from which he was working (fos. 18–19 and 22–3 of the exemplar), and the large chunk, lines 1619–1786, comes from the central bifolium of the exemplar quire (its fos. 20–1).

shire, near the country's juncture with Derbyshire and the West Riding); see iii. 401.

BINDING. Brown leather over millboards, s. xviii, on five thongs. Fo. i is a pastedown from an earlier binding.

PROVENANCE. 'Edmundus Coleman hunc librum possedit' (below his copy of the Pater Noster, and followed by the couplet 'God that made both Sea and land | Give me grace to amend my hand', s. xv ex.); Richard Kydman and his 'Iste liber constat . . .' (perhaps earlier); the couplet 'He that to wrath and anger ys thrall | On his wyt hath no pouer at all' (s. xvii in.) (all fo. iii). In the margin fo. 51: 'Thys byll mayd the x. day of agust In the xxxj. yere of kyng Herri the viij. Wytnes that I Robert Berker Mynstrell In the counte on the one part and Ric' kyrke of Wroxham [Norfolk?] husbandman on the other part' (and the last four lines on the page, 5103–6, repeated in a hand similar to this at the foot). Pasted to fo. i, a modern paper leaf, with (?) Rawlinson's note on Richard Rolle, ascribing him vast tracts of poetry, including *The Prick of Conscience*, and reference to a full MS owned by E. Umfreville.

42. Bodleian Library, MS Rawlinson Q.b.4, frags 92+91

Vellum. s. xv^2 or xv ex. Fos. 2 (rather faded). Overall 220 × 170 (writing area 193 × 90). 35 or 36 lines to the page. Written in Scottish secretary.

CONTENTS. *Speculum Vitae*, a two-leaf fragment with lines 3121–91 (91), 3050–120 (92).

COLLATION. A central bifolium, mounted with the leaves reversed in the guardbook.

TEXTUAL PRESENTATION. At major divisions, two-line red lombards, unflourished. Line initials red-slashed.

LANGUAGE. Although brief, unmistakably Scots, e.g. quham, mycht, ay- and ey-spellings for long *a* and *e* respectively.

PROVENANCE. 'Jan. 27 1718/19 This fragment giuen me by Mr John Murray of London', in the hand of Thomas Hearne; Sally Mapstone would connect the donor with the Murrays of Atholl and Tullibardine, known book owners.

43. Princeton University Library, MS Taylor Med. 11 (P)

Vellum (rather worn throughout, with substantial water damage at front and rear). s. xiv ex. Fos. 112 (foliated 1–110, but 35, 59 [twice] repeated, 95 omitted in the foliation). Overall 350 × 270 (writing area 275–80 × 190). Usually 42 lines to the column, in double columns. Written in a squarish anglicana formata.

CONTENTS

1. Fos. 1ra–96vb: *Speculum Vitae*, complete.

2. Fos. 97ra–104va: the unpublished mid-fourteenth-century prose translation of Ps.-Bonaventura, *Meditaciones passionis Cristi*, inc. 'The tyme neghand and comand of þe rutes and mercyes of the lorde'; see Zeeman, 'Continuity and Change', who did not know this manuscript.

3. Fos. 104vb–110vb: *The Siege of Jerusalem* (*IMEV* 1583), ending fragmentarily at line 1143, with most of the last page illegible, even under ultraviolet light.

COLLATION. $1–2^{12}$ 3^{10} 4^{12} 5^{14} 6^{10} 7^{12} 8^{8} 9^{12} 10^{10} (the final folio used as a pastedown in an earlier binding). Catchwords, no signatures.

TEXTUAL PRESENTATION. Headings in red. Blue lombards (green, on fo. 1 only) with red flourishing at textual divisions (four-line at initia, two-line for medial divisions), line-initials red-slashed; in the prose, elongated ascenders with decorative loops normal on the top line. A full explanatory programme with running titles and marginalia.

LANGUAGE. *LALME* LP 598 (coordinates 366/492, the extreme north-western tip of West Riding, Yorkshire, near Sedbergh); see iii. 651–2.

PROVENANCE. 'liber beate Marie de Bolton in C⟨ ⟩' (fo. 1); the remainder has become progressively illegible, but was clearer when Ker could read 'C⟨rauen⟩' and thus associated the book, *MLGB* 11, with Bolton in Craven (OSA). A. I. Doyle points out to me that Ker's initial reading was 'in T⟨ower⟩', and thus that the book may have belonged to an unidentified private chapel (although not that of Castle Bolton, North Riding, Yorkshire, with a different dedication).

44. Stafford, Staffordshire Record Office, MSS D (W) 1734/4/1/6–8

Vellum. s. xv med. (*c.*1460). Fos. 10 and two strips, used as wrappers (portions of an original foliation survive). Overall 335 × 215 (writing area 240 × 165). 44–6 lines to the column, in double columns. Written in secretary (anglicana *d*).

CONTENTS. *Speculum Vitae*, lines 1655–836 and 2624–820 (wrapping book 7, which also has a strip with a few line-ends), 2920–65 (wrapping book 8, a strip with line openings only), 3197–4284 (the three inner bifolia wrapping book 6), 11696–865 and 12220–392 (the outermost bifolium wrapping book 6).

COLLATION. From a manuscript in eights; the surviving leaves are the original quire 2, leaves 2+7 and 8 (the legible strip is the leading edge of the verso); quire 3, leaves 2–7 (the last three foliated xxj–xx⟨iij⟩); and quire 9, leaves 3+6 ([mis]foliated lxviij and lxix). The strip with line-ends is foliated 'x⟨ ⟩' and was presumably a bit of quire 2.

TEXTUAL PRESENTATION. Headings in red. Two-line blue lombards with red flourishing at textual divisions. Remains of the annotational programme, the customary marginalia written as in-column headings in red.

LANGUAGE. The Lutterworth area, south-west Leicestershire; see Hanna, 'A New Fragment of *Speculum Vitae*', 141.

PROVENANCE. The leaves survive as wrappers around John Whitey's compotus for Lord Paget of Beaudesert, 1550–2, 1552–4, containing accounts of the estate of Misterton, Leicestershire (near Lutterworth).

DESCRIPTIONS. Thorlac Turville-Petre's discovery in March 2002; see Hanna, 'A New Fragment of *Speculum Vitae*'.

45. Tokyo, Prof. Toshiyuki Takamiya, MS 15

Vellum. s. xv^{1}. Fos. 83 (although foliated 1–84 to include the leaf missing after fo. 55). Overall 290 × 200. 50–8 lines to the column, in double columns. Written in textura semiquadrata.

CONTENTS

1. Fos. 1ra–72ra: *Speculum Vitae*, with heading, 'Hic incipit libellus de exposicione oracionis dominice secundum tractatum Ricardi heremite de hampole qui ad salutem animarum multa bona compos(uit?)'; the colophon, 'Explicit libellus de exposicione . . .', as the heading, but with added 'cuius anime pro sua magna pietate propicietur deus Amen'. Lacks lines 12294–518, owing to a lost leaf after fo. 55.

2. Fos. 72ra–76ra: Walter Hilton's exposition of Psalm 90 (*IPMEP* 554).

3. Fos. 76ra–79ra: Hilton on Psalm 91 (*IPMEP* 115.5), separated from the preceding only by a two-line capital.

4. Fo. 79rb: An eight-line prose meditation, 'Blessed is þat soule þat is ay fedde in felyng of luf in his presence', perhaps derived from Rolle.

5. Fo. 79$^{rb–vb}$: The Pater noster in English followed by a prose

exposition, inc. 'We shal vndirstand þat in þis prayer is shortly contened all thinge þat is nedful to vs bodily and gostly'.

6. Fo. 79vb: Instructional lists: the Ten Commandments (in verse, *IMEV* 1129), the seven remedial virtues with the associated vices, the bodily and spiritual wits, the bodily and spiritual works of mercy, followed by a brief paragraph, 'Alle maner of men shulden hold goddes byddynges for withooute holdyng of hem ma⟨y no⟩ man', an excerpt at least citing the opening of the 'standard decalogue tract' (*IPMEP* 48).

7. Fo. 80^{ra-vb}: 'To wytt on what maner and how', a unique poem in couplets, related to texts in BL, MS Additional 37049 ('the Carthusian miscellany', perhaps from Axholme, extreme north-west Lincolnshire).

8. Fos. 80vb–82rb: 'Fayling of frenshippe offt tyme we fynde', another unique poem, ed. Takamiya, '"On the Evils of Covetousness"'.

9. Fo. 82^{rb-vb}: 'Ihesu þi swetnes whoso might se' (*IMEV* 1781).

10. Fos. 82vb–83ra: 'Bona meditacio de bonitate domini nostri Ihesu Cristi. Ihesu of mari þat was borne' (*IMEV* 1786), derived from *Cursor Mundi*.

11. Fo. 83ra beneath the explicit in the scribal hand: 'Exemplum | Erat adam bonus homo qui peccauit contra deum et sic dicit | Allas allas I nel bene isped' (*IMEV* 3825). Fo. 83^{v} was originally blank.

COLLATION. 1–6^{8} 7^{8} (–8) 8–10^{8} 11^{4}. Catchwords (some cut off); all leaves in the first half of each quire originally signed with letter and roman numeral (quires 3–6 = *c–f*).

TEXTUAL PRESENTATION. Alternate red and blue lombards; the decorative bottom line descenders.

LANGUAGE. *LALME* LP 608 ('West Riding, Yorkshire', but unmapped); see iii. 656. Probably the Rotherham-Barnsley area; see Hanna, 'Takamiya MS 15', 125–6.

BINDING. Original oak boards, recovered in modern sheep.

PROVENANCE. 'Ihesus 1486 Detur iste liber Conuentui Fratrum Minorum de lych' super condicione(m?) quod dicant ⟨. . .⟩ missas trigintal' ⟨sancti?⟩ Greg' cum trigint' Placebo dirig⟨?⟩ `[marg.] cum commendac' ⟨?animarum⟩ . . .´ et totidem vij^{te}. psalmi penitenc' ⟨. . .⟩ pro animabus Alicie Iocose et alan⟨. . .⟩; et animabus omnium fidelium defunct⟨. . .⟩' (fo. 83^{v}).

DESCRIPTIONS. Sotheby, 10 December 1969, lot 43 (27–9), a

facsimile, fo. 22^{v}, facing 27; Takamiya, '"On the Evils of Covetousness"', including reproductions of fos. 1ra and 81vb (205–6); further discussion Hanna, 'Takamiya MS 15'. I remain grateful to Prof. Takamiya for lending me a facsimile for inspection, from which I have drawn my description. This is the only copy of *Speculum Vitae* I have not personally examined.

In addition to these copies and fragments, there are excerpts, of varying dimensions. Given that the poem has remained unedited, not even Brown and Robbins were capable of identifying these. They did discover, and indexed as *IMEV* 3648, a quatrain derived from lines 365–70, in two manuscripts.[11] But merely to cite another example, *IMEV* 2671 is also an excerpt, the discussion of usury (lines 6163–340), written in on blank leaves in BL, MS Egerton 2810.[12] Presumably, printing the text will lead to identification of further examples, and thus further evidence for the extent of the poem's influence.

In addition, a very large number of lost copies appears in testamentary records. These have been, in the main, identified and discussed in Doyle's magisterial survey of Middle English religious writing.[13] To these, one can add a few further examples recorded in the early modern period (and thus outside Doyle's survey). The sixteenth-century Halifax (West Riding, Yorkshire) collector Henry Savile of Banke had two copies in his library, his manuscripts 32 and 41, the first certainly related to BL, MS Cotton Tiberius E.vii, described above. There was another among the books of the Norfolk antiquary Sir Henry Spelman (who died 1641); it was MS fo. 85 among his books sold at auction 20–2 December 1709. Given the mechanisms whereby this library was assembled, it may have been the copy later CC 18 in the library of the duke of Kingston-upon-

[11] Similar lack of knowledge of the poem in its full dimensions probably led Robbins, in *IMEV* Sup., to add to the manuscripts BL, MS Harley 5977, fragment 90. It is actually Hoccleve, *Regiment of Princes* 2485–2527.

[12] On this book, mainly a copy of *The South English Legendary* produced in Gloucestershire, s. xiv^{2}, see Görlach, *The Textual Tradition*, 90–2. The hand that added the excerpt, s. xv med., is described as *LALME* LP 495 (hand H of the MS) and placed along the border of south Lancashire and West Riding, Yorkshire, a localization consonant with the book's early modern provenance.

[13] 'A Survey of the Origins', i. 83–9, ii. 46–54. See also Doyle, *The Vernon Manuscript*, 13–14; Keiser's discussion of Yorkshire book ownership, 'Lincoln Cathedral Library MS. 91', 170–5; Johnston, 'William Revetour'; and the description of the Stapletons and their books, Hanna, 'Some North Yorkshire Scribes'.

Hull, Thoresby Hall (near Worksop); it was destroyed by fire when the Hall burned in 1745.[14]

3. AUTHORSHIP AND DATE

Speculum Vitae is resolutely anonymous, although occasionally ascribed in the manuscripts, both to the influential Yorkshire hermit Richard Rolle and to William of Nassyngton. The first ascription, although plainly wrong and long ago (1910) dismissed by Allen as an example of a widespread propensity to link any northerly devotional work with the hermit, is actually somewhat more plausible than the second. The poem includes a versification of part of Rolle's most widely disseminated English work, 'The Form of Living' (lines 5595–834), and the scribes of the three copies offering this ascription may have recognized this fact.[15]

The Nassington ascriptions, although they are universally accepted today,[16] have just as litle to recommend them. They depend upon a version of the poem's conclusion that reads in part (I cite from MS Royal 17 C.viii [R]; the full passage appears in the collations to lines 16079–86 below):

pray specially
For freer Iohn saule of Waldby
þat fast studyd day and nyght
And made þis tale in Latyn right
And preched it with full good chere
To lered \`and´ lewed þat hym wold here . . .
Prays also with deuocion
For William saule of Nassyngton
þat gaf hym als full besyly
Night and day to grete study
And made þis tale in Ynglys tonge . . . .

[14] See, respectively, Watson, *The Manuscripts of Henry Savile of Banke*, 24 and 26 (I would demur from Watson's identification of the first copy with Tiberius itself); Humfrey Wanley, annotations to the Spelman sale catalogue, BL, MS Harley 7055, fo. 235; [Evelyn Pierrepont, 1st Duke of Kingston], *Catalogus Bibliothecae Kingstonianae* ([London, 1726 or 1727]), an unpaginated alphabetical list, the book described under two headings as 'Divine *Poems* on several subjects' and 'A Divine Poem, by way of Paraphrase on the Lord's *Prayer*'.

[15] These are CUL, MSS Ii.i.36 and Ll.i.8; Takamiya MS 15.

[16] e.g. Wallace, *The Cambridge History of Medieval English Literature*, 399, 548, 694; or Peterson, *William of Nassington*.

The first thing to point out about this passage is that it is clearly an interpolation that has occurred in the course of the poem's transmission. There are at this point twenty-seven witnesses to the text, of which only two (Royal and the relatively closely related BodL, MS Hatton 19 [B^6]) provide this information. Moreover, these two copies show every sign of inserting material into the text, having tailored the initial and final couplets of their passage from materials common to all the other copies.

However attenuated this evidence, one might argue these two scribes could have been privy to knowledge unavailable to all other copyists. This tradition claims that the text was translated from the Latin sermons of John Waldeby into English by William of Nassyngton, a York diocesan official who died in 1359.[17] John Waldeby, OESA of York who died *c.*1372, wrote, as a sequence of seven linked sermons, a Latin Pater Noster tract.[18] But, as Allen pointed out long ago (1917, now apparently forgotten), Waldeby's exposition bears no resemblance to the English text. Indeed, *Speculum Vitae*, in the main, renders quite adeptly and literally, not a Latin work, but a French, *Somme le roi*, into English verse (as Allen further insisted). If the ascription of the source to Waldeby (not to mention the assertion of that source's Latinity) is simply wrong, there is no reason to give any credence to the identification of the translator either.

Indeed the Royal–Hatton ascription seems thoroughly programmed by the poem's own reticence as to its origins, evident in the passage the two manuscripts suppress and supplement:

> . . . Pray for hym, bathe alde and yhung,
> þat turned þis boke to Inglisshe tung,
> Whareso he be and in what stede,
> Whethir he lif or he be dede,
> þat Godde almyghty graunt hym mede
> In heuen-blisse for þis dede.
> And yhe sal noght tyne yhour trauaylle;
> Of mede þarefore sal yhe noght faylle. (16079–86)

Something so extensive and so authoritative as this poem must have been produced by a substantial and devout scholar. And the two

[17] For him, see Peterson, *William of Nassington*; Sullivan, 'The Role of the Nassington Family'.

[18] On him, see Morrin, *John Waldeby O.S.A.*

manuscripts provide the text with a suitable, if inaccurate, genealogy; they fill the gap created by the poet's modest refusal to take credit for his work, analogous to more frequent scribal efforts to ascribe *The Prick of Conscience* to Rolle.

The poem may have attracted the name William of Nassyngton because he was apparently identifiable as an English poet, if a minor one, ascribed a single poem. This work, 'þe band of loue' or 'De Trinitate et Unitate' (*IMEV* 11), consists of 432 lines, in the main devoted to the life of Jesus and the hopes of redemption he extends. It is ascribed to Nassyngton in the North Riding gentleman Robert Thornton's great miscellany of s. $xv^{2/4}$, Lincoln Cathedral, MS 91.[19] The only other known copy appears, without this ascription and with the first title cited above, in BL, MS Additional 33995 (A, the base text of this edition) but at the end of the manuscript and in the hand of a second scribe.

This poem is at least reminiscent of *Speculum Vitae* in its verse form and in some of its rhymes (notably 169–70). Moreover, Nassyngton's opening discussion of trinitarian theology certainly resembles that in *Speculum Vitae*. Although commonplace formulations of this subject, the terms, and sometimes the exact language, of *Speculum Vitae* are similar to those of 'þe band' (compare 'þe band' 1–32 with lines 1–3, 275–310, 831–6, 853–904, for example). Again, like the ascriptions of *Speculum* to Rolle, this one may well depend upon perceived affinities between two Northern works. But on the whole, 'þe band of loue' expresses particularly negative, although commonplace Augustinian, views on the human capacity for virtuous action (for example, lines 395–432). If Nassyngton was not there engaged in devotional self-abnegation but actually held such tenets, one would be hard-pressed to imagine him spending a protracted period translating the relatively sunny *Speculum*, with its implicit interest in advancing to a reward for one's virtue.

Nassyngton's Yorkshire career would, however, have overlapped with the period in which *Speculum Vitae* was composed, broadly the third quarter of the fourteenth century. The poem must postdate the manuscript promulgation of Rolle's 'Form of Living', at the earliest 1348 or 1349.[20] A *terminus ad quem* is provided only by the date of

[19] See *Religious Pieces*, 63–75.

[20] The text has traditionally been interpreted as instructions composed for the 1348 inclaustration of Rolle's addressee, Margaret Butler of South Kirkby, in a cell at East Layton (North Riding, Yorkshire); see Allen, *Writings Ascribed to Richard Rolle*, 502–13.

the earliest extant manuscript. This, the most satisfactory witness, BL, MS Additional 33995, was probably copied *c.*1375. (Were the book from a more central locale, with more extensive comparative materials, one might even date it a few years earlier.) A Latin note alleging that the text had been certified for reading on the basis of an examination at Cambridge University in 1384, found in three manuscripts, is irrelevant to the dating (although not to the perceived value of the text) and is, in any event, probably a fabrication of the 1420s.[21]

4. THE POET'S DIALECT

If William of Nassyngton is not the author, one then needs to identify some provenance from which the poem might have emerged. The basis for any such procedure, in the absence of a compelling ascription, can only be linguistic. The poem's great length and its composition in short couplets provide ample rhyming evidence useful in ascertaining the author's phonology and preferred grammatical forms. But analysing these is not a particularly easy procedure, for as the master of the subject, Angus McIntosh, noted, the North is, dialectically, 'the least heterogeneous region of the country'.[22] In my experience, the resistance of Northern texts to localization primarily reflects widespread linguistic conservatism on the part of scribes; whatever their operative phonological behaviour (given widely dispersed and isolated population centres, predictably diverse), the scribes often reproduce received, traditional, and historical spelling systems.[23]

[21] This appears in CUL, MS Ii.i.36; Gonville and Caius College, MS 160/81; and BodL, MS Bodley 446, the first and last from Ely. For the certificate, see Allen, 'The *Speculum Vitae*: Addendum', 148; Doyle, 'A Survey of the Origins and Circulation', i. 82 n. 12. For discussion, see Aston, *Thomas Arundel*, 322–3; Pantin, *The English Church in the Fourteenth Century*, 229–30; and particularly Hudson, *The Premature Reformation*, 416 (with further references).

[22] Lewis-McIntosh, 20.

[23] A single example: the Dalmeny House manuscript of Rolle's prose Psalter was produced by three scribes from extreme West Yorkshire. The first of these shows ample evidence for the coalescence of OE *hw-* with OE *cw-* and routinely writes *qw-* for both sounds. The second scribe, certainly associated with him, never, in my survey, displays this feature, and his spelling observes the historical distinction between the sounds. But one detail, his rendition of 'quake' as *whake*, strongly implies that he shared scribe 1's phonology, if not his orthography. Compare a similarly revealing 'back-spelling' in the work of a proximate copyist (Sawley abbey), responsible for British Library, MS Egerton 927, reported EETS 320, xxxii n.5.

The great majority of the poet's rhymes points to general Northern usage. The poem certainly is, as has always been assumed, 'Northern' and very likely from Yorkshire. The rhymes confirm a broad swathe of features which would typify the language of that county:

1. Earlier OE long *a* has been universally retained, whether alone, as the product of late Old English 'lengthening groups', or in the *au/aw*-diphthong (*ou/ow* in most other parts of England, for example, *sawle/saule*). For examples of the first (generally Old English words in long *a* rhyming with Middle English long *a* in French words and in open syllables), see *mast:wast* 64, *mare:fare* 381, *Gast:tast* 667, *brade:made* 876, *wate:Pilate* 1285, *rase:Thomas* 1325. For late Old English/Middle English long *a* before lengthening groups, see the frequent half-rhyme *halde:called* 89, 134, 162, 370, 410, etc. And for the diphthong, see another repeated rhyme, *knawe:lawe* 125, 695, 983, 1230, 1802, etc.[24]

This feature indicates that it is highly unlikely that the poet wrote in south-Humbrian Yorkshire, southern portions of the West Riding, where OE long *a* is rounded to long open *o*, as in the rest of England.[25] But the poet's broad extension of the feature would exclude quite substantial southerly portions of the county, broadly any part of the Vale south of the River Wharfe, as well as probably the East Riding. Rhymes confirm that such forms as *walde* 'would', *þare* 'there', *whare* 'where', and *ware* 'were', at best recessive in these areas, appear universally. See the rhymes *walde:called* 2044, 11561, 11704, 13731, 13913; of *þare* with *care* 1302, with *bare* 10568, with *fare* 15050, and with *mare* 8675; of *whare* with *mare* 4246 and with *are* 'before' 5541; and of *ware* with *care* 1311, with *bare* 7141, with *þare* 7735, and with *spare* 11132.[26]

[24] As in all other citations, I restrict myself to five or six examples out of a very great many. (For minor forms, attested in fewer than five instances, I give the complete evidence.) Exceptions to these forms are extremely rare. Some uses of Midland forms in long *o* are constrained by proper names in rhyme, for example *go:Pharao* 699–700; *also:Placebo* 13817–18, *so:Eccho* 13825–6; but notice also *so:do* 7603–4, *throte:bote* (pt.) 13035–6. The majority of apparent counter-examples (although *lorde* always rhymes *o*) are capable of alternative explanations, for example *ilkone:Ione* 671–2 as representing *ilkane:Iohane* (compare 1295–6) or *come* (pt.)*:home* 12411–12 as *came* (not the poet's usual form in long *o* < OE c[w]ōm)*:hame* (compare 12445–6, 12469–70). Before 'lengthening groups' the only exception I spot is 5345–6 *tolde:golde*.

[25] The dialectical peculiarities of this area, vis-à-vis the remainder of Yorkshire, go back to the Anglian settlement period; historically, this was long the contested 'march' between the Mercian kingdom and Northumbrian Bernicia.

[26] *LALME* provides a detailed map for 'where', ii. 213–15; for 'ware', 'thare', and 'wald', see dot maps 131, 319–20, and 168 (i. 337, 384, 346), respectively.

2. The rhymes also confirm those verbal inflections customarily viewed as restricted to Northern use. For *-(e)s* in the present third person singular, see 110, 141, 639, 727, 740, 761. For *-(e)s* in the present plural, see 200, 506, 647, 941, 983.[27] And for the present participle in *-and(e)*, see 173, 238, 310, 488, 752, 853. In addition, the poet generally follows the 'Northern personal pronoun rule', whereby a verb with adjacent pronoun has no ending or *-e*; see 234, 332, 2366, 2897, 3028.

3. There is sporadic evidence that, in at least some phonetic environments, earlier long *o* rhymes with earlier *u*, either short or long.[28] The two clearest examples in the text are provided by *boke:Luke* 11375 and *fruyte:bote* 15844. There is also extensive evidence for the development in words with earlier *-os*, e.g. *rosed:accused* 9999 and repeated examples involving *dose/duse*, for example 3586, 4462, 4897, 4984, 5736, 15235.[29] Other sequences providing evidence include earlier *-ōm*, for example instances of *dome:com* (v.) and *toom:com* (v.) at 1828, 9222, 10447, 10766, 10774; and probably earlier *-ōr*, involving *pouer* 'poor' at 4799, 6572, 7057, 8114, 8690, 11598.

4. Rhyme confirms a wide range of other Yorkshire features (I simply present type-spellings indicative of the rhyme evidence): *þa* 'those' (12, 3469, 12824), *sho* 'she' (14513, 15763), *swilk* 'such' (934), *agayne* for both 'again' and 'against' (326, 1138, 2307, 4399, 6652), *yhit* 'yet' (583, 3207, 5397, 7729, 15217), *mykell* 'much' (1973, 4089), *kirk* 'church' (607, 830, 947, 1029, 1411), *brynn* 'burn' (6981, 7138, 9760, 9826), *dede* 'death' (1082, 1291, 2712, 2980, 5016, 5247), *rynne* 'run' (1667, 8031, 9631, 9558, 15410),[30] the distinction *werk* n./*wirk* v. (the noun at 714, 1208, 1340, 1528, 1561; the verb at 905, 1534, 1879, 3947, 9087), *-hede* '-hood' (109, 599, 1154, 1260, 1282).[31]

[27] Notice such cross-rhymes of singular and plural verbal inflections as 347–8, 511–2, 633–4, 821–2, 861–2, 1533–4. For the terminations of the present, see *LALME* iv. 108–11; and for the present participle ii. 237–9.

[28] *LALME*'s keyword for this feature is *gode*, perhaps an unfortunate, if obvious (given the frequency of the word's occurrence), choice. In the poem, forms in earlier *-ōd* rhyme only with one another, and *u*-spellings are decidedly scattered throughout Yorkshire. In the sample I will examine in detail below, forms of the type *gude* appear a little fitfully, only in LPs 53, 358, 410, 488, 526, 1349 (of the thirteen literary texts surveyed) and 349, 360, 377, 1245 (of eight documents); compare the detailed presentation *LALME* ii. 279–81.

[29] But contrast frequent *to:do* (213, 459, 481, 1163, 1211) or *done:fone* 'few' 6893.

[30] In the sample I examine below, *ren(ne)* is the general form, *rin*-types only recorded in LPs 211, 358, 460, and 1349.

[31] See the following presentations in *LALME*: for *þa*, dot map 615 (i. 461); for *sho*, detailed presentation at ii. 9–11; for *swilk*, ii. 39–41; for *agayne* 'again', iv. 66–7; for *agayne*

However, any close placement of the poem's origins cannot be predicated upon the most distinctive features of Northern English. These are precisely those usages that appear most ubiquitously and offer least purchase on local usage. Thus, localizing the author must rely upon relatively minor unusual forms, a mode of procedure generally seen as perilous.[32] Such linguistic details, mapable through the huge database provided by *LALME*, may identify an authorial locale from which one might imagine the poem's transmission as emanating.

Using *LALME* in this way is not entirely unproblematic (and indeed, runs quite counter to the wise anti-phonological theory that animates that project). A certain portion of the evidence presented in the atlas raises problems of circular argument, since a number of *Speculum* manuscripts provide mapped evidence in relevant areas. This possible circularity is of special concern, given the *LALME* editors' sometimes laconic reportage. Many *Speculum* scribes, regardless of their dialects, report Northern forms when they seem necessary (for example, for rhymes, like the frequent *called:hald*). But the only viable evidence for localizing the scribes should be that of unconstrained usage (whether the scribe will use 'hald' within the line, for example), and *LALME* does not always make clear which principles have guided the editors' report of forms. Further, that conservatism of spelling systems I have already mentioned might suggest that the forms I will discuss shortly may have been considerably more widespread than is now apparent, may be veiled under traditional spellings in other books, and may, in the Middle Ages, not have been so distinctive as they now appear.

Moreover, proceeding in this fashion raises a further problem about *LALME* reportage: many such oddments, because not immediately obvious dialect criteria, will not have represented overt queries in the questionnaires from which *LALME* was constructed. One cannot be certain whether all *LALME* surveyers will have routinely noted and reported them, and thus the evidence for dispersal of some features may well be incomplete.

There is yet a further problem to consider. At least one prominent

'against', ii. 153–5; for *yhit*, ii. 171–3; for *mykell*, ii. 75–7; for *kirk*, ii. 249–51; *brynn* is unsurveyed; for *dede*, dot map 728 (i. 480); for *rynne*, dot map 503 (i. 430); for *werk*, dot map 309 (i. 382); for *wirk*, dot map 314 (i. 383); for *-hede*, iv. 303.

[32] Compare 'a preliminary localisation that relies on rare forms or statistically unstable distributions is inherently likely to lead to an impasse' (Benskin, 'The "Fit"-Technique Explained', 17).

rhyming feature provides fairly clear evidence that the author's usage is not that of a 'natural dialect', that is one reflecting the usage of a definable speech/writing community. In rhyme, the consistent and frequently repeated forms for 'is' and 'are' are *es* and *ben(e)*, respectively. This feature is unlikely to reflect a natural Yorkshire dialect, where *er(e)* and *ar(e)* appear well nigh universally for the latter form; the combination of *es* and *bene* as majority representation is attested in only three Yorkshire LPs.[33] Rather, the choice appears to represent an adopted convenience to facilitate rhyme; the poet has ample forms at his disposal for rhymes in *er/ar* (mainly derivatives of earlier *-er(e)* and those common words in long *ar* I have mentioned above), but relatively few for rhymes on *-e(e)ne*.[34]

But a number of features shows, insofar as can now be determined, narrower areas of use. In spite of all the qualifications I have expressed, the evidence does allow some reduction of possibility. On the basis of forms discussed above, a good deal of Yorkshire may be excluded from consideration—the East Riding, the extreme south, and the extreme west. The author's dialect, although it corresponds with no single LP, would make most sense in the area covered by the Ordinance Survey's Landranger map 104 and areas a little to the west (as far perhaps as LPs 18, 364, and 406); it might extend a good deal further north into the North Riding. The handling of earlier long *a* would imply that the poet's forms reflect those from the northern half of the area presented on the OS map, but that same eclecticism shown in rhymes on *bene* also appears as strong and persistent evidence for a range of minor forms largely recorded in LPs from southern portions of this map.[35]

[33] For examples of *es* in rhyme, see 156, 223, 281, 307, 330; for *bene*, see 241, 342, 538, 557, 812. For the distribution of these forms, see *LALME* iv. 32–3 and 35 (full mapping of 'are' at ii. 81–3). The three examples of *es/bene* are LPs 398, 473, and 605 (just south of York City, south-east West Riding, and extreme south West Riding, respectively). The first, at least, is plausibly adjacent to what will emerge as 'the authorial dialect area'; the last two, perhaps predictably, reflect blending with more southerly forms in South Yorkshire. In the LPs surveyed below, *es/er* are nearly universal: *ar* in LP 211, majority *ar* with *((er))* in LPs 410 and 500; *is* in LP 211, majority *ys* but *((es))* in LPs 53 and 410. The documents in this survey, universally from the south of the area, generally show only *ar(e)/is*.

[34] The evidence of the A scribe for the feature here described is salutary: *bene* 'are', although almost universal in rhyme (*ere* 7737 is the single counter-example), is negligible in in-line use: it occurs only 39 times in the entire poem, in all cases probably echoic of the rhymes; in contrast, *er* appears 80 times before line 2900 (*ere* 3 times only, at lines 3696, 7737, 10940).

[35] Landranger Map 104 includes the following *LALME* LPs: 4 (marking the central western limit of the area), 32, 53, 211 (marking the south-eastern limit of the area), 358, 410, 460 (the manuscript here collated as L), 488, 494, 500 (a *Speculum Vitae* manuscript),

The relevant items attested in rhyme include:[36]

1. In alternation with the customary full forms (see 424, 1532, for example), the poet frequently rhymes on the contracted forms *mas(e)* 'make(s)', *tas(e)* 'take(s)', and *tan(e)* 'taken'; for examples of the first, see 567, 660, 5449, 7883, 10251; of the second, 1393, 4549, 6201, 6259, 6436; and of the last, 72, 121, 564, 860, 958. Compare this usage with *tase* in LP 526; *mase* in LPs 32, 410, 500, 526, 592; *tane* in LPs 4, 53, 500. In Yorkshire, these are distinctly 'western' forms, although at least known in the East Riding (and occuring in the unsurveyed *York Play*).

2. The poet's rhymes show his reflex of OE *ĕ̄h* (from 'Anglian smoothing' of earlier *ĕ̄ah/ĕ̄oh*) to be long *e*; compare *nest(e)* (OE nĕ̄ahsta) rhyming with *brest* 902 and with *prest* 6797 and 9422; *the* (OE þēoh, þēh) rhyming with *me* 4549;[37] and probably *legher* (OE lēoger) rhyming with *forswer* 6643 and 14019 and with *maner* 13977. LPs from the poet's dialect area will include forms like *ee(n)* 'eye(s)', *he(e)* 'high', *dee(de)* 'die(d)'.[38] Compare this usage with *de* in LPs

526 (the manuscript here collated as S, marking the northern limit of the area), 592 (with deversified excerpts from *Speculum Vitae*, marking the north-western limit of the area), and 1349 (marking the north-eastern limit of the area). Additional fragmentary evidence is provided by eight legal documents surveyed in *LALME*, of which LP 377 marks the south-western limit of the area. The others include LPs 133, 348, 349, 360, 378, 1128, and 1245. One could draw (although I have not) further evidence from two Rolle manuscripts unsurveyed in *LALME* but both representing southern portions of the area, Aberdeen University Library, MS 243; and CUL, MS Dd.v.64 (III). See further EETS 329, pp. xv and xxix, respectively.

The area can be divided into southerly and northerly portions on the basis of handling of long *a*. Generally, the *au/aw*-diphthong is universal in this area (and well further south in my experience), while *a* before 'lengthening groups' shows some variation: *ald(e)* 'old', for example, is foreign to LPs 211, 488, and 500 (with *olde*), while LP 32 shows split usage (and compare LP 1349 *holde* 'hold'). For such items as *þa*, *þare*, *ware*, *walde*, forms in *o* or *e* are fairly universal in LPs 211, 488, 494, and 500, and variously mixed usages typify the centre of the area. (For *walde*, note the highly localized form *wild*, also recorded in extreme West Yorkshire, in LPs 32 and 592; it also occurs twice in the printed text below, at lines 5238 and 15561.)

[36] For summaries of the general distribution of these features, necessary contextualization for the LPs cited above, see *LALME* iv. 215 and 260 (**feature 1**); iv. 163–5, 195–7, 225, and 150–2 (and compare ii. 255–7, 261–3, 285–7, (2); iv. 306–7 (3); iv. 267–8 (4); iv. 173–5 (5); iv. 299–300 (6); iv. 291 (7); and iv. 181 and 211–2 (8), respectively.

[37] Although complicated by routine OE oblique forms in *þe(o)-*.

[38] Generally, the poet rhymes two forms of equivalent etymology (e.g. OE *ēage* with OE *hēah*), and the rhyme provides no phonological evidence. In surveying Yorkshire for comparable forms, one can logically neither exclude nor include such representations as *eie(n)*. In such forms, the *i* may only be a graphemic indication of vowel length, but may equally represent a diphthong (rather than simple long vowel). But in either case, the form is distinguishable from more usual Yorkshire representation as *eghe(n)*.

133, 211; *ee(n)* in LPs 211, 1349; *he* in LPs 211, 410, 488, 500; and more distantly *deyghed* in LP 500, *eye(n)* in LPs 494, 500; *hey* in LPs 4, 358, 494.

3. In the poet's usage, the suffix OE *-scip* rhymes on long *e*, for example at 452, 669, 966, 1050, and 1376 (all with *kepe*). Compare from these LPs forms like *-s(c)hep(e)* and *-chep(e)* (rhyme does not allow one to determine the quality of the initial consonant) in LPs 4, 32, 410, 500, 526; and *worschepe* only in LP 494.

4. The poet's reflex of OE *þridda* rhymes as if 'thredde', with short *e* and without metathesis to 'third', at 1539, 3655, 3703, 4379, 7242, 12433. Compare the unmetathesized spellings with *-e-* in LPs 500, 526, 592.

5. In the poet's usage, the suffix and French morphological element *-is(c)h* rhymes on *-s(s)*; compare the rhymes of the adjective *Inglisshe* at 9819 and 14541 (and *Frankisshe:þis* 10205–6), as well as the rhymes involving French forms at 6008 (*Cryst:noryst*), 7690, 7733, 10304, 10312, and 12550. However, the poet's normal form for 'flesh', the only word of this type surveyed in *LALME*, was not unambiguously a *fle(i)s(s)*-type (see 5928, 13229, and 14759). In the relevant LPs, the only clear example is minority *flese-* in LP 410.

6. The concluding OE sequences *-amb* and *-imb* have been simplified in the poet's usage, and rhyme on *-am* and *-im*. See *hym:clym* 1529–30 (similarly 12776), *came:wame* 'womb' 1587–8, *clomen: -commen* 6040. Compare the simplified forms for the surveyed *-amb*: *-amm* in LP 53, *-ome* in LPs 494, 500.

7. The poet consistently rhymes the word 'worse' on *e*; see 26 (*maners:wers*), 7102, 14448, 14554. Compare spellings in *werse/werst* from LPs 410, 460, 488, 494, 526. The majority form in the area appears to be *warr/werr*, but *werse*-forms typify the entire western half of the North Riding, including LPs adjacent to Landranger Map 104, for example LP 174.

8. The verbs 'give' and 'live' rhyme, both with each other (see 2019–20) and with other forms in *-eve*, for example, 'give' at 441, 1642, 1654, 2975, and 5811; 'live' at 1057, 1761, 2929, 4528, and 7398. Spellings like *leue* and *geue*, which should appear in LPs from the poet's dialect area, are presumably evidence for 'Northern' lengthening of short *i* in open syllables (although the prevalence of *geue* would probably owe a great deal to ON gefa). The development is otherwise ill-attested in the poem's rhymes; compare repeated examples of the type *wit* (OE witan, not 'Northern' *wete* or *weet(e)*),

for example at 186, 583, 1333, 3207. Within the LPs surveyed, this is a distinctly recessive feature, but see *geue(n)* (pp.) in LPs 348, 377, 378. Both forms are more widely attested in the East Riding, *leve* quite extensively so.

But the poet does, as he wished, remain resolutely anonymous. One can place the poem generally, but offer no narrow provenance. However, the area does provide evidence of at least a foretaste of the poem's inherited reliance upon the petitions of the Pater Noster as a structural device. Fountains Abbey, the great Cistercian house situated just north of Landranger Map 104, distributed an English Pater Noster certificate about 1340.[39]

5. THE POEM'S SOURCES AND THEIR HANDLING

In the main, *Speculum Vitae* is a careful, although in earlier parts of the text, often selective, translation of Fr Lorens of Orleans OP's French *Somme le roi*. This work, customarily dated 1279 and written for King Philippe IV, who employed Lorens as his confessor, was one of the international spiritual classics of the later Middle Ages.[40] The authority of *La Somme* appears to have been widely recognized in England, and *Speculum Vitae* is far from unique in Middle English in showing the imprint of the text. It is one of at least seventeen surviving translations, full or part, of either Lorens's text or the closely related *Miroir du monde*.[41] Moreover, it is the most widely distributed of all by a very large margin, and the only example in verse.[42]

Somme le roi achieved this authoritative status because it was a well-organized (as well as divertingly exemplified, through the provision of sermon 'figurae') vernacular example of 'septenary

[39] See Fairfax-Blakeborough, 'Fountains Abbey Parchments'.

[40] On Lorens, see Kaeppeli, *Scriptores Ordinis Praedicatorum*, iii. 63–4; for surveys, see *BVV* pp. xi–xxxi; Carruthers, *La Somme le Roi*; and, with extensive discussion of the original and its format, Tuve, *Allegorical Imagery*.

[41] See Brayer, 'Contenu, structure et combinaisons'.

[42] Nine of the prose versions appear under Jolliffe A.1 (cf. *IPMEP* 55 [*Ayenbite*], 668 [*BVV*]). On A1.c, see Wilson, 'Sir Robert Shottesbrook' and Hanna, 'Sir Thomas Berkeley', 905–6. A.1h has now been edited; see *Book for a Simple*. Other translations appear in Jolliffe as A.3 (*IPMEP* 209), A.6 (a good deal of this version absorbed into Jolliffe A.2; see Jones, 'Jesus College Oxford, MS 39'), and L.1. Ignored in Jolliffe are *IPMEP* 565 (book 1 only), 817, and 824; a partial trilingual version in Oxford, Magdalen College, MS lat. 188, fos. 9^r–102^v, has passed unnoticed. *IPMEP* 209 and 817, as mentioned above, are not directly from the French but derivatives of *Speculum Vitae* itself. See also *BVV* pp. xxxii–xl.

instruction'. In this scheme, a sweeping range of Christian basics was arranged in a ready mnemonic order through grouping diverse topics into analogous and linked patterns of sevens. These, in developed forms of the septenary, aligned instructional sets of quite disparate origins into a whole. In Lorens's account, ultimately dependent upon sophisticated Latin moral theology of the mid-thirteenth century,[43] this system puts in parallel five different sets of items: the seven petitions of the Pater Noster (from Matthew 6: 9–13), the seven 'gifts' communicated by the Holy Spirit (from Isaiah 11: 1–3), the seven deadly sins, the seven 'remedial virtues' (those which, following thirteenth-century catechetical lore, combat the sins, rather than the set of three theologicals and four cardinals), and the seven beatitudes of the Sermon on the Mount with their associated rewards (Matthew 5: 3–10).[44]

Lorens's text is customarily considered to be a sequence of six tracts of quite uneven size.[45] The French Dominican is most emphatically interested in his septenary (it approaches two-thirds of the whole, over 80 per cent if one adds to it the sins, given separate treatment). The pattern of the *Somme* as a whole suggests Lorens's commitment to septenary patterns, an implicit model of the Christian life as engaged in ceaseless ascent from sin.

The poet of the *Speculum* undertakes some quite elaborate restructuring and rationalization of what he found in Lorens. In particular, he deals with the least satisfactory part of *La Somme*, its opening. Lorens's first two tracts explicate the Decalogue and the Creed, and while they state the grounds of Christian conduct, they have an air of being tacked on, here only in deference to the widely adapted instructional programme of Lateran IV and outside Lorens's real instructional interests.

[43] Particularly the *Summa de viciis et virtutibus* of Guillaume Peyrault ('Peraldus'); for him, see Dondaine, 'Guillaume Peyrault'. Peyrault's influence is abundantly evident in such details of handling as the myriad subdivisions of Sloth (see Wenzel, *The Sin of Sloth*, 75–7, 80–3) or the reformulation of Gluttony as 'Gula' *and* 'Mala Lingua'.

[44] See lines 3361–510 for the poet's concise statement of these relationships and the handy table, Tuve, *Allegorical Imagery*, 442, as well as her extensive discussion. A brief early English example (the text is in Anglo-Norman verse with Latin glosses) appears in CUL, MS Gg.iv.32 (London, *c.*1320); see Meyer, 'Les Manuscrits français de Cambridge', 342. Behind Lorens's treatment stretches a range of learned exegesis, going back so far as Augustine's 'De sermone Domini in monte' 1.3–4 (PL 34: 1233–6) and prominently including Anselm of Laon and his school (see Lottin, *Psychologie et morale*, iii.2.1: 329–456; vi. 42–92, 445–77). An early example of such an effort appears in Hugh of St Victor's 'De quinque septenis' (PL 175: 405–14).

[45] See Tuve, *Allegorical Imagery*, 81.

Lorens's septenary analysis begins with a famous and influential depiction of the seven-headed 'beast from the sea' (Apoc. 13: 1) and the introduction of the sins. He moves from this discussion to his septenary proper through an extended introduction to Virtue: a discussion of the art of dying, followed by one of 'living well', and a description of a 'hortus deliciarum'. The garden description emphasizes the Tree and Well of Life, associated with the beatitudes and the exuding grace conferring the Gifts of the Holy Spirit; this provides the format underlying the remainder of Lorens's presentation.[46] This order of argument might also, like the opening two tracts, be seen as problematic. In following his ascendant pattern, Lorens detaches the sins from his analysis of their virtuous extirpation and its rewards.

The accommodation in *Speculum Vitae* may be equally awkward, but it is at least clever.[47] The translator chooses to unify the entire work as a discussion of the basic prayer Pater Noster, and manages to provide full explication of all Christian responsibilities by analysing the prayer twice in different ways. Only the second exposition, beginning after about 2,300 lines, consistently derives from Lorens.

What precedes, as a fairly overt 'prologue', could form a full poem in its own right (or any other poet's sense of literary propriety). *Speculum Vitae* begins with Lorens's fifth tract, the exposition of the prayer (*BVV* 97), and the poet integrates the Decalogue and Creed into it, as part of the discussion of the phrase 'Qui es'. (Similarly, a brief sacrament tract is built into the discussion of the 9th article of the Creed, at lines 1378–1420.) Lorens's beast from the sea, learn to die, and garden of virtue are simply suppressed, and when he arrives at the sins, the Middle English poet, while following Lorens's discussion verbally, reorganizes the order of presentation to provide a careful alternation between the sins and their opposed virtues.

In making these large-scale structural adjustments, the poet provides, as Lorens had done, a complete Christian catechesis—but in the guise of a 'book of vices and virtues'. Supplementing his freedom with Lorens's original plan, he intermixes other sources into *La Somme*. So far as I can see, he knew (as the poets of *The York*

[46] Compare the available English text, *BVV*: the opening tracts at 1–9, the beast from the sea at 10–11, the introduction to Virtue at 68–97. The garden metaphor, of course, plays upon the traditional language of 'extirpating' sin and 'inserting' virtue in its stead (see e.g. *Speculum Vitae*, lines 2321–8).

[47] Compare Nelson's discussion, *Myrour*, xxx.

Play did later) a very wide range of circumambient Yorkshire literature.

This knowledge is particularly evident in the major adjustments to the opening of the text. In reformulating his primary source, the poet relies upon a Latin septenary tract. This 'tabula de vtilitate oracionis dominice' has actually been adapted from *La Somme* itself. In the form the poet has it, it is no longer a 'tabula', a schematic presentation, but argumentative prose, a form attested in only two of its manuscripts (of the six extant), both Yorkshire books.[48]

Nor is this a unique intrusion into Lorens's text. Thus, in his rendition of Lorens's penitential tract, the poet derives instruction about how one should organize one's confession in advance from the list of sins under four headings in Rolle's 'Form of Living', chapter 6 (lines 5595–834).[49] Neither of the resituated first two tracts exactly follows Lorens, and the poet's discussion of the Creed has certainly been reformulated on the model of extant local discussions. Moreover, odd touches throughout the poem, what Vincent Gillespie, in the only extended study, has called 'lyric pools',[50] are plainly derived from earlier Yorkshire vernacular writing—one-off images imported from *Cursor Mundi* and discussions, usually predicated on patristic citations, that roughly correspond to comparable efforts in *The Prick of Conscience*. Perhaps the most notable of these is the poem's prologue, in its list of offensive romances to be ignored and its comments on the pragmatic efficacy of English translation, clearly inspired by *Cursor*.[51]

The poet's freedom with the opening of his poem contrasts with his usual behaviour throughout most of the text. Early portions of *La*

[48] See Bloomfield no. 8834 (the title 'Flos florum' is not that of this text but of the full collection forming the Burney MS; see Pantin, *The English Church*, 277–9). The two copies resembling the poet's source are BL, MS Harley 1022 (composite, with English Hilton and Rolle; cf. *LALME* LPs 4 and 15) and BodL, MS Rawlinson C.72 (its flyleaves include a reference to a Ros of Hamlake woman who was a London minoress—the family seat was at Helmsley; the book includes the rules for hermits printed in Oliger, 'Regulae tres Reclusorum', and Northern forms appear in its copy of *IMEV* 2320). See further the text in the Appendix below.

[49] See *Richard Rolle*, 11–13 (lines 329–98). The passage appears commonly as an excerpt (exceeded only by ch. 9, lines 610–25): in CUL, MS Hh.i.12; BL, MS Arundel 507; BodL, MSS Ashmole 1393 (in these three within larger excerpts), Bodley 554, and Douce 302. This versification is quite distinct from that of the 'Form' (*IMEV* 1442), unique to BL, MS Cotton Tiberius E.vii, which also includes *Speculum Vitae*.

[50] Gillespie, 'The Literary Form', i. 132–40.

[51] The *Cursor* prologue, as Jean-Pascal Pouzet has pointed out to me, also appears interpolated, although not at the head of the text, into a handful of *Prick* manuscripts.

Somme are typically abbreviated (especially with regard to Lorens's frequent pulpit *exempla*). But, from about one-third of the way through the text, the poet gradually adapts a pattern of relatively full reproduction.[52] And at isolated points, he offers quite extensive expansions, perhaps most notably in the treatment of Avarice. For example, *Somme le roi*'s extremely brief notice of 'the crafts of folly' ('mauuais mestiers') occupies only eight manuscript lines and identifies only three such 'crafts'. In contrast, the *Speculum* poet comes up with an unparalleled profusion, nine 'crafts' in all (lines 7093–236).[53]

6. METRE AND STYLE

Christine Robinson's 1987 dissertation (from whose electronic transcription this edition has been derived) was undertaken to examine the possible common authorship of *The Prick of Conscience* and *Speculum Vitae*. In an acute metrical analysis, Robinson found such a view untenable. Her researches demonstrate that while *The Prick* is written in conventional Middle English octosyllabics, *Speculum Vitae* is not.

Rather, the poem represents an older, looser tradition, customarily called 'native four-stress verse'. In this metrical system, the line is defined by stress-weight alone, its inclusion of four chief and stressed syllables. The number of unstressed syllables is left indeterminate; while they may, as in conventional octosyllabic verse, alternate with the stresses, a metrical line does not require that they do so regularly. More than one unstressed syllable may separate two stressed ones, and, usually within certain limits, an intermediate unstressed syllable may be completely suppressed, potentially creating 'clashing stresses' within the line.

Perhaps the most obvious proof that the poet pays little attention to syllable count comes from line openings. On a very large number of occasions, he suppresses the initial unstressed syllable that one would expect to find at the opening of an octosyllabic line. For

[52] Excepting Lorens's extensive discussions of each of the Gifts of the Holy Spirit (for instance, *BVV* 188–90 on 'the gift of Counsel' becomes only the ten lines, 6111–20). Only the last of these, 'the gift of Wisdom', the fully reproduced climax, appears in anything approaching the extent of the source.

[53] A number of these have clear echoes or tastes in *Piers Plowman*; see 7094 n. and the further references there.

example, in the normalized sample I provide below (fifty-four lines), the technique appears on twelve occasions (631, 633, 637–8, 646, 648, 671–4, 676, 681). Such a 'headless line' is, of course familiar from Chaucer's use of the form as an occasional variant. Here it represents more than a variant, rather a signal of a differently conceived metrical form dependent upon stress-, not syllable-count.

In addition, the line tolerates unstressed sequences greater than a single syllable. One such expansive case from the sample below is provided by line 633:

> Ane es a synne þat men Prydë calles
> C x x C x x C x C (x)

While one might (as I do below) elide the first of the unstressed sequences, the second is not subject to that treatment.

A second important feature of the verse concerns mechanisms whereby the poet avoids stress-clash, even in lines of considerable concision. The technique is well illustrated in line-ending sequences, as in that cited above. In final position, stress is fixed by the rhyme, but frequently the rhyme-word is preceded by a syllable that appears to bear stress. Many, although far from all, of these possible collisions actually testify to a divide between the poem's graphemic presentation and any likely metrical performance. For in a vast number of instances, actual clash has been precluded by the poet's careful reliance on etymological or grammatical *-e*. For example, in something like twenty-five or thirty of the poet's first hundred lines, his third and fourth stresses potentially appear to clash. However, the first six of these instances will provide sufficient examples of the technique:

4 we trowe mast (*trowë* < *-en* of the present plural)
12 til alle þa (*allë* < plural adjective in *-e*)
17 with gode wille (*godë* < inflected dative of the adjective in *-e*)
45 of Warwyke (*Warëwyke* < waering-wic)
68 Ingelande (*Ingëlande* < OE Engla land)
69 mast shewed (*mastë* < OE māste adverb)

In the poet's system, other apparent stress-clashes may well have been construed equally evanescent on the basis of an intruded caesura, understood to equal in weight an unstressed syllable. And there seems fairly clear evidence that the poet did not respect the 'Chaucerian' rule that *-e* should be routinely suppressed before following vowels and before *h*- (for example, *hert es* 2100, 2574; *hertë* < OE heorte).[54]

This metrical system frequently seems to have been as unfamiliar to the scribes as it is to us. Many of them probably did not actively use -*e* and thus had no entrée into one key feature of the metre. The collation is littered with variants probably inspired by metrical confusions, perhaps most frequently the provision of extra words to separate apparently colliding stresses. But about equally often, the scribes suppress what appear to them excess syllables, an effort to impose on the lines a more familiar octosyllabic norm. Given the poet's clear usage, I have tended throughout to follow my copy-text and not to engage in metrical tinkering; the poet's verse form does allow extra unstressed syllables, and thus deciding that one or another sequence is erroneous, on the basis of some scribes' omissions, is a hazardous business.

The text presented below is one largely in the substantive form provided by a single good manuscript, my copy-text A. I make no effort to normalize it to indicate its underlying metrical system. But since this is an unfamiliar verse form and since I think the overwhelming preponderance of lines I print metrical within it, it is appropriate to give some sense of what might underlie the printed text. For this purpose, I provide a sample from early in the poem (lines 631–84), marked to indicate how I imagine its metrical realization. I use the diaeresis to mark necessarily pronounced final -*e* and provide the letter in brackets where the scribe has ignored it; I indicate several examples of at least possible elision by an apostrophe and italicize places where one might reduce potentially extraneous syllables (-*e*, -*es*, -*en*) graphemically represented in the manuscript:[55]

þis word Noster þat es myghty
Vs ken*nes* to hate thre thyng*es* nam*e*ly
Ane's a synne þat men Prydë calles
Anothir's Hatred þat oft[e] falles

[54] On the grammatical rules underlying such treatment, see Donaldson, 'Chaucer's Final -*e*'. Whatever historical linguistics may have postulated about the status of -*e* in spoken Northern English, often described as 'lost' by *c.*1325, it was still functional as an optional alternative (not all potential uses are necessarily sounded) for this poet. Compare the analogous findings on alliterative usage, Duggan, 'The Shape of the B-Verse' and 'Final -*e* and the Rhythmic Structure of the B-Verse'.

[55] Rhymes, for example the frequent *halde:called*, show the poet engaged in such reduction.

þe thriddë thynge es Auaryce
Ouer-many men haunt*es* þat vyce
Pride þat yhern*es* to haf maystry
Put*tes* a man out of cumpany
For when a man to Prydë drawes
He wald b'obou[e]n alle his felawes
þat man war noght here worthy
To dwellë langar in cumpany
For Pryde oft brekës felawshep
And put*tes* a man vnto shenshep
Als Lucifer for Prydë was
Cast*en* to helle for his trespas
He was putt out als clerkës telles
Of þe cumpan'of aungel[e]s
Hatred þat felaws persayuë can
Out of cump'ny put*tes* a man
For if a man his felaw hate
And fondës to fordo his state
Al þe felawshepe greuës he
In cumpany suld he noght be
Au'ryce put*tes* a man I wene
Out of cumpany þat's clene
For when a man noght comon wille
With his felaws aftir skille
Ne with þam part of þat he has
Bot þat he wyn*nes* his aw*en* it mas
Swilk a man methynk suld sone
Out of cumpany be done
þarefore to swilk God vouch*es* noght saue
þat þai part of þe Pater Noster haue
þis worde Noster vs shew*es* by skille
þat God*de*'s our awën if we will[e]
With þe Fader and þe Son and þe Haly Gast
Als we thurgh right[e] trouth may tast
If we hym louë and worshepe
And hys commandëment[e]s kepe
Als God says to vs ilkone
In þe god*de*spell of Saynt Io[ha]ne
Certayne hope we suld haue ay
When we þe Pater Noster say

For þis word þat Noster's called
Wille þat we Hope in hert[e] halde
To spede of þat we aske and craue
If it be skilfull þat we wald haue
For he's our godë Fader of myght
And we'r his awën[56] childer right
þarefore we hopë better by skille
þat he our askynge wil fulfille
Sen he's our Fader and we er his
We hope of þat we sal noght misse

This verse form proves exceptionally supple in the poet's handling. He makes routine use of variable stress patterns, as well as manipulating *-e*, to fit accurately and economically into his metrical template the French prose from which he is working.[57] The verse is also typified by grammatical inversion and often intricate syntactic patterns involving well more than a single couplet. And there is frequent use of enjambment and run-on of the sense past the initial rhyme of its couplets.

Stylistically, the poem is an interesting amalgam. Although the poet has a very large specifically Northern vocabulary, he is remarkably restrained in using it—a feature which may have helped stimulate the wide readership the poem enjoyed. The glossary includes a large number of specifically Northern words, but a very great many of them appear quite sparingly (many only in a single passage, many more fewer than five times). Equally, although not by any means averse to replicating the language of his source, actual carryover of French lexis is also relatively limited.

As his prologue in some measure implies, the poet sets himself up as an 'anti-romance' versifier, a purveyer of sober doctrine, rather than unrestrained delight. But in his conversion of French prose into English verse, he relies heavily upon what one might see as a romance persona—and more prevalently upon 'romance diction', those tricks of rhyming fillers that typify Middle English popular

[56] Or *aw[ne]*, the plural (and in a weak position, as *gode* in the preceding line); compare line 666 above.

[57] For example, the five-syllable plural *com-'maund-e-'ment-es* seems required by the metre of line 670 above (as well as in line 943). But in the first thousand lines of the poem, the word also potentially occurs as tri- or quadrisyllabic (the trisyllabic singular at 132, 985; plural at 435, 956, 975; the quadrisyllabic singular at 124, 434, 995; plural at 435, 956, 975). (These are, in the context, the minimal readings, and all the forms might potentially be of four or five syllables.)

poetry. Some poetic behaviours strike me as potentially irritating repeated tics—a very great number (perhaps defensible, given the announced programme of vernacularizing clerical subject matter) of books telling and clerks reading, rather fuzzy uses of constructions involving *see* and *sight*, the verb *feel*, or the past participle *sought*. But on the whole, the technique works as it should—to facilitate ongoing sense within a fairly restricted poetic idiom. Certainly, one seldom feels in the presence of such an overreliance upon conventional padding techniques like that which renders the earlier 'Surtees Psalter' (*IMEV* 3103) virtually unreadable, even for sense.

7. CONSTRUCTING A TEXT: THE RELATIONSHIP OF THE CENTRAL MANUSCRIPTS

The poem has a disquieting editorial history, comprehensible given its length and the profuse number of extensive copies. Nelson examined nearly all these and discussed the first half of the poem in two Sydney dissertations.[58] The second of her studies forms an edition of a quarter of the work, lines 3357–7320, from the relevant manuscripts, thirty-five in all (she did not know P). And Nelson continued to work on a full text for some years, before abandoning the project. In addition, the Society accepted in 1962 a proposal from Prof. James D. Gordon of the University of Pennsylvania for an edition from all the manuscripts. Gordon's work, on the basis of unpublished correspondence A. I. Doyle has generously supplied me, had proceeded quite far but was interrupted by his death in the early 1980s. Inquiries to the University of Pennsylvania have failed to locate any surviving papers.[59]

Given this history of incompletion, I present here a partial edition,

[58] Nelson, 'The Middle English *Speculum Vitae*'.

[59] Nelson reports in print one version of Gordon's results—it does not agree in all particulars with the unpublished correspondence; see *Myrour*, 23–4. Her extensive discussion of the transmission occurs at 'The Middle English *Speculum Vitae*', 35–117. In addition, Gordon K. Green projected an edition and in his dissertation provided ('On the Text of the Middle English "Mirror of Life"', 134–85) a trial version of about 200 lines (1–90, 7643–86, 16017–96). Green based his work, which involved full collations of thirty manuscripts, on the local manuscript L, but saw that this text required frequent correction from closely related copies. For these purposes, he presented L in parallel with E, whilst recognizing the relatively close relationship of both to ASB[7]. He also identified the copy in Tiberius E.vii as having been subjected to revision and presented its readings in full. Like Gordon's work, any further papers associated with Green's project have subsequently disappeared.

what I call 'a reading text', and one at an uncertain number of points apt to be much less than definitive. In doing so, I rely upon Nelson and Gordon's agreement in one substantial finding. They discovered that five early manuscripts, all Yorkshire productions, communicate a distinct and usually more satisfactory form of the text than the remaining copies. These are the books above identified as:

A BL, MS Additional 33995
E BodL, MS Eng. poet. d.5
L Liverpool University Library, MS F.4.9
P Princeton University Library, MS Taylor Medieval 11
S BL, MS Stowe 951

My edition, in the main, is predicated upon a full collation of these five copies (for what is reported here, see further below). Further, both Nelson and Gordon agreed (and my collations have led me to concur) that any edition should be based upon the Additional MS, as the most satisfactory single rendition of the poem.

The initial evidence for the uniqueness of this group of five books is extensive. However, the most flagrant examples do not directly constitute genetic evidence, that is, the agreement of these five books in error. On the contrary, they provide quite extensive evidence of these scribes' avoidance of error. On perhaps two thousand occasions (!) through the whole text, the five, or a majority of them, preserve a reading better than the overwhelming majority of copies. Frequently, large numbers, as many as twenty-five on some occasions, of the manuscripts agree in the same error against the five.[60] I have devoted a considerable portion of the Commentary on the Text to offering a limited number of examples.

The five manuscripts thus might be seen as genetically similar on the basis of 'the rule of congruence' (see *Piers B*, 19–20). That is, in the presence of overwhelming repeated evidence that all other manuscripts agree against them (although with various defaulters that preserve the original in scattered individual readings), they must form a group to themselves.

However, positive evidence that the five books form a genetic group is difficult to assemble. These manuscripts, as I have suggested, almost always offer plausible readings. A relative handful of shared errors involving four or five of the copies, in statistical terms thoroughly overwhelmed by profuse agreement in

[60] See the brief example cited in Hanna, 'The Yorkshire Circulation of *Speculum Vitae*'.

minor variation elsewhere in the tradition, testifies to the genetic status of the group:

163 it made] *trs.* AEPS; 294a–b *the couplet om.* AELPS; 2870 gladly] gastly AELS, cladely P; 3992 thre] *om.* AELS, *int. later* P; 4422 hym] hym wele AELPS; 4750 saule] *altered from* awen *?later* A, awene ELS; 4806 vyce] vyces AELS; 5840 awne ere] avener AELS, ane ere P; 5935 and[2]] and alle AELS, and þe P; 6253–4 *the couplet added vertically in the margin later* A, *the couplet om.* EPS; 6553 so fre] to se AELS; 9420 of] and AELS, þat 'of' P; 10258 nedes] erand AELS; 10332 ou-] ouer- AL, outher- ES, aur- P; 10700 sese] lette AELS; 11239 For] And AELS; 11610 foule] fole AELPS; 11892 nane] þe name AELPS; 11940 and] with AELS; 12061 many] may AELS, many *int. later* P; 12488 hym bi] *om., with various fillers to repair the short line* AELS, *phrase later in the line* P; 12735 þa] þat AELPS; 12820 To] þat AEPS; 12881 sal] to AELS; 13630 balde] gode AELS, balde *earlier in the line* P; 13865 eren] yren AELS; 14346 Godde þam] þam was AELS; 15966 Alle] Als AEPS

This showing throws up two immediate anomalies regarding the distribution of these errors. The first, the resolution of which will require further study of the whole tradition, concerns the distribution of errors shared by the group through the poem, which is far from uniform. A substantial cluster of such readings occurs over about 4,000 lines rather late on, mostly near the end of a relatively unexciting discussion of Chastity. I have a strong sense, from my collations, that this portion of the poem may have stimulated a considerable level of scribal inattention; certainly, variation here becomes quite profuse for no ostensibly good reason. Moreover, quite unusually for this text, a substantial number of readings here appears to be incorrect, misrepresentations of the poet's holograph, in all copies I know.[61]

The second distributional anomaly appears in situations where only four of the books agree in error. All twenty-eight readings appear in three manuscripts only, AES. L lacks four of them, and, counting generously, P shares only fourteen of the errors.[62]

[61] I identify such 'archetypal error' on about twenty occasions in the text; about three-quarters of these occur within lines 10500–14250. See the Textual Commentary, notes to 3090, 3221, 3923, 7776, 10564, 10867, 11300, 11544, 11960, 12180, 12219, 12555, 12665, 12796, 13146, 13253, 14036, 14056, 14220, 15651.

[62] Further examples of AES alone in error appear at 2583 þat] *om.*; 2633 þat] And (þat al P); 7557 es] *om.*; 8630 gode] a gode; 11515 lyf] *add* and; 11994 fra] *add* alle; and compare 9912 Agayne] And agayne AES+W. On the basis of the discussion in the following several paragraphs, these readings may provide further attenuated evidence for the five-manuscript group, representing occasions where L and P seek readings from other sources.

P, a book of *c.* 1400, has been subjected to a conscientious and heavy series of fifteenth-century corrections. I have collated them all against other copies and find that only very rarely do they correct from or to a reading genetically identifiable; rather, they indicate a corrector's desire to amend a sometimes haphazard copying job. But if the corrector shows only the most minimal evidence of correcting the text from an alien source, such is not the case with the exemplar from which scribe P himself was copying.

Collating P against two copies from the general transmissional tradition of *Speculum Vitae*, for which I have used R and W (see further below), demonstrates conclusively that the exemplar available to the original scribe was a thorough conflation. As I will show in a moment, P agrees in error with one of the other books from among AELS around 250 times; but it agrees 117 times in isolated error with R, 121 times with W, and 108 times with both of them. Its inclusion of about half the distinctive errors of the group (and its omission of the rest) depends upon the selective procedures in the tradition behind this manuscript. At some point in its descent, P's version was copied by a scribe with continuous access to two copies with rather different textual histories. (So far as my spot checks allow me to tell, P's second copy is most apt to have resembled the books I assign the sigla B^3 and B^8; see further below.)

Within the group of five, further distinctions may be made. A, the base text here, stands apart from the remainder; it errs most infrequently, and its agreements with other copies are exiguous.[63] The total agreements in isolative error between any two from among the other four books, consistent over the entire run of the text, are:

EL	84×	LE	84×	PE	36×	SE	121×
EP	36×	LP	195×	PL	195×	SL	319×
ES	121×	LS	319×	PS	41×	SP	41×

To this information, one may add strong evidence for a three-text group ELS, generally consistent throughout the text[64] and, on the basis of spot checks, frequently unique in the entire tradition. This group occurs 178 times, that is more frequently than any variant

[63] I am aware that my particular practice of copy-text editing may contribute to this impression. ELPS appear apart in error about thirty times in the text.

[64] Variations in the usual rate of attestation (about 12–15 times per thousand lines) occur in the first 3,000 lines and in roughly lines 10000–11000 and 12000–13000. One might note that the last two blocks of diminished agreement correspond to the area of textual anomaly I have noted above.

combination except LS, about the same as LP. This set of three is further distinguished by a more profuse tradition of marginal annotations to the text than visible elsewhere (not counted among the variants above).

On this basis, one could represent the descent of this group as {A [E (LS)]} P.[65] Such a showing throws up a further anomaly, however, since it must ignore profuse agreements of the group LP, the second most strongly attested in the sample. This may be explained by a further, and completely independent, act of conflation. Not reproduced above, because alien to the five-text group, is L's second strongest showing of common readings, 256 agreements in error shared only with the non-group member R. These errors, which fluctuate in intensity over the text, are probably the result of sporadic but relatively continuous consultation of a book from the general tradition of transmission by the scribe L or one of his predecessors.[66] On this basis, this scribe supplies a series of readings that converge with the general tradition (for example, in his avoidance of four of the twenty-eight group-defining errors above) and with some portion of P readings otherwise alien to the five-text group.

Editing the text must obviously begin by identifying readings from the archetype of the five superior copies I have been discussing. In this procedure, the Additional MS will clearly be of more importance than simply as a base text. The partial stemma constructed above implies that the evidentiary value of this book is roughly equivalent to that provided by the other four copies (so long as they follow this textual tradition). But however good the text constructed on these grounds may be, it needs some form of confirmation and external check upon its readings. There remains no assurance, in isolation, that at any point in the text, the version provided by AELPS remains anything other than plausible.

[65] Identification of LS as closely linked on textual grounds confirms *LALME*'s suggestion (iii. 636) that the language of the pair is comparable. (It of course raises the question as to whether that language is anything more than a common inheritance from the shared exemplar; plainly the scribes, writing nearly half a century apart, had no direct connection with one another.)

[66] This caveat is necessary, because the erroneous group LSR occurs 64 times and the group LSRW 29 times. The next sentence is predicated on similar data: LPR occurs 71 times, LPW 36 times (two-thirds of these before line 7000), LPRW 33 times.

8. CONSTRUCTING A TEXT: CHECKS ON THE CENTRAL MANUSCRIPTS

Thus, the edition below, on a varyingly selective basis, attempts to assess the quality of the text these five books provide. For this procedure, I have supplemented the readings of these central manuscripts with three other evidentiary sets.

First, I have collated in full the readings of two good but genetically dissimilar copies of *Speculum Vitae*. After study of Nelson's full collation of a quarter of the poem and from my rather distant knowledge of Gordon's work, I have chosen for this purpose two copies already mentioned:

R BL, MS Royal 17 C.viii
W Aberystwyth, National Library of Wales, MS Peniarth 395

The readings of these two books will, in a general sense, give students of my collations some sense of the parameters of the more usual transmission of the poem.

In many instances, readings of RW quite substantially query the value of the central manuscript readings. In assessing these variants, I have brought into play a wider, yet still selective, group of copies. In general, where RW (and sometimes P with them) agree against the central copies, or where various of the central copies present interesting variants, I have spot collated against nine further books. For this purpose, I use the remaining substantial manuscripts held by the Bodleian Library:

B^1 MS Bodley 48
B^2 MS Bodley 446
B^3 MS Eng. poet. a.1
B^4 MS Greaves 43 (fragmentary)
B^5 MS Hatton 18
B^6 MS Hatton 19
B^7 MS Lyell 28
B^8 MS Rawlinson C.884
B^9 MS Rawlinson C.890

In general, I have checked these books selectively, universally in cases of (P)RW agreement, more selectively for agreements of the types PR, PW, and ELS. Selected readings provided by these copies (as a group, referred to as 'B-MSS') appear only in the discussions of the Commentary on the Text. There I adduce them to indicate the general attestation of individual (P)RW readings (and the corresponding isolation of the central manuscripts). While convenience has obviously driven my choice of witnesses here, Nelson and Gordon's efforts at constructing a transmission history (see above) indicate that these books adequately display something of the genetic breadth of the entire tradition.[67]

But given that the poem is a painstakingly accurate translation, its sources provide the ultimate guarantor of its readings. I have confirmed the readings of my text from them, mainly, but not exclusively, from *Somme le roi*. For this purpose, one must return to the manuscripts; in spite of its very great cultural importance, *La Somme* has no modern edition, indeed has not appeared in print since two Parisian efforts of *c.*1500. I cite in the Commentary the readings of selected *Somme* manuscripts produced or used in fourteenth-century England.[68] For this purpose, I rely on the two reasonably complete copies of Lorens's *Somme le roi* in England in the early fourteenth century:

C BL, MS Cotton Cleopatra A.v
BSG Paris, Bibliothèque Ste-Geneviève, MS 2899

The first of these volumes was no. 1504 in the late fifteenth-century catalogue of St Augustine's abbey, Canterbury. The second was produced in 1297 in Paris for Fr Jordan de Kingston and donated by him to the Southampton Franciscans in 1317.[69]

[67] These copies, following Nelson, may be associated with various prominent genetic groups: R is a slightly less adequate representative of a group best represented by B^7 and more distantly by B^2B^6 (on the scribal interpolations into B^2 and other copies, see Nelson, 'The Middle English *Speculum Vitae*', 74–8). And B^4, not extant for Nelson's portion of the poem, appears also associated with this group, whose common archetype was probably the most responsible among those available in the general tradition. B^3B^8 form a distinct genetic form of the text (also in BL, Add. MS 22283); my placement of one linguistic layer of B^8 a bit east of Lichfield suggests that scribe's geographic proximity to the other two books' frequent source of materials. (However, the heavy Northern admixture in B^8 implies that this version may not have been specially tailored in Lichfield, as does P's possible access to a text of this sort.) Finally, W is closely connected with B^1B^9 (on their distinctly deviant form of the text, see Hanna, 'Takamiya MS 15', 130–2) and more distantly B^5.

[68] For the most useful surveys, see *BVV*, xix–xxi; Gradon, 53–6, 112–14.

[69] See Ker *MLGB* 180 and 306 (BSG) and Sup. 12 and 82 (the donor was 'abbas Thomas') (C), and for a description of BSG, Kohler, *Catalogue des manuscrits*, ii. 530–1. Both books probably resemble fairly closely the now-lost copy from which Michel of Northgate translated *Ayenbite of Inwyt* in 1340 and which he subsequently donated to St Augustine's Abbey (where it was no. 1548 in the catalogue). All three lack Lorens's tract

In these annotations, I give priority to BSG, although it is incomplete. After production, the book was equipped with a careful index, keyed to an added set of folio and line numbers; the book thus forms the most precise system for textual citation from *La Somme* available. I cite C explicitly only when it varies from the readings of BSG and in those instances when BSG has omissions. And to facilitate use of the notes, I give the parallel locus in the most frequently cited Middle English translation, *BVV*. I use the source largely to decide probable anteriority in cases where the manuscripts of *Speculum Vitae* offer variation; I have occasionally noted places where I would suspect all manuscripts I know of transmitting English corruptions, but, lacking knowledge of the complete English transmission, I have only rarely emended the text on this basis.[70]

9. THE FORMAT OF THIS EDITION

The edition relies upon A as its copy text. I reproduce the spellings of this manuscript and note its interlineations explicitly (marked '. . .' in the text). I have, in text, collations, and notes, disambiguated the single grapheme (*y*) all my copies use for both *y* and *þ*. (The feature resists easy normalization, since the relevant contrast, familiar in Yorkshire writing, is not between *y/þ* but initial *yh/y*, the first representing more customary *ȝ*, the latter more customary *þ*.) In transcribing A, I have construed a pronounced loop on *-r* to indicate *-re*, in accord with a range of full and unambiguous spellings

on the Works of Mercy. To fill this gap in both books, and to resolve a few recalcitrant readings elsewhere, I occasionally cite as SJ the fourteenth-century French copy in Cambridge, St John's College, MS 31 (B.9).

Also worth mention are two further copies, both incomplete and thus incapable of being used as a full check on the text: (1) Cambridge, St John's College, MS 256 (S.30). This book is London work of the 1320s, with illumination comparable to the Queen Mary Psalter; a flyleaf has later accounts from the Peterborough area (although the book was still in London, s. xiv$^{3/4}$, when it received English additions). The volume includes only the first exposition of the Pater Noster, not the second with the developed septenary. See James, *A Descriptive Catalogue . . . St John's College Cambridge*, 291–3. (2) Lambeth Palace Library, MS 298. This volume, copied s. xiv in., was in the Preston area, 1535 × 1545; it breaks off about halfway through, in the discussion of Avarice. See James and Jenkins, *A Descriptive Catalogue*, 418–20.

[70] See n. 61 above. Probably my most adventurous departures from the seven books I usually collate are the minor examples at 2698 and 12665, both discussed in the Commentary on the Text.

(occasionally such a signalled *-e* is metrically necessary). I have ignored as otiose occasional marks over *-þ* and sporadic extended loops on *-g*. All punctuation (including division into verse paragraphs, though I have often attended to A's divisions) and capitalization are my own; both are heavier than customary, since I have tried to disambiguate complex grammatical sequences and to mark the poet's abiding interest in Vices and Virtues. All alterations are signalled, positive emendations in brackets ([. . .]), letters or words omitted by '+'.

I suspect that, in the Middle Ages, the text is unlikely to have been read straight through, as if it were a continuous narrative. Rather, it seems designed to function as a compendium of spiritual lore, for consulation by topic. To facilitate this kind of selective reading, virtually all copies subject the text to some form of *ordinatio*, a system of subdivision and of directive finding tools. At the fullest, as typified in the central copies, this includes both running titles, giving a threefold entrée to the text (gift, virtue or vice, petition), and a series of marginal indications of topic.[71] These I reproduce from A, and correct (and supplement), as seems necessary, from the other central copies.

At the foot of each page presenting the poem, I give the full variant apparatus for the text. This collects all substantive and grammatical variation (and all ambiguous variation which might be so), with a few exceptions. The scribe of L seems especially frequently to have taken up a little more copy than he could recall while writing and to have produced inadvertent minor transpositions of material; where these are unsupported elsewhere in the manuscripts I collate, I ignore them. I have collated all the corrections made to P, but only report them if they correspond to a variant in one of the other collated copies.

I have taken as non-substantive many common examples of variation: between *outher* and *other*, between *þat* and *at* (and *to* and *at* before infinitives), between *ilk(e)* and its fuller forms *ilka* and *ilkane*, between *es* and *er* and *was* and *war* (often used interchangeably with plural subjects), between marked and unmarked genitives (*Godde/Goddes*), between *oft* and its variant *of*, between *y-* and *yh-* (for example, does *y(h)ow* represent 'thou' or 'you'?), between *riches* and *richesse*, and between *thing* (the old uninflected neuter plural) and

[71] See Gillespie, 'Vernacular Books of Religion', 318, 332–5, with an illustration of the apparatus as it appears in MS Bodley 446.

thinges. Because of their impenetrability (some forms have been overlooked by the editors of *LALME*), I have been liberal in recording variation for 'although' (particularly the form 'if'; see 6367 n.) and 'yet' (particularly the form 'it'). In three cases, I have fully collated (and subjected to genetic analysis) variant types which I here suppress:

1. Alternation of *o* with *of* and *on*: the first may be the ambiguous archetypal form, and I limit the published collations to its full manifestations, variation between *of/on*.
2. Frequent alternation between *þa* and *þai*: while substantive variation, either form potentially represents the reading more explicitly signalled by the other ('those' and 'they', respectively).
3. Frequent apparent alternation between singular and plural, or between marked and unmarked verbal forms, in stems ending in sibilants (including *-ch-*), for example, *vice/vices*. Given widespread tendencies to apocopation in such phonetic contexts (compare Chaucer's *this* 'this is'), it is never clear whether even grammatical variation occurs here. For discussions of examples, see 1943 n., 4018 n.

I streamline the collations slightly through a series of abbreviations: *om.* = omit(s), *trs.* = transpose(s) (usually of an adjacent pair of words, but sometimes a pair of nouns '*trs. nouns*' or phrases '*trs. phrs.*');[72] *precs.* = the reading precedes; *int.* = the reading has been marked for insertion, usually above the line (occasionally in the margins); *illeg.* = the reading is illegible (mostly in opening damp-damaged folios of P, only consistently legible from line 85); *add(s)* I imagine to be self-explanatory.

[72] This signal alternates with '*after*', where a scribe has radically shifted the position of the word in the line.

BIBLIOGRAPHY

I. EDITIONS CITED

Baugh, Nita S. (ed.), *A Worcestershire Miscellany* (Philadelphia, 1956).

Book for a Simple and Devout Woman . . ., ed. F. N. M. Diekstra (Groningen, 1998).

Councils and Synods . . . II, A.D. 1205–1313, ed. F. M. Powicke and C. R. Cheyney, 2 vols. (Oxford, 1964).

Fischer, Erna, 'Ein nordenglisches moralisch-religiöses Versfragment aus dem 15. Jahrhundert', *Englische Studien*, 60 (1925–6), 252–61.

Fragments of an Early Fourteenth-Century Guy of Warwick, ed. Maldwyn Mills and Daniel Huws, Medium Ævum Monographs, NS 4 (Oxford, 1974).

Green, Gordon K., 'On the Text of the Middle English "Mirror of Life"' (BA thesis, University of Liverpool, 1950).

Gunn, Agnes D., 'Accidia and Prowess in the Vernon Version of Nassyngton's "Speculum Vitae": An Edition of the Text and a Study of the Ideas' (Ph.D. thesis, University of Pennsylvania), *Dissertation Abstracts International*, 30 (1969), 4945A.

Horae Eboracenses . . ., ed. [Christopher] Wordsworth, Surtees Society, 132 (Durham, 1920).

Hübner, Walter (the second part with K. Schreiner), 'The Desert of Religion, mit dem Bilde des Richard Rolle of Hampole . . .', *Archiv für das Studium der neueren Sprachen und Literaturen*, 126 (1911), 58–74, 360–4.

Jacob's Well, an English Treatise on the Cleaning of Man's Conscience, ed. Arthur Brandeis, EETS OS 115 (London, 1900).

Langland, William, *Piers Plowman: The B Version . . .*, ed. George Kane and E. Talbot Donaldson (London, 1975).

—— *Piers Plowman: The C Version . . .*, ed. George Russell and George Kane (London, 1997).

Mandeville's Travels: Texts and Translations, ed. Malcolm Letts, 2 vols., Hakluyt Society, 2nd ser. 101–2 (London, 1953).

Meyer, Paul, 'Les Manuscrits français de Cambridge. II — Bibliothèque de l'université', *Romania*, 15 (1886), 236–357.

The Middle English Mirror*: Sermons from Advent to Sexagesima*, ed. Thomas G. Duncan and Margaret Connolly, Middle English Texts, 34 (Heidelberg, 2003).

A Myrour to lewde men and wymmen: A Prose Version of the Speculum Vitae,

Edited from BL MS Harley 45, ed. Venetia Nelson, Middle English Texts, 14 (Heidelberg, 1981).
Mulder-Bakker, Anneke B., et al., *Mary of Oignies, Mother of Salvation* (Turnhout, 2007).
Nelson, Venetia (ed.), 'The Middle English *Speculum Vitae*: A Critical Edition of Part of the Text from Thirty-five Manuscripts', 2 vols. (Ph.D. thesis, University of Sydney, 1974).
The Northern Homily Cycle: The Expanded Version . . ., ed. Saara Nevanlinna, 3 vols., Mémoires de la Société Néophilologique de Helsinki, 38, 41, 43 (Helsinki, 1972–84).
Religious Pieces in Prose and Verse edited from Robert Thornton's MS . . ., ed. George G. Perry, EETS, OS 26 (London, 1867, 1914).
Reliquiae Antiquae: Scraps from Ancient Manuscripts, ed. Thomas Wright and James O. Halliwell, 2 vols. (London, 1845).
Richard Rolle Prose and Verse, ed. S. J. Ogilvie-Thomson, EETS 293 (Oxford, 1988).
Robinson, Christine M., 'A Machine-Readable Edition of the Text of the *Speculum Vitae* as Attested in British Library MS Additional 33995, with Introduction, Glossary and an Investigation of the Claims for the Common Authorship of the *Speculum Vitae* and the *Prick of Conscience*' (Ph.D. thesis, Edinburgh University, 1987).
The Simonie: A Parallel-Text Edition, ed. Dan Embree and Elizabeth Urquhart, Middle English Texts, 24 (Heidelberg, 1991).
Smelz, John W., '*Speculum Vitae*: An Edition of British Museum Manuscript Royal 17C.VIII' (Ph.D. thesis, Duquesne University), *Dissertation Abstracts International*, 38/vii (1978), A4151–2.
Ullmann, J., 'Studien zu Richard Rolle de Hampole', *Englische Studien*, 7 (1884), 415–72.

2. SECONDARY WORKS

Aarts, F. G. A. M., 'The Pater Noster in Medieval English Literature', *Papers on Language and Literature*, 5 (1969), 3–16.
Aers, David, *Community, Gender, and Individual Identity: English Writing 1360–1430* (London, 1988).
Allen, Hope E., 'The Authorship of the *Prick of Conscience*', in *Studies in English and Comparative Literature . . . Presented to Agnes Irwin*, Radcliffe College Monographs, NS 15 (Boston, 1910), 115–70.
—— 'The Desert of Religion: Addendum', *Archiv für das Studium der neueren Sprachen und Literaturen*, 127 (1911), 388–90.
—— 'The *Speculum Vitae*: Addendum', *PMLA* 32 (1917), 133–62 [i.e., an addendum to 'The Authorship'].

—— *Writings Ascribed to Richard Rolle, Hermit of Hampole, and Materials for his Biography* (New York, 1927).

Anderson, M. D., *Drama and Imagery in English Medieval Churches* (Cambridge, 1983).

Aston, Margaret, *Thomas Arundel: A Study of Church Life in the Reign of Richard II* (Oxford, 1967).

Beadle, Richard, 'Middle English Texts and their Transmission, 1350–1500: Some Geographical Criteria', in Margaret Laing and Keith Williamson (eds.), *Speaking in Our Tongues . . .* (Cambridge, 1994), 69–91.

—— 'Prolegomena to a Literary Geography of Later Medieval Norfolk', in Riddy (ed.), *Regionalism*, 89–108.

Benskin, Michael, 'The "Fit"-Technique Explained', in Riddy (ed.), *Regionalism*, 9–26.

Blake, N. F., '*The Form of Living* in Verse and Prose', *Archiv für das Studium der neueren Sprachen und Literaturen*, 211 (1974), 300–8.

Bradley, Ritamary, 'Backgrounds of the Title *Speculum* in Medieval Literature', *Speculum*, 29 (1954), 100–15.

Brayer, E., 'Contenu, structure et combinaisons du *Miroir du Monde* et de la *Somme le Roi*', *Romania*, 79 (1958), 1–38, 433–70.

Britton, Derek, 'Unknown Fragments of *The Prick of Conscience*', *Neuphilologische Mitteilungen*, 80 (1979), 327–34.

Brundage, James A., 'Prostitution in the Medieval Canon Law', in Judith M. Bennett et al. (eds.), *Sisters and Workers in the Middle Ages* (Chicago, 1989), 79–99.

Carruthers, Leo M., 'Allegory and Bible Interpretation: The Narrative Structure of a Middle English Sermon Cycle', *Journal of Literature and Theology*, 4 (Mar. 1990), 1–14.

—— '"Know thyself": Criticism, Reform, and the Audience of *Jacob's Well*', in Jacqueline Hamesse et al. (eds.), *Medieval Sermons and Society: Cloister, City, University* (Louvain, 1998), 219–40.

—— *La Somme le Roi et ses traductions anglaises: Étude comparée* (Paris, 1986).

—— 'Where Did *Jacob's Well* Come From? The Provenance and Dialect of MS Salisbury Cathedral 103', *English Studies*, 71 (1990), 335–40.

Catalogue of the Stowe Manuscripts in the British Library, 2 vols. (London, 1895–6).

Colker, Marvin L., *Trinity College Dublin, Descriptive Catalogue of the Mediaeval and Renaissance Latin Manuscripts*, 2 vols. (Aldershot, 1991).

Daichman, Graciela S., *Wayward Nuns in Medieval Literature* (Syracuse, NY, 1986).

de la Mare, A. C., *Catalogue of the Collection of Medieval Manuscripts bequeathed to the Bodleian Library Oxford by James P. R. Lyell* (Oxford, 1971).

Donaldson, E. Talbot, 'Chaucer's Final *-e*', *PMLA* 63 (1948), 1101–24.

Dondaine, Antoine, 'Guillaume Peyrault, vie et oeuvres', *Archivum Fratrum Praedicatorum*, 18 (1948), 162–236.

Doyle, A. I., 'A Survey of the Origins and Circulation of Theological Writings in English in the 14th, 15th, and Early 16th Centuries with Special Consideration of the Part of the Clergy Therein', 2 vols. (Ph.D. thesis, Cambridge University, 1953).

—— 'University College, Oxford, MS 97 and its Relationship to the Simeon Manuscript (British Library Add. 22283)', in Michael Benskin and M. L. Samuels (eds.), *So meny people longages and tonges* (Edinburgh, 1981), 265–82.

—— (introduction in) *The Vernon Manuscript: A Facsimile of Bodleian Library, Oxford, MS. Eng. poet. a.1* (Cambridge, 1987).

Duggan, Hoyt N., 'Final *-e* and the Rhythmic Structure of the B-Verse in Middle English Alliterative Poetry', *Modern Philology* 86 (1988), 119–45.

—— 'The Shape of the B-Verse in Middle English Alliterative Poetry', *Speculum*, 61 (1986), 564–92.

Fairfax-Blakeborough, J., 'Fountains Abbey Parchments', *Notes and Queries*, 12th ser. 10 (1922), 128.

Gillespie, Vincent, 'The Literary Form of the Middle English Pastoral Manual with Particular Attention to the *Speculum Christiani* and Some Related Texts', 2 vols. (D. Phil. thesis, Oxford University, 1981 [BodL, MS D.Phil. c.3674–5]).

—— '*Lukynge in haly bukes: Lectio* in Some Late Medieval Spiritual Miscellanies', *Analecta Cartusiana*, 106 (1984), 1–27.

—— 'Postcards from the Edge: Interpreting the Ineffable in the Middle English Mystics', in Piero Boitani and Anna Torti (eds.), *Medieval and Modern: The J. A. W. Bennett Memorial Lectures: Perugia 1992* (Cambridge, 1993), 137–65.

—— 'Strange Images of Death: The Passion in Later Medieval English Devotional and Mystical Writing', *Analecta Cartusiana*, 117 (1987), 110–59.

—— 'Vernacular Books of Religion', in Jeremy Griffiths and Derek Pearsall (eds.), *Book Production and Publishing in Britain 1375–1475* (Cambridge, 1989), 317–44.

Goldsmith, Margaret, *The Figure of Piers Plowman: The Image on the Coin* (Cambridge, 1981).

Gordon, James D., 'The Articles of the Creed and The Apostles', *Speculum*, 40 (1965), 634–40.

—— unpublished correspondence concerning his in-progress edition of *Speculum Vitae*, to A. I. Doyle and Toshiyuki Takamiya, 28 January, 22 March, and 8 May 1977.

Görlach, Manfred, *The Textual Tradition of the South English Legendary*, Leeds Texts and Monographs, NS 6 (Leeds, 1974).

Hanna, Ralph, *London Literature, 1300–1380* (Cambridge, 2005).

—— 'A New Fragment of *Speculum Vitae*', *Journal of the Early Book Society*, 6 (2003), 137–42.

—— 'Sir Thomas Berkeley and his Patronage', *Speculum*, 64 (1989), 878–916.

—— 'Some North Yorkshire Scribes and their Context', in Graham D. Caie and Denis Renevey (eds.), *Medieval Texts in Context* (London, 2008), 167–91.

—— 'Takamiya MS 15: Some Liminal Observations', in Takami Matsuda et al. (eds.), *The Medieval Book and a Modern Collector: Essays in Honour of Toshiyuki Takamiya* (Woodbridge, 2004), 125–34.

—— 'The Yorkshire Circulation of *Speculum Vitae*' York MSS conference volume, ed. Linne Mooney, forthcoming.

—— 'Yorkshire Writers', *Proceedings of the British Academy*, 121 (2003), 91–109.

Harris, William O., *Skelton's* Magnificence *and the Cardinal Virtue Tradition* (Chapel Hill, N.C., [1966]).

Henry, Avril, '"The Pater Noster in a table ypeynted" and Some Other Presentations of Doctrine in the Vernon Manuscript', in Pearsall (ed.), *Studies in the Vernon Manuscript*, 89–113.

Howard, Donald R., *The Three Temptations: Medieval Man in Search of the World* (Princeton, 1966).

Hudson, Anne, 'A New Look at the *Lay Folks' Catechism*', *Viator*, 16 (1985), 243–58.

—— *The Premature Reformation: Wycliffite Texts and Lollard History* (Oxford, 1988).

Hussey, Maurice, 'The Petitions of the Paternoster in Mediaeval English Literature', *Medium Ævum*, 27 (1958), 8–16.

James, Montague R., *A Descriptive Catalogue of the McClean Collection of Manuscripts in the Fitzwilliam Museum* (Cambridge, 1912).

—— *A Descriptive Catalogue of the Manuscripts in the Library of Gonville and Caius College*, 2 vols. (Cambridge, 1907–8).

—— *A Descriptive Catalogue of the Manuscripts in the Library of St John's College Cambridge* (Cambridge, 1913).

—— *The Western Manuscripts in the Library of Trinity College, Cambridge: A Descriptive Catalogue*, 4 vols. (Cambridge, 1900–4).

—— and Jenkins, Claude, *A Descriptive Catalogue of the Manuscripts in the Library of Lambeth Palace* (Cambridge, 1930–2).

Johnston, Alexandra F., 'The Plays of the Religious Guilds of York: The Creed Play and the Pater Noster Play', *Speculum* 50 (1975), 55–90.

—— 'William Revetour, Chaplain and Clerk of York, Testator', *Leeds Studies in English*, 29 (1998), 153–71.

Jones, Edward, 'Jesus College Oxford, MS 39: Signs of a Medieval Compiler at Work', *English Manuscript Studies*, 7 (1998), 236–48.

Kaeppeli, T., *Scriptores Ordinis Praedicatorum Medii Aevi*, 4 vols. (Rome, 1970–93).

Keiser, George, 'Lincoln Cathedral Library MS. 91: Life and Milieu of the Scribe', *Studies in Bibliography* 32 (1979), 158–79.

Kempson, E. G. H., 'The Vicar's Library, St Mary's, Marlborough', *Wiltshire Archaeological and Natural History Magazine*, 51 (1945–6), 194–215, 344–5.

Kohler, C., *Catalogue des manuscrits de la Bibliothèque Sainte-Geneviève*, 2 vols. (Paris, 1893–6).

Lottin, Odin, *Psychologie et morale au XIIe et XIIIe siècles*, 6 vols. in 8 (Louvain, 1942–60).

Lyall, Roderick J., 'The Lost Literature of Medieval Scotland', in J. Derrick McClure and Michael R. G. Spiller (eds.), *Bryght Lanternis: Essays on the Language and Literature of Medieval and Renaissance Scotland* (Aberdeen, 1989), 33–47.

MacCracken, Henry N., 'Quixley's Ballades Royal (? 1402)', *Yorkshire Archaeological Journal*, 20 (1909), 33–50.

Marx, William, *The Index of Middle English Prose, Handlist XIV: Manuscripts in the National Library of Wales* . . . (Woodbridge, 1999).

Morrin, Margaret J., *John Waldeby O.S.A., c. 1315–c. 1372* . . ., Studia Augustiniana Historica, 2 (Rome, 1975).

Nelson, Venetia, 'Cot. Tiberius E.vii: A Manuscript of the *Speculum Vitae*', *English Studies* 59 (1978), 97–113.

—— 'Problems of Transcription in the *Speculum Vitae* Manuscripts', *Scriptorium*, 31 (1977), 254–9.

—— 'The *Speculum Vitae*: An Introduction', *Essays in Literature*, 2, iii (University of Denver, May 1974), 75–102.

—— 'The Vernon and Simeon Copies of the *Speculum Vitae*', *English Studies*, 57 (1976), 390–4.

Oliger, Livarius, 'Regulae tres Reclusorum et Eremitarum Angliae, saec. XII–XIV', *Antonianum*, 3 (1928), 151–90, 299–320.

Owst, G. R., *Literature and Pulpit in Medieval England* (2nd edn., Oxford, 1961).

—— '*Sortilegium* in English Homiletic Literature of the Fourteenth Century', in J. Conway Davies (ed.), *Studies Presented to Sir Hilary Jenkinson* (London, 1957), 272–303.

Pantin, W. A., *The English Church in the Fourteenth Century* (Notre Dame, Ind., 1963).

Pearsall, Derek (ed.), *Studies in the Vernon Manuscript* (Cambridge, 1990).

Peterson, Ingrid J., *William of Nassington: Canon, Mystic, and Poet of the* Speculum Vitae (New York, 1986).

Post, Gaines, et al., 'The Medieval Heritage of a Humanistic Ideal: "Scientia donum dei est, unde vendi non potest"', *Traditio*, 11 (1955), 195–234.

Renevey, Denis, *Language, Self and Love . . .* (Cardiff, 2001).

Riddy, Felicity (ed.), *Regionalism in Late Medieval Manuscripts and Texts* (Cambridge, 1991).

Robertson, D. W., Jr, and Huppé, Bernard F., *Piers Plowman and Scriptural Tradition* (Princeton, 1951).

Robinson, P. R., *Catalogue of Dated and Datable Manuscripts c. 737–1600 in Cambridge Libraries*, 2 vols. (Cambridge, 1988).

Rubin, Miri, *Corpus Christi: The Eucharist in Late Medieval Culture* (Cambridge, 1991).

Salter, Elizabeth, 'The Manuscripts of Nicholas Love's *Myrrour of the Blessed Lyf of Jesu Christ* and Related Texts', in A. S. G. Edwards and Derek Pearsall (eds.), *Middle English Prose: Essays on Bibliographical Problems* (New York, 1981), 115–27.

Sandler, Lucy F., *The Psalter of Robert de Lisle in the British Library* (London, 1983).

Scase, Wendy, *'Piers Plowman' and the New Articlericalism* (Cambridge, 1989).

Stevenson, William H., *Report on the Manuscripts of Lord Middleton . . .*, Historical Manuscripts Commission report 69 (London, 1911).

Stover, Edna V., 'A Myrour to Lewde Men and Wymmen: A Note on a Recently Acquired Manuscript', *The Library Chronicle* [University of Pennsylvania], 16 (1950), 81–6.

Sullivan, Matthew, 'The Role of the Nassington Family in the Medieval English Church', *Nottingham Medieval Studies*, 37 (1993), 53–64.

Takamiya, Toshiyuki, '"On the Evils of Covetousness": An Unrecorded Middle English Poem', in Richard Beadle and A. J. Piper (eds.), *New Science Out of Old Books: Studies in Manuscripts and Early Printed Books in Honour of A. I. Doyle* (Aldershot, 1995), 188–206.

—— 'Richard and Robert as False Executors in Late Medieval England', *Anglistik*, 8/1 (Mar. 1997), 49–59.

Tubach, Frederic C., *Index Exemplorum: A Handbook of Medieval Religious Tales*, Folklore Fellows Communications, 86 (Helsinki, 1969).

Turville-Petre, Thorlac, and Johnston, Dorothy, *Image and Text: Medieval Manuscripts at the University of Nottingham* (Nottingham, 1996).

Tuve, Rosemond, *Allegorical Imagery: Some Mediaeval Books and their Posterity* (Princeton, 1966).

Wallace, David (ed.), *The Cambridge History of Medieval English Literature* (Cambridge, 1999).

Warner, George F., and Gilson, J. P., *Catalogue of Western Manuscripts in the Old Royal and King's Collections*, 4 vols. (London, 1921).

Watson, Andrew G., *Catalogue of Dated and Datable Manuscripts c. 700–1600 in the Department of Manuscripts, the British Library*, 2 vols. (London, 1979).

—— *The Manuscripts of Henry Savile of Banke* (London, 1969).

Wenzel, Siegfried, *The Sin of Sloth: Acedia in Medieval Thought and Literature* (Chapel Hill, N.C., 1967).

Wilson, Edward, 'Sir Robert Shottesbrook (1400–1471): Translator', *Notes and Queries*, 206 (1981), 303–5.

Wyatt, Diana, 'The English Pater Noster Play: Evidence and Extrapolations', *Comparative Drama*, 30 (1997), 452–70.

Young, John, and Aitken, P. Henderson, *A Catalogue of the Manuscripts in the Library of the Hunterian Museum in the University of Glasgow* (Glasgow, 1908).

Zeeman (Salter), Elizabeth, 'Continuity and Change in Middle English Versions of the *Meditationes Vitae Christi*', *Medium Ævum*, 26 (1957), 25–31.

SPECULUM VITAE

lines 1–9062

THE CONTENTS OF *SPECULUM VITAE*

Pater noster qui es in celis, sanctificetur nomen tuum; aduen*i*at regnum tuum, etc. fo. 1ra

Almyghty Godde in Trynyte,
In wham anely er persons thre,
Fader and Sone and Haly Gast,
þat er a Godde als we trowe mast,
Spede vs now at þis bygynnyng
And graunt vs alle gode endyng,
And gif me grace swilk wordes to say
þat may be mast Godde to pay
And to hym louyng and worschepe,
And to þe fende shame and shenship,
And to yhow þat me heres alswa
Hele of saul and til alle þa
þat has nede of gode counsaylle,
And mede to me for my trauaylle.
Prayes alle now *par charite*
Specially þat it swa be,
And þareto ilk man with gode wille
Bidde a Pater Noster stille.
  Gode men and wymmen, I yhou pray
Takes gode kepe to þat I say
And takes no rewarde to my dedes,
Al-if I be synful þat redes;
Ne to my persoun ne to my body
þat I hald feble and vnworthy.
For al-if I be of ille maners,
þe wordes I rede er neuer þe wers,
For alle gode wordes men suld prayse
And noght lacke ne loue þat þam says.
þarefore takes na rewarde to me
Wethir I am gode or ille to se,
Bot to my wordes anely takes kepe
And whyle I speke, kepe yhou fra slepe.
And on alle þat heres me right

heading: *om.* LSW, *ends* celis R   6 graunt] bryng L   gode] to gode L   8 to] vnto R   10 to] *om.* L   15 alle now] *trs.* ELR   16 *written on same line as 15* E   it] it may L   17 gode] a gode L   18 stille] and a aue stille E, þaretill L   22 þat] þat it E   25 al-if] if all L, alle W   26 I] that I R   30 Goode or euel wheþer I be R

þe benysoun of God mot lyght.
  I warne yhow first at þe bygynnynge,
I wil make na vayne carpynge
Of dedes of armes ne of amours,
Als dose mynstraylles and iestours
þat mas carpynge in many place
Of Octouyane and Isambrase

fo. 1rb And of many othir iestes,
And namely whan þai cum to festes.
Ne of þe lyf of Beuis of Hamptoun
þat was a knyght of grete renoun,
Ne of Sir Gye of Warwyke,
Al-if it myght sum men lyke,
I thynk my carpynge sal noght be,
For I hald þat noght bot vanyte.
Bot þis sal be my carpynge
To carp of mast nedefull thynge
þat sykirest es for saul and lyf
To man and womman, mayden and wyf.
þarefore gode men þat er here,
Listens me, and yhe may lere
How yhe sal rewell here yhour lyf
And gouerne wele yhour wyttes fyue;
How yhe sal folow Goddes wille
And knaw bathe gode and ille,
And what yhe sal chese and what forsake
And what way yhe sal to heuen take.
  In Inglische tunge I sal yhow telle,
If yhe so lange with me wil dwelle.
Na Latyne wil I speke ne wast
Bot Inglische þat men vses mast,
For þat es yhour kynde langage
þat yhe haf mast here of vsage.

34 mot] *om.* R, *add* on þaim SR 35 first] *om.* L 36 I] That I R vayne] ⟨g⟩ayn? R 37 dedes] dede? L amours] armours L 39 many] many a R 40 and] and sire ELS, and of R 41 And] *om.* L othir] maners þai telle of L 43 Beuis] Boys ELP 48 I . . . noght] that I hold R 49 be] be all R 50 carp of] speke of þe L 54 lere] here W 56 wele] you wyth L 58 And] And lere to R 62 If] And L so . . . me] *trs. phrs.* R 63 wil] nyl W 64 Bot] Bot in R 65 For] Forwhy R yhour] oure L kynde] kyndly R 66 yhe] we L mast here] *trs.* LR

þat can ilk man vnderstande
þat es borne in Ingelande,
For þat langage es mast shewed
Als wele amonge lered als lewed.
Latyne, als I trowe, can nane
Bot þa þat has it of skole tane;
Summe can Frankische and na Latyne
þat vsed has court and dwelled þarin;
And som can of Latyne a party
þat can Frankys bot febilly;
And som vnderstandes Inglische
þat nouthir can Latyn ne Frankische.
Bot lered and lawed, alde and yhunge,
Alle vnderstandes Inglische tunge.
þarefore I hald it mast siker þan

To shewe þe langage þat ilk man can, fo. 1va
And al for lewed men namely
þat can na manere of clergy.
To kenne þam war mast nede,
For clerkes can bathe se and rede
In sere bokes of Haly Writte
How þai sal lif, if þai loke itt.
þarefore I wil me haly halde
To þat langage þat Inglisch es called.
  Gode men, vnderstandes me now:
þe right way I sal kenne yhow
þat yhe may halde whyle yhe lif,
And swilk a lessoun I sal yhow gyf
þat *Mirour of Lyf* to yhow may be
In whilk yhe may al yhour lyf se.
First wil I speke of þe grete profyte
Of þe Pater Noster þat comes of it,

69 shewed] vsede W 71 Latyne] For latyne R nane] þai nane W 73 Frankische] frankes L, fraunce S, franche RP 74 vsed has] *trs.* P 76 Frankys] fraynche PR bot] *om.* W 77 Inglische] in Inglysce L 78 Frankische] frankes L, franche R 79 lawed] *om.* E 80 vnderstandes] *adds* in S 81 siker] ⟨n⟩ede P 82 þe] þat L 83 al] *om.* W men namely] mens sake anely R 85 kenne] teche W þam] þaime what L, þam it R, hom þen W 87 In sere] And se her W 88 loke] con loke W 89 þare-] Whare- S 92 kenne] telle S, teche W 96 In] In þe ELS 97 wil I] *trs.* PS

And of þe fruyt and þe dignyte
Of þat prayere, als men may se;
And specially of þe seuen askynges
þat on þe Pater Noster hynges;
And of þe seuen Giftes of þe Haly Gast
þat þe seuen askynges may to vs hast;
And of seuen syns þat mast may smert
þat þe seuen Giftes puttes out of hert;
And specially of vertus seuen
þat may be sette in þair stede euen;
And of þe seuen blissedhedes
To whilk þe seuen vertus vs ledes;
And of þe seuen medes alle
þat to þe blissedhedes suld falle.
Of alle þise poyntes I thynk to say;
Whaso wil, here þam alle he may.
  þe Pater Noster first men leres,
For it es heued of alle prayers.
It es a prayere mast sufficiaunt
Til alle þa þat it will haunt,
And mast siker, whareso þai ga,
For þis lyf and þe tothir alswa.
Wharefore ilk man þat has tane
þe trouth of baptym at þe funtstane
þat prayere suld lere and tent
Thurgh Halykirkes commaundement.

fo. 1vb And þa þat wil noght lere ne knawe
þat prayere dispyses Goddis lawe.
[*De dignitate oracionis dominice*] þarefore þe manere es þis to loke:
When first a chylde es sette to boke,
þe Pater Noster he sal first lere
For it \`es´ mast precious prayere.
þat lessoun Godde almyghty
Taght his discyples specially;

99 and[2]] and of LR 100 Of] And of L als] þat W 102 on] in P 103 þe[1]] *om.* PR 104 þe] þase L, *om.* R 106 of] of þe L 107 of] of þe L 108 stede] stedes LS 111 of] to R 112 -hedes] -hede W 113 alle] *om.* P 114 -so] -som S alle] *om.* E 118 þa] *om.* PR it will] *trs.* S 119 -so] -sere W þai] þi S 122 at] of P þe[2]] *om.* W 125 ne] and LS 127 *sidenote*: *om.* A, *as in-column heading at 115* R 132 Taght] Thaght S discyples] *adds* full L

þarefore may it be right callede
Goddes prayer, als we it halde.
Wharefore þai þat vnderstand wille
þis lessoun als þai suld thurgh skille,
þai suld become bathe meke and mylde
And debonere als a chylde.
Swilk er þe verray skolers right
Of our wyse mayster Godde of myght,
þat of his wisdome oft þam leres
And teches þam als his awen skolers.
Bot we may fynde many a man
þat þe naked lettre anely can
Of þis prayere þat Cryst wroght,
Bot þe vnderstandynge can þai noght.
þarefore thynk þam it sauourles
For þarein fele þai na swettenes;
Ful litell deuocioun haue þai
In þat prayere when þai it say.
Bot whaso vnderstandes it wele
A swete prayere þai may it fele.
 þis prayere suld be praysed ay
Byfore alle þe prayers þat we say,
For it es priuyleged, als we se,
By þe resoun of thynges thre.
Ane es dignyte þat heghe es;
Anothir thynge es shortenes;
þe thridde thyng es grete profyte
þat on many wyse comes of it.
First þis prayere may be called
A prayere of dignyte, als I halde,
For Cryst [it made] first to say
And taght his disciples so to pray.

133 þare-] Whare L be right] wele be L callede] tolde W 135 vnderstand wille] vnderstandes well S 137 suld] *om.* L bathe] als L 138 And] And als LR 140 of[2]] all- L 142 his] *om.* E awen] *om.* L 144 anely] *om.* L 145 Cryst] gode R 148 þarein] þare P 152 swete] sweter R may] *om.* R 153 praysed] ?prayed P 154 *line om.* L þe] othir P we] ?to P 155 se] se may L 156 þe] *om.* L thynges] skilles P 157 heghe] heghest L 159 grete] *om.* LW 160 on] of P, in W comes] may com L of] on R 161 þis] *om.* P called] talde E *163 it made] *trs.* AES

fo. 2ra A prayere of shortnes we it calle,
For in short wordes Cryst made it alle.
A prayere of profyte it es right,
For thurgh it we ask of Godde of myght
Al þat es nedeful for þis lyf here
And for þe tothir þat es more clere.
þis prayere es short in worde wroght;
It es in sentence lange in thoght.
It es light to say prayande;
It es sutill to vnderstande.
Short in worde es þis prayere,
For men it suld lyghtlyar lere
And thurgh shortnes of it by kynde,
Haf it þe titter in þair mynde.
In sentence it es lange to se
For þe mare deuocioun þarein suld be.
For þe naked lettre þat es noght heuy
Men suld say by mouth anely,
And alle þe sentence of it
Vnderstande and in hert knytt.
It es also light to say
For men suld thurgh it ofter pray.
Sutill to vnderstande es it
For men suld mare sette þair witte
On þe sentence of it namely
Thurgh grete bisynes and study.

De vtilitate oracionis dominice

þis bede puttes alle ille oway
And al þat gode es wynnes vs ay.
It festens in vs alle gode to last
And mas our hert to Godde stedefast.
In þis prayere er askynges seuen;
Whilk þai er I sal þam neuen.
Of whilk seuen I fynde thurgh skille
Thre þat dose away alle ille.

166 short] ?fone P 167 it es] *trs.* P 168 ask] may aske L of] all- L 169 þis] þe L 172 lange] langgar E 176 it suld] *trs.* W suld] sulde þe L lyghtlyar] lyghter W 178 it þe] þarein L titter] ofter W in þair] þe L 179 it es] *trs.* PS (es lang [*expunged*] it S), is R 180 þe] *om.* LP 181 es noght] *om.* L 183 þe] þe grett R 184 in] in þe L 185 to] for to L 186 thurgh it] *trs.* E it] it þe L 189 On] In P 191 *sidenote*: *illeg.* P 192 es] es it L, *om.* P 195 er askynges] es askyng L 196 þai] þat þai L sal þam] wyll you L 197 Of] Of þe P

I fynde also thre othir askynges
þat alle þat gode es to vs brynges.
Yhete es þare ane, als I can telle,
þat festens our hert in alle gode to dwell,
So þat ilkane of þa askynges sere
Has sere offices, als yhe sal here.

First thre dose away alle ille
fo. 2rb
Pro omnibus malis amouendis
þat oft falles, loude or stille;
For alle manere of ille we calle
Outhir þat was or es or þat may falle.
For þe ille þat has bene done
Pro malo preterito: v^{a}. peticio
þus we say to fordo it sone:
Et dimitte nobis debita nostra sicut et nos dimittimus debitoribus nostris.
In þis we ask to cleren our thoght
Forgifnes of þat we haf wroght.
For ille þat men may after do
Pro malo futuro: vj^{a}. peticio
þus say we als falles þarto:
Et ne nos inducas in temptacionem.
In þis we ask sum sleght to se
Agayne alle ille þat may be.
For þe ille þat we do ilka day
Pro malo presenti: vij^{a}. peticio
We say þus to put it away:
Sed libera nos a malo.
In þis we ask ryght abstynence
Of alle ille þat fyles our conscience.
Yhete es þare othir askynges thre
Pro omnibus bonis assequendis
For allekyn gode þat may be;
For alle manere of gode outhir bodily es
Or gastly gode or gode endeles.

199 askynges] askyng L 202 festens] fest P 204 sal] may L 206 oft] *after* or E, be- L, *om.* P falles] falled R *sidenote*: De omnibus malis L, *illeg.* P omnibus] *om.* W 208 falle] befall R 209 *sidenote*: *illeg.* P malo] malis W (*the following word illeg.*) v^{a}.] vj. W 210 to] *om.* P 210a *ends* dimittimus E, *ends* nostra L, *added in upper margin, ends* nos P, *ends* nos SR 212 wroght] myswroght R 213 *sidenote*: vj peticio P, *with remainder illeg.* 214 say we] *trs.* LR 215 In] ȝet in P 216 ille] illes L 217 þe ille] illes L *sidenote*: vij^{a} peticio P, *with remainder illeg.* vij^{a}. peticio] *om.* L 218 it] þaime L 218a *line om.* L 220 fyles] fylles R 221 askynges] askyng L, thynges P *sidenote*: *om.* W, *illeg.* P Pro] ⟨ ⟩ Peticio pro L 223 of] *om.* W outhir] þat W

Pro bono corporali: iiij^{a}. peticio

For bodily gode here to haue
Our sustenaunce þus we craue:
Panem nostrum cotidianum da nobis hodie.
In þis we aske strength and myght
For to sustayne our lyf here right.

Pro bono spirituali: iij^{a}. peticio

For gastly gode here to stir vs
To luf Godde we say þus:
Fiat voluntas tua sicut in celo et in terra.
In þis we ask nyght and day
Stedfast wille Godde to serue ay.

Pro bono eterno: ij^{a}. peticio

For gode to haue withouten end
We say þus, whareso we wende:
Adveniat regnum tuum.
In þis þe blisse of heuen we craue
And grace to be worthy it to haue.

Confirmacio ceterarum peticionum pro perseuerancia in bono: j^{a}. peticio

For festenyng of our hertes to stande
In gode þus say we prayande:
Sanctificetur nomen tuum.

Pater

fo. 2va

In þis we ask wille stedefast
Withouten faylyng in gode to last.
Swilk maner of askynges bene
In þis haly prayer sene.
Bot þis prayer bygynnes right

De iiij^{or}. verbis in principio oracionis dominice que dici possunt prologus eiusdem, scilicet pater, noster, qui es, in celis

With four wordes of grete myght,
On whylk at þe bygynnynge hynges
Al þe spede of þe seuen askynges
Thurgh four wordes þat may we fele,
If we vnderstande þam wele,
How we sal rewel vs by skille

225 here] he R to] for to L *sidenote*: *om*. (*as are the next three*) W corporali] temporali LPS, tempora R iiij^{a}.] viij. R iiij^{a}. peticio] *om*. L 226 þus] þusgates R 226a da nobis hodie] *om*. L hodie] *om*. S 228 here] now R 229 to stir] styres E 230 we say] þan say we R 230a et in terra] *om*. L 231 ask] ask both R 232 Godde] *after* serue LR 233 *sidenote*: ij^{a}. peticio] *om*. L, *illeg*. P 234 We say þus] þus we say L, þan say we þus R 236 to^{2}] for to L 237 *sidenote*: *mostly cut away* L, *mostly illeg*. P Pro . . . peticio] *om*. S j^{a}. peticio] *om*. R 238 þus] þusgates R 239 wille] þe wyll L, wel W 240 faylyng] fallyng R in gode] for P 241 maner] maners W askynges] askyng LS 244 *sidenote*: *ends* dominice E, *om*. LSW, *illeg*. P, *ends* noster R 245 On] On þe LP 246 þe^{1}] *om*. L 247 four] þase foure L þat] þan L 248 If] If þat L we] we won W

To do þat mast es Goddis wille.
þarefore first byhoues vs nede,
If we sal of our askynges spede,
þise four wordes vnderstande
And lede our lyf als þai commande;
Elles er we noght worthy
To be herde of Godde almyghty.
þise er þa four wordes to here
þat er þe entre of þis prayere:
  Pater / noster / qui es / in celis.
þise er on Inglische þus to neuen,
'Fader our þat es in heuen'.
þise four mykell mater byndes,
Als clerkes in þair bokes fyndes.

Pater

þe first worde es 'Pater' right.
þat es a worde of grete myght,
For it may make vs sone to spede
Of our askynge, when we haf nede,
Als we may bathe se and fele,
If we vnderstande þat worde wele.
For Saynt Bernard says þat þe prayere *Bernardus*
þat bygynnes right on þis manere,
With þis swete name to neuen
þat es called 'Fader of heuen',
Gyues ane hope to purchace
Al þat we ask here of grace.
  þis worde 'Fader' to vndirstande,
þat makes swete al þe remenande,
Shewes vs what we sal trowe
And what we sal do here and howe.
It shewes þe lengthe of Goddes beynge
þat es ay withouten endynge,

249 How] How þat LR we sal] *trs.* W rewel vs] reules W 250 mast es] *trs.* LW 252 sal] *om.* P askynges] askyng LSR spede] sped sall spede P 255 er] ne er R 257 þa] þe EPS 259 þise] þai L on] in P neuen] men S 261 four] *adds* wordes S mater] maters S 262 clerkes] clerk L 262a heading: *marg.* P, *om.* RW 266 askynge] preyer L, askynges W 267 may] *om.* P 269 þat] *om.* P *sidenote*: *illeg.* P, *om.* R 270 right] *om.* LP 271 þis] þe P 272 Fader] þe fadyr P 273 ane] ?in P 276 þat] *om.* L 278 sal do] *trs.* P 279 shewes] shewes vs S beynge] beginyng P

Pater

fo. 2vb For Godde withouten bigynnyng es,
And his lastynge es endeles.
He es bigynnyng withouten bygynnyng,
And he es ende withouten endyng,
þat ordayned þam þat his ware
To lif with hym for euermare.
For yhe sal wele vnderstande þan
þat first when Godde maked man,
Ilk man to gode destayned he,
Bot he wist what ilk man wald be—
Wha wald be gode, wha wald be ille—
For he gaf ilk man a free wille
For to chese or for to halde
Gode or ille, whethir þai walde.
[For he destayned no man to blisse
Bot anely þam þat wold be his.]
   Yhete 'Pater' stirs vs to knawe euen
Thre thynges in Godde, Fader of heuen,
And thre thynges in his sons to se
þat lufs þe Fader with hert fre.
First in Godde þe Fader es Myght
And þarewith Wisdome and Godenes right;
In Godde þe Fader er alle þise thre,
For he es a Godde in Trynyte.
   Might es ay in hym anely,
For he es Godde, Fader almighty,
Mayster and Lorde, als clerkes can telle,
Of heuen and erthe and of helle,
And of alle thynge maker he es
And bigynnynge of alle godenes.
Swa men may, als I vnderstande,
Knawe his Myght þat es ay-lastande.

282 his] is P es] withoutyn P 285 þat[1]] And L 286 for] *om.* PW 287 For] *om.* R 288 maked] shuld make RW 289 to] to be W destayned] þan ordaned R, ordende W 291 gode] gode and R 293 or] and LS 294 þai] sa þai L, he R *294ab *lines om.* AELPS, *supplied from R in the forms of A* 294b anely þam] þo only W 295 euen] full euen L 296 Fader] þe fader EL 297 sons] sonne LPS 299 in] *om.* L es] es of L 302 a] *om.* LSR 303 ay] *om.* L *sidenote*: Potencia ES 305 can] *om.* P 306 and[1]] of LP 307 thynge] thinges R 309 men may] *trs.* R als] *om.* E

In Godde þe Fader es Wisdome
þat of hymself anely byhoues come,
Thurgh whilk he his menyhe ledes
And gouernes þam wysely and spedes,
And namely his childer þat he wroght
þat lufs hym wele in hert and thoght.
So may men knawe, whaso wille,
His Wisdome by kyndely skille.
In Godde þe Fader es Bounte,
þat es þe thridde thynge to se,
For Godde þe Fader his childer loues
And somtyme here he þam proues:
And when he sese þat þai do wronge,
He betes and chastyes þam amonge;

Pater

And if þai forsake hym for certayne, fo. 3ra
And sithen wil turne til hym agayne,
He þam resayues debonerly
And fayne es of þaire cumpany.
So may men knawe þe Godenes
þat in Godde þe Fader es.
þarefore suld his childer alle,
Als oft als þai 'Fader' calle,
Knawe in hym þise thynges thre,
Might, Wisdome, and Bounte.
Yhete in his childer men may knawe
Thre thynges to telle here on rawe
þat þai haf of þe Fader mast,
Als I wil shewe yhou in hast.
þe twa bene Nobillesce and Ritches;
þe thridde es Beute, als I gesce.
Nobillesce first es, als I wene,
In þam þat Goddis childer bene,

310 þat] *after* Knawe P 311 *sidenote*: Sapiencia ES 312 anely] *om.* LP byhoues] most W 316 in] wyth P 317 men] mon W 319 *sidenote*: Bonitas ES 320 to] for to L 323 þat] *om.* L 324 chastyes] chastes W amonge] he mange R 327 debonerly] bonerly S 331 suld] *after* childer P 332 þai] þai hym LS 333 in hym] *trs.* P 336 telle] tell þam R here] *om.* L on] in P 338 yhou] to you R 339 twa] *om.* P ritches] rycchnes P 340 beute] bounte ES I] a W 341 Nobillesce] noblete W first es] *trs.* EL *sidenote*: Nobilitas ES

For mare nobillesce may na man se
þan it es Goddis childer to be,
þat es so heghe ane emperour
And kynge of alle kynges of honour.
Ritches also to þam falles
þat men Goddis childer calles,
For mare ritches may na man haue
þan Godde on his childer vouches saue.
For Godde mas þam his heyres right
Of þe kyngedome of heuen bright,
þar alkyn ritches þat may falle
Er sene and alkyn delyces withalle.
Beute in Goddis childer es,
For Godde þam made to his liknes
And after his shappe þat es so fayre,
He made þair saulles of þe ayre.
Mare beute myght neuer be sene
þan in his lickenes es, als I wene,
For so grete beute als es þarin
Na hert may thynk na imagyn.
þarefore his childer suld thynk ay,
Als oftsithe als þai 'Fader' say,
O[n] þise thre thynges þat þai haue
Of þe Fader þat wele vouches saue

Pater

fo. 3rb Swilk thynges on þam for þair byhoue;
þarefore þam awe wele þair Fader luf.
Also þis worde þat 'Fader' es called
Askes of vs sex thynges to halde
þat I wil recken here on rawe.
þis sex suld his childer knawe:
Luf and Drede and Obedience,

Hoc uerbum 'pater' ad vj. nos ammouet, scilicet amorem, timorem, obedienciam, seruicium, honorem, reuerenciam

343 nobillesce] noblete W 344 þan] ?þat P it] *om.* S to] *om.* P 345 heghe] hight R ane] and W 347 also] *after* þam PW to] vnto R *sidenote*: Diuicie ES 350 on] in E 351 his] *om.* E 353 þar] þat S alkyn] alle W falle] befalle L 354 delyces] delytes EW with-] *om.* P 355 Beute] Bounte S *sidenote*: Pulcritudo ES 356 to] eftyr P 359 neuer] ?non P 360 es] *om.* W 361 grete] mykell L 365 *On] Of AL 366 wele] will E, *om.* LS, wele will R 367 on] of L 368 þam awe] þai howe W awe] aght L luf] to loue ES 369 *sidenote*: Pater E, *om.* PSR (*faded* W) 372 sex] sex thinges L

Seruyse, Honour, and Reuerence.
  þe first thynge þat Godde askes of vs *Amor*
Es Luf, þat we luf hym þus:
With al our hert in body wroght,
With al our saul, with al our thoght.
With al our hert, þat es to say
þat we on nathynge, nyght ne day,
Sette our hert to luf mare
þan on Godde, hou so we fare;
Na in nathynge þat man may neuen
Haf mare delyte þan in Godde of heuen.
  With al our saul we suld hym luf;
þat es to say, if we wil proue,
We suld tittar thole, if we war wis,
Our lyues be parted fra our bodys
þan fra Godde departed be,
þat es our Fader, ful of pyte.
þat es, we suld þe dede are take
Ar we suld our Fader forsake.
  We suld hym luf with al our thoght;
þat es to say þat we suld noght
Our wytte, ne our vnderstandynge,
Ne our thoght thurgh imagynynge
About nathynge mare occupy
þan in Godde, Fader almyghty.
  þe secund thyng es Drede alswa *Timor filialis*
To haue in hert, whareso we ga,
þat we Godde drede with al our myght
Thurgh Sones Drede (þan do we right),
And noght thurgh drede þat men calles
Carls Drede þat oft falles. *Timor seruilis*
For carls dredes þair louerdes thurgh awe,
And noght for luf, als men may knawe.

375 *sidenote*: *add* integer ES, *om.* LPW 376 þat] hym þat P 377 body] bodely R 378 saul] saul and P al] *om.* P 379 *sidenote*: Cum omni corde ES 383 in] *om.* P 385 *sidenote*: Cum tota anima ES 387 if] and L 388 lyues] lif W 389 Godde] oure god L 390 es] *after* Fader P 391 þat es] *om.* P we . . . dede] *trs. phrs.* S 392 suld] *om.* R 393 *sidenote*: Cum tota mente ES 394 þat[2]] *om.* LR 396 Ne] *om.* P 398 Godde] gode our R 399 *sidenote*: filialis] *om.* W 402 þan] þat R 403 drede] þe drede W 404 Carls] Carle L falles] befalles L *sidenote om.* W 405 louerdes] lorde PSW thurgh] for L, be P 406 for] be P

þe gode sons thurgh luf has drede
To wreth þair fader in worde or dede;
þis may wele be Sones Drede called.
Swilk Drede in hert suld we halde
And drede ay mare Goddis greuaunce

Pater

fo. 3va þan payne of helle or his vengeaunce,
For drede of payne anely to se
Es drede withouten charyte.
Al þat men dose in swilk a drede
Sal turne þam to litell mede.
  Bot first thurgh ferdnes may Drede bygyn
Anely for vengeaunce of synne,
Thurgh whilk men may bygynne do wele
And afterward a swete luf fele,
þat þe Haly Gast with Drede sal knyt
In þair hertes to stable þair witte.
Drede mas a man synne forsake,
And Luf mas a man gode vertus take.
þai þat þise twa in hert wil halde
'Goddes sonnes' may right be called;
þa sonnes may calle here baldely
Godde þair Fader almyghty.
Obediencia þe thridde thynge Obedyence es,
þat es to say Bouxsomnes,
þat we be bouxsom to do Goddis wille
And alle his commaundements to fulfille;
For þe sonnes suld be obedyent
To do þe fadirs commandement.
His commandements, whaso wil loke,

407 gode sons] sonnes of god L sons] sone P thurgh] for E 408 þair] his P or] and L dede] drede S 409 Sonnes drede may þis wele be called L 410 Swilk] Whylk L we] we ay R 412 þan] þan þe L payne] pyne S 414 charyte] any charite L 415 swilk a] þat P 416 to] vnto R 417 first, drede] `drede', first P thurgh] ?be P 419 do] to do LPS 422 witte] wittys P 423 forsake] to forsake LP 424 gode] *om.* L take] to take LR 425 wil] *after* þat LS (*as well as here* S) 426 sonnes] son R may right] wyth ryght may L right] þai ryght E 427 þa] And þaa L, þaȝ P here] here ryght E 429 *sidenote*: *adds* iij[a]. ER, *om.* P 430 say] *om.* P 431 do] *om.* PR 432 to] *om.* P 433 sonnes] sone W 434 do] *om.* E þe] þaire L, hys þe R 435 -ments] -ment E

He may fynde þam aftir in þis boke.
  þe ferth thynge es Seruyse, *Seruicium*
For we er halden of office
To serue Godde our Fader to pay
With al þe bisynes þat we may,
And al our hert and our wille gif
To do þat hym es mast lieue.
Swilk seruyse may mast ly
In alle þe Werkes of Mercy,
Als men may fynde in þis boke
Aftirward, whaso wil loke.
  þe fift thynge es Honour tolde, *Honor*
þat we suld alle, yhunge and olde,
Loue Godde with grete talent
Of alle godes þat he has vs sent.
On whilk gode we suld take kepe
And spende þam in his worshepe,
And in na ryots ne in folys,
And if we do, we er noght wys.
For vs byhoues acount to gif

Pater

Of þat we do whyle we here lif, fo. 3vb
And of alle þat Godde here wil vs sende
And shew how we haf þam spend,
And of alle þe folys þat we do,
And of ilkan hour and tyme þarto.
þarefore we suld Godde honour
Ilka tyme and ilkan hour,
Outhir in worde or in dede

436 may . . . aftir] sall þaime fynde efterwarde L   fynde þam] *trs.* S   aftir] afturward W   437 *sidenote: adds* iiij^{a}. ER, *om.* P   438 of] also of R   441 al] *om.* P   hert] hert gyf L   and^{2}] and al W   wille] and all wylle hym (and our *canc.*?) P   442 hym es mast] mast is hym P   443 Swilk] And swylk L   may] þat may L   444 werkes] werk L   445 Als] Whylk L   447 honour] reuerence P   tolde] calde S   *sidenote: adds* v^{a}. ER, *om.* P   448 alle] bathe L, hold both R   450 Of] And E   alle] all þe LP   451 On] Of LS   gode] godenes L, gooddes R   452 þam] hitt P   in] ay in R   453 in^{2}] in na L, *om.* RW   454 And if] An P   do] do þat L   455 to] *om.* LPW   *sidenote*: Quia reddituri sumus racionem S   456 here] *om.* P   457 here] *om.* L   here wil] *trs.* R   458 how] how þat P, howgates R   haf þam] þaime haues S   haf] *om.* W   þam] *om.* R   459 of] *om.* L   461 þarefore] And þerfore L   463 or] or ȝit R

Or in thoght hym honour bede,
And thank hym oft and loue hym ay
Of þat he dose vs nyght and day.
So suld þe gode sonnes by skille
Honour þe Fader—þat es his wille.
Reuerencia Reuerence es þe sext and þe last,
For we suld with hert stedefast
Do Godde alle maner of reuerence,
And namely here in his presence,
In kirk and in stedes withoute
þar his body es borne about.
We suld thurgh Reuerence knele doun,
Be it in felde or be it in toun.
His presence here es ouer-alle
þar we may speke to hym or calle.
Bot Halykirk his hous I halde,
þat es mast 'stede of prayer' called.
þare suld we hym mast reuerence do
With deuocioun þat falles þarto,
For when we speke to Godde or pray,
We suld do hym reuerence ay,
þat es to say lout or knele
With vncouerd heued—þan do we wele.
And when we noght knele, we suld stande
(If we may wele, þat war semand)
And noght sitte þare with couerd hede
To speke with Godde in haly stede.
Ne in kirk þat falles his hous to be,
We suld noght speke of vanyte,
For lesse reuerence we do hym þan
þan we wald do ane erthely man.
For if we war, als I vnderstand,

464 in] in our R honour] to honour W bede] to bede P, be dede W 465 loue] honour L 467 þe] we R 469 es] *om.* L *sidenote*: *adds* vj[a]. E, *om.* R 470 suld] shuld all R 472 here] *om.* L 473 in[2]] other R 475–6 *couplet trs.* L 475 thurgh] wyth LS, *om.* W 476 or] *om.* ELS 478 may . . . hym] *trs. phrs.* L to hym] *after* may P 479 his] es hys L *sidenote*: Domus mea domus oracionis vocabitur ES 480 es mast] *trs.* P 483 to] wyth L 484 hym] to hym R 485 or] and W 488 may] myght R war] is P, whar R 489 sitte] stand R þare] *om.* P 491 falles] *om.* P to] `sulde´ P 492 noght] *om.* L of] na L 495–7 If we befor a kyng shuld stand | þat lyf and lyme has in his hand | For to besek hym of his ⟨grace?⟩ R

In þe kynges chaumbre of Ingelande
To pray þe kynge of his grace,
How wald we bere vs in þat place?

Noster

Wald we noght þare in his sight fo. 4ra
Do hym reuerence with al our myght,
And kepe vs so þat we nathynge
Suld say þat myght displese þe kynge?
Mikell mare reuerence þan suld falle
To Godde, þat es mast kynge of alle;
For he es kynge of alle kynges
Of wham al grace and godenes springes.
þarefore to Godde þat we to pray
We suld do þe reuerence þat we may,
So may we al our askynge haue,
If it be skilfull þat we craue.
Swilk Reuerence to þe Fader falles
Of his childer þat on hym calles.
  þarefore we suld, nyght and day
When we þe Pater Noster say,
Als meke childer and bouxsom be
To our Fader, ful of pyte.
Als we will þat he be to vs
A gode Fader and a gracious.
And if we wil his gode childer be,
Vs byhoues alle folys fle
And loke þat we be clene within,
When we sal [þe] Pater Noster bygynne.

Noster

In þis worde ligges a questyoun
At þe bygynnyng of þis orisoun:
Why a man 'our Fader' says ay

499 noght] do nathing L 500 Do] Bot do L with] att P 501 nathynge] dyd nathing L 502 Suld say] *om.* L myght] walde L þe] vnto þe L 506 springes] ?spryng P 508 þe] *om.* LP þat we may] euer and ay L 509 askynge] askynges R 511 to] vnto L 512 on] to L 513 we suld] *trs.* R 517 þat] *om.* L he be] itt be he E 518 A gode] Fauorable L a^2] *om.* LW 519 gode] *om.* L *522 þe] *om.* AW 522a heading: *adds* I^o. (?Iohannes) E 523 ligges] is W 524 *sidenote*: Questio S 525 Why] Why þat L

And may noght als wele 'my Fader' say?
And wha falles felaw with hym be
When he says 'gif vs', and noght 'gif me'?
At þis may men answer sone
And telle skill why it es done.
Thurgh skill suld none 'my Fader' say
Bot he þat es Goddis sone verray
Thurgh kynde withouten bigynnyng
And withouten ende and fayllyng.
Bot thurgh kynde his sonnes er we noght
Bot in als mykell als we er wroght
To his lickenes, als es sene,
Als bathe Ieus and Sarzynes bene.
Per adopcionem Bot we bene his childer thurgh grace
And thurgh his chesyng to folow his trace.

Noster

fo. 4rb Als men may fynde in som lande
Swilk a law, als I vnderstande,
þat he þat es a riche man knawen
þat here has na childe his awen
May chese a pouer mans chylde þat es fayre
And make it his sone and his ayre.
þis grace vs dide Godde Fader of myght,
Paulus Als says Saynt Paul þe apostel right,
When he made vs thurgh þat grace com
To right trouth and to Cristendome,
þat war first pouer and naked to telle
And childer of wreth and of helle.
Wharefore when þat we say þus
'Our Fader' and says 'gif vs',
We gader to vs our brethir alle
þat to grace of baptym God wald calle,

527 wha] *om.* P, wham R, we W felaw] felawes W with hym] *om.* R be] to be LSRW 528 gif[2]] *om.* ES 529 At] Bot R 530 why] why þat LPR it] *om.* R 534 and[2]] neuer P fayllyng] fallynge R 537 To] Vnto R als] as itt P 539 *sidenote om.* PRW 542 als] *om.* R 544 þat] And L childe] childer R his] of hys LPSRW 545 chese] chesche E mans] *om.* P 546 it] hym W 547 vs dide] *trs.* P, cf. dyd god vs S 548 þe apostel] in þe pistyll R *sidenote om.* EPR 549 þat grace] grace to ES, *om.* R 550 to[2]] *om.* S 552 wreth] wrecches W 553 þat] *om.* ELS 555 to vs] togedder EL 556 þat to] *trs.* P to] to þe L calle] calde L

þat þe childer of Halykirk bene
Thurgh trouth of baptym þat es clene.
 þis worde 'Noster' vs shewes þarby
þe largesce and þe curtaysy
Of Godde, þat tittar inoghe gyues
þan lytell to þam þat here lyues,
And soner to many þan to ane
þat here has þe right trouth tane.
For Saynt Gregor spekes on þis manere *Gregorius*
And says þat a right prayere,
þe mare þat men it comon mase,
þe mare it es worth and vertu has—
Als a candell es brighter to kenne
þat serues til an halle ful of men
þan þe candell þat serues of light
Noght bot anely to a mans sight.
 þis worde 'Noster' vs biddes alswa
Loue Godde our Fader whareso we ga,
And with al our hert thank hym sone
Of þe grace þat he haues vs done,
Thurgh whilk we bene his childer fre
And his heyres ordayned to be;
And þat we luf byfore alle othir
Ihesu Cryst, our eldest brothir,
þat in þis grete grace vouched saue
Vs his awen brethir to haue.
 þis worde 'Noster' vs commaundes yhete

Noster

þat we right kepe with al our witte fo. 4va
In our hertes þe Haly Gast,
þat es wytnes here to vs mast
Of þe grace of chesyng `of´ vs. *Gracia adopcionis*
þat may thurgh skille be called þus

558 trouth] throgh E, *om.* L, trough R of] þe L 559 þis] þese W 560 largesce] largeste S 562 lyues] `l´yn es P 565 *sidenote om.* R 566 right] rightwys RW 567 þe] þat R 568 worth] worthy L 569 a] þe P es brighter] þat serues is bryght R 570 til] in W 576 haues] has with P, has for R 577 Thurgh whilk] Wharethurgh L whilk] þat ES 581 þis] his S, ys R vouched] vouches R 582 brethir] brother L 583 vs] *om.* S 587 of[1]] of þe W *sidenote: partly illeg.* P, *om.* RW

Als a wede þat es mast to prayse,
Paulus Als Saynt Paul þe apostell says,
Thurgh whilk we er siker bi right
To haf þe heritage þat es vs dight
Of Godde, our Fader þat es rightwys—
þat es þe blisse of Paradys.
   Yhete on þis worde 'Noster' hynges,
Amange alle othir, twa thynges
Hoc verbum 'noster' nos amouet ad duo, scilicet ad dileccionem proximi et certam spem
þat we suld hald in hert ay
Als oft als we þe Pater Noster say.
Ane es Luf of Brothirhede;
Anothir es syker Hope to spede.
   Luf suld we thurgh þis worde fele
þat ilkane of vs luf othir wele,
For we er alle, bathe heghe and lawe,
Brethir, als ilka man suld knawe,
Of a fader and a moder right.
Our fader es Godde, mast of myght,
And our moder es Halykirk,
Aftir wham vs bihoues wirk.
Ilkane suld luf als syster and brothir,
[And] nane of vs suld dispyse othir.
Bot ilkane othir suld honour
And help in nede and socour,
Als dose þe lyms of a body—
Ilkane helpes othir kyndely.
   Lyms of a body er we alle;
þat body Halykirk we calle,
Of whilk body Godde es þe hede.
þarefore suld ilkane othir rede
And ilkane here for othir pray,
Iacobus Als men may here Saynt Iame say.
For þat prayere may to alle avaylle
þat dose Halykirkes counsaylle,
For he þat mase hys prayere comoun

589 wede] worde ELS 590 *sidenote om.* R 591 whilk] skyll L bi] of R 592 es] he W es vs] *trs.* L dight] hyght ES 595 on þis] in þat P 597 *sidenote: om.* ESR ad^{2}] *om.* L proximi] cristi PW et] et ad L 599 luf] þe lufe P bro-] bre- L 600 to] of W 605 fader] feder S 608 wirk] to wyrk R 609 luf] *adds* other S *610 And] Bot AELP 611 othir suld] *trs.* RW 612 and] and in P 617 Of] Of þe P 620 Iame] Iacob P *sidenote om.* R 623 mase hys] makys R

With gode hert and deuocioun,
He mase hym felawe of þe commonyng
Of alle Halykirk in alle thynge.

Noster

And for ilka Pater Noster þat he says, fo. 4vb
Night or day, when so he prays,
He wynnes hym, als I vnderstande,
Part of ane hundreth thousand.
  þis worde 'Noster' þat es myghty
Vs kennes to hate thre [thynges] namely.
Ane es a synne þat men Pryde calles;
Anothir es Hatred þat oft falles;
þe thridde thynge es Auaryce—
Ouer-many men hauntes þat vyce.
  Pride þat yhernes to haf maystry
Puttes a man out of cumpany,
For when a man to Pryde drawes,
He wald be oboun alle his felawes.
þat man war noght here worthy
To dwelle langar in cumpany,
For Pryde oft brekes felawshepe
And puttes a man vnto shenshepe,
Als Lucifer for Pryde was
Casten to helle for his trespas.
He was putt out, als clerkes telles,
Of þe cumpany of aungels.
  Hatred þat felaws persayue can
Out of cumpany puttes a man.
For if a man his felaw hate
And fondes to fordo his state,
Al þe felawshepe greues he—
In cumpany suld he noght be.

625 þe] all þe P 628 or] and L when . . . prays] wharesa he gase L so] *om.* W so he] *trs.* P 629 als] *om.* P 632 kennes] teches W *thynges] synnes ARW, thyng P *sidenote*: Superbia Odium Auaricia (later) R 633 a] þe P synne þat] *int.* P þat] *om.* L 634 -red] -reddyne P oft] of tym R falles] befalles L 635 thynge] syn R 637 *sidenote*: Superbia ESR (R later) 640 alle] *om.* W his] his awen P 643 oft] oftsithes R 644 vnto] to PW, to gret R 645 for] thurgh PRW 648 Of þe] Oute of L 649 -red] -reden LPW felaws] folows R *sidenote*: Inimicicia ES, Odium (later) R 651 felaw] felaughs L 652 to] for to L

Auaryce puttes a man, I wene,
Out of cumpany þat es clene.
For when a man noght comon wille
With his felaws aftir skille,
Ne with þam part of þat he has,
Bot þat he wynnes his awen it mas—
Swilk a man methynk suld sone
Out of cumpany be done.
þarefore to swilk Godde vouches noght saue
þat þai part of þe Pater Noster haue.
þis worde 'Noster' vs shewes by skille
þat Godde es our awen if we will,
With þe Fader and þe Sone and þe Haly Gast,

Qui es

fo. 5ra Als we thurgh right trouth may tast,
If we hym loue and worshepe
And hys commandements kepe.
Als Godde says to vs ilkone
In þe goddespell of Saynt Ione,
Certayne Hope we suld haue ay,
When we þe Pater Noster say.
For þis worde þat 'Noster' es called
Wille þat we Hope in hert halde
To spede of þat we aske and craue,
If it be skilfull þat we wald haue.
For he es our gode Fader of myght,
And we er his awen childer right.
þarefore we hope better by skille
þat he our askynge wil fulfille.
Sen he es our Fader and we er his,
We hope of þat we sal noght misse.

655 *sidenote*: Auaricia ESR 660 it] *om.* R 661 suld] *om.* L 662 be] sulde be L 663 to] *om.* L 666 if] if þat L 667 þe[2]] *om.* EPW þe[3]] *om.* W 668 right] þe right P 672 *sidenote*: Euang' S, Iohannes W 676 hope in hert] in herte hope E in] and 'in' P 677 spede] speke L 679 es our] *om.* L 680 er] *om.* EL 684 of þat we] þat R

Qui es

þis worde 'Qui es' shewes what God es
And þe ground of his sothfastnes.
For our Fader, als clerkes telle can,
Es verray Godde and verray man,
A substaunce in Trinite,
And nane othir Godde es bot he—
Thurgh wham alle manere of thing es wroght,
Withouten wham ne may be noght.
þarefore es synne in Haly Writte
Called 'noght', for Godde neuer made itte.
Men fyndes writen, als clerkes can knawe,
In þe secund boke of þe Alde Lawe
þat Godde apered in a mountayne
Vnto Moyses (and þat was certayne)
And sayde to hym þus, 'þou sal go
Into Egipt to Kynge Pharao
And bidde hym deliuer in quert and hele
My folk, þe childer of Iraell,
þat he in seruage haldes thurgh myght.
Say I sent þe to hym right'.
'Louerd,' quod Moyses, 'if men ask me
þi name, what sal myne answer be?'
þan sayde he, 'If men ask my name,

Qui es

þou sal say, "I Am þat Am". fo. 5rb
þus saltou say and noght it hele
Vnto þe childer of Iraele:
"He þat Es has me sent
Hider on yhou to take tent." '
þarefore say`s´ þis noble clerkes

684a heading: *om.* LS, Qui es in celis R 686 his] *om.* S soth-] sted- L 688 Es] þe R 690 othir] nothir P es] *om.* L 692 ne] *om.* LPW *sidenote*: Sine ipso factum est nichil (*adds* id est peccatum S) ES 693 es] *om.* L 694 Called] Es calde L noght] es noght ES 696 alde] *om.* W *sidenote*: Dominus apparuit moysi (later?) R 698 and] *om.* LP 699 þus] *om.* L 703 thurgh] wyth E 705 if] and L 707–8 *couplet fused as single line* E, *couplet trs.* P 707 if . . . name] *om.* E ask] aske þe W *sidenote*: Ego sum qui sum ES 708 þou sal say] *om.* E þat] þat I EP Am^{2}] I ame EPS 712 on] to EW tent] entent PR 713 says] *corr. later* A þis] *om.* L

And haly men of haly werkes
Þat amange alle þe heghe names to neuen
Þat es sayde of Godde of heuen,
Þe first and þe proprest es þis,
Þat mast bi skille may vs wisse
And kenne to knawe what Godde es
Thurgh knawyng of sothfastnes.
For alle othir names þat may be,
Als when men spekẻs of his Bounte
Or of his Wisdome or of his Myght—
Als we here clerkes þus calle hym right
Þe Right Gode, þe Right Fayre and Semely,
Þe Right Wys, or þe Right Myghty,
And many othir wordes men says
Of hym when men wil hym prayse—
Þat says noght proprely to herynge
Þe righte sothe of Goddis beinge.
  Bot we, þat rude er and vnsleghe
To speke of swilk thing so heghe,
Speke we of Godde als we can
Als we speke of ane erthely man,
Of wham we knawe noght þe name;
Þan er we noght mykell to blame.
Men says a man es a kynge of myght;
'He es an erle'; 'he es a knyght';
'He es gode'; 'he es curtays',
And many swilk wordes men says,
Thurgh whilk we may bi worthynes
Knawe a man whatso he es,
Al-if we knawe noght his name.
So may we speke of Godde þe same,
Many a worde fynde we may
Þat shewes what war of hym to say.
  Bot þare may na worde \`so´ propre be
Als þis worde 'Es' þat we here se.

714 werkes] werk L 715 amange] a mon W þe heghe] holy W 718 mast] may S may vs] *trs.* PW 719 kenne] teche W Godde] *om.* L 722 his] ?vs (*later over eras.*) P bounte] *a minim short* P 726 or] and W 730 of] to S 731 vn-] noght P 732 swilk] swylk a R thing] thinges L 736 to] at L 741 we] he PS, wordes we E 742 whatso] wele what R, what W 743 Al-if] And if L, If all P we] he S noght] noȝt wele R

þat neuens þe name so proprely
And so shortly of Godde almyghty,
In als mykell als we vndirstande
He es anely Godde al-weldande.

Qui es

He es alane ay-lastandely, fo. 5va
And withouten bigynnyng þe same myghty;
And so he es withouten endynge—
þat may men say of nane othir thinge.
He es sothfastly ay to last,
For he es verray and stedefast.
  Ouer-alle thing he wroght thurgh Myght
þa þat er his creatures right;
Alle his creatures, als men sese,
War noght elles bot vanytese—
Als Salamon says þat was witty— *Salamon*
And to regarde of Godde anely.
And alle suld turne vnto noght,
Warne Godde þam sustayned þat þam wroght
Thurgh his grace and his vertu,
And so he dose al for our pru.
He es al ane sothfastly and fast,
For he es þe same ane ay to last
And ay in þe same poynt of festenynge,
Withouten any maner of lousynge
And withouten chaungyng of powere
And withouten stiryng in any manere.
  Als says Saynt Iame, þe haly man, *Iacobus*
þise wordes, als I shewe yhou can:
'Alle othir thynges may stired be,
Of what kynde so þai er, bot he.'
Wharefore, als Haly Writte beres wyttenes,

753 alane] ay ane E ay] *om.* L 754 And] *om.* L 755 he es] *trs.* EL 759 thurgh] by P 760 þa] þam R 763 *sidenote om.* LS 764 And] As R anely] namly P 765 And] *om.* R vnto] to LP 766 Warne] Warn R, Nade W þam[1]] *om.* L þat] and W 769 ane] *om.* W 770 ane] þat E, and LSW ay] *om.* S to] sall LS 772 maner] more W lousynge] lossyng R, leusynge W 774 in] of L 775 says] *after* Iame R þe] þat L 776 als] says þat L shewe yhou] *trs.* LW 778 kynde] *om.* L kynde so] kond sere W 779 haly] *om.* E *sidenote*: Sacra scriptura ESR

He es called proprely 'He þat Es',
For he es sothfastly to se
Withouten any vanyte.
He es stedefastly in alle thynge
Withouten any stirynge.
He es ay-lastandely to dwelle
Withouten any ende to telle,
Withouten 'was', withouten 'sal be',
For na passyng es of hym to se.
   Now may yhe vnderstande wele
þat nathynge may be better to fele
þan to knawe þat þat Godde es,
In wham we fynde allekyn godenes.
Bot nathinge so harde es to knawe right
Als knawe what Godde es and his myght.
þarefore ilk man be war thurgh witte
And muse noght ouer-mykell on it,
For men myght so erre and wrange wirke

Qui es

fo. 5vb Agayne þe trouth of Halykirke.
It es inoghe to ilka man
þat þe Pater Noster can
To say, 'Our Fader þat es in heuen',
þat ay-whare þar men may hym neuen—
In erthe, on lande, and in þe se,
In helle and in heuen—es he.
Ouer-al men may fele his myght,
Al-if men may noght se hym right;
Bot we may se in many stede
His blissed body in fourme of brede.
Bot face to face we se hym noght
Til we be til heuen-blisse broght;
þare sal he be mast proprely sene

780 *sidenote*: Ego sum qui sum ES 783 stede-] soth- S -ly] *om.* L 789 yhe] we L, the P 791 to] for to L þat þat] what L, þat PR 792 -kyn] *om.* L 794 Als] Als es to L, And P 796 muse] mase L, mynd P, muse hym W on] of L 797 men] ȝe P 798 trouth] troght E, throut P 799 to] to telle L ilka] a R 802 þat] *om.* L þar] *om.* L, is þere P, þat W hym] *om.* P 803 on] in L þe] *om.* W 804 and] *om.* L es] alsswa es L 807 many] many a LSR 810 til] in L

And honured with þam þat þare bene.
He es alsso, gastly to say,
In haly mens hertes nyght and day
þat heghe er, als þe heuen es sene,
And er ay clere als heuen and clene.
For in swilk hertes es Godde ay cledde
And þarein sene, lufd, and dredde,
And loued ay and worshiped wele,
For swilk hertes may hym fele.
þis worde 'Qui es' yhete vs calles
To twa thynges specially þat falles.
Ane es right Trouth þat vs sal saue;
Anothir es Drede in hert to haue.

Hoc verbum 'qui es' nos ammouet ad duo, scilicet ad fidem et spem

De fide

First þe Trouth we suld halde right
þat we trowe here with al our might
Specially in þise twa thinges
On whilk al our trouthe + hinges,
In þe Sothfastnes of Godde to wirk
And in þe powere of Halykirke.

De veritate Trinitatis

In þe Sothfastnes of Godde trowe we
þat he es a Godde in Trynyte,
Fader and Sone and þe Haly Gast,
þat er a Godde thurgh Trouth to tast.
For he es a Godde in threhede
And he es thre in anehede.
And if yhe wil wyte hou þat may be,
Bihald þe sonne and yhe may se,
Whareby Godde vndirstanden es
For he es called Sonne of Rightwysnes.
In þe sonne þat shynes bright
Yhe may se thre thynges right.

813 to] forto L 815 þe] *om.* P 816 ay] als ELS 817 For] *om.* L es] *int. after* Godde P 819 loued] lufed L worshiped] -ipp' R 820 fele] ay fele R 821 *sidenote*: *om.* R scilicet] *om.* P et] et ad L 822 specially þat] *trs.* LW 823 vs sal] *trs.* R 825 *sidenote*: *om.* R, Fides W 828 On] On þe E our] other R *hinges] here hinges ASW 831 *sidenote om.* R 832 he] *om.* L a] *om.* E 833 Sone] þe sone P þe] *om.* ELRW 837 yhe] we L þat] þai W 838 Bihald] In L and yhe] we L se] it se L 842 Yhe] Menne L right] schyne bryght L

Qui es

fo. 6ra

Tria sunt in sole, videlicet decor, splendor, et calor, que tamen sunt inseparabilia. Si quis velit ?inde splendorem segregare, mundum priuet sole; `et´ in calorem temptet distinguere, careat sole

Ane es fayrnes als fyre grete,
Anothir es brightnes, þe thridde es hete;
And nane of alle þise thynges thre
May fra othir departed be.
If men did away þe brightnes,
þan bihoued men be sonneles;
Or if men did þe hete þarefra,
þan bihoued men þe sonne forga.
For whare ane es, þare bihoues be alle;
It may nane othir wise bifalle.

Per decorem solis intelligitur Pater

In þe fayrnes als of fyre semand,
þe Fader first we vndirstande;

Per splendorem Filius

In þe brightnes þat comes of it,
þe Sone we vndirstand thurgh witte;

Per calorem Spiritus Sanctus

In þe hete of þe sonne to tast,
We vnderstand þe Haly Gast.
þise thre persones er alle ane,

Tria sunt Trinitati appropriata, videlicet Patri potencia, Filio sapiencia, Spiritui Sancto bonitas

And nane may be fra othir tane.
þe Trinyte men þise thre calles,
And to þise thre thre thinges falles:
To þe Fader first falles Myght,
And to þe Sone Wisdome right,
And to þe Haly Gast Godenes—
Alle falles to a Godde þat es.
To wase liknes we er wroght
In sawll, als we may se thurgh thoght,

Tria consistunt in anima per quem similitudo Trinitatis in ea inspici potest, videlicet memoria, intelligencia, voluntas siue amor

Bi thre thinges þat mase it like
To Godde þat es in heuenrike.
þa thre bene Mynde and Vnderstandyng
And Wille or Luf withouten fayllyng.

843 als] als of PRW *sidenote*: *om.* ESR, *mostly in gutter* P, *faded badly* W et[1]] *om.* PW velit] *om.* L si] *om.* W et in . . . sole] *om.* L in] *om.* W 845 nane of] *om.* P 846 May] May noght P 851 ane] any W bihoues] behoued W 852 wise] wayes W 853 of fyre] fyre es L, of þe fyre S *sidenote*: *om.* ES, *faded* W, Pro decore R 854 first] fast W we] I P 855 *sidenote*: *om.* ES, *faded* W, Pro splendore R 856 witte] Itt P 857 *sidenote*: *om.* ESR, *faded* W 860 *sidenote*: *om.* ESRW, Etiam sunt tria . . . ? P potencia] *om.* L 863 To] Vnto LR first] *om.* P 864 Sone] Son falles R 866 to] vnto R a] *om.* L 867 To] Vnto R 868 sawll] saules P thurgh] in ELS 869 Bi] Why R *sidenote*: *om.* ESRW, *in gutter* P consistunt] sunt appropriata L 870 in] of L, *om.* P 871 þa] þe whilk R

Thurgh Mynde suld we thynk right
On Godde þe Fader ful of myght
þat thurgh his Myght alle thing made,
Heuen and erthe and þe werld brade
And ilka thynge in right kynde;
So may his Might cum to our Mynde.
  Thurgh Vnderstandyng may we se
Godde þe Sone þat boght vs fre
And ordaynes alle thyng thurgh Wisdom
þat may to our Vndirstandyng com.
  Thurgh Wille or Luf we may fele
Godde þe Haly Gast right wele
þat alle Godenes in hym has,
To wham our Wille and Luf gase.
þus we may in our saul se

Qui es

All þe haly Trinyte. fo. 6rb
Of þise thre mans saul made es
Aftir Goddis image and his lickenes,
For aftir þe Sone we er made right
þat þe image es of þe Fader of Myght.
þarefore we se þe Fader lickenes
Bi þe Sone þat his image es.
  If þat we wille trowe ay þus,
Godde thurgh Trouth es þan in vs.
Forwhy, als þe apostell telles, *Apostolus*
Cryst in þe Trouth ay dwelles,
And þe Trouth es in þe thoght,
And þe thoght in þe hert es broght,
And þe hert es in þe brest,
And þe body about it nest,
þat es þe warde of þe castell
Of þe hert þar þe Trouth sal dwell.

876 þe] þis L, all þe P, *om.* W   brade] sa brade L   877 in] in his W
881 ordaynes] ordende W   885 alle] alkyn L   886 and] or E   luf] oure luf L
887 we may] *trs.* S   saul] saules P   890 þerfore we seye þe fader lickenes (= 893) W
his] *om.* P   892 þe^{1}] *om.* W   897 *sidenote om.* ELPRS   898 þe] *om.* R
900 es] *after* thoght P   broght] wroght EP (*a corr.* P)   901 es] *om.* L   903 þe^{1}] *om.*
E, *int.* P

Bot we suld on þis manere wirk
Thurgh þe Trouth and be noght irk.
We suld thynk on hym þat vs wroght
And honure hym þat vs alle boght
And hym habyde þat vs wil saue
And yherne þe blisse þat we wald haue
And knawe wele thurgh Trouth þat Godde es
Ful of Mercy and Rightwisnes.
Whaso þus dose, he trowes right
In þe Sothfastnes of Godde of myght.
De potestate ecclesie In þe powere of Halikirk alswa
We suld trowe whareso we ga.
Ilke a kirke es Goddis hous,
Bot al Halykirke es Goddis spouse
Þat we suld our moder halde
Als Godde es our Fader called.
For of Halykirk we er borne
Thurgh baptem—elles war we lorne;
Thurgh Halykirke vs bihoues be ledde
And with Haly Writte vs bihoues be fedde.
For als a womman thurgh kynde knawen
Norishes a childe þat es hir awen
With þe mylk þat comes out
Of hir pappes þat sho beres about,
Right so Halykirk, our modir dere,
Norisches vs on þe same manere

Qui es

fo. 6va And vs sustaynes and fedes alswa
With þe mylk of hir pappes twa
Þat gifs many stremes of mylk;
In Haly Writte men may fynde swilk.
Of þe ta pappe springes stremes ten
And of þe tothir twelf to kenne.

909 wil] all wyll L saue] geue W 910 we] *om.* S, he R 912 and] and of W 913 dose he trowes] trowes he dos E 914 of] all- L 915 *sidenote om.* ELSRW 916 We suld] Sall we R 918 Bot] And LP 919 we suld] *trs.* PRW 920 es] we L 921 of] *om.* W we er] *trs.* LP 922 elles] and elles R lorne] forlorne P 924 And with] *trs.* E 930 on] vpon L 931 vs sustaynes] *trs.* R 933 many] full many R 934 men] we PW, *int.* R 935 þe ta] a P 936 And] *om.* LS þe] þat L

þat mylk, whaso vnderstandes it,
Es called bi skille Haly Writte;
þe twa pappes er þat I talde
þe New Testament and þe Alde.
þe ten stremes þat out sprentes
Er called þe Ten Commandementes;
Bi twelf stremes þat er springande
Of þe tothir pappe I vnderstande
Twelf Articles of þe Trouth right
þat we suld kepe bathe day and night.
þus sustaynes vs Halykirke
And teches vs gode werkes to wirke,
Thurgh Haly Writte þat es so swete
þat mas vs with gode vertus mete.
It es gadered, for it es trewe,
Bathe of þe Alde Law and of þe Newe.
þe twa lawes togider er gode;
Of þam comes al our saul-fode,
For of þe Alde Lawe, als es knawen,
Er þe Ten Commaundementes drawen,
And of þe Newe Lawe bi it ane
Er Twelf Articles of þe Trouth tane.
þise er þe Commaundementes Ten *x^{cem}. precepta*
þat byndes here alle Cristen men.
þe first es þis, withouten errour,
þou sal na fals goddis honour.
Anothir es þis, þat es certayne,
þou sal noght take Goddis name in vayne.
þe thridde es þe haly day þou kepe;
þe ferth es fader and moder þou worschepe;
þe fift es sla na man willefully;
þe sext es with na womman þou foly;

938 skille] swylk R haly] of holy W 939 talde] halde S 942 called] *om.* L *sidenote*: x. precepta decalogi E (cf. 959) 943 Bi] Be þe LPW er] er oute L 945 *sidenote*: xij. articuli fidei E 948 vs] *om.* L 949 Thurgh haly] þat ⟨haly⟩ P 950 mete] to met R 952 Bathe] *om.* P of] *om.* SR 954 al] *om.* L 955 als] þat W es] wele es L 957 And] *om.* L lawe] *om.* W 958 Er] Ere þe ELP, þe W tane] ar tane W 959 *sidenote*: *illustration of the two tables ('quoad deum' and 'quoad proximum'), one in each margin, with full texts of Ex. 20* E, *om.* P 960 byndes] byddes ES, er boden L, bydes W here] to L alle] all and L Cristen] maner of R 961 þis] *om.* L 962 þou] þat þou LP sal] *om.* L 963 es þis] es and L, þer is P 965 þe^{2}] þi LW 967 es] es þou L sla] sla yn R 968 es] þe R þou] þou do L, yn R

þe seuent, stele noght þat othir mens es;
þe aghtned, bere na fals wittenes;
þe neghent es loke þou couayte noght

Qui es

fo. 6vb þi neghpur wyf thurgh wille na thoght;
þe tende, couayte noght, whareso þou gase,
Nathinge þat þi neghpur has.
  þise ten commandementes on rawe
Er alle taken of þe Alde Lawe
þat Godde gaf first to Moyses,
þat he for his prophete chese
Opon þe Mount of Synay,
þar Godde spake with hym apertly.
þise commaundementes er na fables;
Forwhy Godde wrate þam in twa tables
With his fynger, als clerkes knawes,
And þa bitokenes þe twa lawes.
  In þe tane er commandementes thre
þat bene onentes þe Trinite;
In þe tothir seuen bene
Onentes our neghpur, als I wene.

Primum preceptum quoad Deum: Non adorabis deos alienos

  þe first es þis, withouten dout:
'þou sal na fals goddes lout',
Bot men suld Godde almighty honoure
And hym ane serue thurgh gode labour
And sette þair luf and þair lykynge
In þat Godde bifore alle thinge.
  Thurgh þis commandement to fele
Ilk man may bithynke hym wele
If he haf leelly Godde honured ay;
If he haf serued hym wele to pay;

969 stele] es steyle EL 970 bere] es bere EW 971 es] *om.* R 972 thurgh] in W na] or `ne´ P 973 tende] tende es E -so] sere W 975 on] on a W 977 to] vnto L 978 þat] Whame R for] fyrste for E, vntill R, before W 980 þar] þat W 981 þise] þis twa E 982 Forwhy] For L twa] hys R 983 fynger] fingres LPSW 984 þa] þat P, ay W bi-] *om.* L 985 er commandementes] commandment ar P 987 In þe tothir] And þase other L, And þe other R 988 als] a W 989 þis] *om.* L *sidenote: in gutter* P, *om.* L Primum . . . deum] *om.* R 990 goddes] godde P 991 Godde almighty] *trs.* S 992 ane] ay RW 994 alle] all oþer PRW 995 þis commandement] his `co´maundmetes W 998 haf] has W

If he haf lufd Godde ouer alle thynge;
If he haf done withouten grochynge
þe seruyse þat he aght thurgh right
To Godde þat es mast of myght;
If he haf fulfilled here
Al his penaunce on right manere;
If he haf to Godde done right
Al þat he in baptem hight.
Al may he se if he take tent
Bi þis first commandement.
þis vs forbedes alle mysbileues
And alle outrages þat Godde greues.
þis commaundement ordaynes euen
A man to Godde þe Fader of heuen.
þe secund commaundement folwand

ij^{m}. quoad Deum: Non assumes nomen Dei tui in vanum

Qui es

Es þis, als I vnderstande:

fo. 7ra

'þou sal noght take Goddis name in vayne.'
þis comaundment falles to ordayne
A man to Godde þe Sone þat es
þat says þus, 'I am Sothfastnes'.
Whaso wil kepe þis commandement
Bihoues be war and take gode tent
And with al his myght hym forbere
þat he na maner of ath swere,
Bot in tyme when it war nede
To trye a soth þat es in drede.
þe thridde es 'Halugh wele þi haly day',

iij^{m}. preceptum quoad Deum: sabbatum sanctifices

þat es þus mykell for to say:
þou sal kepe þe Sonendays clene,
And alle þe solempne festes þat bene
þat es ordayned thurgh Halykirke,

1000 grochynge] hert-g. L, grewynge R 1001 he] *int.* P, hym R 1003 If] And if L 1005 If] If þat L 1006 Al] *om.* L he] he hym LS 1007 if] and L 1009 vs] vs fyrste E 1010 And] *om.* P outrages] outerage LPS greues] greued W 1011 euen] full ewen L 1012 þe] *om.* EPS 1013 *sidenote*: *in gutter* P, *faded* W ij^{m}.] ⟨ ⟩ preceptum L ij^{m}. . . . deum] *om.* R 1017 þe] *om.* E 1023 war] is R 1025 halugh] haly L *sidenote*: *in gutter (and brief?)* P, *om.* L, *unfilled in-column blank* R preceptum] *om.* EW Sabbatum sanctifices] *om.* W 1027 þe] þi LP -days] -day R 1028 alle] hald W þe] *om.* L 1029 es ordayned] ordaned er R

Fra alle werk of seruage to wirke,
þat es to say fra werkes of body
And fra werkes of syn and of foly.
For synne es a wretche thralledome
þat som men hauntes of custome.
þis commaundemente ordaynes mast
A man to Godde þe Haly Gast.
þise thre commaundementes to fele
Kennes hym þat vnderstandes þam wele
How he sal haue hym þat he be
Acordande to þe Trinite.
  þe othir seuen may a man kenne
How he sal haue hym onence alle men
þat here his euencrysten bene
And onence himself to kepe him clene.

iiij[m]. preceptum, primum quoad proximum: honora patrem et matrem

  þe first es 'Fader and moder honour';
So suld men do and þam socour,
And als wele þam þat gastly bene
Als þa þat er bodily sene.
And on twa maner, whaso tas kepe,
Men suld fader and moder worshepe.
Ane es to þam men suld be bousom
And do þam reuerence of coustom;
Anothir es, als clerkes can rede,
Men suld þam helpe in þaire nede
And in alle thinge counsaylle þam right
With al þa`i´r conyng and þaire myght,

Qui es

fo. 7rb So þat þai may lengar lyue
Opon erth and noght Godde greue.

1030 Fra] For P werk] werkes LSRW, ware P of . . . wirke] *om.* S 1031 *line om.* S 1032 And fra werkes] *om.* S of[2]] *om.* P, *int.* S 1036 to] fro W Godde] *om.* R 1038 þat] þat ord L þam] it P 1039 How] How þat L sal] *om.* W þat] to þat L 1040 -dande] -daunt SR to] wyth L 1041 þe] þase L othir] tother R a] *om.* E 1043–4 *couplet om.* ES (*at a page boundary* E) 1045 first es] ferthe L *sidenote: faded and illeg.* W *if there, unfilled in-column blank* R iiij[m]. preceptum primum] iiij[a]. peticio `prima´ P (*and sim. the remainder*) preceptum] p. quoad deum L primum] p. preceptum ES Honora . . . matrem] *om.* L 1046 þam] *om.* L 1047 And] *om.* P als] *om.* W 1048 þa] þam R 1049 And] *om.* E maner] maners SRW 1051 to . . . suld] *trs. phrs.* PW 1053 Anothir] And a. E als] *om.* R clerkes] clerk S 1054 þam helpe] ay help þam R 1055 And] *om.* L thinge] *adds* allswa L 1056 and] and alle E 1057 may] may þe LP

To honour þam men suld vouche saue
Thurgh wham þai þair lyf here haue,
For he þat wil noght thurgh Bouxsomnes
Worship þam thurgh wham he es,
It is noght right þat he lange be
þat þat he es here to se.
Anothir es 'þou sal noght sla'.
Ilk man be war he do noght swa,
For thre maners of Slaghter bene
Fra whilk man suld kepe him clene.
A Slaghter es thurgh hande smert,
Anothir thurgh tunge, þe thridde thurgh hert.
Thurgh hande es Slaghter when men strikes
With any wapen þat men likes.
Thurgh tunge also may be sone
Slaghter on twa maners done.
Ane es thurgh commaundement namely
Of a man þat es myghty,
For whasoeuer þe slaghter mas,
He þat comaundes it, he slaas.
Anothir es thurgh suggestyoun
Of a man þat mas hym boun
To wrye a man or to gif rede
Wharethurgh he may be done to dede.
Whaso þus a man wil dere
He may be halden a manslaere.
Thurgh hert also may Slaghter be
On twa maners als men may se.
Ane es when a man thurgh thoght
Wald anothir to dede war broght;
In als mykell als his wille es þan,
He es slaer of þat man.

v^{m}. preceptum, ij^{m}. quoad proximum: non occides

1060 here] *om.* L 1064 þat on fader and moder wyll na menske se L, Her on lyfe for to se P 1065 *sidenote*: v^{m} . . . proximum] *om.* RW ij^{m}.] *om.* E, quoad deum ⟨ij.⟩ L Non occides] *om.* L 1066 he] *om.* L 1067 For] Bot L maners] maner R slaghter] slaghtes W 1068 man] ilka man LP 1069 es] þer is P 1070 thurgh] es þurgh L, with P 1071 es] *om.* L men] þow P strikes] smytes W 1072 any] a W men] þe P 1073 be] be done L 1074 on] of P 1075 es] *om.* R namely] anely [*canc.*] namely E, anely P 1076 Of] Als of P 1077 þe] at LW 1078 it he] *trs.* L he] *om.* E 1079 thurgh] *om.* L 1081 To wrye] At wrathes W to gif] geues W 1082 -thurgh] *om.* L 1083 wil] wylle do L 1084 man-] mans R (*and similarly other uses to 1104*) 1085 also] als W 1088 broght] wroght W

Anothir manere es, certayne,
He þat tholes a man be slayne
And may hym sokour and noght wille;
He + es manslaer thurgh skille.
And als bodily slaghter es, right swa
Men may gastly a man þus sla.
Þat es when a man thurgh Enuye

Qui es

fo. 7va Anothir hates in hert dedely,
Or hym backebytes, arely or late,
Or hym sclaunder`s´ his loos to abate
Thurgh attry wordes and felle sawes;
Or fra þa þat nede has withdrawes
Þe lyflade þat þair lyf suld halde—
A manslaer he may be called.

vj^{m}. preceptum, iij^{m}. quoad proximum: non mechaberis

Þe thridde commandement es þis þan:
'Þou sal noght foly with woman.'
In þis commaundement Godde forbedes
Alle manere of fleschely dedes
Þat falles bitwene man and womman
(Als clerkes teches þat best can)
To saue þe dede of sposaylle.
Þat es thurgh Halykirkes counsaylle
Leeffull and lawefull to fulfille,
If it be done als þe lawe wille.
Alle fleschely dedes bot þat anely
May be called dedes of Litchory,
Þat er werkes of grete vnclennes
Þat drawes a man to payne endeles.
Bot whaso yhernes to be sene
In heuen-blisse with a lyf clene,
He suld kepe hym here haally

1094 *es] þat es AEPSRW, þat es a L thurgh] be L 1095 And] Ane L 1096 a man þus] þus a man E þus] *om.* LRW 1100 sclaunders] *later corr.* A 1101 attry] *om.* L and] or E *sidenote: illegible* W 1102 þa] þaim EPS, hym R 1105–22 *om.* R 1105 es þis þan] it ys þoon W þis] *om.* L *sidenote: om.* L, *faded* W vj^{m}.] ⟨v^{m}.⟩ E vj^{m} . . . . proximum] *om.* R 1106 noght] *om.* P with] with na ELPS 1110 clerkes] þir clerkes L 1111 To] *om.* L 1114 If] *om.* S 1116 called] told W 1117 grete] *om.* L 1120 a] *om.* W 1121 here] here alle E, *om.* S

Fra alle corrupciouns of body.
þe ferth es 'þou sal noght stele',
vij^{m}. preceptum, iiij^{m}. quoad proximum: non furaberis
If þou wil be halden leele.
In þis commandement namely
Es Theft forboden and Robbery,
Okir als and Extorsyouns,
And alle vnleffull raunsiouns,
Fals Marchaundys and Gylery,
And Sacrilege and Simony,
And alle vnleeffull takynges,
Alle withhaldynges, and wrange hidynges
Of othir mens gode withhalden stille
Agayne þair wytynge and þair wille.
And whaso may be funden gilty
In any of þise, he es noght worthy
To haf þe lyf þat es ay certayne,
Bot he al yhelde haally agayne

Qui es

þat es wrange tane, if he be mighty,
fo. 7vb
Or elles, aftir his might a party.
For he þat yhernes to haf þe lyf
þat ay sal last withouten stryf,
He suld fra na man take with wrange
Ne þat he has tane withhalde ouerlange,
Na mare þan he wald war tane
Or withhalden fra himself alane.
For elles þis commandement brekes he
And es out of right charite.
þe fift 'þou sal bere na fals wyttenes'
viij^{m}. preceptum, v^{m}. quoad proximum: non falsum testimonium dices
Ne nathynge say þat fals es
Agayne þi neghpur thurgh ille wille
þat him may dere or greue ille.

1122 corrupciouns of] corrupcioune of hys L 1123 *sidenote*: *om*. LR vij^{m}.] vj^{m}. E, viij^{m}. W 1124 If] If þat LR 1127 als] *om*. L, and als P, allso S and] and all maner of L 1132 Alle] And L -dynges^{1,2}] -dynge P hidynges] wynnynges R, heydynges W 1133 gode] godes LRW 1136 In] Of L he es] be R 1137 ay] *om*. L certayne] clayn R 1138 Bot] Bot if L he al] yf W 1139 if] and L 1140 a party] apertely W 1141 þat] *om*. W 1144 þat he] *trs*. E tane] *om*. L 1147 For] Or LS 1149 *sidenote*: *om*. L, viij. W viij^{m} . . . . proximum] *om*. R v^{m}.] iiij^{a}. P 1152 him may] *trs*. ELS greue] greue hym ER, greue oght L

Ilka man here suld haf grete drede
To leghe or to say falshede
To greue his neghpur namely,
And if he do, he es worthy
þe blisse of heuen for to tyne
And in helle to haue endeles pyne.
For þise twa þan dispyses he,
Sothfastnes and Charyte.
And whaso thurgh hymself wil noght
Greue a man thurgh malyce soght,
When othir men hym harme wil do,
He suld nane wyse assent þarto.
In þis commaundement to loke
Es forboden, als says þe boke,
Alle manere of leghe and lesynge,
Alle fals falaces and forswerynge,
Alle maner of false losengeryse,
And alle fals conspiracyse.

ix^{m}. preceptum, vj^{m}. quoad proximum: non concupisces vxorem proximi tui

  þe sext 'þou sal noght, by þi lyf,
Couayt here þi neghpur wyf'.
þat es to say a man suld noght
Yherne his neghpur wyf in thoght;
Ne yhete nane othir womman
Suld man couayte þat witte can,
Ne a womman a man in foly
Anely thurgh likynge of body.
A man suld noght couayte to haue

Qui es

fo. 8ra His neghpur mayden, ne his knaue,
Ne his ox, ne his asse þat gase,
Ne na moble þat he hase—

1154 to^{2}] for to R 1159 þan dispyses] *trs.* E 1161 -so] *om.* LW 1162 malyce] malycez E soght] thoght P 1164 nane] o na LS assent] consent L 1167 leghe] leghes R lesynge] lesynges R 1168 falaces] fallacy L, fautes *corr. to* fa\`l\'utes? P, falce W -rynge] -rynges R 1169 -geryse] -gery LS 1170 -racyse] -racy LS 1171 *sidenote*: *om.* L ix^{m} . . . . proximum] *om.* R preceptum] *om.* W vj^{m}.] Sextum preceptum E Non . . . tui] *om.* W proximi tui] *om.* S 1172 here þi neghpur] nan other mannes L 1173 to] at E 1175 yhete] *om.* L womman] sulde na womman L 1176 man] nane ELP 1177 a^{1}] na L a^{2}] *om.* R 1178 of] of hyr L, of his S 1180 mayden] mayde W 1181 þat gase] *om.* L 1182 Ne] Ne ȝit R na] nanekynne L moble] mobels L, othyr thynge P, moumple W þat] *om.* L

Nouthir robes, ne vessele,
Ne siluer, ne gold, ne iuele.
þise men may fynde þat gifs tent
Contende in þis commaundement.
þe seuent of þis last seuen
And þe last of þe ten to neuen
Es þis: 'þou sal noght thurgh langynge
Couayt to haue þi neghpur thynge',
Nouthir his hous ne his lande,
Ne nathyng, als I vnderstande,
þat haally may noght lifted be
Fra þe ground, als men may se.
In þis commaundement last sene
Es forboden, als I wene,
Alle manere of Couatyse
þat es vnskilfull and wrangwyse.
þise twa commaundements to fele
To twa bifore acordes wele.
þat es to say þou sal noght fleschely
Synne with na wommans body,
Ne þou sal na mans gode stele
Ne othir mens godes hyde ne hele.
For he þat has in hert ille wille
Or if his entencioun be ille,
He may noght lange, als says þis clerkes,
Kepe hym wele fra wicked werkes.
þarefore methink wele, if a man
Or a woman þat right skille can
Wille na dede of Litchery do,
He suld noght þan assent þarto,
Ne to þam in þair foly

x^{m}. in numero omnium, vij^{m}. quoad proximum: non concupisces rem proximi tui

1183 vessele] dessayle L 1184 Ne . . . gold] Golde na syluer cornne L iuele] mayle P 1185 þise] þo W þise men may] þus may þu R men may] *trs.* L tent] entent R 1187 *sidenote*: *om.* L x^{m} . . . . omnium] x^{m}. preceptum ES x^{m} . . . . proximum] *om.* R in] *om.* W vij^{m} . . . . proximum] *om.* W 1188 ten] tende LW 1189 þou] þat þou L noght] *marg., later* P noght thurgh] thurgh na ES 1193 haally may noght] may noght godely L noght] *om.* W 1194 als] þat L may] ma E 1196 Es] Ys clene R 1197 Alle] Allkyn R 1200 To] To þe L 1201–2 þou . . . fleschely] *om., remainder fused as single line, and then adds line* Ne teche none to wyrk foly P 1201 fleschely] foly W 1203 gode] guddes R 1204 godes] gode LW 1205 þat] *om.* W 1206 if] *om.* E, of R 1207 þis] *om.* P 1212 þan] *om.* E assent] consent L

þat has wille to do litchery.
And if a man wil noght stele
Bot wald be halden gode and leele,
He suld noght couayt in hert lange
Othir mens gode to haue with wrange.
  þise er þe Commaundementes Ten,
Of wilk falles þe thre to kenne
Vnto þe luf of Godde of heuen,

Qui es

fo. 8rb And to þe luf of our neghpur ⟨s⟩euen.
þise commaundements er now talde,
Bathe þe Newe Lawe and þe Alde,
þe whilk Goddis childer thurgh right
Suld knawe and kepe with al þair might.
For he þat þe trouth in hert wil haue
Suld kepe þise commaundements and saue.
De articulis fidei   On þe tothir syde shewes þe New Lawe
Twelf Articles of þe Trouth to knawe,
þe whilk þe twelf apostels made
þat þe grace of `þe´ Haly Gast habade.
For ilk apostell by and by
Of þe Crede made a party,
And ilka parte an article es called,
And in þe Crede er twelf to halde.
For after þe noumbre þat was sene
Of twelf apostels twelf articles bene
þat ilka man here bihoues haue
And halde in hert þat wil be saue.
Bot þe ground of þe trouth bihoues be
To trowe trewely þus in þe Trinite:
þat þe Fader and þe Son and þe Hali Gast

1215 a] *om.* S noght] nathinge R 1216 Bot] And L 1218 gode] godes S haue] halde L 1220 þe] *om.* LPR 1222 to] to (*expunged*) vnto S 1224 þe[1,2]] of þe LP 1225 þe] Be L, Of R thurgh] sulde L, *om.* RW 1226 Suld] *om.* L 1227 þe] *om.* LPR 1228 Suld . . . commaundements] þir c. he sulde kepe L þise commaundements] þis commavndment R 1229 On] In PR þe[2]] ne E *sidenote*: De] De xij. R 1230 of] to S 1231 þe twelf] *trs.* LP 1232 of] *om.* P 1233 For] Of P 1235 And] On L parte] party R 1236 er] on W to halde] talde L 1237 was] was þan L 1239 here] *om.* P haue] to haue W 1241 ground, trouth] *trs. sbs.* W be] to be W 1242 þus] *om.* P þe] a L, *om.* E 1243 þe[3]] *om.* L

Er a Godde in thre persones to tast.
Þe twelf articles I shewe yhou sal
And þair names þat made þam alle.
Þe first article es þis to rede
Of þe twelf þat er in þe Crede,
'To trowe in Godde Fader almyghty
Þat heuen and erth made craftyly'
And alle thing, als says þe boke.
Petre first þis article toke.

j^{us}. articulus per Petrum

Anothir es to trow with mynde
'In Ihesu Cryst his Sone thurgh kynde',
Þat a lorde es mast rightwys
Of heuen and erth and Paradys.
For a man suld trowe with al his myght
Þat þe Sone es lyke to þe Fader right
And euen with hym, als clerkes may rede,
In al þat falles to his Goddehede.
And þe same es to vndirstandynge
Þat þe Fader es in alle thynge,
Bot þat þe Fader of Rightwisnes

ij^{us}. articulus per Andream

Qui es

Es othir persone þan þe Sone es,
Als þis clerkes in boke can shewe;
Þis article toke Saynt Andrewe.

fo. 8va

Þe thridde article nest folwande
Es to trowe and to vnderstande
Þat 'Ihesu Cryst of myght mast
Conceyued was of þe Haly Gast
And of þe Virgyne Mary borne'—

iij^{us}. articulus per Iacobum maiorem, scilicet fratrem Iohannis euangeliste

1244 tast] last W 1245 I] *after* yhou SR I shewe yhou] *trs. pronouns* L 1246 þair] þe L 1247 *sidenote*: *om.* L (*as all others in this series*), Per Petrum Petrus (split) W j^{us}. articulus] Credo in deum patrem omnipotentem creatorem celi et terre (*and similar citations of the appropriate, but unnumbered, article for the remainder*) R per] per sanctum S (*which splits all these notes, the number of the article at the head of the discussion, the ascription to an apostle at the end*) 1249 in] in a L 1252 Petre] Saynt Peter L 1253 with] in LW *sidenote*: *om.* W per Andream] sanctus Andreas S, Andrew R 1254 his] *om.* W 1256 heuen] heuenene E 1258 þe[1]] *om.* E 1259 may] can S 1260 In] Itt in (?) E, *om.* L þat] *om.* S 1261 to] to þe L 1263 þat] *om.* P 1264 othir] another L 1265 in boke] *om.* L boke] bokes ES 1266 toke] made L 1267 *sidenote*: Per . . . euangeliste] Iacobus maior R maiorem] minorem P 1268 to[2]] *om.* E 1269 myght] myghtes LPR 1270 of] þurgh LS

Elles had we bene alle forlorne.
Þat es to say specially
Þat Crist conceyued was in Mary
Thurgh vertu of þe Haly Gast right
(And noght thurgh werk of mans myght)
And þat sho bifore þe birth was
Clene mayden withouten trespas,
And in þe birth was mayden clene,
And after þe birth, and ay has bene.
Þis article falles, whaso tas hede,
To þe Sone onence his manhede.
Þis article ordayned nane othir
Bot Saynt Iame, Saynt Iohan brothir.

iiij^{us}. articulus per Iohannem euangelistam

Þe ferthe es to trowe, als clerkes wate,
Þat 'Cryst tholed vndir Pounce Pilate'
Mikell reproue and vilanye
Þat to hym was done thurgh envye.
For Pilate was in Ierusalem þan
A iustys and a domesman,
Thurgh wham Cryst was demed to dede
Falsely after þe Iewes rede,
'And his body on þe croyce done
And dede was and biryed sone'
In a sepulchre wroght of stone.
Þis article made Saynt Ione.

v^{us}. articulus per Thomam

Þe fift es, als clerkes can telle,
To trowe þat 'Cryst went doun til helle
Aftir his dede, ful gode spede',
In saul anely with his Goddehede,
To delyuer þe saules fra care
Of þe haly faders þat war þare.
Þat es to say of ilka man
Þat þan was dede fra þe werlde bigan,

1272 alle] *om.* LW 1273 say] say þus R 1274 conceyued was] *trs.* LS 1275 vertu] þe vertew S 1276 werk] werkes L, vertu W 1277 birth] byrthen L 1281 hede] kepe hede L 1282 To] Vnto L 1284 Saynt[2]] *om.* P 1285 *sidenote*: Per . . . euangelistam] Iohannes euangelista R 1291 demed] don W 1292 after] thurgh EL 1293 þe] *om.* S 1295 a] *om.* R 1296 þis] þis is þe P made] of P, ordaned R 1297 fift] fyfte article E es] *om.* P als] als þis? S *sidenote*: per Thomam] *adds* apostolum S, Sanctus Thomas R 1298 doun til] vnto L 1302 þe] *om.* LP war þare] þair ware P þare] *om.* W 1303 *line om.* W 1304 þe werlde] ward P

In verray trouthe and hope certayne
þat þai suld be delyuerd fra payne

Qui es

And thurgh Cryst, Goddis Sone, boght fo. 8vb
And to þe blisse of heuen be broght.
þarefore als sone als Cryst was dede,
He went doun right to þat stede
þar þe haly faders ware
And broght þam out of sorow and care.
Bot to depe helle went he noght
To take þam out þat þider war broght,
For þai trowed noght in his comynge
þarefore þare es ay þair wonynge.
And afterward 'On þe thridde day
He rase fra dede', als we here say
Alle Haly Writte to fulfille,
Als it was his swete wille.
And sone þareafter appered he
To his disciples, als þai myght se;
And for he wald proue his vpperysyng,
Yhete made he here lengar dwellynge
Fourty days after he rase.
þis article made Saynt Thomas.
  þe sext article alsso to neuen *vjus. articulus per Iacobum minorem*
Es to 'Trowe þat he stey to heuen'
þe fourtyde day of his vprysynge
Withouten any manere of lettyng,
Alle his disciples þat seande,
'And sittes on his Fadir right hande'.
þis article bihoues vs alle wit
For Saynt Iacob ordayned it.
  þe seuent article es alswa *vijus. articulus per Philippum*

1307 And] *om.* W Goddis Sone] gode dedes sone W 1308 þe] *om.* P be] *om.* R 1310 to] vnto R 1313 went] ne went R 1314 þam out þat] out þam `þat' P 1316 wonynge] dwellyng W 1319 to] for to R 1320 swete] faders L 1321 sone] *om.* P 1322 his] *om.* L als] þat L myght] mot P 1324 made he] *trs.* W 1327 alsso] es als L *sidenote*: Iacobus W Per] *om.* SR minorem] maiorem P, *om.* R 1328 Es] And L þat] how L 1329 fourtyde] fourty LW, fourtende S of] fra L, aftyr P 1331 þat] *om.* L 1333 vs] *om.* L 1334 Iacob] Iame S 1335 *sidenote*: Per Philippum] Philippus R

To trowe right, whareso we ga,
þat 'Godde sal com at domesday
To deme ilk man, þat es to say
Bathe quicke and dede', als says þis clerkes,
And gode and ille after þair werkes,
þe gode to ioy, þe ille to payne.
þis sal we trowe; þat es certayne.
þis article made Saynt Philippe;
þarefore we wil it noght ouerhippe.
viij^{us}. articulus per Bartholomeum þe aghtned article in hert to tast
Es to 'Trowe in þe Haly Gast',
þat es to trowe thurgh stedfastnes
þat þe Haly Gast sothfastly es
þe gift and þe luf of þe Fader and þe Sone,

Qui es

fo. 9ra Als þai in heuen togider wone,
Of wham comes alle godes of grace
In seuen giftes to purchace
þat for our saulles best suld be,
Als ye sal after here and se.
And þat þe Haly Gast es right
þe same Godde, ay ful of myght,
And þe same Lorde in sothfastnes
þat þe Fader and þe Sone ay es,
Bot þat þe person we othir halde
þan of þe Fader and þe Sone es called.
þis article þat I þus shewe
Ordayned first Saynt Berthelmewe.
ix^{o}. articulus per Matheum þe neghent article þat I shew now
Es 'In Halykirke to trowe
And also in þe comonynge
Of alle haly mens lifynge'.
For Halykirk, als men may kenne,

1336 whareso] so whar R 1337 at] on LW 1339 þis] *om.* P 1341 ille] euele E 1344 we] ȝhe W we wil] *trs.* R it noght] *trs.* LS 1345 aghtned article] *trs.* E *sidenote*: Per Bartholomeum] Bartholomeus (*later?*) R 1349 þe^{2}] *om.* P þe^{4}] *om.* LW 1351 godes] godenes LP 1352 In] In þe P to] for to R 1353 saulles] soule W 1355 þe] *om.* W es] of E 1356 ay] *om.* L 1360 of] *om.* P 1361 þis] Ys R 1363 *sidenote*: Per Matheum] *om.* S, Matheus R 1367 For] Of L

Es gaderyng of alle Cristen men
þat in þe trouth of Cryst has bene,
And chosen for gode men and clene,
And þat er yhete, whareso þai wende,
And þat sal be to þe werldes ende.
Alle sal þai be in a company
In heuen with ioye and melody,
And we sal trowe, if we vs kepe,
To comon with þat felawshepe.
On þis article þat men to tentes
Hinges þe seuen sacramentes,
In þe whilk ilka man suld trowe *vij^{tem}. sacramenta ecclesie*
And þa sal I shewe yhow nowe.
  Baptem, þat first es, halde I ane
þat falles at þe funt be tane;
Anothir es to vndirstande
Confermyng of bischop hande.
þe thridde es Penaunce, mare or lesse;
þe ferth þe sacrament of þe auter es;
þe fift es Order of grete myght;
þe sext es Matrimoigne right;
þe seuent es Last Enoyntynge.
þise seuen in our trouth suld hynge.
  Baptem clenses a man withinne *i^{m}. sacramentum baptisma*

Qui es

Of þe grete originall synne fo. 9rb
þat he of our formast fader tas,
And thurgh þat Baptem grace has.
Confermynge of bisshop at þe last *ij^{m}. sacramentum confirmacio*
Festes þe Haly Gast fast

1368 alle] haly L 1370 and] and for L 1371 þat] *om.* LS er] *om.* L, here W 1372 þat] *om.* LW 1373 in] *om.* R 1376 comon] come W 1377 þis article] þir articles L 1379 suld] aughe to L *sidenote: items numbered marginally through 1389* E 1380 Whylk þat þai er I sall schew þou L þa] þaim P yhow nowe] vnto you R 1381 þat] þe L halde I] called L, halden PW 1382 be] to be L 1384 of] of þe LS 1386 þe^{1}] is þe L auter es] messe ELS (*whole line canc.*, s. xvi? S) 1387 es] þe P 1389 es] es þe LW 1390 suld] *after* seuen P 1391 clenses] clens R *sidenote* (*as well as the other indications of the sacraments*): *om.* LSR, Baptismus PW 1393 þat] þe (*expunged and altered later*) A 1394 thurgh] of L 1395 of] of þe R, seruyng of W *sidenote*: *om.* L ij^{m}. sacramentum] *om.* W sacramentum] *om.* P (*and similarly for these two copies throughout the series, except as noted*) 1396 Festes] Festens LP Gast] gostes W

In hym þat baptized es right
To strengthe him agayne þe fendes might.
iij. sacramentum penitencia Penaunce fordose, als clerkes wate wele,
Bathe dedely synne and venyele.
iiij^{m}. sacramentum þe sacrament of þe auter dight
altare Es a thynge of grete myght,
þat es Goddis awen flesshe and blode
þat of brede es made to saul-fode.
þat sacrament may fest and knytte
Grace in hym þat receyues itte,
þat repentaunt es and clene withinne,
þat he falle noght agayne in synne
And may recounsaylle hym agayne
And in gode werkes hym sustayne.
v^{m}. ordo Order gifs power to wirk
þe sacramentes of Halykirke.
vj^{m}. matrimonium Matrimoigne es grete and mighty,
For it fordose synne dedely
Of dede bitwene man and womman,
If þair entent be skilfull þan.
vij^{m}. sacramentum Last Enoyntyng þat oft es done
extrema vnctio To seke men may alegge sone
Bathe body and saul of payn withinne
And clense a man of venyall synne.
þis article þat I þus rede
Saynt Mathewe sette in þe crede.
x^{us}. articulus per Simonem þe tende article þareaftir es
To trowe 'To haf forgifnes
Of alle synnes' to whilk men tentes
Thurgh vertu of þe sacramentes.
þis article made Saynt Symon;
Alle our ˋheleˊ hynges þareon.

1401 *sidenote*: *om.* W altare] sacramentum altaris EP 1404 of] *om.* L to] for P saul] soules W 1405 fest] fasten W 1408 And thinkes na mare to falle þerin L in] to P 1410 in] *om.* P 1411 Order] Oþer W *sidenote*: v^{m}.] v^{m}. sacramentum E 1412 sacramentes] sacrament R 1413 *sidenote*: vj^{m}.] vj^{m}. sacramentum E 1415 Of] Of þe P bitwene] bytwyx P 1417 Last] þe laste LW oft] *om.* L 1419 of] *om.* L, *int.* P 1420 clense] clenses L 1422 in] itt in PR 1423 þare-] here- P, þat W *sidenote*: *om.* P x^{us}. (*by 1417*) S per Simonem] *om.* R (*as all subsequent references to the apostles*) 1424 to^{2}] for to L 1425 synnes] *om.* ELS to] in P to whilk] þe whylk þat L 1426 sacramentes] sacrament S 1428 hele] *later* A, troght ELS -on] -opone E

xj. articulus per Iudam fratrem [Symonis]

þe elleuent article folwande
Es þis namely to vnderstande
And to trowe withouten fayntyse:
'þat alle men sal at domesday ryse'
Out of þair graues in flesshe and felle
And, body and saul, togider sal dwelle

In celis

fo. 9va

Euermare withouten ende,
Whethir þai to ioye or payne wende.
þis article, amange alle othir,
Made Iudas, Saynt Simons brothir.

xij^{us}. articulus per Mathiam

þe twelft article and þe last
Es to trowe with hert stedefast
þat þe gode men þat sal be saue
'Endeles lyf þan sal haue'
In heuen with þe Trinite,
þar ioye and blisse sal euermare be.
Bot þe wicked sal wende þat day
To þe fire of helle þat lastes ay,
For þan sal be shewed na mercy;
Ilka man sal haue als he es worthy.
þis article þat es sette shortly
In þe crede made Saynt Mathy.
þise er þe twelf articles knawen
þat of þe Newe Lawe er drawen.

De timore

Yhete þis worde, when we it rede,
'Qui es', stirs vs to haue Drede.
For al-if we Godde our Fader halde
And we be here his childer called,
He es rightwys and sothfast
And wil yhelde vs at þe last
Aftir our dedes (and þat es skille),
Be þai gode or be þai ille,

1429 *sidenote*: *om.* L Symonis] EPSW; eius A, *om.* R 1432 sal at] *trs.* W at] on L 1434 sal] *om.* EL, to R 1436 Whethir þai] *after* payne L þai] *after* payne W 1438 Saynt] *om.* LW 1442 þan sal] þan sal þai ER, sall þai LS 1444 euer-] *om.* E 1446 To] Vnto R 1448 Ilka] Bot ilk R 1449 sette] *adds* here þus L 1450 made] sett P 1453 *sidenote*: Ad timorem ES, *adds* Qui es L, *om.* P 1455 al-if] if all LP our] for our L 1456 his] for his L called] tald R 1458 vs] vs all PR 1459 and] *om.* R 1460 or] *om.* R

And þat sal be at domesday sene.
Wele es hym þat þan es clene,
For þan wil Godde rewarde sone
To ilka man after he has done.
þarefore we suld ay haf drede
To do ille thurgh worde or dede,
For we sal gif acount þat day
Of ilk idell worde þat we say.

In celis

þis worde 'In celis' es wele semand
To þam þat wil it vnderstand,
Bot bi þis worde þat þus es tane,
It semes þar er ma heuens þan ane,
And þat es sothe to proue bi skille

In celis

fo. 9vb Whaso vnderstande it wille.
For þare es na heuen of sikernes
Bot anely þare þar Godde es,
And whareso Godde vouches saue to dwelle,
þare men may heuen bi skille telle.
In many places Godde may be
Alle at a tyme, als men may se
By a mirour, on þis wyse,
þat es crased in sere partyse.
In ilka pece, grete and smale,
Man may se ay a thynge hale
Alle at anes in þe mirour bright,
And alle may be a thynge in sight.
So shewes Godde him in many place
Al at a tyme thurgh myght and grace.
In heuen and in erthe he es sene
And in haly mens hertes clene,

1461 sal] moun L 1462 þan] þaim ES 1463 wil] moun L 1465 þarefore] And þarefore L we suld] *trs.* R ay] euer L 1467 sal] moun L 1468 Of] For P 1468a heading: *om.* L, *marg.* P 1471 bi] *om.* R 1474 -stande] -standes W wille] wele W 1476 þar[2]] os P, whar R, hor W 1478 men may] *trs.* R 1480 men] ȝe L 1482 þat] *om.* P in] into P, on W 1483 grete] both grett R 1484 Man] ȝee L ay] *om.* LSW 1485 þe] þat L 1488 at] *om.* R grace] space R 1489 in[2]] et E, *om.* LPW

And ilka hert þat Godde may halde
Bi skille may be heuen called.
For als þe heuen es clene and clere,
So er þair hertes on þe same manere;
þair hertes er ay ful of blisse.
Gastly men suld vnderstande þis,
For in Godde anely es al þair thoght;
On othir thynge ne think þai noght,
Bot in þe luf of Ihesu Cryst
Er alle þair hertes thurgh thoght rauyst.
In þat þai haue so grete delite
þat þai it think a ioy parfyte.
  Thurgh thoght in hert þan may þai se
þe mast blisse þat in heuen may be,
þat es þe sight of Godde almyghty
þat þai may se in hert gastly.
þarefore es heuen bi þis skille best
In ilka place þar Godde wil rest,
þat es in þe hertes of haly men
þat in erthe mast wille hym kenne.
  Bot in heghe heuen, als es proued,
He es mast worshiped and loued
With alle þe halughs þat þare bene,
Of wham he es þare bodily sene.
For alle þat comes to þat place
Sal se him þare face to face,

In celis

And þat sight es þair souerayne blisse; fo. 10ra
Wa es hym þat þat sal mysse!
  þis worde 'In celis' vs stirs to se
þe heght of Goddis maieste,
For he es so heghe þat al wroght

1492 be heuen] *trs.* LP (by P) 1493 For als] Als and E, And als L þe] *om.* L heuen es] heuenes ben W clene] bryght P 1495 ful] fulfyllyd R 1498 ne] *om.* LPSRW 1500 hertes] hert S thoght] lufe ES 1502 þai] þaim R þai it think] þaime think it L 1503 þan] *om.* L 1505 þe] of þe L 1508 ilka] twa P þar] whare L 1510 in] here in R mast . . . hym] will hym mast R, will most hym W 1511 es] wele es L 1512 He es] *trs.* L, He es he R 1514 þare] *before* he P 1515 alle] he L to] in P 1517 þair] *om.* L 1518 Wa es hym] Full waa er þai L þat[2]] itt E sal] moun L

þat obown hym may be noght,
Bot vnder hym es alle thinge
þat euer had any bigynnynge.
And whaso yhernes to cum so heghe
Hym bihoues clym vp bi a steghe
þat suld be made, als says þis clerkes,
Of harde penaunce and haly werkes.
For þider comes na man to hym
Bot he wil bi þis steghe clym.
Bot whaso wille his syn forsake
Bigynnes þan þis steghe to make,
And þa þat of na penaunce irkes,
Ne of almusdede, þis steghe wirkes.

Hoc verbum 'in celis' nos ammouet ad iij^a^., scilicet ad veram humilitatem, vigorem, et probitatem

þis worde 'In celis' vs askes thre thinges
þat tittest a man to heuen bringes.
Ane es called verray Mekenes;
Strengthe of wille anothir es;
Pruesce of hert es þe thridde.
With þise thre men suld be ledde,
For þare may na man to heuen com
Bot he be meke here and bouxsom.

Nota: qui se humiliat exaltabitur, et qui se exaltat humiliabitur

For Godde says þus, als clerkes knawes,
'He sal be heghed þat hym lawes;
And he þat hymself here heghe wille,
He sal be lawed', and þat es skille.

þarefore we suld thynk and knawe
How heghe Godde es and we so lawe,
And þat we haue noght þat gode es
Of ourself, bot wickednes.
For al þat we haue of grace and witte,
Al comes of Godde þat sendes vs itte.
þarefore, if we wil wisdome seke,
We haf grete mater to be meke,
For so heghe to heuen wynne we noght

1523 alle] allkyn R 1527 þis] þe P 1530 steghe] *om.* L 1532 þan] *om.* L 1533 þa] þam R na penaunce] penaunce noght L 1534 of] *om.* RW 1535 vs askes] *trs.* R *sidenote: flaked and illeg.* P, *om.* RW ad[1]] *om.* S 1539 es] call I R 1541 For] *om.* W 1542 here] *om.* S 1543 *sidenote: faded* P, *om.* RW, *clauses trs.* L nota] *om.* EL 1544 þat] þat here L hym] hymself R 1545 here heghe] *trs.* R 1547 þarefore] And þarefore L 1549 þat[1]] *om.* P 1551 of] *om.* R and] and of L 1552 vs] *om.* LSR 1553 wil wisdome] *trs.* LR 1555 wynne] ne wyn R

Bot we thurgh Mekenes þider be broght.
We may noght cum on heght so fer
Bot verray Mekenes vs vp bere.

In celis

Verray Mekenes als falles to be *fo. 10rb*
Shewes it in þise thinges thre, *De vera humilitate*
In hert, in mouthe, and in werke.
Ilkane of þa may be a merke,
Als I sal recken þam here on rawe,
Thurgh whilk men may Mekenes knawe.
Mekenes falles in herte to dwelle *Humilitas cordis ostendit se quadrupliciter*
Thurgh þise four thynges þat I sal telle:
Thurgh Oft Bithinkynge vp and doun
And thurgh Verray Contriscioun;
Thurgh gode Suffraunce withouten grochyng,
Thurgh Haly Delyte withouten chaungyng.
Thurgh Oft Bithinking may Mekenes com *Per meditacionem*
And make a man meke and bouxsom
þat him bithinkes of his wrechednes
And what Godde has done hym, mare and lesse.
For if he lat his thoght noght passe;
And hym bithynk what he first was;
And whethen he come, if he right se;
And what he es and whare es he,
And what he sal be at þe ende,
And whiderward he sal þan wende,
He may fynde skilles and knawe
Wharethurgh he suld him meke and lawe.
He suld think he was first noght *Meditacio quoad seipsum*
And sithen conceyued in syn, wroght

1557 heght] hegh EPSW 1559 *sidenote om.* LW 1560 in] þurgh L þise] *om.* EL 1561 in^{1}] *om.* E 1562 Ilkane] In ilkane L þa] þer P 1563 Als] And L recken] schew P 1564 may] may her R 1565 *sidenote*: *om.* PR Humilitas] Meditacio W se] *om.* W 1566 þat I sal] to LS 1567 bithinkynge] bysekyng P, -ynges ? R 1569 Thurgh] And thurgh W 1571 bithinking] bythynge R *sidenote om.* PR 1574 hym] *before* has W 1575 thoght] herte E 1576 hym] vm- L 1577 whethen] when L if he] and L 1578 whare] ware E 1579 þe] *om.* L, þe last W 1580 þan] *om.* L 1581 may . . . and] sall be many skilles L 1582 Hym for to meke and for to lawe L him] be P, *om.* W 1583 suld] sulde fyrste E *sidenote*: *om.* R quo-] et i^{o}. P 1584 in] and in W syn] syn and R

De miseria propria Of a porcioun of foul matere—
þat es a wlatsom thing to here.
Fra a foul herber he þan came—
þat was fra his moder wame.
  What he es he suld think,
For he es noght bot filth and stynke;
Na fruyt of himself may com
Bot filth and stynk—þat es wlatsom.
To alle wickednes he es heldande,
Bot in alle godenes he es fayllande;
Of himself, withouten ne withinne,
Comes noght bot filth and synne.
He es here in a mirke vallay,
þar dole and anger es night and day;
þat ful es of drede and trauaylle
And of vanyte þat sal faylle;

In celis

fo. 10va And of perils þat oft here falles—
þat vallay men þis werlde calles,
þat to þe se may lickened be.
For it ebbes and flowes als dose þe se
With grete waghes þat lang lastes,
þat vppe and doun a man ay castes.
þarefore whaso traystes on it,
It sal desceyf him ar he wit.
  And when þe werled has him faylled
And þe dede him has assaylled,
þan sal his body noght elles be
Bot wormes mete and erthe to se.
His body men sal in a pitte lay,
And þe saul sal wende anothir way;

1585 *sidenote*: *om.* R de] et P (*run together with prev. marg. note*) miseria propria] *trs.* E 1586 a] *om.* S to] of to L 1587 herber] herberth S he þan] *trs.* R 1588 þat] And þat L his] þi L 1589 What es he oft suld he think L 1590 es noght] ne is P stynke] think L 1591 of] fra E 1593 alle] *om.* L 1594 Bot in] And to S 1596 Comes] Ne comes R noght] nathing LR 1597 a] *om.* R 1598 and anger es] es anger L 1599 ful es] *trs.* LP 1600 vanyte] vanites L sal] nede sall R 1601 oft] *om.* R oft here] *trs.* P here] *om.* L 1603 may] *after* þat L; may so P may lickened] *trs.* S 1604 þe se] he LW 1605 waghes] valayes W 1606 ay] oft vp L 1607 þarefore] And þ. L 1608 ar] er þat W 1610 him has] *trs.* ELPS 1612 wormes] worme L

Whethir it wende to ioye or payne,
Na man wate here for certayne.
Bot after þe endyng þat he sal make,
He sal his right iugement take;
Be it gode or be it ille,
He sal be demed þaraftir thurgh skille.
Also if he wald bithynk hym sone *Meditacio quoad Deum*
What godenes Godde haues hym done,
And what gode he dose him, night and day,
And what he sal do hym and do may,
He suld luf him and drede in thoght
Mare þan anythynge þat es wroght;
And luf and drede in alle thinge
May sonest a man to Mekenes bringe.
He suld think ay wele in thoght *De beneficiis Dei*
How Godde made him first of noght
Aftir his image and his lickenes
And ordayned him to ioye endeles;
And gaf him witte to knawe and skille
What es gode and what es ille;
And how he boght hym agayne
When he was dampned to helle payne
Thurgh our formast fader synne
þat made first Godde and vs to twynne;
And what payne he tholed and reproue
And how he dyed for our luf.
Al tholed he mekely þat might greue
Ensaumple of Mekenes vs to gieue.
Also he suld think, when he may,

In celis

What Godde him dose, night and day. fo. 10vb
He sendes him ilk day his sustinaunce;

1615 or] or to L, oþer W 1617 endyng] ende P 1618 right] *om.* P 1619 it[1,2]] he PR 1621 Also if] Also if so E, And swa and L, ȝhit W *sidenote om.* LR 1622 What] Of þe L Godde] þat godde P hym] *om.* P, for hym (*before* Godde) W 1623 he] *om.* EL night and] ilk P 1624 sal] *om.* E hym] *om.* L 1625 in] hym in R 1628 sonest] semiest W 1629 think ay] *trs.* EL wele] *om.* L *sidenote: here and repeated at 1643* ES, *om.* LR 1631 lickenes] lickes P 1633 witte] *om.* R and] by gud P 1643 he[1,2]] we L (*and continues in* we-*forms through 1658, unnoted except in conjunction with other errors*) 1644 him dose] he dose vs L, *trs.* S dose] duse bath R 1645 ilk] al- W

He saues him here fra alle meschaunce;
He helpes him when he has nede;
He strengthes him in alle gode-dede;
Witte and strengthe he hym sendes
And fra þe fende he hym fendes.
He spares him ay in his foly
And to forgif him he es ay redy;
Al-if he him gretly greue,
When he askes mercy, he wil forgif.
And ay when he to hym turne wille,
Did he neuer so mykil ille,
He wil receyf him als his sone
And ordayne him in blisse to wone.
Bot he þat here vouches noght saue
To turne hym to hym and mercy craue,
After þis lyf he sal wende
To payne of helle withouten ende.
Of swilk thoght comes luf and drede
Þat may a man to Mekenes lede.

Humilitas se ostendit in corde per veram contricionem

Also thurgh Verray Contriscioun
Mekenes it shewes in hert boun.
For when sorow in a mans hert rynnes,
When he bithinkes him of his synnes
And of þe vnkyndenes þat he has wroght
To Godde þat hym so dere has boght,
Þan tenders his hert for hys synne,
And Mekenes lightens sone withinne.

Per pacienciam

Thurgh Gode Suffraunce also we se
Mekenes falles in hert to be.
For when a man tholes with gode wille
Angers þat er sharp and ille,
Be it sekenes or be it pouert,

1646 He] And L alle] all maner of L 1647 him] vs here L 1648 He] And L gode] his gud P 1650 fendes] defendes LR 1651 He] And P ay] euer L 1652 him] *om.* E, vs L he] *om.* SR ay] euer L, *int. later* P 1653 Al-] And LP he] þat he R 1654 wil] wyll vs L 1655 *lines 1655–6 appear after 1658 in order 1656, 1655* E ay] *after* he E, *om.* PW to hym] *om.* R 1656 Did] Do W 1657 his] *om.* LP 1658 ordayne him] ordaynde vs L 1660 hym to hym] his lyf R to hym] *int.* P 1661 he sal] þa sall he R sal] wil W 1662 To] To þe L 1663 Of] For 'of' P swilk] whylk L 1665 Also] All W *sidenote*: *om.* R Humilitas se] Humiliter W 1669 þat] *om.* L 1672 lightens] lyghtes LSW lightens sone] sone l. hym L 1673 *sidenote om.* LR 1676 sharp] hard W 1677 seke-] meke- W

Mekenes shewes it þan in hert.
  Yhete fynde I þat thurgh Haly Delyte
Mekenes shewes it in hert tyte.
For when a man his hert settes right
To luf Godde with al his myght,
Lastandly withouten fayllynge,
And has delyte in nane othir thing,
In þe hert þar swilk Delyte es
Schewes it verray Mekenes.

Per sanctam dileccionem

In celis

  In mouth Mekenes shewes it ay
Thurgh þise four thynges þat I now say:
Thurgh oft Wreghyng in Shrift of ille;
Thurgh Deuoute Prayere, loude or stille;
Thurgh hertly Continuele Louynge;
Thurgh gode Shewyng and Techynge.
  First thurgh oft Wreghyng in Shrift
þat þe saul toward Godde may lift,
Mekenes amange alle othir thewes
Openly in þe mouthe it shewes.
For when a man es ay redy
To wreghe hymself in shrift namely
Of alle þe synnes þat he has wroght
In worde, in dede, and in thoght—
And namely of þe Hede-synnes Seuen
þat er mast principall to neuen,
þat es to say Pryde and Envye,
Ire and Slewth and Litchery,
Glotony and Couatyse.
If he war gilty on þis wyse
And mare walde say if he couthe,

fo. 11ra
Humilitas in ore se ostendit quadrupliciter

Per propriam accusationem in confessione

1678 *lines 1678–9 om.* LS; S *then recopies from 1675, again omitting the lines* shewes it] *trs.* W 1679 *sidenote*: *om.* R dileccionem] di⟨ . . . ⟩tacionem P 1680 shewes it] *trs. and adds* þen W it] *om.* L 1681 his hert settes] *trs. phrs.* EL 1683 Lastandly] And l. L 1684 delyte] na lite L 1685 þar] *om.* L, þat PW 1687 shewes] schew L ay] may L, way R *sidenote*: *partly cut off* L, *much in gutter* P, *om.* RW 1688 þise] *om.* L now] salle E, think to L 1691 hertly] hert LP 1693 oft] *om.* LW, of R *sidenote*: Per confessionem ES, *mostly in gutter* P, *om.* LRW 1696 þe] *om.* R 1698 namely] anely L 1702 er] er þe P 1703 *sidenote*: Septem peccata principalia E 1705 and] *repeats* P 1706 on] in L þis] any of þis L, any P 1707 if] and L

þan shewes Mekenes it in mouthe.
Per deuotam oracionem
Yhete thurgh Deuoute Prayere semes
Mekenes in mouth, als men demes.
For when a man prayes deuoutly
To our Louerd Godde almyghty
With al þe wille þat in hym es,
þan semes in his mouth Mekenes.
Per continuam laudacionem Dei
Thurgh Continuele Louynge bi sight
Mekenes shewes it in mouth right.
For when a man loues Godde ay
And thankes hym, bathe nyght and day,
Of alle gode þat he has hym done,
þan shewes it Mekenes in mouth sone.
Per bonam instruccionem et bonam doctrinam
Thurgh Teching and Shewyng of lare
Mekenes shewes it openly þare.
For when a man es bisy to kenne
And to shewe gode lare to alle men,
It semes wele bi his mouth fre
þat Mekenes suld in hym be.
Humilitas in opere se ostendit quadrupliciter
In werke Mekenes may be sene
Thurgh þise four thinges þat here bene:
Thurgh Qwyting of al þat Dette es,
Thurgh leel bodyly Bouxsomnes,

In celis

fo. 11rb
Thurgh Wirkyng of Gode Werkes namely,
Thurgh Harde Lyf þe flesshe to chasty.
Per satisfaccionem debiti
First thurgh Quytinge of alle Dett
Mekenes in werk es right sette.
For when a man wil right knawe
Alle manere of dette þat he awe,
Bathe to Godde þat es ful of myght
And to his euencristen right,
And mase asseth to Godde and man,

1708 mekenes it] *trs.* LW it] *om.* PS in] in his P 1709 *sidenote*: *in gutter* P, *om.* RW 1712 To] Vntyll R 1714 þan] þat P his mouth] hym L 1715 louynge] lokynge R bi] in L *sidenote*: *in gutter* P, *om.* RW continuam] deuotam L 1716 shewes it] *trs.* R it] *om.* P 1719 alle] all þe LR 1720 þan] þat P it] *om.* L, hegh P 1721 *sidenote*: *om.* RW bonam] deuotam L 1724 shewe] tech R 1727 *sidenote*: *om.* RW, In (Per E) opus perfectum ES in . . . ostendit] *trs. phrs.* P 1731 -yng] -ynges R namely] anely P 1733 *sidenote om.* ESRW

Mekenes shewes it in werk þan.
  Thurgh Bouxsomnes, als I wene, *Per obedienciam*
Mekenes may in werk be sene.
For when a man with al his myght
Es bouxsom bathe day and nyght
Vnto Godde and to Halykirke,
þair commaundmentes leelly to wirk,
And to his soueraynes aftir skille
Es bouxsom to folow þair wille,
In hym semes Mekenes ay redy
þat shewes it þan in werk apertly.
  Thurgh Wirkynge of Gode Werkes in sight *Per bona opera*
Mekenes in werk shewes it right.
For when a man es bisy ay
To do al þe gode þat he may,
And namely þe Werkes of Mercy
þat ouer alle othir er mast worthy,
þan may men Mekenes se and fele
þat in werke shewes it wele.
  Thurgh sharpnes of Harde Lyf to lede *Per asperitatem vite*
Mekenes shewes it in werk and dede.
For when a man in penaunce lifs
And thurgh penaunce his flesshe greues,
And flees delytz and kepes him chast
And forsakes þat his flesshe yhernes mast,
To chasty it and to putte it lawe,
þan may men Mekenes in werke`s´ knawe.
  Now haf I shewed here twelf thinges
On whilk verray Mekenes hynges,
þat mas þair cours bi thre ways,
Als þe boke bifore right says.

1740 werk] hert W 1741 *sidenote om.* RW 1742 werk] hert LR 1744 bathe] bath be R bathe . . . nyght] for to do ryght P 1745 to] *om.* ERW 1746 þair] And þaire L -mentes] -ment L leelly] for P 1747 his] *om.* W 1749 ay] ay and R 1750 þan] *after* werk RW 1751 Thurgh] þurgh gode L gode] godes L *sidenote*: Per opus coram hominibus ES, *om.* LR 1752 werk] hert L 1753 For] *om.* P bisy] redy L 1754 þe] *om.* R þat] *om.* L 1757 mekenes] wickednes L 1758 werke] hys werk(es) L 1759 *sidenote*: Per artam viam (vitam S) ES, *om.* LR 1760 shewes it] *trs.* R it] *om.* L werk] worde L 1762 greues] he greues P 1763 flees] slays R delytz] delite ELS 1764 yhernes] lufes ELS 1765 to] *om.* L 1766 werkes] *later corr.* A, hert LPR, werke W 1767 here] *om.* L

þe twelf skils þat yhe herd me neuen
Ledes verray Mekenes euen
Bi thre partys and mase it light

In celis

fo. 11va In hert, in mouth, and in werk right.
Withouten þa twelf in þise thre
Verray Mekenes may noght be.
  þis worde 'In celis' with gode skille
Askes of vs Strengthe of wille.
Forwhy þe way þat we oft layte
To heuen es so narow and strayte
þat na man may passe þarby
Withouten gastly Strengthe namely.
þat es to vndirstande þus:
Bot he be, als þe boke says vs,
With haly werkes strengthed wele
And gode vertus þat he suld fele;
De vij[tem]. virtutibus principalibus And namely with þise vertus seuen
þat I wil now specially neuen.
þat es Trouth, Hope, and Charyte;
Sleght þat thurgh witte bihoues be;
Methfulnes, Strengthe, and Rightwisnes
Thurgh whilk ilk gode man gouerned es.
þe thre + Dyuyne Vertus men calles
And þe four after Cardynalles.
Virtutes theologice Dyuynes men calles þe first thre,
Trouth and Hope and Charyte.
For þise thre ordaynes specially
Al þe hert to Godde almyghty.
Fides   First Trouthe, als says Saynt Austyn,
þat es þe first Vertu Dyuyne,

1771 neuen] say P   1772 euen] full euen L, ay P   1774 in[2]] and W   in werk] werkes W   1775 þa] þe W   in] and LS, þe W   þise] ys þise R   1776 may] ne may R   1777 with] by PRW   1778 of[1]] *om.* P   of[2]] and L   1780 so] bathe L   and] and so R   1785 haly] al haly E   1787 þise] þe E   *sidenote om.* R   1788 now] you L   1789 trouth] strenghe L, thurgh W   1790 Sleght] And sleght L   witte] *om.* L   be] to be W   1791 Meth-] Meke- W   *1793 thre] thre 'first' *added marg. later* A, thre first R   1794 cardynalles] ordynalles W   1795 *sidenote*: theologice] theologie R   1796 and[1]] *om.* EPR   1798 to] of W   1799 Saynt] *om.* P   *sidenote*: *adds* Augustinus W

Puttes vs here vnder Goddis lawe
And makes vs þat Lorde to knawe
Of wham we halde, als he vouches saue,
Alle þe godes þat we here haue.
Right Trouth, als says þis clerkes, *Fides sine operibus mortua est*
Es bigynnyng of alle gode werkes;
Trouth withouten gode werk es dede,
For of alle gode werkes it es hede.
Thurgh werkes anely na man may
Withouten Trouth Godde wele pay.
  Hope es a siker habydynge *Spes*
Of gastly gode aftir our endynge,
Thurgh þe godenes of Godde almyghty
And thurgh our gode dedes a party,
For to com, when we hethen wende,
Vnto þe blisse þat neuer sal ende.

In celis

And noght anely in ouer-grete trayst fo. 11vb
Of Goddis godenes þat men may frayst,
Ne alanely als witte vs ledes
In trayst of our awen gode dedes,
Bot in trayst of þam þat faylles noght
When þai er bathe sammen broght.
  For nouthir we sal so fer falle
Intil Wanhope, mast synne of alle,
þat we ne sal trayst to haf blisse
If we wele do and leue our mysse;
Ne we ne sal so fer com
Intil Ouerhope thurgh our awen dome
þat we sal trayst als men witteles
So mykell in Goddis godenes
þat we sal hope þat blisse to haue

1801 Goddis] gode W 1802 þat] to þat W 1804 godes] godnes L 1805 Right] þurgh S þis] þe P *sidenote*: *om.* R, *prec. by* Nota AW 1807 werk] werkes ELPW 1808 hede] þe hede L 1809 anely] sauely L 1811 *sidenote om.* W 1812 gode] godes L 1813 godenes] godes L 1816 Vnto] To LW 1817 ouer] our P trayst] straste E 1818 þat men may] for to L 1819 al] noght L, *om.* W 1820 awen] *om.* L 1823 we sal] *trs.* R 1824 mast] þe maste L 1825 ne] *om.* L to] for to R haf] haue þe L 1827 sal] sal noȝt R 1828 ouer-] our PW 1830 mykell] outragely R 1831 sal] *om.* W þat blisse] *om.* L

Withouten gode dedes and be saue.
Augustinus Hope, als Saynt Austyn says,
Vs may to Godde vplift and rayse;
And mas vs stalward and myghty
And smert and wight, and hardy
To vndirtake for hym in right
þat þat passes here mans myght.
Caritas Charyte of þe thre es last
þat enioynes vs to Godde fast,
For Charyte es nane othir thinge
Bot dere anehede with hert-lykynge.
Charyte wil þat we Godde luf
Ouer alle thyng, als men may proue;
And our euencrysten luf suld we
Als ourseluen with hert fre.
We suld luf Godde for hymself anely
And our euencristen for God almyghty.
For þe tane may noght, als I fele,
Withouten þe tothir be lufd wele.
Iohannes apostolus Als Saynt Ione in his pistell says,
Whase sawes er mykell for to prays,
'þat commaundement (he says) we haue
Of Godde namely, als he vouches saue,
þat whaso lufs Godde als he can
He lufs his euencrysten þan'.
For he þat lufs noght with hert fre
His brothir wham he may se,
How suld he luf in hert right
Godde, of wham he has na sight?

In celis

fo. 12ra Charyte þat es right tane
Mas þe hert and Godde al ane.
Paulus Als says Saynt Paul, Trouth þar it es

1832 gode dedes] dede gode L 1833 *sidenote om.* LR 1835 mas] make R vs] *om.* L myghty] hardy P 1836 hardy] myghty P 1837 -take] -stand R 1839 þe] þir L 1840 vs] *om.* L fast] sa faste L 1845 And] All L 1846 *sidenote*: Nota R 1847 for] *om.* W 1851 *sidenote*: *partly in gutter* P, *om.* RW 1852 for] *om.* LRW 1855 -so] *om.* W 1857 he] *om.* W 1858 wham he] whaime þat he L, when he ay R 1859 How] He E in] god in L 1860 Godde] *om.* L 1863 þar it] þat W es] es tane S *sidenote om.* SW

In Godde sees souerayne sothfastnes;
Hope his souerayne heght may se,
And Charyte his souerayne bounte.
þise thre vertus departed bene
Thurgh thre degrees of Luf clene.
Forwhy for thre thynges fynde I can
þat men specially lufs a man:
Outhir forthy þat men has herde
Grete gode of hym þat he wele ferde,
Or forthy þat men bides to haue
Grete gode of him als he vouches saue,
Or forþi þat men has had namely
Grete gode of hym of curtaysy.
Bot þise thre maners of Luf clene
In þise thre first vertus er sene.
For Luf of Trouth heres and wirkes
And of gode werk neuermare irkes;
Luf of Hope þat alle gode waytes
Feles þe right sauour and baytes;
Luf of Charyte resayues at þe last
And sees and tastes and haldes fast.
þe four lattar vertus to halde
Er þe Vertus Cardynals called,
Of whilk spekes þair auyse
þis philosofers þat war wys.
Bot þe Haly Gast gyues þam wele
Ane hundrethfalde better to fele,
Als Salamon says in þe *Boke*
Of Wisdome, als clerkes may loke.
Ane es Warnes, als I right halde; *Virtutes cardinales*
Anothir es Methefulnes called;
Strengthe also þe thridde vertu es,
And þe ferth es Rightwisnes.

1864 In Godde sees] þar is godde P soth-] *om.* L 1865 his] *om.* L, es W se] be LS 1866 his] es L 1869 for] *over eras. and squeezed in* E, *om.* LPR 1870 þat] þat for S 1871 forthy] for LP has] had W 1872 he wele] we R 1873 bides] abides L 1874 vouches] vouched S 1875 had] herde LSR namely] anely P 1876 of] *om.* R 1878 thre] *om.* W first] *om.* R first vertus] *trs.* ES er] þat fyrst er L 1879 heres] here S 1880 of] for W werk] werkys LPRW 1882 þe] *om.* E baytes] laytes PRW (y *int.* P) 1887 Of] Of þe L 1891 þe] a L *sidenote*: Salamon L 1892 als] þat W may] cane E 1893 *sidenote om.* L

þise four vertus men comonly calles
By skille þe Vertus Cardynalles,
Forwhy þai er, als men may se,
Mast principalle aftir þe first thre.
For thurgh þise four vertus sere
A man may gyen himseluen here,

In celis

fo. 12rb Als þe pape thurgh his cardynals
Gouernes Halykirk, als falles;
And als þe herre gouernes þe dore
And beres it vp fra þe flore.
Right so þai may a man right kepe
þat he falle noght doun ouer-depe.
Prudencia Warnes vs wisses ay war to be
And þe wathes of þis werld to fle.
For it kennes vs to knawe bi skille
Whilk es gode and whilk es ille,
And also to sundre haally
þe tane fra þe tothir party,
And þe ille ay to forsake
And þe gode anely to take,
And of twa gode to chese þe bettir
þat to þe saul may be swettir.
Warnes kepes ay wele a man
þat his witte right rewell can,
þat he be noght deceyued namely
Thurgh wicked wyles of þe enemy.
Methe kepes þat he be noght
Corrumped thurgh fals luf in thoght.
Strengthe him kepes þat he noght be
Ouercommen thurgh drede or aduersyte.

1900 þe first] *int.* P first] *om.* R 1901 thurgh] *om.* E, wyth L 1902 gyen] ken P, rewle S, led R, kepe W 1904 als] þat L 1905 And] *om.* L 1907 right] *om.* L, wele P 1908 he falle] falles L ouer-] or R 1909 war] whare LPW *sidenote om.* R 1910 þe] *om.* L þis] þe L werld] word PW (P *corr.*) 1913 sundre] breke W 1915 to] for to EPS 1917 of] *om.* R gode] godes PW 1918 be] be þe LS 1919 kepes ay] *trs.* P 1922 þe] *om.* P 1923 kepes] kepes a man L, hym kepys R be] *om.* W *sidenote*: Temperancia EL 1924 Corrumped] *om.* R luf in] lyf and W 1925 noght be] not (*canc.*) be noght E *sidenote*: Fortitudo EL 1926 or] and R aduersyte] dyuersite W

Rightwisnes him settes thurgh myght
In order and in state right
Onence alle othir, mare and lesse,
For it kepes to ilk man þat his es.
  þise four vertus þat er dyuers
Er als four tours in four corners
Of þe haly mans hous so fre
þat mas þe hous siker to be.
Warnes it kepes thurgh purueaunce
Toward þe est fra perils and chaunce;
Methe it kepes toward þe southe
Agayne wicked hetes vncouthe;
Strenght toward þe north es sette
Agayne þe wicked coldes to lette;
And Rightwisnes westward socours
Agayne þe wicked rayne shours.
  þise four vertus has offyces sere
þat sal be keped on sere manere,

In celis

Als a philosofir says þat ight fo. 12va
Placius in a boke right
þat he made of þise four vertus,
And parted þam sleghely and sayd þus:
þat Warnes has offices thre,
Forwhy thurgh him, als men may se,
Al þat euer a man sal do
Or say in alle þat falles þarto,
Alle ordaynes he and ledes at wille
And rewels bi þe lyne of skille;
And nathing wil do, day ne nyght,

1927 *sidenote*: Iusticia E 1928 in[2]] in gode S 1929 alle] *om.* S 1931 dyuers] ordeyners W 1932 als] all W 1933, 1934 hous] *with int. gloss* hert R, hert W 1935 *sidenote*: Prudencia ES, Temperancia L 1936 þe] þe soule þe W 1937 it] *om.* L þe] þe flesch W *sidenote*: Temperancia ES 1938 wicked] þe wycked S hetes] hetes and L, hetes and lustes W 1939 es] þe fende ys W *sidenote*: Fortitudo ES 1940 þe] *om.* L coldes] *om.* E, calde LS, caldeys W lette] *adds* hatred and enuye W 1941 socours] suctores R *sidenote*: Iusticia ES 1944 sal] sulde L sere] diuers W 1946 *sidenote*: Placius W 1947 þise] þe L 1948 sleghely] sleghtly R sayd] says ELS 1949 offices] of office W *sidenote*: Prudencia ES 1950 him] itt PRW 1953 ledes] dose L 1954 bi] wyth L lyne] lyfe LS of] and R

Bot þat þat es resoun and right;
And in alle his werkes, mare and lesse,
He puruays hym, als sikerest es,
Aftir þe ordynaunce and þe wille
Of Godde þat alle gode wil fulfille.
A grete lorde he may be called
þat has þis vertu and may it halde
And gyes hym in þise thre thinges,
Thurgh þis vertu þar grete myght hinges.
Temperancia Methe also has offices thre,
For þe hert þat has þat vertu fre
Nouthir couaytes ne has talent
To do thinge þat him may repent;
In nathynge he passes forby
Ne ouer-skille vnmesurabilly;
And vnder þe yhock of resoun right
He settes, and dredes day and nyght
Al þe couatyse þat regnes mykell
In þis werlde þat es ful fykell.
þat es to say whaso has
þis vertu, whareso he gase,
He kepes hym þat he be noght
Corrumped nouthir in wille ne thoght
Thurgh thre thynges, als Saynt Ion says,
þat man confoundes and Godde myspays—
þat es Lust of Flesshe and Pryde of Hert
And Couatyse of þe Werlde so smert.
Fortitudo Strengthe also has, als I wene,
Thre offices, als here es sene.
For þe hert þat has þis vertu right

In celis

fo. 12vb Rayses itseluen on heght thurgh myght
Oboun alle perils þat may be

1963 gyes] gyfes L, kepes SW in] *om.* L þise] þes vertus P 1964 þar] þat P 1965 *sidenote om.* LR 1966 þat] *om.* W 1967 couaytes] he c. E ne] he ne R 1968 thinge] þe thyng E him may] *trs.* ELPR 1971 resoun] resonus S 1972 settes] sittes LP, betes W 1974 ful] so E 1976 -so] -sere W 1977 hym] *om.* L, hym ay R 1978 ne] na in L 1979 Thurgh . . . thynges] Thre thinges er L *sidenote*: Iohannes ES, Iohannes euangelista L 1980 Godde] man L 1981 lust] luf LPS 1983 also has] *trs.* R has] *om.* L als] I als S *sidenote om.* LR 1984 Thre] Haues thre L 1986 on] of W

In þis werlde þat we here se.
He dredes nathinge bot vilany,
And angre and welthe he bers sadly,
And suffirs euenly wo and wele,
Welth or angre, whethir he fele.
So þat his hert es neuermare
Ouer-heghe here for na wele-fare,
Ne ouer-laghe here, on þe tothir syde,
For nane ille-fare þat may bityde.
Bot stifly withouten fayntyse
Standes agayne alle his enemyse,
Whethir þat þai bodyly be
Or gastly þat men may noght se,
So þat na foul temptacioun
Make him lightly to falle doun.
A gode knyght he suld be talde
And ane hardy bachilere and a balde
þat in þise thre thinges to fele
War appertly proued and wele.
   þise thre vertus armes a man
And ordaynes hym sikerly þan
And saues him ay in gode quert,
When he has þise thre thinges in hert,
Als þai ly in brede and lengthe—
þat es Resoun, Luf, and Strengthe.
Warnes right kepes þe resoun
þat it be noght deceyued thurgh tresoun;
Methe kepes þe luf ay fre
þat it noght corrumped be;
Strengthe kepes þe strengthe right
þat it be noght ouercomen thurgh myght.
   Rightwisnes right wille may gif *Iusticia*

1988 here] maye ELS 1990 angre] angres E welthe] w`r´ethe P 1991 and[2]] or L 1992 angre] angers L he] sa he LP 1993 neuer-] neuer þe L 1994 Ouer-] Na ouer- L here] *om.* LR 1996 nane] na LW þat] here þat W 2000 may] *om.* E 2001 foul] *om.* L 2002 lightly] lyghly W 2003 talde] cald PS 2004 And[1]] *om.* LP hardy] harde E bachilere] batheler S 2006 and] *om.* L 2009 ay] *om.* LR 2010 has] haue S 2013 right] *after* resoun L þe] þat W *sidenote*: Prudencia ES 2014 þat tresoun to deceyfe haue na myght L thurgh] with P 2015 *sidenote*: Temperancia ES 2017 kepes] ay kepys R right] ay ryght L *sidenote*: Fortitudo ES 2018 thurgh] by P 2019 wille] wele PRW *sidenote om.* R

Til a man ordaynely to lif
Onence ilk man, bathe mare and lesse,
To do to þam al þat right es.
For als þe philosophre says wele,
þis es þe vertu, als men may fele,
þat mas a man do þat hym awe

In celis

fo. 13ra Onence ilk man, bathe heghe and lawe.
For it yheldes reuerence, als es sene,
To þam þat oboun hym bene,
And lufrede on gode manere
To þam þat bene euen with hym here,
And grace to þam with hert fre
þat vnder hym falles to be.
  Thurgh þise four vertus þat I prays,
Als þe wys philosophre says,
A man es worthy thurgh fauour
þat he be made right gouernour,
First of hymself, als es mast nede,
And aftirward of othir to lede.
  In þise four vertus þat I sayde last
þis olde philosophres studyed fast
And to forsake þe werlde vouched saue
Vertu and wisdome for to haue.
þarefore þai war here right called
Philosophres þat lif þus wald,
For philosophye, als we se,
Es a worde of grete dignyte
And es þus mykell for to say
Als 'luf of wisdome'; þat lykes ay.
And philosophre es noght elles

2021 ilk man] ilkane R bathe] *om.* R 2022 to] *om.* L 2023 þe] a R -sophre] -sofyrs P wele] full wele L 2024 þe] a R 2025 do] to do EL hym] he R 2027–8 *couplet trs.* L 2027 For] *om.* L es] oft es L, *int.* P 2028 To] Vnto R 2029 -rede] -reden LP, *om.* RW 2030 bene euen] *trs.* R 2032 vnder] vndernethen R hym] *om.* P 2033 I] I now L 2034 þe . . . philosophre] þes . . . philo`so´fres P 2035 fauour] ryght fauour L 2037 als es] þat es þe L 2038 of] *om.* E to] *om.* P 2040 -phres] -pher LW studyed] studyes PW 2041 And] *om.* L vouched] he vouched L 2045 se] se may L, may se R 2047 es] *om.* P 2048 of] and R 2049 And] And a LP, A RW -phre] -phi S

Bot 'lufer of wisdom', als clerkes telles.
Lorde! how vs aght to drede sare
þat þa þat sumtyme paens ware
And war withouten certayne lawe,
And þe grace of Godde couth noght knawe
Ne þe gift of þe Haly Gast,
Bot folwes þair awen witte mast—
And yhete þai climned in þe mountayne
Of Parfytenes of lyf certayne.
þus þai did, als I shewe yhow,
Anely thurgh þair awen vertu,
And þam deyned na mare to loke
To þe werlde þat þai forsoke.
And we þat Cristen men er called
And has þe verray trouth to halde
And knawes Goddis commaundements mast

In celis

And has þe grace of þe Haly Gast— fo. 13rb
þat in a day anely, if we wille,
We may mare profyte, loude or stille,
Thurgh þe grace þat we haue here
þan þai may in al a yhere—
We weltre here als swyne vnclene
In þe sloghes of þis werlde here sene.
þarefore says Saynt Paul right wele, *Paulus*
Als clerkes may fynde in boke and fele,
þat þe paens þat has na lawe
And dose þe lawe þat þai noght knawe
At domesday sal vs deme
þat þe lawe has and noght wil it yheme.
Bot forthy þat þai haf noght here
þe right trouth in þe hert clere

2051 how] *om.* P 2052 þa] *om.* W þa þat] *om.* P paens] paynynis S, paynes W 2056 folwes] folled R witte] wittes W 2057 climned] climmed EPSRW, clymbbe L 2062 To] Vnto LPR 2063 And] þane E 2064 verray] vertw of S trouth] way (*int. later*) R 2066 þe[1]] *om.* L 2067 þat] And S in] on L anely] *om.* LS 2068 mare] *om.* L or] and R 2072 þis] þe RW 2073 þare-] And yare- L right] full L, *om.* P *sidenote om.* R 2074 Als] And L in] it in L boke] bokes L 2075 paens] paymys E, paymyns S þat[2]] *om.* W 2077 At] On L sal] þan sall L, þai sall R 2078 þe lawe has] *trs.* LPW has] had S 2080 þe[2]] *om.* LR

Ne þe grace of þe Haly Gast,
Alle þair vertus er dede and wast,
For þai haf na quyk vertu of myght,
Semed it neuer so fayr in sight.
For, als men may se in som stede,
Bitwene a quyke cole and a dede
Or a dede man and a lifande,
þus es þe vertu to vndirstande
þat withouten brightnes es
And þe vertu þat has brightnes,
þat es þe valu and þe bounte
And þe lyf of othir vertus to se.
Augustinus Wharefore Saynt Austyn, als I fynde þus,
When he spekes of þis four vertus,
He þam departes for our bihoue
Proprely thurgh four manere of luf,
And also thurgh four thynges þarto
þat verray luf here may fordo.
He says first þat þe vertu of Warnes
Bi skille þe luf of þe hert es,
Thurgh whilk þe hert forsakes ay
Alle thing þat lette or harme him may,
And cheses, aftir he can se and fele,
Alle thing þat may help him wele

In celis

fo. 13va To haf þat he lufs namely,
þat es our Lorde Godde almyghty.
þe vertu of Methe, als he says,
Es luf of hert þat Godde payse,
Thurgh whilk he gifs him with wille chast
To Godde anely þat he lufs mast.
þe vertu of Strengthe es luf of hert
Thurgh whilk he tholes al þat may smert

2082 þair] þese W þair vertus] vertuz fra þaime L 2084 Semed] Seme PR in] to þe L 2088 þus] And S þe] þis þe S 2090 has] es E 2093 I fynde þus] he fyndus W *sidenote*: *later ?* S, *om*. RW 2096 manere] maners LPW 2098 here] hyt W 2099 first] *int*. P, *om*. R *sidenote*: Prudencia ES 2102 him] it L 2103 cheses] chese LP and] or L 2105 þat] all þat R 2106 our] *om*. P 2107 methe] mete W *sidenote*: Temperancia ES 2108 of] of þe L 2109 with] þat R 2111 *sidenote*: Fortitudo ES 2112 may] is P

Stalwardely, withouten fayllynge,
To haue þat he lufs ouer alle thing.
þe vertu of Rightwisnes may be
Bi skille þe luf of hert fre,
Thurgh whilk he serues þat he mast lufs,
þat es Godde þat þe hert proues.
þarefore vnderfote he settes
Alle othir thinge þat swilk luf lettes.
Wharefore Rightwisnes settes wele
A man in his right state to fele,
þat es abowen alle thinge soght
And bynethen Godde þat alle thing wroght.
Withouten þise four vertus clene
Na man may clym wele, als I wene,
Into þe mountayne of Parfytenes
þat þe right way to heuen es.
For whaso wil clymbe so heghe,
He suld flee welth and angre dreghe.
Forwhy na man comes to þat place
Bot he first folow here Goddis trace.
He suld haf Warnes on alle wyse;
þat may make him þis werld dispyse.
And him bihoues haf Strengthe withalle;
Elles he myght here ful sone falle.
þat gifs him grace to vndirtake
þat þat strayte es for Goddis sake.
He suld haf Methe, als we se,
þat he noght ouercharged be.
Rightwisnes he suld haf ay
þat him may lede bi þe right way
And him shewe to se gastly
þe kingedome of God almyghty,

2113 fayll-] fall- P 2115 *sidenote*: Iusticia ES 2116 hert] *illeg. int.* P 2117 whilk] þe whylk L 2118 þat[2]] as R hert] *adds* maste L 2119 settes] ?sittes W 2124 þat] þat haues L 2125 vertus] vertu R 2127 Into] Vnto L þe] *om.* E 2128 þat] þer W to] of W 2129 so] vp so R 2130 angre] angers L 2132 Bot] Bot if P here] *om.* LW trace] grace E 2133 *sidenote*: Prudencia ES 2135 *sidenote*: Fortitudo ES 2136 myght] may L ful] foule P 2137 him] *om.* LW 2139 methe] *om.* L, mete W als] alsswa L *sidenote*: Temperancia ES 2141 *sidenote*: Iusticia E 2142 bi] *om.* L 2143 to] for to R

In celis

fo. 13vb Als God to Iacob did thurgh myght,
Als þe *Boke of Wisdome* says right.
He þat had þise vertus alle
A parfyte man men myght him calle,
For he war blissed in þis werlde here
And in þe tothir þat es mare clere.
Forwhy he suld be in gode quert
And ay in rest and pees of hert,
And in gastly ioy and delyte dwelle,
Als men may here þis clerkes telle.
Hym suld faylle here nathynge
þat gode ware to his lifynge,
And at þe last, he suld wende
To þe delitz withouten ende.
  Now haf I talde yhow als I can
þe vertus þat mast strengthes a man
With gode werkes, þat specially springes
Of twa maners of right lifynges.
Ane es called right Actyue Lyue;
Anothir es Lyf Contemplatyue.
Vita actiua Actyue Lyf, als says þis clerkes,
Es lyf of trauaylle in gode werkes.
For he þat hauntes þat lyf es bisy
To do ay þe Werkes of Mercy.
þat es þe hungry and þe thristy to fede,
To lene and frist þam þat has nede,
To clethe þat naked bene and bare,
To viset þe seke þat feles sare,
To herber in house with gode hert
Pouer men þat comes ouerthwert,

2146 right] full ryght L 2150 þe] þat W clere] dere W 2151 Forwhy] Forþi L 2153 in] *om.* R and] and in L, in P 2155 faylle] *om.* P, falle W nathynge] *adds* mysse P 2156 to] vntill R his lifynge] *trs.* P lifynge] likynge W 2157 þe] *om.* L 2158 delitz] delite L, delices R 2160 a] *om.* LPW 2161 werkes] vertues W 2162 Of] On L maners] maner R lifynges] lyfing S 2163 Ane] And W 2164 lyf] cald R 2165 þis] þe`s' (*later*) P *sidenote*: *as in-column heading* R, *om.* W 2166 in] and LW 2167 es] es euer L 2168 ay] all L *sidenote*: Nota de opera misericordie L, Opera misericordie corporalia R 2169 þe[1]] *om.* LW þe[2]] *om.* LRW 2170 lene and frist] *trs. verbs* R and frist] *om.* P 2171 þat . . . and] þe naked þat er L 2172 feles] er L

To help þat in prisoun er bunden,
To biry þam þat dede er funden;
To counsaylle þam þat er redeles,
To teche vnconande al þat gode es,
To amende misdoars and chasty,
To comfort þam þat bene sary,
To forgif with gode wille sone
Trespas and wranges þat es done,
To rewe on þam þat angre has,
To pray for fr'endes and for faas,

In celis

To acorde þam þat bene at debate, fo. 14ra
To do penaunce arely and late—
Werkes of Mercy alle þise men calles.
Swilk werkes to Lyf Actyue falles.
  Contemplatyue Lyf es þis, *Vita contemplatiua*
Haally study about heuen-blisse.
Contemplatyue Lyf hauntes he
þat lifs in clene charyte
And settes his hert in Godde anly
And leues þe werlde þat mase men bisy.
Contemplatyue Lyf withouten semes
A lyf of rest, als men oft demes.
Bot he þat ledes þat lyf rightly
He es in hert in thre thynges bisy,
þat es to say in redynge,
In prayinge, and in bithynkynge.
  In redynge has he grete delyte
Of lyfs of haly men parfyte
And of Haly Wrytte þat clerkes lokes,
þat es wryten in dyuers bokes.

2175 þat] þam þat ELR 2177 *sidenote*: Opera misericordie spiritualia R 2178 teche] *add* þe LP 2181 gode] *om.* R gode wille] *trs.* E 2182 Trespas] Trespasses R wranges] wrange EPS es] here ben W 2183 rewe on] rewen W angre] angers LS 2184 frendes] r *int. later* A 2186 and] or L 2187 alle] of all L 2188 werkes] vertus P 2189–90 *couplet om.* P 2189 es] yit ys R *sidenote*: *as in-column heading* De v. c. R 2190 study] stodying L 2194 mase men] *trs.* P 2195–8 *lines om.* ES 2195 semes] seruice L 2196 als] es als L 2197 ledes þat lyf] þat (*int.*) lyf ledes P rightly] lightly P 2198 in] of P 2202 lyfs] lyfe R men] men and LR 2203 wrytte] wyrte R

Yhete haly ensaumples wil he rede
To rewell his lyf bi þam and lede.
In prayinge es he bisy and boun
With alle manere of deuocioun.
He es ay prayand, loude or stille,
And shewes to Godde al his wille.
His prayere ful of yhernynge es
To com to blisse þat es endeles.
He prayes also, whareso he wendes,
For his faas and for his frendes.
When he prayes, his hert es broght
Clene out of alle idell thoght,
And bot he praye on þis manere,
Godde wil noght here his prayere.
In bithynkyng ful bisy he es,
When he thinkes of his wrechednes,
Bathe of saul and of body,
And of þe godenes and þe curtaysy
Þat Godde has done him and dose ilk day,
Als yhe haf herde me bifore say.

In celis

fo. 14rb Þus may Contemplatyue Lyf be
Reweled in þise thinges thre.
Bot Contemplatyue Lyf es noght clene
Bot Actyue Lyf þarewith be sene.
Of þise twa lyues, als says þis clerkes,
Comes alle vertus and alle gode werkes.
Þis worde 'In celis' þat we say þus
Pruesce of hert askes of vs.
For heuen es swilk a kingedome
Þat na man may þider come
To bere þe coroun of blisse þareinne,

2205 Yhete] þat S he] þai L, I R 2206 lede] drede L 2209 or] and W 2210 al] haly R 2211 prayere] prayers W 2213 also] als W whareso] whar R 2215 When] When þat L 2216 out] *om.* L 2217 And] *om.* E þis] ?þes W 2218 here] tent to L here his prayere] *trs.* R 2219 ful] oft full L bisy] besyly W 2220 of] on ELPSR 2222 þe[1]] *om.* P and[2]] and of L þe[2]] *om.* PW 2223 him] *om.* L 2224 haf] *om.* P 2225 þus] þis W lyf] *om.* W 2229 lyues] lyfnes R þis] þe P 2230 alle[1]] all gode L alle[2]] *om.* R 2231 þat] ȝhet W *sidenote*: In celis S 2232 of[2]] *om.* P 2233 kinge-] kyn- W

Bot he it here appertly wynne
Thurgh Pruesce and thurgh victory,
To ouercom þise thre faas namely:
þe Werlde, his Flesshe, and þe Fende
þat hym assaylles and wald shende.
  þe Werlde assaylles on aythir syde *De mundo*
A man þat wil it here habyde.
On þe right syde, als I gesce,
It assaylles thurgh welth and ritches;
And on þe left syde alswa,
It assaylles thurgh angre and wa.
Bot ay when it a man assaylles
Thurgh welthe and ritches þat oft faylles,
It may sone ouercommen be
Thurgh Willeful Pouert, als we se.
And when it assaylles thurgh angre a man,
It may lightly be ouercommen þan
Thurgh stedefast Suffraunce of hert,
Be þe angre neuer so smert.
  þe Flesshe assaylles a man egrely *De carne*
Thurgh grete lust [and] lykyng of body
þat may be ouercommen thurgh skille
Thurgh Abstinence of fre wille.
  þe Fende assaylles a man sleghely *De diabolo*
Thurgh Pryde of hert and Vayneglory,
And he may thurgh verray Mekenes
Be ouercommen and made myghtles.
þarefore whaso may on þis wyse
Ouercom þise thre fals enemyse,

In celis

He sal noght þan of heuen mysse fo. 14va
þar he sal haue þe coroun of blisse.

2236 Bot] Bot if L here] *om.* L 2237 thurgh[2]] *om.* E 2238 þise] his S thre] *om.* L namely] anely P 2239 his] þe L 2240 wald] fayn wold R 2241 on aythir] another W *sidenote om.* PR 2243 On] Opon R 2244 welth and] or R 2245 And] *om.* L þe] *om.* P left] ryght W 2247–8 *couplet trs.* W 2247 Bot] *om.* W it] hom W a man] men L assaylles] sayles W 2249 sone] full son L 2250 se] may se L 2253 suffraunce] souerans R 2255 *sidenote: twice (both inner and outer marg., similarly, all other examples to 2293)* W, *om.* R *2256 and] *om.* APW 2257 þat] It L be] be wele R 2259 sleghely] sleghtly W *sidenote om.* RW 2260 and] and of R 2262 myghtles] les R 2264 þise] þe L 2266 þar] *om.* S

þat may he chalange rightwisly
When he of þam has þe victory.
Now haf I talde þe vndirstandynge
Of þise four wordes at þe bigynnynge:
Pater / noster / qui es / in celis.
Whaso wil þise four wordes halde,
Goddis sone he may be called,
þat es to say, if he folow wille,
þe vnderstandynge of þam bi skille,
þe whilk men may lightly bere,
If þai it in þair hert sper.
Pater þe first worde shewes to our knawing
þe lengthe of Goddis ay-lastyng.
And thurgh kynde of þe Faderhede,
He askes of vs Luf and Drede,
Bouxsomnes and Honour to do,
Seruyse and Reuerence þarto.
Noster þe secund worde vs shewes to se
þe largesce of Goddis charyte,
And askes of vs, when we it rede,
Luf þat falles to brothirhede
And Hope withouten dout to haue
Alle þat we rightwisly craue.
Qui es þe thridde vs shewes, als writen es,
þe depnes of his sothfastnes,
And askes of vs Trouth stedefast
And Drede of þe dome þat sal be last.
In celis þe ferth worde shewes, als falles to be,
þe heght of Goddis maieste,
And askes of vs namely thre thinges.
Ane es Mekenes þat in hert springes;
Anothir Strengthe of wille suld be,
þe thridde es Pruesce of hert fre.
þus may men vndirstande shortly

2267 he] be L 2268 þe] *om.* PS 2270a *om.* L *sidenote*: Pater W 2271 wordes] *om.* L 2272 sone] seruaunde L he] *om.* R 2273 if] and L wille] welle W 2274 of þam] *om.* S 2276 it] *om.* P þair hert] *trs.* E hert] hertes walde L, hertes R 2277 our] ȝhor W 2284 Goddis] his PRW 2286 Luf] þe luf L 2288 craue] will craue R 2292 þe] *om.* L 2293 worde] vs PW, *om.* R *sidenote om.* L 2295 namely] *om.* W 2297 Anothir] *adds* is P 2298 pruesce] prowest LR

þise four wordes with lytell study.
And whaso vndirstandes þam right
And aftir þam dose with al his might
And fulfilles ay Goddis wille,
He es his gode sone thurgh skille.

In celis

Whatso he of þe Fader wil craue fo. 14vb
þat skilful es, he sal þan haue.
And he þat wirkes þareagayne,
He says his Pater Noster in vayne.
After þise four wordes at þe bigynnyng
Folwes euen þe first askynge,
And if we þa four fast fest in vs,
þan may we say sikerly þus:
Sanctificetur nomen tuum.
þise four wordes er þe prolouge called
Of þe Pater Noster, als I halde,
þat es right als ane entree
Of a toun or of a cyte.
Into a cyte na man may
Com bot bi ane entre of way.
So sal we com on þe same manere
Bi þis proloug to right prayere.
After þat folwes seuen askinges
þat purchaces and to vs bringes
þe Seuen Giftes of þe Haly Gast,
þat to clene lifyng vs may hast.
þe whilk out of þe hert drawes
þe Seuen Hede-synnes þat within gnawes,
And sette⟨s⟩ seuen maner of vertus
Instede of þam þat men suld vse.
þe whilk a man euen ledes

2301 whaso] swa L vnderstandes] vnderstande L 2302 To do efter þaime whasa haues myght L 2305 Whatso] And whatsa L þe] his L wil] *after* he P 2306 sal þan] mouuen L þan] itt P 2311 we] *om.* E fast fest] *trs.* LPW 2312 say sikerly] *trs.* LR (say *int.* R) sikerly] seker W 2312a *marg.* L, *adds sidenote* Sanctificetur W 2313 er] es (*after* prolouge) L, *int.* S þe] *om.* W 2316 a^2] *om.* R 2318 bot] *om.* L bi] *om.* P of] of a LPRW 2320 to] of P 2323 *sidenote*: 7. dona spiritus sancti W 2324 vs] oft P 2325 out] þat oute L 2326 þe] *om.* R within] wyth hym L 2327 maner] maners L 2328 Instede of þam] In þaire stede L suld] sall P 2329 euen] euer? P

To seuen manere of Blissedhedes.
  Of þise seuen askynges þe first thre
Mase a man here haly to be,
And þe four þat aftir lys
Mase a man here rightwys.
Forwhy al þe halynes of a man,
Als þise clerkes shewe vs can,
Þat es made right lyke to be
To þe image of þe Trynyte
Aftir thre thynges þat er sene
In þe saul, þat þise thre bene—
Mynde, Vndirstandynge, and Wille—
Þat es in þise thre thinges thurgh skille.

In celis

fo. 15ra In þat þat þe saul in þe body
Be clensed in þe Wille parfytely
Of allekyns maner of fylynge,
And lightend wele in þe Vndirstandyng,
And parfytely confermed in þe Mynde
In Godde and with Godde þat toke mankynde.
And þe mare largely þat þe saul fre
Resayues of Godde þise giftes thre,
Þe mare proprely it neghes nere
To his kynde beute þat es clere,
Þat es to þe beute þat come mast
Of þe Fader and þe Sone and þe Hali Gast.
Þat es when Godde þe Fader fre
Confermes in mans hert Mynde to be,
Godde þe Sone withouten lettyng
Lightens his Vndirstandynge,
And Godde þe Haly Gast to fele
His Wille at þe last clenses wele.
Þise thre thynges þat we suld haue

2331 þise] whylk L thre] of thre S 2332 here] *om.* L to] for to L 2336 clerkes] clerk S shewe vs] telle L, schewen W 2340 þat] þare L 2342 þat] þare L es] *om.* P 2343 In] *added marg.* P In þat] If L 2344 clensed] closede P 2345 -kyns] *om.* L -kyns maner] þe maners P 2347 þe] *om.* L, *int.* P 2349 þe[2]] *om.* S fre] es fre LP 2350 giftes] thinges L 2353 to] of R to þe] *om.* L come] comes LSR 2354 þe[2]] *om.* PW þe[3]] *om.* W 2355 þe] þi R 2358 -tens] -tendes L 2360 þe] *om.* L

We aske ilk day here and craue
Thurgh þe first thre askinges
þat in þe Pater Noster hynges.

De prima peticione, scilicet Sanctificetur etc.

First we suld bigynne to pray
At þe heghest when we þus say:
Sanctificetur nomen tuum.
Here shewe we at þe biginnyng
To our Fader our mast yhernynge
þat we suld in hert haf ay
While we wone here nyght and day.
þat es shortly to say þus
þat 'his name be halwed' in vs.
Wharefore when we say als bousom,
'*Sanctificetur nomen tuum*',
þus we say for thing mast certayne,
'Lorde, þis es our yhernyng souerayne;
Ouer alle thinge þis aske we

Sanctificetur nomen tuum

þat halwed mot þi name be. fo. 15rb
þat es þi knawynge and þi trouth right
Be festend in vs, day and nyght'.
þarefore in þis first askynge
We ask bifore alle othir thinge
þe first Gift of þe Haly Gast,
þat es þe Gift of Wisdome, to tast,
þe whilk festes þe hert ay fast
In Godde þe Fader ay to last,
And ioynes and knyttes it to him so
þat it may noght depart him fro.
Wisdome es sayde of sauour
Of thinge þat swete es and noght sour.

2362 here] *om.* L 2363 first] *om.* L 2364a De . . . peticione] Prima Peticio LS scilicet] *om.* S scilicet . . . etc.] *om.* R etc.] nomen tuum ELS 2366 þus] *before* when W 2366a *om.* ELS 2370 wone] lyf L 2372 his] es þi L 2373 Whare-] þare- L 2377 þis] þan L, þus R, þes W 2378 mot] myght R 2380 festend] festene E day] bothe day P 2381 *sidenote*: Spiritus sapiencie ES 2385 festes] festens LR ay] *after* festes P 2387 And] At W ioynes] ioynenes L it] *om.* W 2389 sayde] sad W of] of a L

For when a man es bouxsom
To resayue þe Gift of Wisdome,
He tastes þe sauour what it es
And feles of Godde þe swetnes,
Als he þat wil and may tast wele
þe swetnes of gode licour, and fele
Bi þe mouthe, if he tast right,
Better þan he may bi þe sight.
  And forthy þat þa þat er vnconande
Suld þe better vnderstande
þis askynge þat we say þus,
'þi name mot be halwed in vs':
Men suld knawe and right halde
þat þis worde þat haly es called
Es als mykell to say als clene,
Als withouten erthe to be sene;
Als halwed to Goddis seruyse
And to alle werkes þat bene rightwys;
Als litted in blode ay to last,
Als confermed and festened fast.
  On þise thre wyse þe Gast of Wisdome
Halwes þe hert þat es bouxsome.
First he clenses and fynes it right,
Als fyre fynes gold þat es bright.
Aftirward I fynde alswa,
He puttes away alle erthe þarfra,
þat es to say, als clerkes can proue,

I[a]. peticio Sanctificetur nomen tuum

fo. 15va He dose away al erthely luf
And alkyn flesshely affeccioun
þat reues a man deuocioun,
And mase it bicom fade to þe sight

2392 þe] þis PW gift] gyftes E 2393 þe sauour] and sauours L 2394 Godde] *om.* L 2396 gode] goddes P 2398 þe] *om.* L 2399 þat[1]] *om.* LRW 2401 þis askynge] þese askynges W 2402 mot] *om.* P 2403 right] full ryght L 2404 worde] world R haly es] *trs.* E 2406 Als] And L erthe] ergh P 2407 Als] And L halwed] hawed W to] vnto L Goddis] god ESW 2410 Als] And L 2411 þise] *om.* L 2413 it] *om.* EP 2414 gold] þe golde L 2416 away] *om.* R 2418 erthely] erth R 2419 alkyn] ilke a P flesshely] erthly W 2420 reues] rewes L 2421 it] to L fade] sad R, fadet W to þe] in L

Al þat bifore semed clere and bright,
Als water semes fade in shewyng
To hym þat to gode wyne has lyking.
  Afterward he halwes it euen
To þe seruyse of Godde of heuen
And puttes it fra alle bisynes
Of thoght and of þat vanyte es.
And mase it to think on Godde ay
And to luf Godde wele and serue to pay,
Als þe kirke es on þe same wyse
Halwed here to Goddis seruyse,
So þat men sal nathinge wirke
Bot Goddis seruyse in Halykirke.
  Also he littes þe hert in blode
þat precius es and clene and gode.
For he puttes it, als I vnderstande,
In swilk a grete luf brynnande
And in swilk a deuocion namely
Of our Lorde Godde almyghty
þat when he thinkes, vp and doun,
On Cryst and on his passyoun,
It es thurgh-litted in þe blode
þat Cryst shedde for hym on rode,
Als a soppe es of warme brede
þat es dipped in wyne rede.
So es þe hert þat es clene to fele
In þe blode of Cryst + litted wele.
  þis es a newe baptyme sene
To make þe hert bright and clene,
For als þe boke beres wittenes,
Ly`t´tynge and baptyme al ane es.
þarefore he festes þe hert right
In Godde þat es mast of myght

2423 semes] becomes L, comes S   fade] sad R, faded W   2426 To] Vnto L
2428 of[2]] þat (*canc.*) of S   þat] þat þat L   2429 to] *om.* P   2430 Godde] hym PRW   wele] *om.* R   to] hym to R   2432 Goddis] god E   2434 in] and W
2435 he] le W   þe] þi R, þat W   þe hert] his E   2438 grete] *om.* L   grete luf] *trs.* W   2439 in] *om.* L   a] *om.* P   2441 þat] And R   2442 On[1,2]] Of P
2444 on] on þe ER, opon þe L   2446 dipped] bidded RW   wyne] vyne L
*2448 litted] es litted AELPSW   2452 Lyttynge] t *int. perhaps orig. hand* A
2453 festes] fested R

So þat it may noght fra God wynne,
For nathinge may þam sundre ne twynne.

I[a]. peticio Sanctificetur nomen tuum

fo. 15vb þan may we say þis worde þus,
'þi name mot be halwed in vs'.
  þat es to say on þis manere:
Graunt vs þe Gast of Wisdom here,
Wharethurgh we be fyned clene
And clensed of alle filthes þat bene;
Wharethurgh we be so filled of þi luf,
þat swettest es of alle thing to proue,
þat alle othir swetnes may be
To vs ay bitter; þus aske we.
Wharethurgh we may so on all wyse
Vs gif to þe and to þi seruyse
þat we alle othir seruyse forsake
And to þi seruyse anely vs take;
Wharethurgh we be noght anely
Wasshen bot litted in grayne þarby
And renoueld thurgh grace and myght
And eft baptyzed and wasshen right
In Crystes blode, precious to proue,
Thurgh deuocioun and fast luf;
Wharethurgh þe name of our Fader fre
Mot in vs so fast festened be
þat he be our gode Fader of myght
And we his childer and his ayres right,
So festend fast þat nathinge
May greue na louse þat festnynge.
  A grete grace es þis at þe last,
When þe hert in Godde es so rotefast

2455 it] þai L may] *om.* P 2456 sundre] part W ne] *om.* P 2458 Haloghed be þi name in vs L name mote] myght R be halwed] *trs.* ES 2460 þe gast] grace L 2461 be] may be R 2462 And clensed] *after* filthes S alle filthes] *trs.* (-s *later*) E 2465 swetnes] þat L, swettest S 2466 ay] be L bitter] better PSW þus] þat L 2467 so] *om.* L, se W 2470 vs] we us E 2471 we] þat we R 2473 renoueld] reneweld E, rewled L, renewed S, reuolued W 2474 right] bright P 2476 fast] stedfast ELS 2477 -thurgh] *om.* P 2478 fast] *om.* R 2483 es] þis R at] atte E 2484 es] *before* in P so] *om.* S rote-] sted- E

þat þe wille and þe deuocioun
May noght be loused thurgh temptacioun,
And so fulfilled in þe luf anely
Of þe swetnes of Godde almyghty
þat it ne may na solace gette
Bot of Godde þar þe thoght es sette.
þan es þe hert þat þis may fele
Fested in Godde parfytely and wele.
On þis manere aske we ay
Als oftsythe als we þus say,
Sanctificetur nomen tuum.

ij[a]. peticio Adueniat regnum tuum

þat es to say shortly þus, fo. 16ra
'"Fader, halow þi name" in vs
þat er þi childer here thurgh skille
þat we do noght agayne þi wille,
Bot þat we mot here in alle thing
Bouxsomly do al þi bidynge'.

De secunda peticione, scilicet Adueniat etc.

And forthi þat we er noght mighty
To do Goddis wille here parfytely
Whyle we dwell in þis werld here,
þarefore we say on þis manere,
Adueniat regnum tuum.
þat es to say, 'þi kyngedome
Hastily mot to vs com'.
Our Lorde says þus in þe godespell
To his discyples, als I now tell,
'þe kyngedom of God es within yhou';
þat it may so be vnderstandes now,
When God gyfs a grace thurgh myght

2485 þe[2]] þi R 2487 -filled] fast W þe] þi R 2489 ne] *om.* L gette] gyte R 2490 þar] whare L thoght] solace L 2492 Fested] Festened LR and] *om.* L 2494 -sythe] *om.* L 2494a *marg.* L 2496 halow] haly S þi] we þi W 2497 þat er] And here L here] *om.* L 2500 al] *om.* L 2500a *marg.* ELPW scilicet] *om.* ESW scilicet . . . etc.] *om.* R etc.] regnum tuum LS 2501 mighty] worthy S 2504a *line om.* ELS 2506 to] itt to EW 2508 now] you L 2509 kynge-] kyn- W within] inwyth L 2510 it] *om.* R -standes] -stand L, -stand as R

In mans hert þat es called right
þe haly Gift of Vnderstandyng;
þat may a man to clene lyf bringe.
For als þe sonne puttes away
þe mirkenes of night and mas day
And wastes þe cloudes þat myrk bene
And þe mornyng mistes þat er sene,
Right so þis gift þat men tastes
Al þe mirkenes of þe hert wastes,
And shewes his syns thurgh clerenes
And alle his defautes mare and lesse.
So þat he þat wenes he es clene
Sal fynde in þe hert, als I wene,
So mykil poudre þarein dwelle
Of synne withouten noumbre to tell,
Als þe sonnebeem shewes right
Poudre and motes þar it shines bright.
  þareafter he shewes thurgh his clernes
Noght anely þat þat withinne es

ij^{a}. peticio Adueniat regnum tuum

fo. 16rb Bot þat þat es withouten to telle
And þat es bynethen him in helle
And þat es obowen in heuen
And þat es obouten him euen.
þat es to say þe fayre creatures
þat Godde ay loues and honures
And witneses here sothfastly
How wys Godde es and how mighty,
How mykell, how gode, and hou debonere,
How swete, how lufly of chere.
And þe mare clere he sees thurgh sight
þe creatures þat Godde made right,

2513 of] þurgh L, of þe W *sidenote*: Spiritus intelligencie E 2516 þe] In R mirke-] derke- W of] of þe R day] þe day LR 2517 myrk] derk W 2520 wastes] it wastes L 2522 And] *om.* P alle] *om.* L mare] bathe mare L 2523 þat^{2}] *om.* L þat wenes] *trs.* S he^{2}] þat he ELPW 2526 synne] syniz? P 2527 Als] And L -beem] -bemes L 2528 þar it] þat L it] ine E 2529 þare-] Whare- S thurgh] *om.* R 2530 þat^{2}] it R 2532 þat] þat at R 2533 þat] þat at RW in] hym in PR 2534 þat] þat at RW 2537 And] Als S -fast-] *om.* S 2540 how] and how LR 2541 he] *om.* P

þe mare he es yhernand in thoght
To se þat Lorde þat þam wroght.
Bot he sees wele þat vnclene es he
And vnworthy þat Lorde to se.
þan chaufes he þe hert thurgh maystry
And waxes wrathe to himself anely.
þan tase he a picke sharp and smert
And grubbes and mynes about þe hert
Ay til he withinne þe hert be
þar he may alle his defautes se.
And when he has myned and es within,
þan fyndes he þare so mykell syn
And so many vyces of vnclennes
And so many defautes, mare and lesse,
And so mykell poudre þat his sight spilles
Of wicked thoghtes and of ille willes
þat he mas dole and has grete tene
For swilk filth es in þe hert sene.
þan biginnes he alle filth outcast
And mas þe hert clene at þe last
Of alkyn thing þat lettes þe sight
Of Godde, our Fader mast of myght.
And þat dose he thurgh tunge swift,
When he wryes himself in shrift.
Bot when he has lang grubbed about
And al þe filth has casten out,

Adueniat regnum tuum

þan fyndes he in þe hert thurgh grace fo. 16va
Pese and rest, ioy and solace,
So mykell and so grete to telle
þat him think þis werld noght bot helle,
To regarde of þat clerenes
And of pees þat þan in þe hert es.

2544 þam] hym haues L 2547 þan] þat L chaufes] shaufes R, schewes W he] here L 2550 þe] his R 2551 he] *om.* R 2552 may] *om.* L 2555 of] and R 2556 defautes] fautes P 2558 of[2]] *om.* P 2560 þe] *om.* E, hys LP 2561 filth] fylte to E, *adds* to S, fylthes W outcast] out to caste L 2562 þe[1]] hys L þe[2]] *om.* L 2563 þe] þi R 2565 þat] *om.* W dose he] *trs.* R 2566 When] When þat L, When so R 2567 grubbed] g`r´opet W 2568 þe] *om.* W 2572 noght] is P, *om.* L 2574 þan] *om.* L

And þis aske we, bathe nyght and day,
Thurgh þis askyng when we it say,
Adueniat regnum tuum.
þat es to say, 'Fader of pyte,
Graunt vs here, if þi wille be,
þat þe Haly Gast vs light within
And clense our hert of al filth of syn,
So þat we may here worthy be
In our hertes þe ay to se;
And [þat] þou vouche saue to com
And wone in vs with þi kyngedom
Als kynge and lorde and gouernour,
Als chief mayster and comandour,
So þat our hert be al þine awen
And þou kyng þarof to vs ay knawen;
So þat we may of þe haf sight
In our hert, bathe day and nyght.
þis es þe lyf þat we mast craue,
þe kingedome of Godde in vs to haue'.
þarefore says Godde on þis manere
In þe gospell, als men may here,
Mattheus in euangelio 'Godde es als a tresour kidde,
þat in a felde es priuyly hidde',
þat es in þe hert ful of clennes,
þat es mare þan al þis werlde es.
þus in þe Pater Noster aske we
Thurgh þis askynge, als yhe may se,
Adueniat regnum tuum.
þat may be shortly sayde þus,
'Lorde, thurgh grace here regne in vs,
þat we thurgh blisse may regne in þe
In þe tothir werld þat ay sal be'.

2576 it] *om.* R 2576a *marg.* EL 2578 wille] whilles L 2579 vs light] *trs.* LW 2580 hert] hertes R of[1]] fro P of[2]] and S 2582 þe ay] *trs.* P 2583 *þat] *om.* AES *sidenote*: De iij[a]. peticione Fiat voluntas t⟨ua⟩ L 2584 in] wyth ELSR with] *om.* L 2586 chief] *adds* and P 2587 hert] hertes L al] ay L þine] his P 2590 hert] hertes LP 2591 þis] þat S mast] ay P 2592 Godde] hewyn R 2594 men] we P 2595 a] *om.* W kidde] hyde kyde E *sidenote om.* ELPSRW 2596 a] *om.* R hidde] hede R 2597 in] *om.* R þe] *om.* W 2600 als] and R 2600a *om.* ES, *marg.* LP 2601 be shortly] *trs.* LP 2602 grace] þi grace L

iij[a]. peticio Fiat voluntas tua sicut in celo et in terra

And þis same say we comonly fo. 16vb
For þam þat er in purgatory.

De tercia peticione, scilicet Fiat uoluntas tua etc.

And forthy þat we may noght haue
Blisse in heuen þat we craue
Bot we in erthe here do his wille,
þarefore we say þus thurgh skille:
Fiat uoluntas tua sicut in celo et in terra.
þat es to say on þis wyse sone,
'Fader þi wille in vs be done
In erthe als es in heuen sene'.
þat es als in aungels þat þare bene,
þat er so lighted and fested fast
In Godde thurgh blisse þat ay sal last,
þat þai may yherne nane othir thing
Bot þat þat es to þi likynge.
þis askyng may noght auaylle
Withouten þe Gift of Counsaylle.
þat es a Gift of þe Haly Gast
þat teches vs here Goddis wille mast
And turnes our wille to his likynge
And so to do his wille in alle thinge.
þat na self-wille ne -witte in vs rest
Bot his wille anely þat es best,
þat it be huswyf and lauedy
Of al þe hert withinne haally
And gouerne it with resoun and skille
And do in vs whatso it wille,

2606a scilicet] *om.* ELS scilicet . . . etc.] *om.* R etc.] sicut in celo et in terra E (Fiat . . . terra *as running title*) E, *om.* S 2608 Blisse] þe blysse L we] we þus R 2609 here] *om.* LS do] dos E 2610 we say] *trs.* R say þus] schal W 2610a *om.* LS sicut . . . terra] *om.* R 2611 þis wyse] hys L 2613 es] *om.* L, *int.* P 2614 als in] *om.* L 2615 -hted] -htend L, -ht R -sted] -stend LR 2618 þi] goddys R 2619 noght] nothyng R *sidenote*: Spiritus consilij ES 2622 here] *om.* L 2624 so to do] do tyll R do] *om.* PW 2625 ne witte in] wythine E 2627 be] by W 2628 *sidenote*: iiij[a]. Peticio Panem nostrum cotidianum L 2629 gouerne] goueren P 2630 do] *om.* W it] he ES

Als it dose and es done right
In þe aungels of heuen bright,
[þat] dose Gods wille in alle thinge
Withouten any agaynestandynge.
Al þis in our askynge lyes
When we say þus on þis wyse,
Fiat uoluntas tua sicut in celo et in terra.
þat es shortly, 'þi wille be done
In erthe als in heuen sone'.
þat es þus mykell for to say,
'Graunt vs myght and grace here ay

iiij[a]. peticio Panem nostrum cotidianum da nobis hodie

fo. 17ra To do ay here with gode talent
Alle þat es þi commandement,
And þat þou forbedes to leue sone
In erthe als es in heuen done'.
þise er þe first askynges thre
þat we in þe Pater Noster se,
þat of alle þe tothir heghest bene
And þe mast worthy, als es sene.
In þe first we ask als childer bouxsom
Of our Fader þe Gift of Wisdome;
We aske in þe secunde askynge
þe heghe Gift of Vnderstandynge;
And in þe thridde þat may vs vaylle
We aske þe haly Gift of Counsaylle.
þise thre we noght anely craue
For we þam suld here parfytely haue.
Bot we shewe our Fader our yhernyngs
þat specially on our hert hynges,

2631 es] has P 2633 *þat] And AES, þat al P alle] ilk P 2634 any] *om.* L agayne-] gayn- P 2636a *marg.* EL tua . . . terra] *om.* L 2637 þi] þat P 2638 in] ys in R 2640 myght and grace] *trs. sbs.* LR 2641 ay] *om.* L 2643 to] *om.* L sone] it sone R 2644 es] *om.* PW 2645 first] *om.* L askynges] askyng LR 2647 þe tothir] þase other L, þe other W 2650 gift] gaste P 2652 heghe] *om.* E 2653 And] þat L þat] *om.* L vaylle] avayle LS 2654 gift] gaste ELPR 2655 thre] *om.* L we . . . anely] only noght we W 2656 þam] *after* here P suld] *before* haue W 2657 Bot] þat R our] here oure L yhernyngs] yernyng S 2658 on] in LP

þat bene or suld be in þat sone
þat þise thre askynges war in vs done
And confermed in vs and fested fast
And fulfilled in þe luf þat ay sal last.
In þe tothir four þat after lyse
We say to our Fader on þis wyse,
'Graunt vs, forgif vs, and kepe vs,
Delyuer vs'—þa four shew we þus.
And bot we þise four askynges haue,
We may noght wele our lyf here saue,
Forwhy þise four ful nedeful bene
In þis lyf þat here es sene.

De quarta peticione, scilicet Panem nostrum etc.

And forthy þat we may noght fulfille
Whyle we lif here al Goddis wille
Bot we haf sustynaunce of body,
þarefore we say þus specially,
Panem nostrum cotidianum da nobis hodie.
þat es to say shortly þus,

iiij^{a}. peticio Panem nostrum cotidianum da nobis hodie

'Our ilk day brede today gif vs'. fo. 17rb
Our gode mayster vs kennes hereby
Mekely to speke and wysely,
When he kennes vs þus to say,
'Our ilke day brede graunt vs today'.
What may þe sone better craue
Or aske of þe Fader here to haue
þan brede anely, withouten mare,
For þe day als nedeful ware?
He askes nane outrage þarby,
Nouthir fisshe ne flesshe, bot brede anely;

2661 fested] festend LPR 2663 þe] þase L tothir] other LP 2664 to] vnto W 2665 vs^2] -es L 2666 þa] þer P four] for R þus] vs L 2667 bot] bot if PR 2668 wele] here R here] *om.* L, wele R 2670a scilicet] *om.* ELS scilicet . . . etc.] *om.* R etc.] cotidianum ELS, cotidianum da etc. W 2671 And] Now P may] *om.* S 2672 al] *om.* E, as R 2674 say] pray L 2674a *line om.* EL 2676 day] dayus W 2681 þe] *om.* R 2682 here] for L 2686 fisshe ne flesshe] *trs. sbs.* R

And þat askes he noght for yhere ne woke
Bot for þe day, als says þe boke.
Now semes þis a lytell thinge
þat we craue in þis askynge,
Bot a grete thing may he it fele
þat can vnderstande it wele.
  When a man wil ane abbot praye
And hym aske þe brede of his abbay,
He askes, after his entent,
þe brothirhede of þe couent,
And part of þair lyf religious,
And of alle þe + godes of ˋþeˊ hous.
Swa askes he Godde þat says þus,
'Lorde, our ilke day brede today graunt vs'.
In þis he askes for his mast nede,
þe company and þe brothirhede
And part and right in þe godes alle
þat in heghe heuen-ryke may falle.
  þis es þe brede of þat blisseful couent,
þe brede of heuen þat he sal hent,
þe brede of aungels profytable,
þe brede mast delycius and delytable,
þe brede of mast sikernes,
þe brede of lyf þat es endeles.
For a siker lyf mas þat brede
And kepes þe saul fra gastly dede.
þat brede may be talde right
Fode of grete vertu and myght,

Panem nostrum cotidianum da nobis hodie

fo. 17va For it may staunche wele and fille
Al þe hunger of þe werlde bi skille,

2687 þat] ȝhyte EL askes] asked S askes . . . ne] forther noght for þe L noght] nouther E, *om.* P 2689 þis] hit W 2691 it] by it R 2692 vnderstande it] *trs.* P 2693 When] For when P ane] haue R 2694 hym] a man R aske] askes L 2695 after] euer wyth L 2696 þe[2]] hys L, þat P 2698 *godes] gode dedes AELPSRW þe[2]] *int. later* A 2699 *sidenote*: Panem nostrum E, p. n. cotidianum L, p. n. c. etc. S 2700 Lorde] *om.* L today] to E, þis day L graunt] gyfe P 2701 for] at L 2702 þe[2]] *om.* R 2703 in þe] of þi R þe godes alle] goddes L 2704 -ryke] *om.* L 2705 þe] *om.* R blisseful] blyssed LPR, blessed W 2706 sal] schuld W 2708 delytable] dilectable PR 2713 talde] cald R 2714 grete] ?grace P 2715 For] And for L staunche] staunce E fille] stille W 2716 Als in bokes er talde be proper skylle L

And so may do nane othir fode
Bot þat brede anely þat es so gode.
   Þat brede men resayues right
[In] sacrament of þe auter dight.
Hastyly men suld ay ete it
And gredily, als says Haly Writte—
Als þe gredy man dose gode mete
Þat so gredily wil it ete
Þat þe gode morsels þat er smale
Withouten chewyng swalowes hale.
Swa suld men with a brynnand luf
Resayue þat mete for þe saul bihoue
And swelow it withouten chewyng
With grete luf of hert and lykyng.
Þat es men suld trowen sothfastly
Þat þis mete es þe blissed body
Of Ihesu Cryst vs to fede
With þe saul of his Godhede,
Alletogider gastly to se
Withouten musyng how þat may be.
Forwhy mare may Godde do al-weldand
Þan any man may vnderstande.
   Afterward of þat blissed mete
Men suld ett als dose þe nete
Þat eftsons chewes þe gresse
Þat he has eten, als his kynde es,
With lytell and litell, als he shewes,
And þat es when he þe cude chewes.
Swa suld a man thurgh deuocioun
Think when he has swelwed þat mete doun
And recorde of[t] in hert and thoght
Þe gode þat God has for him wroght,
And how grete payne our Lorde Iesus

2718 so] anely so P   2720 *In] To AS, Of þe E, To ye L, *adds* þe R   of] on P   dight] bedyght L, bryght R   2721 ay] *om.* LR   2723 gode] þe L   2724 so] ay so R   2725 þat[1]] *om.* L   2726 chewyng] *adds* þaim L   2728 þat] þe L   2731 es] es at P   soth-] sted- L   2732 þis] þat ES   þe] þat S   2735 to] for to L   2736 musyng] mouyng L   þat] *int. after* may P   2737 -weld-] -wend- W   2740 ett] *om.* W   2741 eft-] efter- PW   chewes] schewes S   2743 shewes] chewes W   2744 And] *om.* W   þe] *om.* R   cude] gode L   2746 has] had L   *2747 oft] of A, oft (-t *expunged*) P

Suffred here in erthe for vs.
þan fyndes he þe sauour right
Of þat mete of so grete myght
And conceyues also and tastes þarby
A brynnand luf in God almyghty
And a grete yhernyng, nyght and day,
To thole for hym al þat he may.

Panem nostrum cotidianum da nobis hodie

fo. 17vb And al þis mase þe grete vertu
Of þis blissed brede of valu.
  Forwhy þat brede, als men may fele,
Strengthes and comfortes þe hert wele
To þat þat it be stalward to proue
And to suffre mykell for Goddis luf.
Bot þat may noght be, bot if it tast
þe fierth Gift of þe Haly Gast,
þat es þe Gift of Strengthe talde
þat armes and mas Goddis knyghtes balde
And mas þam rynne to martirdome
And lagh when þai in turments come.
And þarefore when we þis brede craue,
We aske þe Gift of Strengthe to haue,
For als þe brede þat here es bodily,
Sustaynes and strengthes þe body,
Right so þe Gift of Strengthe may make
þe hert stalwarde to vndirtake
And thole ane harde thing to þe body
For þe luf of Godde almyghty.
  þis brede we calle our brede mast
Forwhy it was made of our past.
It es our brede thurgh right tryed,
For it was for vs sothen and fryed.
Sothen it was in þe wambe namely

2751 þe] *om.* S 2752 so] *om.* P 2757 þe] þat E 2759 may] *om.* P 2761 þat[2]] *om.* L 2763 it] he ER 2765 of] *om.* P talde] cald R *sidenote*: Spiritus fortitudinis ES 2766 knyghtes] knyght L 2767 to] to þe L 2769 brede] worde L 2770 aske] awe W 2771 als] all L 2772 Sustaynes and strengthes] *trs.* R 2777 *sidenote*: Nota E 2778 of] for LR past] taste L 2779 thurgh] *om.* LW right] myght R 2780 For] *om.* L for vs sothen] *trs.* E 2781 Sothen] Sithen L þe] *om.* L

Of þe blissefull mayden Mary;
Fryed it was al in blode
On þe croyce anely for our gode,
For he vouched saue to do þus
In þat brynnand luf he had to vs.
  þis brede of whilk I spake bifore
Es þe siker warnystore
þat ay lastes and neuer faylles,
Wharewith he þe shippe vitaylles,
þat Halykirk es to vnderstande,
To passe þe see of þe werlde flowande.
  It es our brede thurgh vnderstandyng,
For Godde, at his last leue-takynge,
Left vs in his last testament
þe body of Ihesu Cryst to tent,
Als þe mast and þe derrest tresore

Panem nostrum cotidianum da nobis hodie

þat he might leue vs here in store. fo. 18ra
And gaf vs it while we here lif
Als þe best iewell þat he might gif,
þat we suld kepe whyle we haf witte
For þe luf of hym þat left vs itte,
And vse it ay when we er worthy
In remembraunce of hym anely.
  It es our, for nathing bi skille
May reue vs it agayne our wille.
For it es a distribucioun
þat es ane ilk day warisoun
þat Godde gifs til his chanouns
Ilke day, instede of þair comouns,
þat his seruyse here dose right
And synges his werkes day and nyght.
His chanouns er called hertes clene

2782 blissefull] blyssed LP 2785 to] for to R do] dy L 2787 whilk] þat L 2788 þe] þe maste L warny-] warene- E, ware in P, warme R 2791 to] I P 2792 flowande] folwande W 2793 thurgh] to E 2794 last] *om.* W 2797 þe^2] *om.* LRW derrest] deppest E, deppest (*corr. by cancelling descenders?*) S 2798 leue] bene P vs] *om.* L 2799 gaf] geue W 2801 suld] mot P whyle] it wele R 2806 vs it] *trs.* PRW 2808 ane] *om.* L 2809 gifs] geue W til] vnto L 2812 day] here day W 2813 hertes] þe hertes L

þat meke to Godde and bouxsom bene,
þat er bisy to do ilka day
Alle þe gode werkes þat God may pay
Thurgh verray luf and deuocioun
In remembraunce of his passyoun.
  Our ilk day brede men calles it þus,
For it es nedefull ilk day to vs,
And ilka day, if we do wele,
We suld resayue it and fele
Worthily in þe sacrament
Of þe auter, with gode entent
Als dose þe prest thurgh wham it es dight,
Or gastly thurgh Trouth take it right.
  þis brede ful noble and precious es
And ful of myght and sothfastnes.
It es a mete real and clene,
In whilk alle maner of delyces bene.
For alle gode sauours þareof may com,
Als þe *Boke* says þus *of Wisdome*:
þis es na mete for knaues and pages
Ne to hors ne cherles for þair wages,
Bot to þe hertes þat er curtays,
Clene and gentell and noble to prays.
þat er þe hertes þat in alle place
Er curtays and gentell thurgh grace
And noble thurgh gode lyf to se

Panem nostrum cotidianum da nobis hodie

fo. 18rb And clene wasshen thurgh shrift pryue.
  Of þe vertu of þat brede
Iohannes Saynt Ione spekes in a stede
And calles þat blissed brede to fele
Ouer alle thinge substanciele.

2816 þe] *om.* PRW 2817 verray luf] *trs.* S 2818 In] In þe P 2819 *sidenote*: Panem nostrum cotidianum EL 2820 For ilk day nedful 'is it' to vs P (*added at page foot*) 2821 And] For P if] and L 2824 with] in L 2826 trouth take] talkyng E, takyng S it] *om.* E 2830 In] In þe L delyces] delytez EPW 2832 þus] *om.* L 2833 þis] It L and] ne PR 2834 hors] howrs R ne] na to LP cherles] karles LS wages] vages E 2835 þe] *om.* W 2837 þe] *om.* L 2838 curtays and gentell] *trs. adjs.* LP 2839 gode lyf] lyf clene P 2841 þe] þat ES þat] þe L 2842 a] þat R *sidenote*: Iohannes euangelista S, *om.* PRW

þat es to say, for mast sustinaunce
It passes obown alle othir substaunce
And alle creatures, mare and lesse,
In vertu and in worthynes.
þar may na man in þis lyue
Bettir þis blisseful brede discryue
þan calle it, als it semes wele,
Ouer alle thinge substancyele.
Men says substanciele es þat mete
In whilk es mayne and substaunce grete.
Mete of substaunce we say þan
Es mete of grete norisshyng to man,
And þe mare þe mete es norisshande,
þe mare substanciele it es semande.
þarefore es vertu and norisshynge
In þis brede ouer alle thinge,
Mare þan any man knawe here may
Or think with hert or with tunge say.
For þe vertu of þis brede may passe
Alle þe mens wytte þat euer was.
  þis brede we ask of our Fader ay
And pray hym graunt it vs today.
þat es to say, 'þou it vs gif
Als lange als we sal here lif
þat we mot here gode iourne make
And g[l]a[d]ly habyde our hire to take'.
þat es þe peny of blisse to kenne
þat Godde gifs to his werkemen
þat in his vyne-yherde trauaylle wille, *Euangelium*
Als þe gospell telles bi skille.
For he comes at euen and mas þair pay,
þat es þe ende of þis lyf to say.

2845 for] *precs.* to L sustinaunce] substaunce PR (R *corr.*) 2846 obown] *om.* W othir] *om.* L substaunce] substinance P 2848 and] *om.* E 2850 blisseful] blyssed LR, blissedful P 2851 þan] Menne L 2853 says] *adds* þat E 2855 Mete] We say it 'mete' P of] is of W we say] *om.* P 2856 to] to a S 2857 þe[2]] þat þe L 2860 *sidenote*: v[a]. peticio Et dimitte nobis debita nostra L 2865 of] *om.* L 2868 sal] *om.* S 2869 gode] som L iourne] iournes P *2870 gladly] gastly AELS, cladely P 2872 þat Godde] Of God þat L Godde] *int.* P, he W to his] vnto all goode (goode *canc.*?) R 2873 vyne-] wyne- ESR wille] wele (*expunged*) wylle E, wele L *sidenote om.* PRW 2874 þe] þe gode L 2876 þis] his W

þarefore þe brede þat best es for vs
Aske we ay when we say þus,
Panem nostrum cotidianum da nobis hodie.

v[a]. peticio Et dimitte nobis debita nostra sicut et nos dimittimus debitoribus nostris

fo. 18va þat may be sayde þus shortly and wele,
'Graunt vs today our brede to fele',
þat es strengthe and hele namely,
Bathe of saul and of body.
Thre manere of brede here aske we
Thurgh þis askynge, als yhe may se.
Ane es bodyly brede of substaunce
þat es our nedefull sustinaunce.
Anothir es gastly—þat es wytte
To vnderstande Haly Writte.
þe thridde es brede of þe eukarist,
þat es þe blissefull body of Cryst,
þat comfortes thurgh grace namely
þe kynde of þe saul and of þe body.

De quinta peticione, scilicet Et dimitte etc.

And for we er na gode worthy
Whiles we here in synne ly,
þarefore we aske of our Fader dere
Forgifnes and says on þis manere:
Et dimitte nobis debita nostra sicut et nos dimittimus debitoribus nostris.
In þis askynge þat we here say
Our Fader of heuen þus we pray,
þat he wil forgif vs sone
Our mysdedes þat we haf done,
Als we forgif with gode wille
To þam þat has done vs ille.

2877 þe] þat L 2878a *marg. with* da . . .] *om.* E, *om.* L 2879 shortly] worthely S 2881 *sidenote*: Panem nostrum cotidianum EL 2883 manere] maners L here] *om.* L 2886 es] *om.* P nedefull] bodely L 2887 þat] and þat L 2889 of] *om.* R þe[2]] *om.* L 2890 þe] *om.* W blisse-] blyssed P 2892 þe[1]] *om.* LW of[2]] *om.* ER þe[2]] *om.* L 2892a *marg.* EL scilicet] *om.* ELS scilicet . . . etc.] *om.* R etc.] nobis ELPSW (*adds* etc. W) 2894 Whiles we] We will P 2895 of] *om.* L 2896a *line om.* ELS 2900 Our] All our R

þis sal be our vnderstandynge
Ay when we sal say þis askynge:
Et dimitte nobis debita nostra sicut et nos dimittimus debitoribus nostris.
þat es to say specially þus,
'Fader, our dettes forgif vs,
Als we alle dettes forgif clene
Til alle þat our dettours bene'.
Our dettes er our synnes ilkane
þat we haf here to frest tane
And sette our saules for þam to halde;
þat es þe best wedde of þe hous calde.
Forwhy a man þat es gilty
Of a synne þat es dedely—
For þat a synne þat comes so tyte
Als onence þe dede and þe delyte—

v[a]. peticio Et dimitte nobis debita nostra sicut et nos dimittimus debitoribus nostris

To so grete oker bonden es he fo. 18vb
þat it may neuer thurgh him quitte be.
For he has nouthir powere na myght
To make assethe þarfore bi right.
þat vsure to vnderstande es
þe payne of helle þat es endeles.
  Also to Godde almyghty he awe—
þat he has wrethed and broken his lawe—
So grete amendes, forsothe to say,
þat he es of na powere to pay.
For in al his lyf while he lifs here, *Nota*
If he lifd ane hundreth yhere
Or mare, if he so lange lyued
And he had anes Godde dedely greued,
He myght noght penaunce inoghe do

2904a *line om.* ES, *marg.*, debita . . .] *om.* L sicut . . . nostris] *om.* R 2906 forgif] þu forgyf R 2907 alle] oure L 2908 þat] þai þat R 2909 er] *om.* W 2910 here] *om.* L frest] first W 2911 sette] settes R 2912 þe[1]] *om.* S wedde] wede ER 2913 Forwhy] For who W 2917 es] here es L 2919 nouthir] na L 2920 assethe] ?a sothe L 2923 Also] As so W 2924 wrethed] wrehed R, *adds* hym L his] þe LS 2926 es of] has E 2927 while] þat EL lifs] leued P *sidenote*: *later?* A, *om.* PLR 2928 If] If þat L, All-if R 2929 if] and L so] had so R 2930 anes] enes PW anes Godde] *trs.* LS

For þat a synne als fel þarto,
If Godde wald vse, þat mercyfull es,
þe grete reddure of rightwisnes.
þarefore bihoued hym specially
Rynne to þe courte of mercy
And cry mercy som grace to wynne
And ask forgifnes of his synne.
Forwhy thurgh right, als writen es,
In þe court anely of rightwisnes
þe synful man suld dampned be
To endeles dede withouten pyte.
þarefore our Lorde Godde, swete Iesus,
For our recouerere kennes vs
To aske hertly when we haf nede
Forgifnes of al our mysdede.
  Bot ilk man suld take kepe þat prays
To Godde our Fader when he þus says,

Et dimitte nobis debita nostra sicut et nos dimittimus debitoribus nostris.

'Lorde, forgif vs our misse þat ders
Als we forgif our mysdoers'.
God wil noght forgif vs our folys
Bot we forgif on þe same wys,
Als clerkes may here himself telle
Openly in þe godspelle.
Wharefore he þat þe Pater Noster says

Et dimitte nobis etc.

fo. 19ra And of forgifnes þe Fader prays
And rankour in hert haldes or envye
Or ire or hatred or felonye,
He prays agayne himseluen ay
When he þe Pater Noster sal say.

2932 als] þat LSW fel] falles W 2933 If] If no L vse] do vs (vse S) ES, *om*. L 2934 reddure] redderour P of] of his L 2935 bihoued] behoues L 2935–40 *lines om*. S 2943 Godde] *om*. L 2944 recouerere] recouere R 2946 mysdede] mysdedes R 2948a *marg*. ESR, *om*. LP sicut . . . nostris] *om*. E, etc. R debita . . . nostris] *om*. S 2949 misse] myssededes L 2952 wys] wyses W 2954 þe] þe haly L *sidenote*: Euangelia E, Euangelium S 2955 þe] hys L 2956 þe] his P þe Fader] he L 2957–8 And rancure or hatreden or enuy | Or ire in 'hert' (*later*) haldes or felony P 2957 haldes] halde S 2958 hatred] hatre(n)dene ELP 2959–60 *lines om*. ES 2960 sal] sulde L

For he prays þat God forgif him noght
þe dedes þat he has wrange wroght,
When he says, 'Forgif me myne ille
Als I othir men forgif wille'.
  And þarefore ilke tyme þat a man
His Pater Noster says als he can
Bifore Godde in pryuyte,
þat knawes his hert and may it se
And persayues al hys entent,
He suld forgif al mautalent
And wreth out of his hert sone cast
And rancour so þat it noght last.
And elles his prayere, als we se,
Sal mare agayne hym þan for him be.
  And if he think it harde, and greue
His mawtalent here to forgif
To þam þat wil hym any ille
Or has mysdone him agayne skille,
þan suld he think, als I hym rede,
þat our Lorde forgaf his dede
To þam þat hym did on þe rode
To gif vs here ensaumple gode
To forgif alle trespas sone
To þam þat has hym mis done,
And yhete mare for þam to praye
And in þair nede to helpe þam ay.
  Forwhy, als þe gospell right says,
It es na grete thinge to prays
Ne grete desert onence God to rose
To do þam gode þat vs gode dose,
Ne to luf þam anely þat here lufs vs,
Forwhy Iewes and Sarzyns dose þus.

2965 man] man wylle L 2966 als he] sal W 2970 al mau-] of all hys L, al `maw´ R 2971 sone] *after* wreth LS 2972 it] *om.* W 2974 hym] hymselfe L þan] ?þer W 2975 if] *om.* E he] hym ELSW, it R it] hym (*canc.*) it R 2976 here] for L, he for S 2977 þam] þaim alle E þat] þat all (*marked for trs.*) S any] anely L 2979 think] hym vmthink L 2981 hym did] *trs.* ELP, tyd hym R 2983 To] And to R 2984 has hym] *trs.* E, vs has R mis] oght mysse L 2988 *sidenote*: Euangelium E 2991–3176 *lines repeated R, following its first copy of line 3176 (fos. 65–9); in this portion of the collation, R = the reading of both versions,* R^1 *= the reading of the continuous text from 2991 alone,* R^2 *= the reading of the second version of the text following 3176 alone* 2991 to] *om.* R^1

Bot we, þat er Goddis childer fre
Thurgh trouth and grace als falles to be,
And has þe name of Cryst to halde
And Crysten men thurgh trouth er cald

Et dimitte nobis etc.

fo. 19rb And er heyrs with Cryst so rightwys
Of þe herytage of Paradys,
We suld forgif ilkane othir
And luf sammen als syster and brothir
And luf our enmys here namely
þat to vs has here envye.
þat es to say, we suld luf ay
þair persones and for þam pray
And helpe þam when þai haf nede;
þan war we worthy to haf mede.
  Forwhy þus Godde vs commandes
In þe godspell, als clerkes vnderstandes;
Wharefore we suld anely hate
þair synnes þat appayres þair state
And luf þair sawles in hert and thoght
þat aftir Goddis image er wroght,
Als a lym lufs of þe body
And forberes anothir lym kyndely.
If þe tane hurt þe tothir sare,
þe tothir venges hym neuer þe mare.
  We er in Cryst alle a body,
Als says þe apostell openly;
And þarefore we suld here luf right
Ilkane othir with al our myght.
And he þat lufs noght þus, I halde
þat he may manslaer be cald,
þat dampnes hymself to payne endeles,

2996 And] þat S thurgh] *om.* L trouth] erth S 2997 heyrs] hired P with] of R 2999 othir] to othir R 3000 sammen] togeder W 3002 to] vnto L has here] *trs.* EL, here had S 3004 persones] person R^1 3005 haf] had LS 3006 to] *om.* R^2 3007 þus] *after* vs LW 3009 Whare-] þare- S 3010 ap-] en- LR 3014 lym] *om.* L 3015 tothir] othyr P 3016 hym] it R þe^2] *om.* E 3017 *sidenote*: Apostolus ES 3018 apostell] bok R^1 3019 here] *om.* E here luf] *trs.* LPW 3021 he] *om.* R^1 3022 þat] *om.* L man-] a mannes L, mans- R 3023 þat dampnes] And dampne S

Als Haly Writte beres wittenes,
þat says he þat wil his brothir dere
Or in hert hates, he es mansslaere.
  þarefore parchaunce swilk wil say
þe Pater Noster when þai pray
þat better war, als semes bi skille,
þai lete it be and helde þam stille.
Forwhy þai moue þair awen iugement
Agayne þamself aftir þair entent.
  Bot neuerþelesse þai suld say
þe Pater Noster ay when þai may
And leue it noght, al-if þai be
In synne and out of charyte.
For þat prayere es so precious

Et dimitte nobis etc.

And so haly and so vertuous fo. 19va
þat thurgh vertu of it and thurgh myght,
Som grace sal þair hertes light
To do þam se al þayr foly
And repent þam and aske mercy.
For als I sayd first and es sene,
In þat prayere seuen askynges bene,
And ilkane askynge may purchace
Of þe Haly Gast a speciall grace
þat þe synful mans hert may fele,
Al be his askynge condicionele.
For in þe Pater Noster we pray
On condicioun when we þus say:
  Et dimitte nobis debita nostra sicut et nos
    dimittimus debitoribus nostris.
'Fader, forgif vs our folys

3025 *line om.* S he þat] *trs.* E 3026 es] es a LS mans-] man S 3027 wil] *om.* E 3028 pray] say R[1] 3029 war] war it L, it war R 3030 þam] it P 3031 moue] make P, mowe S, mon W 3032 Agayne] And agayne ES þam-] þair PR þair] *adds* aughen L 3035 it] þai P, *om.* W al-if] as if W 3039 of it] *om.* L thurgh[2]] þe L 3040 sal] may in L, sall in P 3041 To . . . al] þat may gerre þaime fle fra L do] styrr S se] 'and' (*later*) se S 3044 þat] þis R 3047 hert] *om.* L may fele] fyle R 3048 be] by PW 3050 On] On a L þus] *om.* P 3050a *marg.* ES, *om.* L debita nostra] *om.* E et . . . nostris] etc. R nostra . . . nostris] *om.* S dimittimus . . . nostris] *om.* E

Als we forgif on þe same wyse',
Als wha say, 'If we forgif noght,
Forgif vs noght þat we haf wroght'.
In þis askynge þat we charge mast,
We ask a gift of þe Haly Gast
þat es called þe Gift of Knawyng
þat mase a man knaw his lifyng.
þis gift abates a mans felnes,
For it shewes a man what he es
And whare he es—if he wil se—
And in what perill here es he
And whethen he come and whider he sal
And his misdedes—he shewes hym al—
And what he has tane of frest vnqwitte,
And how mykell he awe it mas him wit.
And when he sees þat he es so sette
þat he has noght to quyte his dette,
þan sal þe haly Gast of Knawyng
Bringe him til a grete forthinkynge
And make him grete and sare sigh ay
And cry God mercy and þus say,
'Lorde, forgif me here my dettes
(þat er my synnes þat my mede lettes),
Forwhy I am, als þou may se,
Gretly endetted onence þe
Thurgh my wickednes þat I haf wroght

vj[a]. peticio Et ne nos inducas in temptacionem

fo. 19vb In worde, in werk, in wille, in thoght;
And for þe gode þat I haf left to do
And þat I haf forgeten þarto
þat I suld haf done thurgh skille,
And myght haf done and had na wille;
And for þe gode þat þou dose me

3053 wha] swa we L 3055 þat] *om.* L we] I PRW 3057 *sidenote*: Spiritus sciencie ES 3058 man] man to L 3060 he] hymself R 3062 *line om.* R in] *om.* P 3063 whider] wheþer R[2] 3064 he] it R 3065 of] on R frest] first PW 3066 it] he ELS hym] hym to L 3069 þe] he se þe L 3070 grete] gode L 3071 him] hym tille E 3074 my] *om.* ES 3076 endetted] entettyd R[2] 3077 -ked-] -kend- P 3078 in] and L 3080 þar-] mare E 3083 *line om.* R[1] þat] *om.* S

And þe vertus þat I haf of þe
þat I vse wrange with my body
And serues þe vnbouxsomly.
And for I may noght þis dette quyte,
Lorde, þat I awe, forgif me tyte'.
And when þe Gift of Knawynge
Has made hym swilk a shewynge
þat he may knawe al his wickednes
And alle his defautes mare and lesse,
þan mas þis gift hym at þe last
Alle rancour out of þe hert cast
And to forgif al mautalent
And alle wranges þat he has hent,
And gifs hym wille to forgif tyte
To þam þat has hym done dispyte.
þan faylles he noght of his yhernyng
When he shewes þis askynge,

Et dimitte nobis debita nostra sicut et nos dimittimus debitoribus nostris.

þat es to say on þis manere,
'Fader, forgif vs our synnes here
þat we haf agayne þe wroght
In worde, in dede, or in thoght
Right als we forgif here wille
To þam þat has done vs ille'.

De sexta peticione scilicet Et ne nos etc.

And forthy þat we er noght worthy
To haf forgifnes of our foly,
Bot we vs kepe forwarde fra synne

3084 þe[1]] for þe R[2] vertus] vertu ELS haf] had W 3085 þat . . . wrange] And dos w. E, And I þus wrang haue done S 3087 may] am R[1] 3088 me] *om.* R[1] 3091 al] *om.* R[2] wicked-] wyk- R[1] 3092 alle] *om.* P mare] bothe more W 3093 þan] þat L þis gift hym] it þus R[2] hym] *om.* W 3094 out] *om.* ES þe] his R[2], *om.* W cast] to kaste EPL, out to c. S 3095 mau-] maner of L 3096 wranges] þe wrang L 3097 gifs hym] forgyfnes he L wille] *om.* P 3098 To þam] All þase L has hym] *trs.* R hym done] *trs.* LW 3099 he] hym L 3100–3100a *lines trs.* P 3100 When] When þat L shewes] has schewed P þis] his W 3100a *om.* E, *marg.* LS *ends* nobis L, *ends* nos P, *ends* debita S, *ends* sicut etc. R 3102 synnes] synne LR[1] 3103 haf] *om.* E 3104 in[2]] and PW 3106a *marg.* ELSW (at S 3087), *om.* R[2] sexta] vij[a] L scilicet] *om.* ELS scilicet . . . etc.] *om.* R[1] etc.] inducas EPS (*adds* etc. P), inducas in temptacione L 3109 Bot] Bot if L kepe] *adds* hethen W

Þat we falle noght agayne þarinne.
Þarefore we pray for drede of fallynge
To God of help thurgh þis askynge,
Et ne nos inducas in temptacionem.
Þat es to say þus shortly,
'Swete Fader, God almyghty,
Lede vs noght withinne temptacioun
Þat we na mare to synne be boun'.

Et ne nos inducas etc.

fo. 20ra Þat es to say thurgh vnderstandyng,
Lat vs noght be ledde in fondyng
Nouthir of þe werlde, ne of þe fende,
Ne of our flesshe þat þe saul may shende.
Þe fende, þat es ay felle and balde,
Principall tempter may be talde,
And þe flesshe and þe werlde he settes
For his seruauntes and his sugettes,
Thurgh wham he may men tittest bring
To flesshe-lust and werldely lykynge
And to alle maner of wicked vyce.
Forwhy þat es his kynde offyce,
Whareof he serues in Goddis hostelle
To proue yhung knyghtes þat with him dwelle.
And if fondynge war noght profytable
To gode men here of hert stable,
Godde, þat alle thinge dose wele,
Suld noght thole men so mykil it fele.
Bernardus Bot when he þat temptes, says Saynt Bernard,
On our backes strykes harde,
He foreges vs corouns of blisse
Þat Godde graunts to þam þat er his.

3112 of] to W thurgh] to W 3112a *om.* EL, *marg.* S in temptacionem] *om.* S 3115 withinne] into P 3116 na . . . synne] *trs. phrs.* S 3117 thurgh] to W 3118 ledde] filde P, felled RW in] into L 3120 our] o þe R[1], þe W þe] oure P 3121 þat] þas E 3122 may] he may E talde] calde LPSR 3123 he settes] sittes W 3125 men] *om.* SR[2]W tittest] tites L, sannest W 3126 flesshe-] fleschly EPRW 3127 vyce] wyce R[2] 3129 he] ye E 3130 him] *om.* R[2] 3134 thole] *om.* L it] *om.* L, to SR[1] 3135 *sidenote om.* RW 3136 On] In L, Vpon R strykes] steres W 3137 foreges] forgyues W vs] till vs LS 3138 þat Godde] And ES, þat L þam þat er] all P er his] here es L

For he þat strykes fast thurgh might
On þe backe of a gode knyght,
He forges him loos and worshepe,
Al-if he þat strykes take na kepe.
Bot þe fende thurgh wyles þat he can
To þat anely he temptes a man,
þat he myght draghe him sleghely
Fra þe luf of Godde almyghty.
þarefore Saynt Paul þat mykel grace had *Paulus*
His disciples prayed and badde
þat þai suld sadly grunded be,
Als a tour þat es stronge to se
And als a tre roted fast
In clene charyte ay to last
So þat na temptacioun
Might stryke þair hertes vp ne doun.
þarefor in þis askynge ask we

Et ne nos inducas etc.

Helpe of God and þe Gift of Pyte. fo. 20rb
þat es a grace þat fresshes þe hert wele
And mas it swete and pitous to fele
And mas it florisshe, als says þis clerkes,
And bere fruyt inoghe of gode werkes
And festes his rotes in þe lande
þar men sal ay be lyfande.
þis grace, whaso tas gode tent,
May be lickend to þe gode syment
With whilk men mas, als men says,
þe strange walles sarzynays
þat na man vnnethes breke þam may,
So harde and so strange er þai;

3140 of] on S gode] dughty R 3142 Al-if] Alle þat if E, Of all L 3143 wyles] whyles E, wylles R 3144 Maste he gernnes to tempte man L To] þat E To þat anely] þat sotely S 3145 þat] How L 3146 þe] þat R^1 3147 *sidenote om.* R 3151 roted] rott R^2 3152 *line om.*, So þat þe wynde hym ne doun ⟨ca⟩st *added marg.* W 3154 þair hertes] þe hert L ne] an W 3155 ask] we ask P 3156 and] and of LP þe] *om.* R^1 þe . . . of] *om.* L *sidenote*: Spiritus pietatis ES 3157 a] *om.* LR^2 3158 pitous] precious R^2 3159 florisshe] fresche ELS þis] þe`s' (*corr. later*) P 3160 bere] beres ES 3161 festes] festyns R 3162 ay] euer R ay be] *trs.* S lyfande] lastande P 3163 tent] intent R^1 3166 walles] walles of ELPSW sarzynays] garrenase E 3167 na] a R^1 þam] *om.* S

Right so þe Gift of Pyte festes
And stables þe hert þar it restes.
þarefore þis worde þus say we
þat falles in þe Pater Noster to be,
  Et ne nos inducas in temptacionem.
þat es to say to vnderstande,
'Swete Fader, God alweldande,
Make our hertes stable and fast
In alle fondynges ay to last,
Thurgh grace to fele als may be
Of þe haly Gift of Pyte,
þat thurgh na blast of temptacioun
Our hertes be stird, nouthir vp ne doun'.
  Bot we pray noght on þis manere
þat we be noght tempted here.
For þis war a foly to pray
And a shameful thinge to vs to say,
Right als a mans sone of grete might
þat war made a new knyght
Prayed his fader on þis wyse
Thurgh faynt hert and cowardyse:
'Gode fader', he says 'I pray þe
Kepe me wele and forbere me
þat I neuer to tournament ga
Na to bataylle, bot kepe me þarfra.'
Swilk a knyght es noght worthy

Et ne nos inducas etc.

fo. 20va To haf loos, als he þat es dughty.
  We suld ay yherne fondyngs to fele
So þat we agaynestande it wele.
For fondyng for our prow may be
On many manere, als yhe may se.

3170 þar] whar R[2] 3172 to] *om.* R 3172a *marg.* ES, *om.* L in temptacionem] *om.* ES, *adds* etc. W 3173 to[2]] and to L vnderstande] þe vnderstandyng P 3174 Fader God] *trs.* S -dande] -dyng P 3175 Make] Meke LS 3176 alle] alkyns L -dynges] -dyng SW *The R repetition ends* 3177 Thurgh] So S 3178 gift] gaste ELS 3180 stird nouthir] *trs.* P nouthir] *om.* L 3181 noght] o noght E 3183 þis] þat L 3184 to[1]] *om.* P 3186 made a new] newly made LR 3187 þis] his W 3191 tournament] torment L 3193 es] war R, ne ys W 3195 yherne] *adds* þat (?*later*) P -dyngs] -dyng PS 3198 manere] maners PW yhe] men L may] ma S

Forwhy we may be thurgh fondynge
Made mare meke in alle thynge
And mare dredefull and mare wys
In alle maners and mare of prys
And mare dughty and mare proued
And of Godde our Fader mare loued.
For als Salamon says þareby, *Salamon*
þat was a wyse man and a wytty,
'He þat neuer was fanded yhete,
He may noght rightly a thinge witte',
Bot als men has vnderstandynge
Of þe bataylle of Troy thurgh here-saying.
Forwhy he may [noght] knawe ne gesce
His awen strengthe ne his feblesce,
Ne þe strengthe of his enemys,
Ne þe sotiltees þat in þam lyse,
Ne howe leel Godde es to help in nede
His awen frende þat es in drede,
Ne fra how many shenshipes
And synnes and perils he him kepes.
And for alle þise skils, als I proue,
He suld noght cun Godde right luf
Ne thank him of his godenes here,
Warne he war fonded on som manere.
  Bot in þe Pater Noster we praye
þat he our hertes kepe, nyght and day,
þat no fondynges þam fordo,
þat es þat we noght assent þarto.
Forwhy of ourself here er we
So feble þat we haf na pouste
To thole assautes of þe fende strange

3199 be] *om.* L -dynge] -dynges L 3200 thynge] thinges L 3202 maners] maner R 3203 proued] pruf R 3204 loued] luf R 3205 *sidenote om.* RW 3206 a[2]] *om.* W 3208 rightly] right P thinge] *leaves blank* R 3209 has] þat haues L 3210 here-] *om.* P 3211 -why] when W may] ne may PR *noght] *om.* AEPRW gesce] gest W 3212 His[1]] Of his L his[2]] *om.* LP feblesce] febellnesse ELPSR, feblest W 3213 þe] *om.* R 3214 þe] ne R sotiltees] sotellnes L, suttelte R in þam] þerin L lyse] es W 3216 His] Als his L 3219 þise] þe P, *om.* S als] þat P 3220 right] ryghtly R 3222 Warne] Nere W he war] we noȝt fonded] foundene E som] þe same W 3225–6 *added scribal line* þat na fandynges dere vs na may, *followed by* 3226, 3225 L 3225 -dynges] -dyng LPSW þam] þanne L 3226 noght assent] *trs.* LP 3227 here] *om.* L 3229 assautes] þe assautes L

Withouten helpe of Godde amange.
And what tyme þat he vs faylles,
We falle when þe fende vs assaylles;
Bot ay when God helpes vs right,
Thurgh his grace and thurgh his myght,
We fight agayne þe fende fast

vij^{a}. peticio Sed libera nos a malo

fo. 20vb And ouercomes hym at þe last.
þarefore we aske in þis askynge
Our Fader helpe in alle fondynge,
Et ne nos inducas in temptacionem.
þat es to say þus shortly,
'Swete Fader, Godde almyghty,
Lede vs noght in fondynge of synne',
þat es lat vs noght entre þarinne
Thurgh wicked consentynge of hert
Or likynges þat comes ouerthwert.

De septima peticione scilicet Sed libera etc.

And forthy þat when God vouches saue
þat we þe godes þat we aske haue,
We er noght siker to halde þam stille
Bot he delyuer vs of alle ille.
þarefore say we þis þarto,
'*Sed libera nos a malo*'.
Saynt Austyne says þat som vyces
Chaces our wille here and entyces
To do mykell mare ille þarto
And to leue þe gode þat we suld do.
For al þat men has done wele
Thurgh þe gift of grace þat men may fele,
Pryde, þat es of alle synnes mast,

3231 þat] sa LR 3233 God] he E 3234 thurgh^{2}] *om.* P 3235 fast] full fast R 3238 alle] oure L fondynge] thynge W 3238a *marg.* ELS in temptacionem] *om.* EL 3244a *marg.* S, *om.* L De . . . peticione] Peticio P scilicet] *om.* EPSRW Sed libera etc.] *om.* RW etc.] nos a malo EPS 3245 forthy] fader W þat] *om.* LW 3246 þe] may þe P aske] aske to E 3248 he] we W 3249 þis] þus S 3251 *sidenote*: Augustinus ES 3252 Chaces] Chates S here] *blank space* L 3254 gode] gode`s´ (*later*) P, gooddys R, gode dedes W þat] *om.* L 3256 þe gift] myght W men] þai L 3257 synnes] syn PW

Eghtels to fordo and wast.
  þarefore þise clerkes þat wisdom can
Says þat when God has gyuen a man
þat he has asked and after prayed
In þe sex askynges bifore sayde,
þan war grete nede, methinke bi skille,
þat he delyuerd ware of al ille.
þarefore þis askynge last we fynde,
Als þe rerewarde þat comes bihynde:
  Sed libera nos a malo.
þat es to say, 'Fader almyghty,
Delyuer vs of alle ille haally',
þat es of our faa þe fende
And of his wyles þat may vs shende,
þat we thurgh Pryde þa godes noght tyne
þat þou has gyuen vs here of þine.

Amen

In þis askynge aske we þus fo. 21ra
þat he þe Gift of Drede graunt vs,
Wharethurgh we be delyuerd wele
Of alle ille þat men may fele.
þat es of alle synnes namely
And of perils of saul and of body
In þis werlde and in þe tothir ay,
And þareto falles vs 'Amen' say.
þat es to say, 'Swa mot it be';
Alle our prayere þus afferme we.
  Bot forthy þat our Lorde Iesus
In þe gospell says vs þus,
'Whatso yhe aske my Fader or craue
In my name here yhe sal haue'.

3258 to] þat L 3259 þise] þe P 3260 gyuen] forgyfen L 3261 he] *om.* W 3262 þe] *om.* P sex] sext LR askynges] askyn R 3263 war] were hit W 3266 rerewarde] rewarde PSRW 3266a *line om.* ELS malo] *adds* etc. W 3268 of] fro W ille] illes L 3270 wyles] whyles E þat] *om.* P 3271 pryde þa godes] þa gates ES, pryde na gates L noght] *om.* L 3272 þat] þa E, Oght þat L gyuen vs] *trs.* L 3275 wele] here wele S 3276 alle] alkyn L 3277 synnes] synn PW 3278 of] of alle E, *om.* W of[2]] *om.* R 3280 say] to say ELPSRW 3282 afferme] askyn P 3283 Iesus] *repeats* E *sidenote*: Amen ES 3284 vs] *om.* L 3286 sal] sall it LPR

þarefore it war gode, whaso wille,
At þe ende to say þise wordes þartille:
Per Dominum nostrum Ihesum Cristum filium tuum qui tecum uiuit et regnat in unitate spiritus sancti deus per omnia secula seculorum amen.
þat es to say on þis manere
In Inglysshe tunge, als yhe may here,
'Thurgh our Louerd þat es ful of myght,
Ihesu Cryst þi sone thurgh right,
þat with þe lifs and regnes mast
In anehede with þe Haly Gast,
þat es þe same Godde almyghty,
In alle werldes of werldes' to say shortly.
þan at þe first may be here sayde
'Amen' after we haf þus prayde.
Now haf yhe herde þe vnderstandyng
Of þe Pater Noster to þe endynge,
þe whilk God teches in þe gospelle,
Als men may here þise clerkes telle.
Bot vnderstandes yhe sal noght say
Als wryten es here when yhe pray,
Bot yhe sal say by mouthe anely
þe naked lettre and think þareby
In yhour hertes on þis manere,
Als I haf tolde on `ilk´ worde here.
And hast yhow noght when yhe sal pray

fo. 21rb Many Pater Nosters to say;
For bettir it es, als I right fele,
To say a Pater Noster wele,
With a right vnderstandynge
And with deuocioun and likynge,
þan a thousant to say ouerthwert

3287 war] is R 3288 þise] þe L 3288a *marg.* ELS tuum] *om.* W *ends* tuum etc. E, *ends* tecum S, *ends* uiuit L 3292 þi] þe L thurgh] *om.* L, of W 3293 with] we R 3296 of werldes] *om.* R 3297 þe] *om.* LSR may be here] m.h.b. L, h.m.b. P 3298 we haf] *repeats, first use cancelled later* A prayde] sayde L *sidenote*: Amen EL 3300 to þe] *om.* E 3302 Als] All S 3304 here] *after* Als W when] when þat L 3307 yhour] oure E 3308 on] of L, ȝhow W ilk] *perhaps later* A 3309 yhow] now P yhe] he P 3310 Nosters] noster ELPW 3311 als I] to L 3314 and[2]] and wyth L

Withouten deuocioun of hert.
For Saynt Paul says þus, 'Leuer had I *Paulus*
Haf fyue wordes sayde deuoutly,
With hert and vnderstandyng right,
þan fyue thousant sayde with tung light,
Withouten hert and deuoute thoght
And vnderstandyng rightly soght'.
And þarefore when we sal here pray
To Godde our Fader, nyght or day,
Our hert suld on our prayere be
Withouten thoght of vanyte.
And bot we pray with hert certayne, *Dum cor non orat in uanum lingua laborat*
Our tung trauaylles al in vayne,
For prayer of tung Godde myspays
Withouten þe hert of hym þat prays.
þarefore when we sal to God pray,
þe hert bihoues think and þe tung say
So þat þe tunge þe hert ay fele
And with þe hert acorde wele.
Elles auaylles noght þat þe tung may do
For Godde taas na rewarde þarto.
Bot he can bathe fele and tast
What our hertes yhernes mast,
If we aske oght with hert fre
þat suld to vs nedefull be.
To graunt vs it he vouches saue
And mare þareto þan we can craue,
For we can noght als wele se
Of what we haf nede als can he.
þarefore we suld first aske and seke *Primo querite regnum Dei etc.*
þe kyngdome of God with hert meke
Ilk day, ar we did othir dede;
þan sal we of our askynge spede
And haf al þat nedefull ware þarby,

3316 of] of þe P 3317 þus] *om.* LR *sidenote om.* RW 3322 rightly] wisly P 3324 Godde] do P, *om.* R or] and ESW 3326 of] or P 3327 *sidenote om.* LR 3329 of] with W 3331 þare-] Whare- L to] *om.* S 3334 hert] *adds* ay L 3335 auaylles] wailles R 3336 taas] mas ES, haues L 3337 Bot] Bot if S 3338 What] þat thing L, þat S 3339 If] If-all L 3340 to] vnto LR 3344 nede] *adds* of L can] *om.* P 3345 first] *om.* ELW *sidenote*: *as in-column heading* R, *om.* L Primo] Primum R etc.] *om.* EPRW 3347 did] do L

Bathe for þe saul and for þe body.
þat aske we and aftir it pray
In þis haly prayere þat we say
þat we our Pater Noster calle,

fo. 21va þe whilk Cryst made for help of vs alle;
And sette Pater at þe bigynnynge
For we suld þareinne haf mare likynge.
þis prayer þat [þ]vs falles to bigynne
vij^{tem}. *peticiones* Has seuen siker askinges withinne,
Als yhe haf herde me bifore telle,
And mare wil say if yhe wil dwelle.
þise seuen vs wynnes and mas vs tast
vij^{tem}. *dona Spiritus Sancti* þe Seuen Giftes of þe Haly Gast,
þat puttes out of þe hert euen
vij^{tem}. *peccata mortalia* þe principall Dedely Synnes Seuen,
With alle þair braunches þat may be sene,
And mas þe hert of alle synnes clene;
And in þair stede withinne settes right
vij^{tem}. *genera virtutum* Seuen manere of vertus of myght,
þe whilk vertus a man right ledes
vij^{tem}. *beatitudines* Vnto þe Seuen Blissedhedes
vij^{tem}. *premia* And to Seuen Medes þat to þam lys,
Als I sal shewe yhow on sere wyse.
þe first askyng of þe seuen
In þe Pater Noster es þis to neuen,
j^{a}. *peticio* **Sanctificetur nomen tuum.**
þat mas a grace in þe hert to com
Donum Sapiencie þat es called þe Gift of Wisdom,
þe whilk drawes out hally

3350 for^{2}] *om.* E 3351 aftir] oft E 3352 say] pray S 3353 our] *om.* W 3354 þe] *om.* W whilk] *adds* þat L help of] *om.* L 3355 sette] *om.* L Pater] þe pater noster LP 3356 þareinne] þarto PR, *om.* W haf] haue þat in W 3357 þis] In þis P *þus] vs A 3358 siker] principales L *sidenote*: *om.* LP; *from this point, all such annotations are lacking in R, unless explicitly noted* 3360 say] *om.* ELS if] and L 3361 vs^{2}] vs to ELS 3362 þe] þise S *sidenote om.* LP 3363 þat] And R of] fra L euen] full euen L 3364 *sidenote*: Septem vicia E; *om.* LP peccata mortalia] *trs.* W 3365 *sidenote*: Septem peticiones S 3366 synnes] synne ELS 3367 þair] þat P 3368 manere] maners LSW vertus] vertuous R *sidenote om.* LP 3370 Vnto] To PW þe] *om.* E blissedhedes] fleschely dedes W *sidenote om.* LP 3371 to] *int.* P, to þe W *sidenote om.* LP 3372 yhow] *om.* R on] in E 3373 þe^{1}] In þe R 3374 es] þat is R 3374a *marg.* ELS *sidenote om.* EPS 3375 in] into E þe] *om.* W 3376 gift] grace L *sidenote*: Donum] Dona S

Of þe hert þe synne of Glotony *Peccatum Gule*
And settes þis in þat stede, þat es *Virtus Temperancie et Sobrietatis*
þe vertu of Mesure and Sobrenesse,
þat a man bringes to þe blissedhede *Beatitudo Pacificacionis*
Of Paysebilnes and to his mede.
þat es þat he sal in heuen wone *Premium Deificacionis*
And be called ay Goddis sone.
Als Godde says, 'Blissed be þai *Beati pacifici, quoniam ipsi filij dei vocabuntur*
þat er paysebil in þis lyf ay,
For þai sal Goddis childer be called
And for his childer he sal þam halde'.
  þe secund of þa askynges sere
In þe Pater Noster es þis to here,
  Adueniat regnum tuum. *ij[a]. peticio*
þis askynge may to vs brynge
þe haly Gift of Vnderstandynge *Donum Intellectus*

þat puttes out of þe hert namely fo. 21vb
þe filthe of þe synne of Litchery *Peccatum Luxurie*
And settes in þat stede to se
þe clene vertu of Chastite, *Virtus Castitatis*
þat may brynge a man thurgh myght
þat kepes it wele, day and nyght,
To þe blissedhede, als clerkes says, *Beatitudo Mundicie Cordis*
Of Clennes of Hert þat God pays
And to þe mede þarefore ay lastand; *Premium Visionis Dei*
þat es Sight of Godde al-weldande.
Als Godde calles þam blissed þat bene
Namely in hert honest and clene,

3378 Of[1]] Fra L þe synne] all þe synnes P *sidenote om.* L 3379 settes] *om.* E þis] *om.* LS þat[1]] þe W 3380 and] and of EL 3381 þat] And L, þe whylk S a man bringes] *trs.* LSR þe] *om.* E, a P, *adds* vertw of S blissedhede] blyssede E *sidenote om.* SW 3382 Payse-] Passa- LS 3383 he sal] *trs.* R he . . . heuen] *trs. phrs.* LW *sidenote*: Beati pacifici *precs.* A, *om.* PS deificacionis] deificacio L, diffi[is] W 3384 ay] *om.* L Goddis] gode W 3385 *sidenote*: *om.* E quoniam . . . vocabuntur] *om.* L ipsi] *om.* S vocabuntur] ro a W 3386 paysebil] passyble LS in] and in W 3388 sal] *om.* L 3389 þa] þe W 3390 þe] þat P þis] *om.* W 3390a *marg.* ELS *sidenote om.* S 3391 to] vnto P 3392 gift] gaste ES 3393 þe] *om.* R 3394 þe[2]] *om.* L 3395 se] be L 3396 chastite] charite W 3398 þat kepes] To kepe L, þat kepyd R 3399 To] *om.* L *sidenote*: mundicie cordis] *om.* W cordis] *om.* S 3401 to] *om.* S þe] *om.* W 3402 sight] dyght E, þe sight PRW al-weldande] ay-lastande W 3403 þat] þai W

Beati mundi corde, quoniam ipsi deum videbunt ‘For þai sal Godde appertely se’;
In þe gospell þus says he.
  Þe thridde askyng es þis to say
In þe Pater Noster when we pray,
iij[a]. peticio **Fiat uoluntas tua sicut in celo et in terra.**
Þis askynge may vs mykell auaylle:
Donum Consilij It wynnes vs þe Gift of Counsaylle
And puttes out of þe hert a vyce;
Peccatum Auaricie Þat es þe synne of Auaryce.
And instede of þat, þe hert to light,
Virtus Misericordie Settes þe vertu of Mercy right
Beatitudo Misericordie Actiue And bringes a man specially
Vnto þe blissedhede of Mercy
Premium Misericordie Passiue And aftirwarde vnto þe mede,
Þat es Mercy when he has nede.
Beati misericordes, quoniam ipsi misericordiam consequentur Als Godde says, ‘Blissed be þai
Þat here mercyable er ay,
For þai sal fully mercy haue’;
When þai haf nede, þat sal þam saue.
  Þe ferth askynge, als we se,
In þe Pater Noster sal þis be,
iiij[a]. peticio **Panem nostrum cotidianum da nobis hodie.**
Þis wynnes vs, als clerkes wate wele,
Donum Fortitudinis Þe haly Gift of Strengthe to fele
Þat drawes þe synne of Slawnes
Peccatum Accidie Out of þe hert þare it es,
And euen instede of it to gesce
Virtus Probitatis Settes þe vertu of Pruesce,
Þe whilk may a man right lede
And bringe him to þe blissedhede

3405 *sidenote*: mundi] mundo SW quoniam] quia W videbunt] etc. S 3408 we] he E 3408a *marg*. ELS in[1] . . . terra] *om*. L sicut . . . terra] *om*. ES, etc. P et in terra] etc. R *sidenote*: *om*. ES iij[a].] 4[a]. W 3411 And] þat RW out] fra L hert] *adds* oway L 3413 -stede] þe stede PSR þe] in þe L 3415 And] þat PSRW 3416 Vnto] To PW 3417 vnto] to ELW *sidenote*: *om*. L passiue] *om*. S 3418 es] *adds* of L he has] we haue LW 3419 says] sayd R *sidenote*: *om*. L quoniam] quia W consequentur] *om*. S 3420 here, er] ere, here ELS mercyable] merciablely W mercyable er] *trs*. R 3422 nede þat] it it L 3423 se] here se L 3424a *marg*. ELS da . . . hodie] *om*. ELS *sidenote om*. ES 3425 vs] *om*. L clerkes] þis clerkes L 3426 gift] gaste ELS, gift *over eras*., *later* P 3429 in-] in þe L 3430 vertu] vertues W 3432 to] into L blissed-] blysful- ES

Of Hungre and Thrist of Rightwisnes
And to þe mede þat þarefore es,
þat es to say gastly Fillynge
Of endeles ioy and likynge.
Als Godde says þus, mast of myght,
'Blissed be þa[i] þat hungres right
And thristes aftir rightwisnes,
For þai sal filled be, als right es'.
  þe fift askynge men þis calles
þat in þe Pater Noster falles,
  Et dimitte nobis debita nostra sicut et nos
    dimittimus debitoribus nostris.
þis askynge may to vs brynge
þe haly Gift of Knawynge
þat out of þe hert smertly drawes
þe synne of Wreth, als þis clerkes knawes;
And instede of it, als falles to be,
Settes þe vertu of Equyte,
þe whilk may a man sone bringe
To þe blissedhede of Gretynge
And to þe mede þarefore thurgh grace,
þat es Comfort and Solace.
Als Godde says right on þis manere,
'Blissed be þai þat sorow has here,
For þai sal be conforted wele
þare þai sal endeles ioy fele'.
  þe sext askyng to telle on rawe
In þe Pater Noster es þis to knawe,
  Et ne nos inducas in temptacionem.
þis wynnes vs, als men may se,
þe haly Gift of Pyte
þat puttes out, thurgh maystry,

fo. 22ra
Beatitudo Sitis et Esurie Iusticie
Premium Saturitatis
Beati qui esurient et siciunt iusticiam, quoniam ipsi saturabuntur
va. peticio
Donum Sciencie
Peccatum Ire
Virtus Equitatis
Beatitudo Luctus
Premium Consolacionis
Beati qui lugent, quoniam ipsi consolabuntur
vja. peticio
Donum Pietatis

3433 and] of R of] and LSW *sidenote*: esurie] *adds* et L 3434 þe] *om.* W 3435 *sidenote om.* ES 3436 and] and of L *3438 þai] þa AS 3440 filled be] *trs.* LR 3441 men þis] *trs.* R 3442a *marg.* ELS sicut . . . nostris] *om.* E, sicut etc. R debita . . . nostris] *om.* LPS *sidenote om.* S 3444 *sidenote*: sciencie] consilij L 3445 þe] *om.* E 3446 *sidenote om.* L 3447 of it] þerof S 3450 To] Vnto R blissed-] blysful- ES 3452 comfort] of comforthe L and] and gret R *sidenote om.* E 3453 on] in W 3455 conforted] comforth LS 3456 þare] For L, þat er R, Whereas W sal] sal be P sal . . . ioy] endles ioy schun W R *adds line* Sed libera nos a malo 3457 to] is to L 3458 þis] *om.* W 3458a *marg.* ELS in temptacionem] *om.* ES *sidenote om.* S

Peccatum Inuidie Of þe hert þe synne of Envye
Virtus Amicicie And instede of þat for to kepe
Settes þe vertu of Frenshepe,
þat ledes a man in wham luf es
Beatitudo Mititudinis Vnto þe blissedhede of Mildenes
And to þe mede þat þarefore sal be,
Premium Possessionis Terre þat es þe lande of mast plente.
Als Godde says, 'Blissed er alle þa
Beati mites, quoniam ipsi terram possidebunt þat here er mylde, whareso þai ga,
For þai sal haue þe lande' of blisse
And of ioy þat þai sal neuer mysse.

fo. 22rb þe seuent askynge, last of alle,
Of þe Pater Noster we þis calle,
vij[a]. peticio **Sed libera nos a malo.**
þis askynge, when we haf nede,
Donum Timoris Domini May make vs haue þe Gift of Drede
Peccatum Superbie þat puttes þe synne of Pryde out
Of þe hert þat es heghe and stout
And instede of it plantes and settes
Virtus Humilitatis Mekenes þat Pryde mast lettes,
þat may a man here lightly lede
Beatitudo Paupertatis Spiritus Vnto þe parfyte blissedhede
þat es to say of Gastly Pouert
þat comes of a parfyte hert,
And to þe mede þarefore thurgh right
Premium Regni Celorum þat es þe kyngedome of heuen bright.
Als Godde says in þe gospell, 'Mast
Beati pauperes in spiritu, quoniam ipsorum est regnum celorum Blissed be þe pouer in gast,
For þairs es þe kyngdome of heuen',
þar mare ioy es þan man may neuen.
'Amen' comes bihynde at þe last

3463 for] settes for L 3466 Vnto] To W Mildenes] mekenes W *sidenote*: mititudinis] miticie W 3467 þarefore] þerto P sal] suld P 3468 *sidenote*: Terra possessionis W terre] *om.* EL 3469 er] be R 3470 here] *om.* W *sidenote*: terram possidebunt] *trs.* L 3472 ioy þat] ioy LR, *trs.* W 3474 we þis] *trs.* R 3474a *marg.* ELS malo] *om.* L, *adds* etc. W *sidenote om.* S 3476 haue] to haue L *sidenote*: *in gutter (as also 3482, 3486, 3488)* P, *om.* EW Domini] *om.* L 3478 heghe] proud W 3479 in-] in þe P of it] *om.* PW 3482 Vnto] To PW 3483 gastly] gasty L 3484 a] *om.* E 3486 heuen] godde P 3488 pouer] meke PRW in] in þe W *sidenote*: pauperes] mites W in] *om.* LW 3490 may] can LS 3491 þe] *om.* L

þat festens al our prayere fast.
Bot al-if we first aske þe mast
And þe heghest gift of þe Haly Gast
And ilkane after othir euen,
After order of þe askynges seuen,
Til we come at þe lawest of alle
þat we þe Gift of Drede calle,
At þe lawest vs bihoues bigynne
Ar we may to þe heghest wynne—
þat es to say þe Gift of Drede,
þe whilk vs may to Wisdom lede.
For þe prophete þat Dauid hight
Says þus in þe Sauter right,
þat Drede of Godde in hert to halde *Inicium sapiencie timor Domini*
Es þe bigynnyng of Wisdom called.
For þe Gift of Drede þat we aske last
þe first and þe mast synne may cast
Out of þe hert þar it es inne;
þat es Pryde, rote of al synne.
For Pryde, þat comes of hert and thoght,
Was þe first syn þat euer was wroght;
Pryde was bigynnyng of al ille;

Pryde es contrarius to alle skille. fo. 22va
Pryde brake first þe company
And þe ordre in heuen þat was semly,
When Lucifer for his beute
Obowen alle othir aungels wald be
And euen with Godde, mast of myght,
þat hym made so fayre and bright.
þarefore fra heuen doun he felle
And bicome þe foullest deuell of helle.
And alle þat war of his assent

3492 festens] festes EPSW *sidenote*: Amen ELSW 3493 Bot] þo R al-if] of all L al-if we] if we alle E we first] *trs.* R 3495 And] *om.* P 3496 After] *add* þe LPW 3497 at] to P þe] *om.* L 3499 bihoues] *adds* to W 3500 may] *om.* R þe] *om.* W 3502 vs may] *trs.* LW 3503 *sidenote*: Dauit ES 3504 þus] *om.* P, vs R 3505 *sidenote*: *in-column* W, *om.* R 3506 þe] *om.* LP 3507 þe] *om.* R 3508 cast] ouercaste L 3510 pryde] *add* þe LP al] *om.* L 3511 comes] is comen P of] of þe L 3513 ille] iwell L 3514 contrarius] contrary S alle] alkyn L 3520–1 *lines trs.* P 3521 doun] dowen euen P 3522 deuell] fende L of] in LSR 3523 alle] *om.* W

Out of heuen with hym doun went
And bicome fendes þat war aungelles,
Of whilk som in þe ayr yhete dwelles,
Bot Lucifer, þat so heghe wald sitt,
Fell deppest doun into helle pitte.
To wham men may licken bi skille
þise proude men of hert and wille,
þat brekes and fordose, al þat þai can,
þe company and þe order of man,
When þai yherne to be myghty
Oboun alle othir, and haue maystry,
And mare praysed wald be ay
þan othir þat er bettir þan þai.
   þis synne of Pryde ful perillous es,
Of wham springes al wickednes.
For it blyndes a man and reues him sight
þat he knawes noght himseluen right.
Pryde yhete may be lickened wele
To þe fendes awen wyne to fele,
þat semes gode and delitious
And es ful strange and perillous,
Thurgh whilk þe fende, als he can,
Mase drunken here many a man
þat bene wys, riche, and myghty,
And noble and wight, balde and hardy—
And comonly to vnderstand
Alle maner of men here lifande,
Bot specially þise men of myght
þat knawes noght þairseluen right,
Ne þair defautes here noght sees,
Ne þair folys, ne þair nycetees,
Bot folwes ay þair awen wille

3524 Out of] Fra L 3526 Of] *adds* þe L ayr] erthe W yhete] *om.* L, *int.* P 3528 into] in PW 3530 þise] þe W and] and of L 3531 brekes] berkes W al] in all L 3532 þe[2]] *om.* P 3533 When] When þat L 3534 haue] *adds* þe L 3535 ay] þai R 3537 ful] *om.* P perillous] perlyus P 3539 blyndes] byndys R him] *adds* hys L *sidenote*: De timore Domini et de superbia S 3542 To] Vnto R fendes] fende L 3543 þat] It L 3544 ful] *om.* L 3545 Thurgh] *adds* þe L he] he wele L 3546 a] *om.* P 3547 wys riche] *trs.* ES, riche wyght L, wyse R 3548 And[1, 2]] *om.* L wight] wyse L 3549 comonly] comly R 3552 þair-] þaim- ELSR right] aryght W 3553 noght] myght R

Al þair lykynge to fulfille. fo. 22vb
Wharefore I hald þis synne namely
þe mast perillous malady
þat any man may fele or se
Of alle othir þat may be.
For in grete perill es þat man
þat na man thurgh medycyne hele can,
To wham alle medycyne þat felle to hym
And alle treacle turnes til venym.
So dose techynge of alle godenes
And chastyinge to hym þat proude es.
For ay þe mare þat men blame him wille
And chasty bi right lawe and skille,
þe mare he es wrethfull and hasty,
And þe mare defendes he his foly.
Pryde þat rote es of alle wickednes
þe fendes eldest doghter es,
þat has parte of his herytage,
þe whilk falles to hir maryage.
And he þat wedde hir vouches saue
þat part with hir he sal haue.
Pride agayne Godde werrays
And agayne his godes, als clerkes says.
And Godde werrays agayne Pryde
And abates hir myght on ilka syde.
Pryde es quene of alle vices
þat to alle wickednes vs entyces.
Pryde es þe gredy lyonesce
þat alle gode swelwes, als I gesce.
Pryde alle grace fordose and vertus
In alle gode werkes þat a man dose,
Forwhy Pryde mas of vertu vyce,
Of almus synne—þis es hire office.

3556 Al] And LP lykynge] lykynges ELSR 3559 fele] here L 3560 alle] *adds* þe L 3562 hele] hale L 3463–4 *couplet trs.* W 3565 dose] *adds* þe L 3566 chastyinge] chastyng S, chastysyng R to] of E 3569 wrethfull] wrechedfull R 3570 þe] *om.* S defendes he] descendes to W 3571 *sidenote*: Superbia S 3572 fendes] fende LPS 3573 has] ys R his] hyr L 3575 þat] *om.* W wedde] wedded E, to wedde L, weds R wedde hir] hyr weddes S 3576 þat] þe L he sal] *trs.* PR 3579–80 *couplet om.* W 3583–6 *lines om. at page boundary* R 3583 þe] a W 3586 In] And LW werkes] vertus ES a man] men LS 3587 vertu] vertews L 3588 þis] þat ELSR

And of al gode þat man may neuen,
Wharethurgh men myght here wynne heuen,
Sho mas a man to wynne helle sone
And wastes alle gode þat he has done.
  Pryde es þe first þat assaylles fast
Goddis knyght and þat leues him last.
For when he has ouercommen right
Alle othir synnes thurgh grace and myght,
þan comes Pryde aftir þat victory
And assaylles hym mast stalwardely.
Pryde mas men heghe state couayte

De dono Timoris Domini De Superbia Sed libera nos a malo

fo. 23ra And maystry ouer alle othir men layt.
Bot Pryde, als clerkes in boke can rede,
May be fordone thurgh þe Gift of Drede.

De dono Timoris Domini

Donum Timoris Domini þe Gift of Drede es a grace
þat vs bihoues first purchace
Bifor alle þe tothir for to haue,
Al-if we it þus last craue,
Thurgh þe last askynge of alle
Sed libera nos a malo þat in þe Pater Noster may falle.
þis gift es þe last in askynge,
Bot it suld be þe first in hauynge,
For it es a bigynnynge to fele
Of þe tothir, als clerkes wate wele.
þarefore at þis we suld bigynne;
Elles may we noght to þe tothir wynne.
Als men biginnes þat wil clym heghe

3589 man] men L, god R 3590 -thurgh] -wyth L here] hyr L, *om.* PS wynne] *adds* þaim P 3591 Sho] So P wynne helle] syne heil R 3592 alle] *add* þe LPSR 3594 þat] *om.* S him] *adds* at L 3597 pryde] prydere R aftir] *om.* P 3598 And] þat L 3599 men] man L state] *adds* to EL 3600 ouer] of W men] *om.* ELS layt] to layte ELW 3601 boke] bokes LSW 3602 þe] *om.* PRW 3602a *marg.* P, *om.* ELS Domini] *om.* R 3603 *sidenote*: *om.* W Donum] De dono P Domini] *om.* L 3604 vs] we R 3605 þe tothir] þis othir L, oþer PR, þe oþer W for] *om.* L 3608 *sidenote om.* W 3609 þe] *om.* W 3612 þe] all L tothir] other LRW 3614 þe] þase L tothir] other LW 3615 wil clym] clymbes L

At þe lawest degre of þe steghe,
For na man at þe heghest may be,
Bot he bygynne at þe lawest degre.
  Þe Seuen Giftes has sere offices
To voyde þe hert of alle vyces
And to sette in þair stede agayne
Alle vertus þat er certayne.
Bot þe Gift of Drede first out-shotes
Of þe hert Pryde with alle his rotes
And with alle his braunches, mare and lesse,
And instede of Pryde settes Mekenes,
Als I sal shewe yhow, if yhe habyde;
Bot first I wil speke of Pryde.
  Pryde has speciall rotes seuen; *De Superbia*
Whilk þai er I sal þam neuen.
Þe first rote, als wryten es,
Es proprely Vnfaythfulnes.
Þe secund es Dispyte þareby;
Þe thridde men calles Surquidry.
Þe ferthe es, als þis clerkes wate,
Couaytynge of Heghe State.
Þe fift men calles Vayneglory,
And þe sext es Ipocrysy;
Þe seuent es Fole Shame to hide.

De dono Timoris Domini De Superbia Sed libera nos a malo

Þise er seuen smale rotes of Pryde. fo. 23rb
Men may bi skille calle þam rotes,
For many braunches out of þam shotes.
  Vnfaythfulnes proprely es *j^a. Infidelitas*
To Godde and man vnkyndenes.

3617 may] *after* man P 3619 sere] seuen ELS offices] office P 3620 of] on P vyces] wise P 3621 stede] stedes L 3622 vertus] vertuous R er] ys R 3624 hert Pryde] *trs.* R with] and E 3625 alle] *om.* P 3626 in-] in þat P 3627 Als] And L if] and L habyde] will bide P, wyll abyde SW 3628 Bot . . . speke] Fra þat I haue spoken mare L I wil] will I you R 3629 speciall] *om.* L *sidenote*: *om.* L, *as in-column heading* R De] *om.* W 3630 Whilk] *adds* þat L þam] þe L, ʒou PSR (*over eras.* P) 3631 als] þat R 3635 es] *om.* P þis] *om.* LPR 3638 es] *om.* R 3639 þe] And þe P Fole] foly E 3640 er] *adds* þe L 3641–4 *trs. couplets* L 3642 many] mo P out] *after* þam L, *om.* RW 3643–4 *lines om.* ES 3643 Vn-] In- R *sidenote*: j^a.] *om.* ELPSW

Vnfaythfulnes has braunches thre;
Rusticitas Vilany þe first may be.
Obliuio beneficiorum þat es forgetyng, þat a man,
þat right witte and gode skille can,
To thank Godde forgetes sone
Of al þe gode þat he has him done.
Demencia þe tothir may be Wodenes talde,
When a man to spende es balde
His tyme wrange of yhouth and elde
And wate him bihoues acount yhelde.
Apostasia Fals Renayinge es þe thridde,
When a man with þe fende es ledde
So þat he his lorde forsake
And to his lordes enemy him take.
A renayed man men comonly calles
Hym þat in dedely synne falles,
Bot specially to our knawynge
In thre thinges may be Renayinge.
þat es when any Crysten wight
Forsakes and haldes noght þe trouth right,
Or thurgh athe þe trouth forsweres,
Or trowes in oght þat fals trouth beres.
ij^{a}. Contemptus þe secund rote es Dispyte,
þat in thre partys spredes tyte.
Ane es when men prayse ne wille
Othir in hert, als falles bi skille,
Bot of þam has grete dedeyne,
Al-if þai fals continaunce feyne.
When men wil noght for honure dwelle
To do þe reuerence þat men felle,
Or when men wil noght bouxsomly do

3646 may] þat may L *sidenote om.* LS 3647 þat[2]] when R *sidenote*: beneficiorum] benefactorum ELS 3648 witte] *adds* haues L 3649 To] Of W 3650 þat] *om.* P 3651 talde] calde SPR *sidenote*: Demencia] Semencia L 3652 When] When þat L spende] spede R 3653 of] in ELS 3654 wate] what RW 3655 *sidenote*: Apostasia] Apostaria ELPS 3656 es] *after* man P 3657 he] *after* lorde P forsake] forsaykes R 3658 lordes] lorde EL him] he hym L take] takys R 3659 renayed] reniand R comonly] comly R 3660 Hym] A man L 3661 to] in L 3663 any] a L 3664 þe] his E 3665 athe] athes L 3666 fals] to fals L, þe W 3667 *sidenote*: *om.* W ij^{a}.] ij^{us}. ramus L, *om.* EP 3668 partys] partes L spredes] *adds* oute L 3669 Ane] And W prayse] peyse R 3672 þai] þaim P, þe R 3674 þe] *om.* LP men] þaime L

To þam þat men suld bowe vnto.
For Vnbouxsomnes first springes *Inobediencia*
Out of Dispyte þat on Pryde hinges.
Vnbouxsomnes som wil noght layne

Donum Timoris De Superbia Sed libera nos a malo

Agayne Godde and his souerayne. fo. 23va
Vnto Godde men suld do ay
Al þe worshepe þat men may
And to his halowes reuerence
And to þair souerayne obedience.
And whaso dose noght, he es to wyte;
Methink he has in hert Dispyte.
Bot comonly na man synnes
þat ne he it thurgh Dispyte bigynnes,
For ilka dedely synne es wroght
Thurgh Dispyte in dede or thoght.
þe thridde rote es Surquydry *iij^{a}. Presumpcio*
þat shewes it oft appertly
In som men þat wald be sene
When þai wrange of þamself wene.
For þai gesce þam of mare prys
þan þai ere, or othir als wys.
þis es þe largest rote of þe seuen
þat sex braunches shotes out euen.
þe first braunche Syngulerte es,
þat es to say self-willefulnes;
Anothir es thurgh pomp and outrage
A Fole Vndirtakynge of costage.
Fole Mayntenaunce es þe thridde
Of motynges and strifs þat wyde er spredde.

3676 men] þai E men suld] *trs.* R vnto] to LPS 3677 Vn-] vm- L *sidenote:* ⟨ ⟩obedia P, *om.* SW 3679 Vn-] Vm- L 3682 men] þai R 3683 his] *om.* W halowes] *adds* do EL 3684 þair] þaim W souerayne] soueraynes L 3685 he] *om.* L es to wyte] vsys wyce R 3686 Dispyte] dispice R 3688 ne] *om.* LPS, *after* it R it] *om.* LSW dispyte] dispice R, spite W 3690 Dispyte] dispice R or] or in S, and W 3691 *sidenote*: iij^{a}.] *om.* ELW, *in gutter* P iij^{a}. Presumpcio] *trs.* S 3692 it] *om.* P appertly] aperly W 3694 þai] þat R wene] bene R 3695 of] in (*over eras.*) P 3696 ere] *om.* R or] *om.* P 3697 þe^{2}] *om.* RW 3698 þat] þareof L euen] full euen L 3699 syngulerte] syngulert R 3701 thurgh] *om.* P 3702 Fole] foly E Vndir-] undun-? W 3704 motynges] motyng PSW strifs] strife P, stryuyng W wyde] ferr L spredde] kyde ELPS

þe ferthe braunche es Fole Vauntyng;
þe fift I halde es Skornynge.
þe sext Frawardnes es called
þat many men in hert wil halde.
Singularitas First Singuler⟨te⟩ es þis bi skille:
When a man folwes his awen wille
And noght wil do als wyser dose,
Bot his awen wille for pompe and rose.
Prodigalitas Anothir es Fole Vndirtakynge
Of outrageous dispendynge:
When a man mas grete outrage
And lettes for na grete costage,
Forþi þat men suld thurgh þat skille
Hym halde mare large and fre of wille.
Aggressio licium et querelarum þe thridde braunche es Mayntenaunce
Of motynges and striues þat falle[s] ochaunce.

Donum Timoris De Superbia Sed libera nos a malo

fo. 23vb *Nota Salamon* For Salamon says þat motynge and strif
Amange proude men es ay ful rif.
Iactancia Vauntynge es aftir þe ferth talde.
þat es when a man waxes so balde
To avaun[t]e him of his noblesce,
Of his witte or of his ritches,
Or of his vertus or of his foly,
Or of his myght or his maystry,
Or of oght þat neuer was sene;
And mas men bi hym so to wene,
Forthy þat men suld him noble halde

3705 fole] foly P vauntyng] avaunseyng L 3706 I . . . es] may wele be calde L, ys cald R es] *om.* P 3707 es] *after* sext P 3709 singulerte] -te *rubbed or erased* A, syngulert R *sidenote*: *adds* j. E, *om.* P 3713 es] *adds* a L Fole] full S -takynge] -standynge R *sidenote*: *adds* ij. E, *om.* P 3714 outrageous] contrarius L, outerages S 3715 a man] þat a L 3716 grete] *om.* L 3717 Forþi] Forwhy S suld] *om.* E thurgh] for L, by P 3718 halde . . . large] large halde S 3719 mayntenaunce] maynteaunces W *sidenote om.* W 3720 motynges] motyng LPW and] of P striues] stryuynges S, stryuyng W *falles] falle A o-] þurgh L 3721 motyng] motynges S *sidenote*: *om.* SW Nota] *om.* ELP 3722 men] *om.* E es ay] *trs.* P ay] *om.* LR 3723 Vauntynge] Avauntyng LS talde] cald R *sidenote*: *adds* iiij. E, *om.* S 3725 *avaunte] avaunce AE noblesce] nobellnes LSR 3727 Or^{1}] *om.* P vertus] vertew LW 3728 or^{2}] or of ELPSRW 3729 neuer] euer R 3730 so] *before* bi LS

For pomp and loos þat he haf walde.
Or to losengeours þat can make dyn
Gyues giftes for loos þareby to wyn.
  þe fift braunche after es Skornynge; *Derisio*
þat es when a man mas hethynge
Of othir men thurgh grete nycete
þat has noght vertus als has he,
And of gode men of gode renoun
For þat þai do þair deuocioun.
  þe sext braunche nest folwand *Rebellio*
Es Frawardnes to vnderstande;
þat es, als I wil yhow telle,
When a man es fraward and felle
And wrath als men [did hym] vilany,
When men hym snybbes of his foly.
Bot he es ful seke, liggand on couche,
þat may thole na man him touche,
And strange sekenes es in hym
When treacle turnes hym to venym.
  þe ferthe rote, als clerkes wate, *iiij. Ambicio*
Es Yhernynge namely of Heghe State,
þat bi twa partys shewes his myght,
Bathe bi þe left syde and bi þe right.
On þe right syde, it passes sleghely
Thurgh giftes and spenses and losengery,
Als when a man couaytes baylly,
To haue powere and maystry,
He dose alle þat he may do
Thurgh procurynge to com þarto.
On þe left syde þus may it hynge

3733 to] vnto L 3734 Gyues] Gyfe RW 3735 *sidenote*: *adds* v. E, *om.* P 3736 hethynge] hethynges S 3737 men] *om.* L 3738 als] I as R 3739 gode] gret P 3741 *sidenote*: *adds* vj. E, *om.* P 3743 wil] sall L telle] *om.* W 3745 And] As R wrath] wrethes L *did hym] *trs.* AW, did `hym´ P 3746 of] for L 3747 on] in L couche] couthe SR 3749 strange sekenes] *trs.* E 3751 rote] es L *sidenote*: *om.* P iiij.] *om.* ELW 3752 Es] Is þe R namely] *om.* R 3754 bi[2]] *om.* R þe[2]] *om.* E 3755 *line after 3758* L 3756–7 *lines om.* ES 3756 and[2]] to L, of RW losengery] losengeres L 3757 a man] men L couaytes] couatyce R baylly] balyes L 3758 and] and grete R 3759 dose] *adds* þan R 3761 On] In E

De Superbia

fo. 24ra Thurgh falshede and backebytynge,
Als when a man anothir deres
þat office or power beres,
And es bisy to brynge hym doun
Thurgh falshede or thurgh tresoun.
For he couaytes oboun hym be
And to haue here mare powere þan he.
v. Vana gloria þe fift rote es Vayneglory
þat in mans hert springes lightly.
Vayneglory es nane othir thinge
Bot in hert a vayne lykynge
Of thinge thurgh whilk men may loos wyn,
Bot som men charges litell þat syn.
Men may him rightly a fole calle,
For he reues Godde þat him suld falle.
To Godde falles louynge and worshepe
For þe godes þat we of hym kepe,
And to vs falles þe auauntage;
He þat yhernes mare dose outrage.
Bot bi som skille can I fynde
þat Vayneglory may be called a wynde
þat blawes alle maner of men doun,
Bathe men of þe werlde and of religyoun.
With Vayneglory felled es he
þat has likynge of vanyte;
And whaso loos yhernes for gode dede,
He sal neuer haf othir mede.
Thurgh Vayneglory to vndirstande
þe fende bicomes a marchande,
þat he haldes his mone of prys
Thurgh whilke he mas his marchandys.
He wendes obout on ilka syde

3762 and] and thurgh R 3764 or] or gret R 3766 or] and P 3767 be] to be ELS 3768 to] *om.* L here] *om.* L þan] and L 3769 *sidenote*: *om.* W v.] *om.* ELPS 3773 thurgh] by P whilk] skyll L 3774 men] man P charges] charge R 3775 rightly] lyghtly LR 3776 For] þat P him] to hym L 3777 louynge] louenyng L 3779 þe] *om.* P 3780 dose] he dose L 3782 may be] es L *sidenote*: Nota E 3783 of] *om.* P 3785 vayneglory] glory wayn R felled] filled R 3786 of] in L 3787 for] of W 3789 to] I L 3792 his] *om.* L

Thurgh þe fayr of þis werlde wyde
þe druryse of ilka man to bie
With þe mone of Vayneglory.
þa drurys bene mens gode dedes,
Wharefore þe fende þat mone bedes.
A grete foly methinke dose he
þat selles his godes for þat mone.
Forthy many men aght to be sory
þat lufs þat mone of Vayneglory.

De Superbia

On thre maners, als I telle can, fo. 24rb
Vayneglory deceyues a man.
Ane es when he es gladde in thoght
Of gode dedes þat he has wroght
And thinkes hym pryuyer þan he es
With Godde, anely for his godenes.
Anothir es when a man heres
þat men prayses his maners
And has a lykynge in hert þan
For men hym haldes a gode man.
þe thridde es when a man him spedes
With al his myght to do gode dedes,
Forþi þat he suld praysed be
With alle þat his dedes may se.
þe sext rote es Ipocrysy; *vj. Ipocrisis*
þat shewes som men ouercomonly.
For when a man shewes halynes
Mare withouten þan withinne es
And wers withinne es þan he semes,
Als ipocryte men hym right demes.
Bot I fynde wryten apertly

3795 to] for to R   3797 þa] þe R   3798 bedes] ledys PR   3800 godes] gude dedes P   3801 Forthy] For þis L, For PRW   men] man LW   3802 þat²] þe LR   3803 On thre] Other E   als] *om.* L, þat P   3804 Vayneglory] How vayneglory L   a] *om.* L   3807 thinkes] thynk P   pryuyer] pryuer L   he] is he P   3808 With Godde] Right good R   -nes] dedes L   3809 a] *om.* L   3811 a] *om.* P   3812 hym] þaime L   hym haldes] *trs.* LS   3815 Forthi] Bycause P   suld praysed] *trs.* LS   3816 alle] *adds* men L, *om.* W   may] myght S   3817 *sidenote*: *om.* L   vj.] *om.* PSW   3818 som men] sommen R   men] *om.* W   ouer-] *om.* R   3821 es] *om.* W   he] hym P   3822 right] *om.* R, *before* men W   3823 apertly] specialy R

Thre maner of Ipocrysy.
Ane es foul þat semes ille,
Anothir fole, þe thridde sutille.
Feda Ipocrisis Foul Ipocrisy may þis be
When a man in priuite
Dose foul synne and reckes neuer when
And semes clene bifore alle men.
Stulta Ipocrisis Fole Ipocrisy es þis called right
When a man with al his myght
Dose gode dedes for men suld wene
þat he war a gode man and a clene.
Subtilis Ipocrisis Suttill Ipocrisy, als I halde,
Es when a man wynne wald
Outhir dignite or benefyce
Or baylif or any offyce,
He beres hym wele and mekely
To make men wene he war worthy
Swilk a grete state for to take,
Als man þat es withouten lake.
Bot when he to þat state may wynne,

Donum Timoris De Superbia De Humilitate

fo. 24va þan he shewes what he es withinne.
He waxes þan bathe felle and stout
And puttes fast his venym out
In pryde and in othir wickednes;
þan may men knawe what he es.
First als a shepe he mas him be sene,
And þareafter he semes a wolf kene;
Bot men may knawe bi þe fruyt þat springes
What þe tree es þat it forth bringes.
Stulta Verecundia þe seuent rote es Fole Shame,

3824 maner] maners L 3825 þat] and S 3826 fole] ys fole R 3828 a] any R 3829 foul] full R synne] synnes L and] þat R reckes] rekenes W 3831 Fole] Foule S þis] he R *sidenote*: Occulta W 3835 als] es als L *sidenote om.* W 3836 Es when] When þat L, Is where W 3838 baylif] baylslyfe E, balyschipp L, baylly PRW any] *adds* grete R, *adds* oþer W 3840 make] gerre L he] *om.* W 3842 man] many E 3843 þat] þe W may] *after* he R 3844 he shewes] *trs.* LR 3845 felle] ⟨h.lle⟩ L 3846 fast] *adds* þan L 3848 knawe] *adds* wele R 3849 be] to be L 3850 þare-] þan P he] hym W 3852 it] *om.* LP 3853 *sidenote*: *adds* vij. E, *om.* W

Wharethurgh a man es worthy blame
þat lettes to do any gode dede
In sight of men for shame or drede.
For when a man in mens sight
Lettes for shame to do þat es right,
Or any dede þat to Godde may pay
For any speche þat men may say,
þan dose he noght Goddis wille
Bot pleises þe werlde—he dose ille.
I halde hym þat na bettir þan wode
þat leues for shame to do gode.
For þat seruaunt es worthy haf blame
þat lettes to serue his lorde for shame.
Bot som es ouerbalde and hardy
To haunt þair synne ay appertly,
And nouthir has here shame na drede
To do in sight a wicked dede.
þat may men calle Folehardynes
þat a part of þe seuent rote es.
þise seuen rotes spredes wyde
þat comes out of þe stock of Pryde.
þe whilk stocke with alle his rotes
þe Gift of Drede out of þe hert shotes
And settes Mekenes in þat stede—
þat es of alle vertus þe hede.
Of þis vertu I wil yhow telle
A party, if þat yhe wil dwelle.

De virtute Humilitatis

Mekenes has seuen degrees *De Humilitate*
And seuen braunches þat men suld chese.

3854 -thurgh] by P worthy] worth L 3856 In] For R for] *om.* R 3857 mens] mans L 3858 þat] þat at R 3859 þat to] to do þat L þat . . . Godde] to god þat S 3861 Goddis] godses S 3862 he] and LR he dose] þen dose he P ille] full ille LR 3863 þat] *om.* PR 3864 leues] lettes ELR to] for to R 3865 worthy] *om.* L haf] to L, *om.* PR 3867 ouer-] euer R 3868 þair] þat L ay] *om.* P 3871 may] many ER calle] calles E 3872 seuent] seuen L 3873 þise] þe L wyde] full wyde LR 3878 es] *after* vertus LR vertus] vertuous R 3879 I . . . yhow] will I now R 3880 A party] Apertly P if þat] of þat if L, if P 3880a *om.* ELPSRW 3881 *sidenote*: *om.* LW, *as in-column heading* R 3882 suld] sall P

De Humilitate Sed libera nos a malo

fo. 24vb Bot first I wil þe degrees neuen
And afterwarde þe braunches seuen.
þe first degre may be þis,
þat when a man knawes his mysse
And his defautes and his freilte,
þan bigynnes he meke to be,
Bernardus Als Saynt Bernard beres wittenes.
'Mekenes', he says, 'swilk a vertu es
þat it mas a man himseluen dispyse,
When he knawes what in him lyse'.
Bot som wate þair defautes wele,
Bot þai can noght þam pleyn ne fele.
  þarefore þe secund degree suld falle
þat a man suld fele his defautes alle.
For he þat feles sare, hym mekes
And blethely til a gode leche sekes;
When he feles filthes within him byte,
He wald fayne it cast out tyte.
  þarefore þe thridde degre es þis,
þat he suld shryue hym of his mysse.
Bot som þam shryues and sighes sare
Bot þai wald nane wist how ille þai ware.
  þarefore þe ferthe es þis bi skille,
þat a man suld yherne to be halden ille.
Bot som feles wele þair foly
And says, 'Na man es so ille als I'.
Bot if ane say, 'Ful sothe saystow',
He wald be wrathe, als I trow.
  þarefore þe fift es on þis manere
A man suld blethely his defautes here.

3883 I wil] *trs.* R degrees] grese W 3887 defautes] defaute L his²] *om.* P 3888 þan] *adds* he S 3889 Als] And ELS *sidenote*: Nota Bene P, *om.* W 3891 it] *om.* LPW a man] *om.* R dispyse] despyces E, to dispyse L 3892 him] hymselfe LS 3893 som] *om.* P þair] þan W 3894 can] *om.* W noght] *after* pleyn W þam] þai L, *om.* R 3897 feles] fele R 3898 blethely] *om.* W 3899 filthes] fylthe L within] in ELS, with P 3900 He wald] þan wald he R 3901 -fore] *om.* L þe] *om.* R 3903 þam] þat P and] þat E 3904 Bot þai wald] Wald þat P þai²] it L ware] fare W 3906 yherne to] *om.* L 3907 Bot] *om.* L som] some mene E wele] fully L 3908 na . . . es] þare es nane L 3909 say] sayde LSR ful] *om.* L 3910 wrathe] *add* þan LR 3911 þarefore] þan L, Wharefore S 3912 defautes] fautes L

For Saynt Bernard þat Godde oft payde *Bernardus*
Says þus, als I herebifore sayde,
þat þe verray meke man wald be
Halden vyle þat men myght se
And noght be praysed als þe meke,
Forwhy he wil na loos seke.
  þarefore þe sext comes aftir tyte,
þat þe meke suld suffre dispyte,
Als Dauid did, þat was king of myght, *Dauid*
þat tholed his seruaunt þat Semay ight
Reuyle him foully and at him cast,
And al suffird he with hert stedfast.

De Humilitate

  þarefore es þis þe seuent degre fo. 25ra
þat þe verray meke with hert fre
Suld yherne ay, withouten fayntyse,
þat men hym reuyle and dispyse.
þis may men calle, right als it es,
þe heght mast of Parfytenes.
þat es verray Mekenes of Hert
þe whilk es called Gastly Pouert.
þarefore sayd Godde, of myght mast,
'Blissed be þe pouere in gast'.
  Here haf I tolde þe degrees seuen;
Now wil I þe seuen braunches neuen
þat springes out of Mekenes right
þat we suld haunt bathe day and night.
Ane es to honure Godde anely,
Bathe with hert and with body.
Anothir es to prayse ilk man;
þe thridde es to lack ourself þan;

3913 Godde oft] *trs.* LS (*marg corr.* L) *sidenote om.* PW 3914 I] *om.* W here] *after* bifore E, *om.* L bifore] *adds* hafe P 3915 þe] he R 3917 þe] for L 3918 Forwhy] For L 3919 comes] come L 3921 *sidenote om.* LPW 3922 þat tholed] He sufferde L 3923 foully] foule PW at] atte E 3924 suffird he] *trs.* LPRW 3925 es þis] he ys R 3927 withouten] *add* any LS 3930 heght] heghest S, heghe RW mast] and þe (*om.* S) maste LS 3931 verray] called L 3932 þe whilk] þat P called] *om.* L 3933 sayd] says W myght] myghtes LPSR 3934 gast] þe gost W 3936 þe seuen braunches now wyll I neuen L 3937 þat] þe whilk R 3939 Ane] And W to] *om.* P 3941 es] *om.* W to] *om.* L

þe ferthe to luf pouert bi skille;
þe fift es to serue with gode wille;
þe sext to fle of alle loos þe cry;
þe seuent to trayst in Godde anely.
Wele es hym þat lufs to wirke
þise seuen poyntes and es noght irke.
  þe first braunche es, als I tolde right,
To honure Godde, mast of myght.
Bot men may on thre maneres
Honure Godde, als þe boke vs leres:
Ane es thurgh symple trowynge;
Anothir may be thurgh leel louynge;
þe thridde es thurgh deuout prayere.
þise thre maners er gode to lere.
  Thurgh symple trowyng whaso wil
May honure Godde þus bi skille,
þat es if he trowe sympilly
þe wordes of Godde almyghty,
Withouten sekynge of skils to se
How Goddis worde myght so be.
Als dose a chylde þat es yhunge
þat trowes wele his mayster tunge.

De Humilitate

fo. 25rb Thurgh leel louynge yhete men may
Honure Godde; þat es to say
When a man with symple mode
Loues and thankes God of al gode
þat he has done hym, and vouches saue,
And þat he hopes yhete to haue.
Als þe pouer þat in pouert lifs
Es fayne when men him almus gifs;
With al his might, he thankes þam sone
þat hym any gode has done.

3943 to] es to ER 3944 es] *om.* P serue] *add* god LP 3945 to] es to E þe] to W 3946 to] es to E 3948 þise] þe W es] *om.* E 3949 es] *om.* L 3950 To] Es to L 3955 es] may be L 3958 Godde] *om.* R 3961 sekynge] lesyng W skils] skyll L 3962 so] sogatys R 3964 þat] *om.* L 3965 leel] lelel E 3967 with] of L 3969 he] *om.* R 3970 þat] *om.* R to] for to R 3971 Als] And L lifs] lyes L 3972 Es] Er L him] þaim L gifs] bedes L 3973 þam] *om.* P sone] loue W 3974 hym] till hym R

Men may thurgh deuoute prayere
Honure Godde on þe thridde manere,
Als when a man him think vnworthy
And prayes to Godde right hertly
With teres of eghe and hert sare
For he hym feles of godenes bare.
Als a chylde þat naked standes
Bifore his mayster and dredes his handes,
Forthy þat he can noght his lessoun—
Ful hertly prayand kneles he doun.
On þis wyse honures he God þan
þat es þe verray meke man.
þe secund braunche, als þe boke says, *ij.*
Es when a man alle othir wil prayse.
Bot þe meke may prayse in þise thre,
In hert, in mouth, and in dede to se.
In hert he may withouten fayntys
Alle othir men prayse on þis [thre] wise:
He trowes othir mens witte vnknawen
Wele mare þan he dose his awen.
He wil þat othir mens wille
Be mare done þan his awen in skille.
In othir mens vertu mare he traystes
þan in his awen þat he oft fraystes.
In mouth alsso þe meke man
On thre wyse othir men prayse can.
Alle othir mens godenes he liftes heghe
And puttes þam bifore his eghe.
He hydes and excuses ilk mans lacke
And puttes þam ay bihynde his backe.

3975 may] *om.* L 3976 Honure] Sulde honour L 3978 to] *om.* P 3979 eghe] eghen PW 3980 hym] *om.* R 3982 *line om.* R 3983 Forthy þat] For L 3984 kneles] falles S kneles he] *trs.* LP 3985 God] his god R þan] and þan W 3987 *sidenote om.* LPSW 3988 Es] *om.* L a] *torn* L 3989 þise] *om.* L 3990 and] *om.* R 3991 fayntys] any fayntese LS 3992 Alle] Als P men] *om.* L prayse] pryse R þis] oþer R *thre] *om.* AELS, *int. later* P, kyn W 3996 in] by P 3997 vertu] vertus ELR 3998 in] of R 3999 mouth] mekenes L 4000 wyse] maners L 4002 þam] *adds* ay R 4003 ilk mans] othyr menes P mans] mane E 4004 ay] *om.* L, away R

Donum Timoris De Humilitate Sed
libera nos a malo

fo. 25va And alle þat may seme gode and ille
To þe mast gode he turnes bi skille.
In dede þe meke prayses othir ay
On þise thre wyse; þat es to say,
He worshepes othir with gode wille
And dose þam reuerence bi skille.
He serues þam als falles þarto
And dose þam þe gode þat he may do.
He puttes othir bifore hym tyte
Til alle worshepe and profyte.
iij. þe thridde braunche þat Mekenes rayses
Es when a man himself mysprayses.
Bot þe meke man on þe same wyse
Als he prayses othir, himself dispyse.
To dispyse himself he has na drede
In hert, in mouth, and in dede.
In hert þe meke wil blethely
Halde hymself vyle and vnworthy
And noght knawe þe gode þat he has ˋdoneˊ,
Bot bihinde his back puttes it sone.
Of his wickednes he thinkes ay right
And puttes þam bifor him in his sight.
In mouth þe meke himself reproues
Of alle his mysse þat in hert houes.
He snybbes his werkes and his dedes,
His wordes, his thoghtes þat he dredes.
He wreyes hymself thurgh tung swift
Of alle his mysdede oft in shrift.
In dede he hym mysprays wille;

4005 seme] sende? P and^{2}] or L 4006 þe] *om.* L bi] þaim be L 4007 othir] *om.* P 4008 thre] *om.* LR wyse] vyses E to] for to L 4010 And] He L 4012 And] He L 4013 othir] all other L 4014 Til] Vnto L alle] alkyn R worshepe] worschippes L 4015 Mekenes] þe meke L rayses] prayses L *sidenote om.* LPW 4018 dispyse] mysprayses R 4019 he has] *trs.* R 4021 blethely] bletly S 4022 vyle] wyle S, wyll R 4023 noght knawe] *trs.* E, knawes noght P 4024 puttes] putte E, he puttes L 4025 Of] On SR 4026 puttes . . . him] þam b. h. he p. P þam] þan R him] *om.* R his] *om.* P 4028 in] on RW 4029 snybbes] sembles W 4030 þat] all þat L 4032 mysdede] myssededes ELPSRW 4033 he] *om.* R hym] *om.* L

He yheldes þat he awes and dose skille.
He dose penaunce for saul-bote
And puttes his flesshe vndirfote.
Almusdede he dose blethely
And alle þe Werkes of Mercy.
  þe ferthe braunche, als men may proue, *iiij.*
Es when a man wil Pouert luf.
So dose þe verray meke in hert;
On four maners he lufs Pouert.
He lufs pouer mens company
And haldes þe maners of þam haly;

Donum Timoris De Humilitate Sed libera nos a malo

He tholes for Goddis luf and assayse fo. 25vb
Hungre and colde and othir mysays;
He begges prayers, whareso he wendes,
Of gode men þat bene Goddis frendes;
Ritchesce he forsakes right
And flees þam with al his myght.
  Ritchesce suld men hate and fle
For thre skils, als yhe may se:
For perils þat in Ritches hynges;
For þe godes þat of Pouert springes;
For Godde himself wald Pouert fele—
þarefore suld men luf it wele.
  þe fift braunche es to serue blethly, *v.*
Als when a man es ay redy
To serue þe nedefull als he can—
So dose þe verray meke man.
To serue and helpe him es right lief
Alle þat has nede and meschief.
þe meke als wele wil hym hast

4034 awes] awe EPSRW, aght L dose] *add* þat is PR 4035 for] for þe L 4036 vndir-] ay vndir his R 4037 -dede] -dedes L 4038 werkes] dedes S 4039 *sidenote om.* LPSW 4044 maners] maner W 4047 prayers] prays RW -so] -sum L 4048 Goddis] god R 4050 þam] fra þaime L with] in L 4052 skils] thinges L yhe] men LW 4053 perils] perel W 4054 For] And for L þe] *om.* P godes] gode LS 4055 For] And L, And for R 4056 þarefore] And þarefore L, For þes skils R 4057 *sidenote om.* ELPSW 4059 nedeful] nedy L 4061 him es] *trs.* P, hym as W right] full L 4062 nede and] any L and] *adds* gret R 4063 hym] help in P

To serue þe leste als þe mast,
Als Godde did þat sympilly lete
When he wesshe his disciples fete.
He gaf vs ensaumple to knawe
To be bouxsom and bere vs lawe.
Bot Mekenes þe meke man leres
To bowe and serue in aght maners.
þe meke him boghes to serue redily
And sympilly with al his body,
And clenly and wele in alle thinge,
And trewely withouten fayllynge,
And comonly with al his myght,
And wightly with gode hert and light,
And stalwardely whareso he wende,
And lastandely to his lyues ende.
þe meke him lawes to serue redyly,
Als þe shipman þat es ay redy
When he has nede, to rynne and skippe
Als he war wode, to gouerne þe shippe.
þe meke hym lawes to serue sympilly,
Als dose þe shepe þat es noght wyly,

De Humilitate

fo. 26ra þat mekely gase withouten stryue
Whider`so´ þe hirde hym wil dryue.
þe meke hym lawes to serue clenely,
Bathe with hert and with al his body,
For he hates nathinge here so mykill
Als to plese þe werlde þat es fikill.
þe meke him lawes to serue trewely,
Als dose þe gode bouxsom lauedy,
þat in foly wil na man plese
Bot to hire lorde anely, for his ese.

4064 als] and P *sidenote*: Nota P 4065 sympilly] symple W 4066 disciples] apostles L 4068 bere] to bere E 4071 meke] mekes W 4074 trewely] *adds* and W 4075 with] at L 4077 stalwardely] stalworly R whareso he] whar he shall R wende] wendes L, to wende R 4078 lyues] lyfe LR ende] endes L 4080 es ay] *trs.* R ay] *om.* S 4081 When] And L and] and to L 4084 noght wyly] ay redy W 4086 Whiderso] Whidir R hirde] hyrdman R hym wil] *trs.* ELSRW 4088 with^2] *om.* L with al] als with R 4089 nathinge here] *trs.* ELPSRW 4090 es] *add* sa LP 4092 gode] *om.* R 4094 to] *om.* R lorde] *om.* P

þe meke hym lawes to serue comonly,
Als dose þe asse þat beres oft heuy,
þat beres als blethely barly als whete,
And als fast for smale gase als for grete,
And als blethely beres stanes als brede
And lede or iren als golde rede.
þe meke him lawes to serue wightly,
Als he þat es light and semy,
When Bouxsomnes him ledes in state
And Goddis wille with his prelate.
þe meke him lawes to serue stalwardly,
Als he þat es strange and myghty
þat al his strengthe thurgh Mekenes
To Goddis strengthe chaunges þat mast es.
þe meke him lawes to serue lastandly,
Als he þat es neuer wery
To boghe hym ay vnto Mekenes
And na mare wery þan þe sonne es,
þat euer þe mare he ryses on lengthe,
Ay þe mare gaders his strengthe.
þe sext braunche es þis to se, *vj.*
Als when a man wil loos fle,
Als dose þe man þat Mekenes ledes
For twa thinges þat he dredes—
For þe wynde of Vayneglory shille
And for þe tempest of tung þat es ille.
First for þe wynde of Vayneglory
þe meke man flees loos sleghely,

De Humilitate

Als God did when he þe folk had fedde fo. 26rb
And held þe seke—fra þam he fledde,
And til a mountayne droghe him nere

4097 blethely] gladly ELS barly] lede L 4098 fast] oft P gase] *after* fast ELSR smale] a smal W for[2]] *om.* S, a W 4099 blethely] wele L 4100 or] and L 4101 wightly] mekely W 4109 lawes] boghes L, laes W 4110 es neuer] *trs.* LSR neuer] neuermare ELR 4111 *line om.* R boghe] boo W vnto] into W 4112 wery] ys wery R 4113 euer] *om.* R he] hyt W 4114 gaders] he geders LR, geders he S his] *om.* R 4115 braunche] *om.* L *sidenote om.* LSW 4117 þe] a W þat] wham R 4118 þat] es þat L dredes] gretely dredys R 4119 shille] shyrlle E, stylle L, þis skill P 4120 þe] *om.* R 4123 þe] *om.* E, ys R

For he wald na loos þan here.
In orysouns þare wald he be
To teche vs how we suld loos fle.
  For tempest of tunge þe meke man
Also flees loos als he can,
Als dose a mayden, in hir flours
Þat lufs a man paramours,
Shames als tyte als sho may witt
Þat any man persayues itte.
So dose `þe´ meke when he heres
Þat men spekes of his maners.
Þan sekes he to places pryue
And to hirnes, loos for to fle.
Þare may he be in pees and rest
And speke with his twa frendes best,
With Godde and with himself anely,
And þan has he a siker company.
Þare may he dresce him to Godde right soght
And Godde to hym thurgh haly thoght;
Þare fyndes he swetnes of solace
Þat Godde him gifs in priue place.
vij.   Þe seuent braunche es þis to frayst,
Ouer alle thinge in Godde to trayst.
So dose þe meke in wham hope hinges;
He traystes in Godde thurgh twa thinges,
Thurgh haly conscience to se
And thurgh hardynes of hert fre.
  He traystes thurgh haly conscience
When he thinkes on Goddis presence
And es rauyst to heuen heghe

4126 For] For þat R   wald . . . þan] of na lose walde L, na losse wold R   4127 orysouns] orysoun LR   þare] þat W   he] *om.* E   4128 loos] louyng L   4129 For] Fra L   tunge] tonges R   4130 Also flees] *trs.* R   loos als] in all þat L, losse in þat R   4131 mayden] mayde W   in hir flours] `þat is´ amerous P   4132 man] *adds* wele R   4133–6 *lines om.* W   4133 Shames] Hir shames R   tyte] sone L   4134 persayues] persayue R   4135 þe] *int. later* A   meke] meke man LR   4136 of] on S   4137 To pryue places þan sekys he R   4138 to[1]] vntill R   for] *om.* SW   4141 with[2]] *om.* L   4142 has he] *trs.* W   4143 he . . . him] drese he hym R   dresce him] *trs.* W   4145 solace] vlace R   4146 him gifs] hymselfe es L   4147 to] *om.* W   *sidenote om.* LSW   4149 hope] help W   4152 fre] so fre R   4153 thurgh] of L   4154 on] of L   4155–6 *lines trs.* ER   4155 es] *om.* P   heghe] so heghe R

Thurgh haly thoght with gastly eghe.
þan seese he þe werld lytell þat tyde
Vnto regarde of heuen so wyde.
He sees it foul thurgh þe ayre
To regarde of heuen so fayre;
Ful vgly semes it to his sight

Donum Timoris De Humilitate Sed libera nos

To regarde of heuen so bright, fo. 26va
And al voyde semes þe werld to be
To regarde of þe grete plente
þat he sees in heuenryke,
Of allekyn gode þat þe hert may like.
þan bigynnes he þe werlde dispyse
For him think it noght bot fayntyse.
þan hates he alle þe ritchesce
Of þe werlde and alle þe nobillesce,
For when he sees it al sammen
Hym think it noght bot a barne-gammen,
Or als a dreme in his slepe.
þan forsakes he þe werldes worshepe.
  Thurgh hardynes of hert stable,
He traystes in Godde so mercyable
When he dar habyde so wele
þe angres of þe werlde and fele,
And allekyns noyes thole and proue
Or take þe dede for Goddis luf.
  þe seuen braunches now haf I redde
þat in þe meke mans hert er spredde.
Alle þai sprynge, bathe mare and lesse,
Out of þe vertu of Mekenes

4157 þan] And S he] *om.* S 4158 Vnto] Ta P, To W regard] warde P, þe regarde R, begard W 4160 To] Vnto LR regarde] þe regarde R 4161 to] vnto L 4162 To] Vnto L, As to R 4163 voyde] wode W 4164 To] Vnto L, As to R þe] þat L, *om.* R 4165 sees] þan seys R 4166 þe hert] *om.* L, hert W 4167 dispyse] to despyse LS 4168 noght] *om.* L fayntyse] fantasyce E 4169 hates he] *trs.* P alle þe] alkyn L, all W 4170 alle þe] *om.* L nobillesce] nobilnes PR 4172 Hym think] He thynkes W it] *om.* P noght] *om.* L 4173 als] elles L in] here in E his] a P 4174 þe] *om.* PR 4175 hardy-] harde- E 4177 When] When þat L 4179 noyes] noye EP 4181 seuen braunches] seuent braunche ELRW 4183 Alle] As R 4184 Out] *om.* L

þat ledes a man bi þe right way
To þe blissedhede, þat es to say,
Of Gastly Pouert þat God pays
And to his mede, als God þus says,

Beati pauperes spiritu, quoniam ipsorum est regnum celorum

'Blissed be þe pouer in gast,
For heuenryke þairs es mast'.
Here may men se, whaso tas hede,
Whareof serues þe Gift of Drede.
It es `þe´ last þat we craue,
Bot it es þe first þat we suld haue.

Sed libera nos a malo

þat gift may þe seuent askynge
Of þe Pater Noster to vs brynge,
þat may vs fra alle ille defende
þe whilk gift Ihesu Cryst vs sende.
Amen

Donum Pietatis

fo. 26vb *De dono Pietatis*

Anothir gift yhete may we gette,
Als here in þis boke es sette,
þat after þe Gift of Drede suld be,
And þat es þe Gift of Pyte,
þe whilk þe sext askyng may wyn vs
In þe Pater Noster so precius.
þis Gift of Pyte es swilke a grace
þat to Charyte it may vs chace,
And our hertes so strengthe and fest fast
þat na fandynge vs may doun cast.
þis Gift of Pyte es ful myghty;
It puttes away þe synne of Envye
Out of þe hert þar it es inne
And settes Frenship in stede of þat synne.

4185 þe] *om.* LP 4188 to] vnto L, *om.* W 4189 *sidenote om.* LPW 4190 þairs] to þaim E, þaire LS 4191 Here] þare L men] ȝe P 4192 serues] it serues PR gift] gyftes W 4193 þe] *int. later* A 4195 *sidenote om.* LPW 4196 to] vntill R 4198a *om.* P 4200 in . . . es] ys in þis bok PR þis] þe L 4202 þat] *om.* P 4202–3 *lines trs.* E 4203 þe sext askyng] sex askynges L wyn vs] *trs.* W 4206 to] vnto L 4207 our . . . fast] str. o. h. and f. s. f. P 4209 þis] þe R 4210 It] And ELS 4212 þat] *om.* W

De peccato Inuidie *De Inuidia*

Envye in thre partys may sprede,
In hert, in mouth, and in dede.
In hert it spredes thurgh thre thinges
þat in þe envyous mans hert hynges.
A Fals Demynge þe first thynge es;
þe tothir es a Wicked Gladdenes;
þe thridde es a Fole Forthinkynge—
þise thre out of Envie may springe.
A Fals Demyng may þis wele be,
When þe envyus may here or se
þe godenes of anothir man
And in hert demes hym falsely þan.
A Wicked Gladdenes þis men calles,
When ioy in a mans hert falles
Of othir mens noye or greuaunce,
Or of any harme þat comes thurgh chaunce.
A Fole Forthynkynge es þis called,
When a man in hert wil halde
Outhir murnynge, dole, or care
For any othir mens welefare.
Envye also spredes in mouthe
Thurgh thre thinges þat er couthe,
Thurgh Myssayinge and Bitternes;
Thurgh Backbytynge, þat þe thridde es.
For at þe dosill men may knawe

De Inuidia

What likour es in þe tunne to drawe. fo. 27ra
Missayinge of mouth first es þis,
When a man spekes oght amysse
Of any othir mens godenes

4212a *om.* ELSW, De Inuidia PR *sidenote*: Inuidia E, *om.* LSW 4215 spredes] springes L thre] *om.* P 4216 mans] man LP 4217 A Fals] Fals P 4220 Envie] þe envye mane E may] moun W 4222 wele] *om.* P 4224 And] þat L 4225 Gladdenes] gladyng ELS 4226 a] any R 4227 noye] angre R 4228 Or] þat L 4229 es þis] may þis be L; *trs.* P þis] ys R 4230 When] When þat L a] any R 4232 any] ay S othir] *om.* P mens] mans LPR 4234 couthe] full couthe LR 4236 þat] *om.* LP es] þat es L 4237 at] in L 4240 When] When þat L a] any R spekes oght] *trs.* R amysse] of mysse LPS, myse RW 4241 Of] Of any P

And paynes hym to make it lesse.
Bitternes es þis bi skille,
When a man heres of othir men ille,
He ekes it and maas it mare
And dose it be knawen wydewhare.
Backebytynge es þis to say,
When a man spekes ille ay
And turnes al þat he may here
Of othir men to þe werst manere.
 In dede spredes also Envye
Thurgh thre thinges specially,
Thurgh Restreynyng of gode bigunne,
Thurgh Fordoynge of gode þat es wonne,
Thurgh Dressynge of wycked wyles—
At þise thre þe fende oft smyles.
Restreynyng may be þis, to lacke,
When þe envyous puttes obacke
A man þat has gode bigynnynge
And wil do wele in alle thynge,
Bathe to Godde and to ilke a man;
Hym lettes þe envyous als he can.
A Fordoinge men may þis telle,
When he þat es envious and felle
Distroys anothir man thurgh myght
Þat to Godde and man dose right.
Dressynge of wyles þat er wycke
Þat in þe envyous man may stycke
Agayne gode men, þat es to abate
Þair gode name and þair state,
Þe whilk þe envyous, nyght and day,
Waytes to fordo in al þat he may.
 Men may licken þe envyous
Vntill a worme þat es venemous

4242 to] for to R 4244 othir men] another mans L men] mennes PS 4245 it] it sone R 4246 it] *om.* S 4249 turnes] turnes aye E 4250 to] on R werst] wers L 4251 spredes also] *trs.* LP 4253 Restreynyng] restrenenyng S, restroyng R bigunne] to bygynne E, bigynnyng P 4254 þat es wonne] wynnyng P 4255 Thurgh] And thurghe R 4256 oft] *om.* PR oft smyles] syn hyles W 4257 Restreynyng] Refrenynge R be þis] *trs.* LPRW 4258 When] When he P 4260 wil do wele] wele dose L 4264 envious] ane envyouse man L 4266 to] god to S, ay to R 4268 þat] *om.* RW þe] *om.* W man] mannes hert PRW 4270 þair] Bath þar R state] astate L 4271 þe] *om.* P 4274 Vntill] To W

þat clerkes calles on Latyn þus,
Als þe boke says, *basiliscus*.
þe whilk distroys, als men has sene,
þe gresse þat growes when it es grene,
And namely a thinge, als we se,
þat es þe corne þat has states thre.
First þe corne semes a gresse
þat waxes ay mare and noght lesse;
Sithen it spyres and florisches fayr

Et ne nos inducas in temptacionem

Thurgh vertu and thurgh kynde of þe ayre. fo. 27rb
þareafter bicomes it corne rype,
Bathe for to bery and for to strype.
þe gresse bitokens, þat first suld springe,
A man þat has gode bigynnynge
To do wele, als his hert es sette;
And þat wil þe envyous man lette,
Als dose þe worme withinne a stound
þat lettes þe gresse þat growes on ground.
þe florisshynge to se and fele
Bitokens a man þat dose here wele.
Agayne hym es þe envyous boun
To distroy hym and brynge hym doun,
Als þe worme dose thurgh his myght
þat distroys þe grysse þat florisshes right.
þe rype corne þat es in sesoun
Bitokens gode men of renoun.
Agayne þam þe envious man
Sekes alle þe wyles þat he can
To fordo here þair gode fame
And to brynge þam til a werldes shame.
For þe mare þat gode men dose wele,
þe mare sorow þe envious may fele.

4275 on] in R 4280 þe] *om.* LP 4281 a] als P 4283 spyres] spredes LR 4285 þare-] þen P 4286 bery] lery W for to^2] to W 4287 bitokens] takens L first] *om.* W suld springe] sprynges L 4288 bigynnynge] -es L 4291 withinne] in L 4292 þat growes] to growe ELS ground] þe grond R 4294 dose here] *trs.* R here] *om.* L 4298 þe] *om.* W 4300 renoun] gode renoun L 4302 alle] ay W þe] *om.* P 4303 fame] name LS 4304 to] *om.* L a] *om.* P werldes] werlde E 4305 þe] ay þe R 4306 þe^2] *om.* E may] *after* sorow PRW

þe synne of Envye es so perillous
þat vnnethes may þe envyous
Come to right repentaunce;
It bringes him til swilk ane encombraunce.
For it es a synne þat Godde hates mast;
It es contrarious vnto þe Haly Gast
þat es of alle godenes þe welle.

Dominus dicit in euangelio: Qui peccat contra Spiritum Sanctum non remittetur ei in hoc seculo nec in futuro

For Godde says þus in þe godspelle
þat whaso synnes and dose ille
Agayne þe Hali Gast thurgh wille,
In þis werlde getes he na mercy,
Ne in þe tothir of þat foly.
For he þat dose swilk a vyce,
He synnes thurgh wille and malyce.
Bot men sal sauely vndirstande
And noght be ouer-mykell dredande,
þat it ne es nane so grete synne done
þat ne Godde wil forgif it sone,
If a man hym wil repent
In his lyf with gode talent.
Bot vnnethes wil a man bigynne
To repent hym of swilk a synne.

Donum Pietatis De Inuidia Et ne nos inducas etc.

fo. 27va

Bot sex synnes fynde I speciele
Agayne þe Haly Gast to fele.
Ane es Presumpcioun of hert balde,
þat es Ouerhope in Inglishe talde.
Wanhope es þe secund synne;
Waa es hym þat endes þareinne.
þe thridde es Hardnes of Hert;
þe ferthe es Dispyte of Penaunce smert;

4309 to] to þe E, vnto R 4310 him] *om.* W 4311–2 *lines trs.* R 4311 a synne] agayn W *sidenote*: Nota E 4312 vnto] to LRW 4314 þe] his R *sidenote*: Dominus dicit] *om.* E Dominus . . . euangelio] *om.* L, Euang' S in hoc . . . futuro] etc. E nec] neque LW 4315 þat] And L 4317 na] neuer L 4318 of] for L 4319 dose] synnes in R 4320 malyce] thurgh malyce R 4321 men] ȝe P sauely] anly W 4323 it] þare LS; *int.* P ne] *om.* LPSW grete] mykell L 4324 ne] *om.* LS 4325 If] If þat L a man] þe synfull L hym wil] *trs.* LPSRW 4327 a] any LS 4328 swilk a] hys L 4329 speciele] specyely E 4330 fele] fle R 4332 in] on SR talde] calde LS 4335 Hard-] hardy- P 4336 es] *om.* L

þe fift es Wereyinge in othir men
Of þe Grace of þe Haly Gast to ken.
þe sext synne þareaftir es
Wereying agayne Sothfastnes.
Ouerhope proprely may be þis, *Presumpcio*
When a man ledes his inwitte mysse,
þat wil noght leue his foly
Bot traystes al in Goddis mercy.
Here mas he Goddis mercy ouer-large;
þis es a synne gretly to charge.
For al-if he lifd ay als a swyne,
He wenes þat Godde wil noght him tyne.
þare haldes he Godde vnrightwys
And his rightwisnes of lytel prys.
So Goddis mercy ouer-large men mas
And his rightwysnes ouer-skars tase,
And thurgh þat men may so lange synne
þat mercy of Godde sal þai neuer wynne.
Anothir synne es Wanhope called,
þat es þis proprely to halde, *Desperacio*
When a man es so ful of foly
þat he traystes noght in Goddis mercy.
He wenes and hopes þat God may noght
Forgif hym þe synne þat he has wroght.
So mas Wanhope Goddis mercy lesse
Als Ouerhope dose his rightwisnesse.
Bot it es nane þat mercy wil haue
þat he ne may haue it if he it craue,
þat es if he wil folow þarto
And shryue hym wele and penaunce do
And make amendes of alle his ille
And turne hym after Goddis wille.

4337 Wereyinge] wreynge R, weryng W in] of P 4338 þe[1]] *om.* S 4339 synne] sone L 4340 Wereying] Weryng S 4341 *sidenote om.* LS 4342 inwitte] wittes PW mysse] omysse S 4346 þis] þat S 4347 he] *om.* P lifd] lyf R, lyues W ay] *om.* LSR 4348 noght him] *trs.* S 4352 -skars] scharse P, schart W 4353 men may] *trs.* P 4356 þis] *om.* L *sidenote om.* L 4357 so] *om.* L 4358 þat] *om.* L 4359–60 *couplet trs.* P 4360 þe synne] *om.* L 4362 Als] And W 4363 it] *om.* P *sidenote*: Nota L 4364 ne] *om.* LS haue] *om.* L it[1]] *om.* LPW if he] if (and P) he wyll LP it[2]] wil W 4367 make] makes L 4368 after] efter to LP

And elles he es noght worthy
To haf forgifnes and mercy,
For Godde says þus in þe gospelle,

Donum Pietatis De Inuidia Et ne nos inducas etc.

fo. 27vb

Scriptum est in euangelio: Non omnes qui dicunt 'Domine, Domine' intrabunt [in] regnum celorum, sed qui faciunt voluntatem Patris mei

Als yhe may here þis clerkes telle,
'Alle sal noght', he says, 'þat says þus,
"Lorde, lorde, haf mercy on vs",
To þe kingdome of heuen wende
To lif in ioye withouten ende,
Bot þa anely þat wil fulfille
In alle thinge my Faders wille'.

Obstinacio

Hardnes of Hert es þe thridde,
Þat es when a man es so stedde
Þat he es hardened in his synne
Þat na man may him out wynne.
For he wil for nathynge him amende
Þat men may warne hym or defende.
Þe ferthe es Dispyte of Penaunce,

Contemptus penitencie

When a man thurgh wicked encumbraunce
Es neuer in wille ne in entent
Of his synne hym to repent.

Impugnacio gracie Spiritus Sancti

Þe fift es Wereynge agayne Grace
Of þe Haly Gast þat we purchace,
Als when a man wald fordo and wast
Men þat ledde er thurgh þe Haly Gast.
For þe envyous wald fayne fordo
Þat þe Haly Gast puttes þam to.
Þe sext synne and þe last þis es

Impugnacio veritatis

Wereying agayne Sothfastnes,
Pryncipally of þe trouth right,

4369 And] Or L 4370 haf . . . and] askes here goddes L 4372 *sidenote*: Scriptum . . . euangelio] Euang' ES, *om.* L omnes] omnis LS (*and singular verbs throughout*) *in] *om.* AW mei] *add* qui in celis (celis est S) ES, *om.* L, *adds* etc. W 4373 he says] *om.* LR 4375 þe] *om.* E 4379 thridde] thryde ledde E 4381 he] *om.* W 4384 hym] *om.* S or] ne R 4385–6 *trs. couplet* P 4386 When] When þat L, With R encumbraunce] combraunce L -braunce] -braunche P *sidenote om.* L 4387 in[2]] *om.* R 4388 hym to] *trs.* ES 4389 Wereynge] weryng P, warnyng W *sidenote*: gracie] gracia L Spiritus Sancti] *trs.* W 4392 ledde er] *trs.* LPR 4393 fayne] gladly L 4394 þat] All þat R 4395 þis] *om.* L þis es] *trs.* EP, es ys S 4396 Wereying] Weryng P *sidenote om.* LS 4397 þe] *om.* L

Als when a man with al his myght
Wytandly haldes þareagayne;
þan getes he na mercy certayne.
For whaso haldes agayne þe faythe,
He dose heresy—þat synne es layth.
þise sex synnes semes þe mast
þat er agayne þe Haly Gast.
So stronge þay er and so fast þai bynde
þat vnnethes I may a man fynde
þat wil in shryft þa synnes graunt
Or for þam wil be repentaunt.
þarefore ful seldom may men se
þat þise synnes forgyuen may be.
On þis wyse þe Gift of Pyte may
þe synne of Enuye putte away,
Out of þe hert þar it es knytte,
And sette Frenship in s[t]ede of itte.

De Amicicia

De virtute Amicicie fo. 28ra

Frendship mas a mans hert fre
And brynges hym to right charyte.
þis vertu has seuen degrees
And seuen braunches, als clerkes sees.
þe seuen degrees er, als I proue, *vijtem. sunt raciones quare quilibet diligeret alium*
Seuen maners of skils of luf,
Why ilk man suld kyndely luf othir
And help hym + als his awen brothir.
þe first skille es þis to neuen, *j.*
For we haf alle a Fader in heuen,
þat made vs alle, mare and lesse,
After his shappe and his lickenes.

4402 þat synne] and þat L 4403 þise] þe W sex synnes] sext synne L þe] *om.* L 4404 þat er] Frawarde L 4405 So . . . er] Strang er þir synnes L 4406 I] *om.* LS a] any S 4407 þa] þes P 4410 þise synnes] þis synne L forgyuen may] *trs.* E 4413 knytte] in knytt L *4414 stede] sede A, þe stede L 4414a De amicicia PRW 4416 And] *om.* ES brynges] To brynge ELS to] to a P 4417 seuen] foure L 4418 seuen] *om.* E sees] says R 4419 þe] *om.* L degrees] grees W *sidenote om.* LW 4420 maners] maner R skils] skyll L 4421 kyndely] *om.* W 4422 *hym] hym wele AELPS awen] *om.* L 4423 skille] kille E *sidenote om.* ES (*and all further until* 4451 *om.* S) 4425 þat] At þat E mare] bathe mare E

ij. Þe tothir skille es, forþi
Þat we er crystened alle haally
In a baptyme and maked fre
And thurgh a pris boght and a mone.
iij. Þe thridde es, forþi þat we haue
Alle a trouth þat sal vs saue,
And er bunden alle with a lawe
Þat to þe luf of Godde sal vs drawe.
iiij. Þe ferthe es, forþi þat we alle
Haf a lorde þat we to calle
Þat haldes vs alle vnder his shelde,
Body and saul and al þat we welde.
v. Þe fift es, als ilke man knawes,
Forþi þat we er alle felawes
In Goddis oste þat ilk day fightes,
Als his soudours and his knyghtes.
And alle habyde we a warysoun,
Þat es of blisse þe coroun.
vj. Þe sext skille es þis to wit,
For we bene alle of a spyrit
To lif gastly, als we lif right
Alle bodyly here of an ayre bright.
Thurgh þat spirit chosen er we
Goddis childer, our Fader so fre.
vij. Þe seuent skill yhete es, forthy
Þat we er alle lyms of a body.
Þat body Halykirke we calle,
And Godde es þe hede of alle,

De Amicicia

fo. 28rb And we lyf here alle with a fode,
Þat es Goddis flesshe and blode.
Þise er þe seuen skilles to proue
Þat stirs a mans hert to luf,

4427 tothir] seconde W es] es þis R *sidenote*: j. W 4428 haally] hailly P 4431 es] *om.* L 4433 er] *om.* P 4434 sal] sulde L 4435 es] *om.* L 4436 to] *om.* W 4437 vs alle] *om.* L 4442 soudours] awn soudʒours R 4444 þe] and of P coroun] heghe croune R 4445 es] *om.* E 4446 a] *om.* S 4447–8 *couplet trs.* R 4451 yhete es] *trs.* ES es] *om.* L 4452 alle] *om.* L 4454 of] of vs P 4456 blode] his blode ELSRW 4458 mans hert] mane hertely E to] vnto R

þat he suld fest in hert and knytte
With seuen braunches þat springe[s] of it,
þe whilk we frayst als seuen vertus,
Als þe lyms of þe body dose.
þat es to say Innocence,
Debonerte, and Obedyence,
Charyte, Pyte, and Rightwisnes,
And Parfyte Luf þe seuent es.
Innocence thurgh vnderstandynge, *Innocencia*
þat es to say Vnderynge,
þat es þat nane sal othir dere,
Bot ilk man suld othir forbere,
Als þe lymes dose of þe body.
Ilkane forberes othir kyndely,
And nane of þam wil othir greue
For ilkane es to other leue.
By þe lyms þat er so lufand
Innocence we vnderstande.
We er als lyms of a body cald;
þarefore we suld þat vertu halde.
Dobenerte may vs lere *Benignitas*
To be mure and debonere,
To suffre and noght seke vengeaunce
On þam þat vs dose here greuaunce,
Ne to hald na wreth in hert
For na greuaunce þat vs may smert.
Als ilka lym, lesse and mare,
Tholes othir þat it hurtes sare
And noght it venges ne smytes agayne,
Fele it neuer so mykell payne.
þus by þe lyms men may se
þe vertu of Debonerte,

4459 he] we R hert] hys hert L 4460 seuen] *om.* W *springes] springe A 4463 say] say þus R Innocence] innocente R 4464 Debonerte] Debonert R 4467 Innocence] Innocent R *sidenote om.* S 4469 þat[2]] to say SR 4471 þe[2]] a SR 4472 Ilkane] Vche mon W 4473 greue] do greyf R 4474 For] *om.* L leue] full leue L 4475 þat] þare E lufand] wele lufand R 4477–8 *couplet om.* R 4477 als] all L cald] talde P 4479 Debonerte] Debonert þan R *sidenote om.* L 4480 To be mure] For to war R mure] mery LS 4481 noght] *adds* to R 4482 On] Of W here] *om.* LP 4483 to] for to LR na] *om.* L wreth] wyrth R 4484 vs may] *trs.* LS, is P may] mas E 4485 lesse] both lesse R 4486 it] hym W 4487 it] hym W venges, smytes] venge, smyt P 4488 Fele it] All felytt R

þat has thre speciele degrees
þat þe debonere man suld chees.
   Ane is þis, þat he venge him noght
For na harme þat to hym es wroght.
Anothir es þat he hald noght lange
Wrethe in hert for na wrange.
þe thridde es þat he kepe him wele

Donum Pietatis De Amicicia Et ne nos inducas etc.

fo. 28va þat he na stiryng of hatred fele
Agayne his neghpur, nyght ne day,
For noght þat he may do or say.
Obediencia   Obedyence of luf may com,
þat es when a man es bouxsom
To his souerayne with hert fre.
So bouxsom suld we alle be,
Als þe lyms bene þat er in quert
To þair souerayne, þat es þe hert.
For alle þe lyms has grete talent
To do þe hertes commandement
Als lange als þai may dreghe
After þe wissynge of þe eghe.
In þis we knawe Obedience right
To wham Luf and Charyte gifs myght.
Caritas   Charyte es a vertu to fele
þat we suld halde and kepe wele.
þat mase vs helpe othir right
And serue þam with al our myght,
Als we wald þai did vs in nede
Withouten any gift or mede.
Als a lyme dose þat es fayne
To helpe anothir þat has payne

4492 þe] *om.* L   4493 þis] *om.* LS   he] he ne W   4495 hald] sshal W   lange] laughe S   4496 Wrethe] Haue wreth W   na] nakyn LR   4497 es] *om.* P   4498 stiryng] thyng P, storyng W   hatred] hatereden LP   4501 com] roume L   *sidenote om.* L   4503 with] *repeats* P   4505 bene] *om.* R   4506 þe] in þe L   4507 For] And L   grete] le grete P   4509 may] *om.* W   4510 wissynge] wilnyng W   4513–16 *lines om.* R   4513 *sidenote om.* LW   4514 halde] haue L   4515 helpe] to helpe L, hegh W   helpe othir] other helpe in þare E   4516 serue] to serue L   4517 did] serued L   4519 dose . . . es] es wonnder L   4520 has] is in P

And ese it on þe best manere,
Withouten couatyse or daungere.
In þis we may knawe and se
þe grete vertu of Charyte.
Wharefore ilk man suld bi skille
Helpe othir with gode wille
þat has defaute or mischief
And withouten helpe may noght lif.
Ilk man suld do to othir sone
Als he wald to hymself war done,
And lat nane othir of helpe faylle
When he may þam helpe or vaylle,
Bot ilkane counsaylle othir and kenne
And to þam þat nede has gif and lenne
For Goddis luf, and for noght elles,
Forwhy Charyte þis men telles.
Pyte es a vertu called *Pietas*
þat we suld ay in hert halde.
þat opens ilk mans hert to fele
When othir fares ille or wele.

Donum Pietatis De Amicicia Et ne nos inducas etc.

Pitee, þar it es verray, fo. 28vb
Puttes a man in a gode way.
It mas a man to sighe sare
For othir mens here illefare,
And to haue ioye and solace
Of othir mens happe and grace.
Als ilk lym feles what othir aylles,
When oght it greues or auaylles,
And ilk lym til hymseluen taas
Bathe gode and ille þat othir hase.

4521 ese] eses L 4522 couatyse] any couatys R or] *om.* P daungere] danengere P 4523 knawe] bathe knawe R 4524 grete] clere R, *om.* W of] of þe W 4526 Helpe] Help ay R 4527 defaute] faute L or] gret R 4529–30 *couplet trs.* P 4529 *sidenote*: Nota Hoc facias alteri quod tibi vis fieri E 4532 When] When þat L, When so R vaylle] avayle LS, \`a´vaylle P 4536 þis men] *trs.* L, þus men R 4537 *sidenote om.* P 4538 ay] *om.* L 4539 þat] þat welle P mans] *om.* S 4541 verray] sa verray L 4542 Puttes] Settes S a^{2}] *om.* LS 4544 here] *om.* LPS 4545 solace] gret solace R 4547 Als] And L feles] fele L 4548 it] hom W

For if men smyte outhir fote or the,
þe mouthe says, 'þou hurtes me'.
By þe lyms of þe body
We may knawe Pyte verrayly.
þat vertu it shewes in twa thinges
Withinne þe hert þar it springes.
Ane es ioy withouten rose
Of gode þat he has or dose;
Anothir es sorow, þat som of irkes,
Of ille þat othir feles or wirkes.
Iusticia Rightwisnes es a vertu of myght
þat mas our hertes boun to do right
And to haue compassyoun and mercy
On alle þat seke er and sary.
For ilk man, after his state es,
Suld rewe of othir þat has sekenes,
And helpe to brynge hym out of bale,
And tent to hym til he war hale.
Als alle þe lyms, lesse and mare,
Eses a lym þat es sare
And helpes it at þair powere
Til it be made hale and fere.
By þis vnderstande we wele
þe sothe of Rightwysnes to fele,
Thurgh whilk men suld ay be bisy
þe misdoers for to chasty,
And þair suggets þat dose ille
Men suld punysshe bi lawe and skille,
And thole his neghþur noght be shent
Bot brynge hym til amendement.
For ilk man suld othir saue
For luf þat he suld to hym haue.
Perfectus Amor Parfyte Luf of swilk myght es talde

4551 the] kne E 4552 hurtes] smytes L 4553 By] þus by R 4555 þat] þe W 4558 gode] godnes L, godes S 4559 sorow] sor`o´is? P of] *om.* E 4560 Of] For W othir] other men L 4561 *sidenote om.* W 4562 boun] *om.* LS 4564 and] oþer W 4566 of] on LPSR 4567 helpe] helpe þaime L hym] þaime L 4568 to hym] *trs.* P hym] þaime L til] whils SR he] þai L 4569 Als] Ryght als S þe] *om.* W lesse] both lesse R 4570 a] þat L þat] when it R 4572 be] *om.* E hale] both hale R 4573 we] we may P 4574 sothe] shothe R 4575 ay be] *trs.* W 4576 for] *om.* PW 4578 punysshe] þaime pones L 4582 he] we L 4583 swilk] whilk W talde] cald R *sidenote om.* W

De Amicicia

þat it mas a man boun and balde fo. 29ra
To putte hymself in grete perill
To saue anothir man fra ille.
Als a lym helpes anothir in nede
And puttes it for hym in drede.
For when a fote bigynnes to skrythe,
þe tothir kepes and sokours it swithe;
And if men at þe heued wil smyte,
þe hande wil kepe þe strake tyte.
þus may a man, when he has nede,
Knawe his frende þat hym luf wil bede.
By þe lyms, als we proue,
Vnderstand we Parfyte Luf,
Thurgh whilk ilke man here suld for othir
In perille hym putte `to' saue his brothir,
Als Godde gaf vs ensaumple ryf,
When he wald for vs gif his lyf.
þise er þe seuen braunches of Luf
þat þe hert of man may oft moue.
þai sprede in vs, if we þam kepe,
Thurgh þe vertu of Frendshepe.
þat bringes a man in wham it es
To þe blissedhede of Myldenes
And to þe mede þat þarefore falles—
þat es þe lande þat men heuen calles.
Als yhe myght here me bifore telle
How Godde says þus in þe godspelle,
'Blissed be bathe yhunge and alde
þat er mylde; þai may be balde,
For þai sal haue when þai hethen wende
þe lande þat lastes withouten ende'.

Beati mites, quoniam ipsi terram possidebunt

4584 it] *om.* P 4588 it] hym L hym] it L, it oft R 4590 kepes] helpes S it] *om.* LSR 4591 And] *om.* S men] a man LS 4592 þe] þat L tyte] full tite L, as tyte R 4595 we] we may PRW 4596 we] may we L 4597 ilke man] ilkane L here] *om.* ES, *after* suld LW 4598 hym putte] *trs.* LR 4599 Als] And W 4600 wald] *after* vs R 4602 oft] *om.* E 4603 þai sprede] þat spredys R 4607 þare-] *om.* S 4608 þat] of L men heuen] *trs.* LS 4609 yhe] þou W here me] *trs.* W me] *om.* PS 4610 says] saide P þus] *om.* P 4611 be] er P *sidenote*: *om.* L Beati] Sancti W terram] domini terram E 4612 þai] and E þai . . . be] for be þai L 4613 For] *om.* L

Here men may se þat tentes þarto
What þe Gift of Pyte vs may do,
þe whilk es a speciall grace
Et ne nos inducas etc. þat þe sext askynge may purchace
þat we in þe Pater Noster neuen;
þat gift vs graunt þe kynge of heuen.
Amen

De dono Sciencie

Donum Sciencie De Ira Et dimitte etc.

fo. 29rb þe Gift of Knawynge may we haue
After Pyte, if we it craue,
Thurgh þe fift askynge, with hert clene,
Et dimitte etc. þat in þe Pater Noster es sene.
þe Gift of Knawyng shewes vs right
What we er and what es our myght
And in what perille we er alle
And whethen we come and whider we sall
And what folys we haf done
And mas vs forsake our synne sone.
þat gift out of þe hert drawes clene
Ire þat mas men felle and kene.

De peccato Ire

De Ira Ire es a synne þat wyde spredes
And bi four partys a man ledes.
Ane es agayne God of heuen,
Anothir agayne a man self euen,
þe thridde agayne his awen meyne;
Agayne his neghpur þe ferthe may be.
Ire a mans hert grettely moues
Agayne Godde oft—als þe boke proues—

4615 men may] *trs.* PR 4616 What] þat S of] *om.* E 4617 a] *om.* W 4618 *sidenote*: *om.* P inducas etc.] *om.* W etc.] *om.* E 4620 gift] gyf L, *int.* P vs] men W 4620a Amen] Amen Amen E, *om.* LSR 4620b *line om.* L 4623 fift] furst R 4624 *sidenote*: etc.] nobis ES, *om.* LPW 4627 in] *after* er P 4628 whethen] when S 4629 we] þat we R 4630 vs] vs to L 4632a *line om.* PW 4633 *sidenote om.* ELPSW 4634 And] þat S 4636 a] *om.* LRW man] hym- LW euen] full euen L 4639 moues] neyes W 4640 oft] *om.* LW

When a man grotches or mas ille chere
Agayne Godde or his halowes dere,
If he þam sclaundre or says vilany
Or says Godde dose noght rightwisly,
For Godde wil noght fulfille his wille
Or for he feles oght þat es ille.
He synnes greefly and maas God wrathe,
For he hym greues and his halowes bathe.
Alle þis comes of þe synne of Ire
þat ledes a man til helle fyre.
  Ire may stir a man also
Agayne hymself and do hym wo,
Als when a man þat es brathe
Agayne himseluen es so wrathe
þat he may nouthir ete na drynke,
Ne comfort in his hert may synke
Bot falles parchaunce in sekenes sone
For his wille may noght be done.
þat wrethe may nane bot himself dere;
Of himself he may be manslaere.

Donum Sciencie De Peccato Ire

  Ire stirs a man agayne his menyhe fo. 29va
For ouer þam he has mast pouste.
His menyhe wyf and barnes men calles
And his seruaunts þat serue hym falles.
Bot when a man es moued thurgh Ire,
Agayne þam þan he fares als fyre.
He bannes and betes and lays on þan
And fares als he war a wode man.
What vessaylle he brekes, he gifs neuer tale;
Bathe pottes and coppes, he leues nane hale.
He fares als he war in wodnes,

4641 When] As when R grotches] grothes LS 4646 Or] *om.* R feles] fele P oght] noght W 4647 He] For he P greefly] gretely EP, greuously LSW 4653 brathe] wrathe S 4654 so] to S wrathe] w`r´ath P, brathe S 4658 may] þan may R 4659 þat wrethe] þe wreche W dere] were R 4660 manslaere] a maneslaere EL, mans slaer SR 4662 he has] *trs.* SR, he hast W 4663–4 *couplet trs.* P 4663 menyhe] meynthe S barnes] barne P, child W 4664 his] þe L serue] to hi serue L 4666 þan] *om.* LPSW he fares] *trs.* R 4667 and[1]] he L þan] þam RW

And so semes it wele þat he es.
  Ire mas a man felle and hasty
Agayne his negheþur þat wones him by.
When Ire ryses bitwene twa,
In seuen thinges it wil forth ga.
Ane es Stryf thurgh wordes smert;
Anothir es Rancour in hert;
þe thridde es Hatred priue;
þe ferthe may be called Medle;
þe fift es Yhernynge of Vengeaunce;
þe sext es Slaghter thurgh myschaunce;
þe seuent es Were þat þan falles sone,
Thurgh whilk many men er fordone.
For when were ryses or debate
Bytwene twa men of grete state,
Mikell blode es þan sene spilt,
And many men dede withouten gilt;
Touns brende and landes distroyed,
And many men on sere wyse noyed.
Som er disherite, and som flemed,
And som er in strayt prisoun yhemed,
And som er raymed and raunsound,
And som has many sare wounde,
And many othir harmes er done
þat many may noght be amended sone.
Ire es þe enchesoun of al þis
þat mas a man tyne heuen-blisse.
þus may of Ire com mykell waa
þat es moued bitwene twa.
How may a man þan þat es gilty
Make amendes of swilke foly?

4672 so] *om.* S it] *om.* L 4673 Ire] It L 4675 ryses] ryse L 4676 wil] bihoues L 4677 stryf] schryft R, first W thurgh] wyth E wordes] wodenes L 4678 rancour] *repeats* E, rancorne W in] of L 4679 Hatred] hatereden LP 4680 be] wele be R 4681 vengeaunce] wengange R 4682 þe . . . thurgh] of þare enmys do haue E es] mans L 4683 seuent] sexte E 4685 were ryses] *trs.* W 4687 þan sene] *trs.* P sene] soyne ES, *om.* L 4688 men] a man L, man R 4690 on] or R noyed] destroyed noyed L, neyet W 4691 disherite] deseryed L, deseret S, dysheryd R flemed] er flemyd PR 4692 er] *om.* L strayt] strang P 4693–4 *couplet trs.* PR 4693 and] and som L 4694 sare] a sare LR 4695 er] *om.* L, *int.* P 4696 many] *om.* LS 4697 þe enchesoun] chosen W 4698 tyne] to tyne W 4701 þan] *om.* LR

De virtute Equitatis Et dimitte etc.

And bot he mendes make of swilk thinge fo. 29vb
I drede þat he in helle mon hynge.
  þis synne of Ire withouten dout
þe Gift of Knawynge puttes out
Of þe hert and settes þareinne
A vertu instede of þat synne.
þat es þe vertu of Euenhede,
þe whilk a mans resoun suld lede.

De virtute Equitatis

  Evenhede es a vertu of skille *De equitate*
þat acordes Resoun with Wille.
Resoun falles be in four thinges
þat to Rightwisnes a man bringes.
Ane es Enqueryng, anothir Demynge,
And þe thridde es Right Bithinkynge;
þe ferthe es Shewyng of Tunge fre.
In þise four falles Resoun to be.
  Resoun mas a man to enquere
And þe sothe of gode men lere,
Whethen a thinge comes and how,
Ar he it sal certaynly trowe.
Resoun suld a man wele yheme
þat falles anythinge to deme,
þat he afferme noght in vayne
Til he be of þe sothe certayne.
Resoun mase a mans witte stable
To think þat may be profitable.
  Resoun wil in þe hert knytte
Thre partys of þe sleght of Witte,
A party to thynk ay sone
Of þe thinges þat es done.

4703 mendes] amendes ELS thinge] thinges L 4707 Of þe] O mans L settes] puttes L 4710a De equitate EP(*marg.*)RS, Equitas W 4713 be] to be LPR, bufore W *sidenote*: De racione ES 4714 to] vnto R 4715 Demynge] es demyng L *sidenote*: Et dimitte nobis Donum sciencie L 4716 And] *om.* L Right] *om.* L Bithinkynge] vmbethinkyng L 4719 *sidenote*: Racio E (*repeated at* 4723, 4727, 4737) 4721 and] or R 4722 Ar] Or it R, þat W sal] *om.* L 4728 think] thing L 4730 þe] *om.* R 4732 Of] On R done] ay done L

Anothir es to vndirstande
And to se þe thinge þat es semande.
þe thridde es to puruay and ordayne
Thinge þat sal byfalle certayne.
  Resoun mas a man take hede
How he sal his tunge right lede,
When he sal speke and when be stille
þat he na wordes in vayne spille.
þus may men se, whaso can,

De Equitate

fo. 30ra How Resoun suld rewell a man.
  Bot Wille suld be with Resoun ay,
For Euenhed ledes þam bathe a way.
Wille falles to be with Resoun
In four thinges for som enchesoun.
þise er þa four: Luf and Drede,
Ioye and Sorow in hert to sprede.
First a man suld nathinge luf
Bot thinge þat war for his + `saule´ bihof,
And nane othir thing suld he drede
Bot thing þat turne him myght to saul-mede.
And of noght elles haf ioy ne delyte
Bot of thinge þat myght make him parfyte,
Ne haf sorow in hert, loude ne stille,
Bot for thinge þat es agayne Goddis wille.
  þe right vertu of Euenhede
Shewes `it´, als men may in boke rede,
In seuen degrees on ilka syde
And seuen braunches þat spredes wyde.
þe seuen degrees er nathinge elles,
Als I fynde and als clerkes telles,

4734 to] *om.* P 4735 and] or and R 4736 Thinge] For thing L, þe thing W 4737 mas] garres L take] to take E 4738 right] *om.* E 4740 wordes] worde ELS 4742 suld rewell] *trs.* P 4744 Euenhed] euen W 4745 to] for to R 4747 þa] þe W 4748 sprede] spede P *4750 saule] *int. later; the original reading,* awen *left uncorrected* A, awene ELS 4751 othir] nother L 4752 turne] turnes P turne . . . myght] moght tornne hym LS myght] noght P 4753 ne] and ELS 4754 of] of þe P myght make] warr to L make him] *trs.* RW parfyte] profitt L 4756 for] for þe P 4758 it] *om.* PRW boke] bokes LS 4759–60 *couplet om.* E 4759 ilka] twa P 4760 spredes] sprynges S 4761–2 *couplet trs.* L 4761 þe] In E, þes R *sidenote*: De vij^{tem}. gradibus equitatis S

Bot seuen maners of clere sight
þat teches a man þe way right.
þe first sight es þis to bygynne
þat a man suld se + himself withinne;
Anothir es þat a man sal se
To þe thynge þat falles vnder him be.
þe thridde sight mas a man sleghe
To se þat es bifor his eghe.
þe ferthe mas a mans eghe glyde
To se clerely on þe right syde;
þe fift a mans eghe may lede
On þe left syde to loke and take hede.
þe sext sight, als says þe boke,
Mas a man bihynde hym loke.
þe seuent mase a man thurgh sleght
Loke oboun his heued on heght.
  First suld a man withinne himself se
His consciens þat es pryue,

De Equitate

And ransake it wele þat tyde, fo. 30rb
And examyne on ilka syde
Ilka thoght and ilka wille,
Whilk es gode and whilk es ille,
And ordayne al his entencioun
After þe rewarde of Resoun,
So þat Resoun and þe Wille fre
May bathe at ane accorde be.
  A man suld loke thurgh clere sight
To thinge þat es vnder him right.
þat es his body þat yhernes likynge,
Of whilk him falles to haue þe kepynge.
For in þat party war grete nede

4763 maners] maner R 4764 right] ful right R 4765 sight] *om.* L *4766 him-] him se him, *the repetition cancelled* A 4767 sal] suld ELS 4768 him be] to be ELS 4769 sight] thing L 4770 se] þat L 4771 glyde] to glyde ELS 4772 on] opon R 4774 and] and to L 4775 sight] es L 4776 Mas] þat makes L loke] to loke ELS 4778 Loke] To loke L 4781 ransake] ransaykede E, rynsake P it] *om.* P 4782 examyne] examin it L, examyn wele R 4785–6 *couplet trs.* P 4786 þe] *om.* P rewarde] regarde E, rerewarde LS 4787 þat] syat L þe] *om.* L, þi R 4788 ane] *om.* S 4791 his body] *trs.* E yhernes] ȝhemes W 4792 whilk] þe whilk L þe] *om.* ELPSR

To halde þe lyne of Euenhede,
And þe right mesure þat it noght faylle,
Als in clethynge and in apparaylle,
In mete and drynk and othir thynge
þat þe body askes thurgh yhernynge.
For þe body yhernes, albeit pouer,
Wel oftner outrage þan mesure.
  Bot a man bihoues lede warly
þe fyue wyttes of his body
Thurgh þe lyne of Equyte,
So þat na witte passe his degre,
And rewell þam so in þair offyce
So þat þai turne fra alle + vyce:
Als þe eghen to se, þe eres to here,
þe nese to smelle sauours sere,
þe mouth to tast and to speke wele,
þe handes and al þe body to fele.
þise er þe yhates of þe saul namely
And þe wyndous of þe body,
Thurgh whilk þe ded entren may
Vnto þe saul by þe neste way.
  A man suld loke thurgh sight clere
To thynge þat es byfore him here.
þat es to say, als men may gesce,
Werldely godes and ricchesce
þat may deceyf a man mast
And þe saul distroy and wast.

Donum Sciencie De virtute Equitatis
Et dimitte etc.

fo. 30va þarefore a man suld hym avyse
For to do þat þat es rightwyse
And passe noght þe lyne of Equite
For na gode þat he may se.

4794 lyne] lyfe LP 4795 þe] *om.* L þat it] and L 4797 othir] in other L 4799 yhernes] askes R al-] all if R be it] *adds* be E, *trs.* R 4800 Wel] Whyle L oftner] ofter EPSR, after LW 4803 lyne] life LPSW *4806 vyce] vyces AELS 4808 smelle] *adds* þe W 4810 and] *om.* P 4813 whilk] þe whilk L, *om.* W þe] *om.* L ded] *om.* E entren] in entre L, entre in S 4816 thynge] þe thing L, thynk RW 4818 godes] gude E 4821 hym] *om.* L, *int.* (later) P avyse] vse L 4822 þat[2]] *om.* L 4823 lyne] lyfe L 4824 he] men L

A man suld loke clerely on þe right syde
And lat nathing his sight hyde,
And þat sight sal him teche and kenne
So to take kepe to gode men,
þat he of þam may witte fele
And ensaumple take to do wele,
So þat his dedes be reweld bi skille,
Als þe vertu of Euenhede wille.
On þe left syde, als says þe boke,
Suld a man thurgh clere sight loke.
þat es a man suld bihalde
Misdoars þat foles er called,
þat þair foly can noght hyde—
þai er als on þe left syde.
To þam a man suld bi twa skils
Take rewarde for alle perilles.
Ane es men suld haue compassioun
Of þair wicked condycioun;
Anothir es men suld be bisy
To fle þair synne and þair foly.
A man also suld be sleghe
And haue bihynd hym a clere eghe.
þat es to say þat he take kepe
Of þe fende, to fle his felawshepe,
þat standes bihynd him waytand ay
Thurgh wyles to wynne him to his pray.
Bot him thar noght his wyles drede
þat folowes þe lyne of Euenhede.
A man suld loke in ilka stede
Thurgh clere sight obown his hede.
For he suld be of his sight sleghe
To haf ay Godde bifore his eghe,
þat es to say in þis condicioun,
So þat alle his entencioun

4825 loke] *om.* R 4826 his] þaire L 4828 to] vnto R 4829 þam] whayme S 4830 to] for to R 4834 Thurgh clere sight a man shuld loke R 4835 suld] shuld ay R 4836 Misdoars] To mysdoers R foles] folyes L 4837 foly] awn foly R 4838 als] as W 4843 be bisy] *trs.* P 4845 *line repeated* S suld] shuld ay R 4848 Of] On R 4850 wyles] whyles E 4852 lyne] lyfe LSW 4854 his] *om.* W 4857 þis] his R 4858–61 *lines om.* ES 4858 *line om.* L alle] *om.* P

Of his hert be symple and clene
In alle his dedes, als may be sene.
For withouten right entencioun,
Als knawes clerkes of discrescioun,

Donum Sciencie De virtute Equitatis
Et dimitte etc.

fo. 30vb Almusdede synne may oft be
And vertu vyce, als we oft se.
Right entencioun es þis,
Als clerkes can vs teche and wisse,
When a man alanely wil proue
To do gode werkes for Goddis luf.
  þise seuen manere`s´ of sightes to rede
Er þe seuen degrees of Euenhede
þat haue`s´ seuen braunches to telle,
Als I sal shewe yhow, if yhe wil dwelle.
For yhe may vndirstande þam þus:
þe seuen braunches er þe seuen vertus
Agayne þe Dedely Synnes Seuen,
Als men may fynde þam sette ful euen.
Ane es Mekenes agayne Pryde
þat spredes ouer alle þe werlde wyde.
Anothir es Luf agayne Envye
þat ouercomes þat synne lightly.
þe thridde es Debonerte
þat skomfites Ire and dose him fle.
þe ferthe braunche Pruesce es
þat may putte away Slawenes.
þe fift es Chastyte of body
þat standes agayne Litchery.
þe sext es Sobrenes to knawe

4859–60 *lines after* 4864 L 4859 his] þe P 4860 als] *om.* L 4861 *line om.* L 4863 -dede] *om.* L 4864 vyce] vices L oft] may L 4865 *sidenote*: Recta intencio E 4868 gode] *om.* L 4869 maneres] manere ER sightes] syght LPW 4871 haues] haue RW 4872 yhow] *om.* L if] and L 4874 er] *om.* L þe^{2}] *om.* R vertus] vertuous R *sidenote*: De vij. ramis equitatis ES 4875 þe] *om.* P 4878 alle] *om.* L þe] þis LR werlde] land full P wyde] sa wyde LW 4880 þat] And R lightly] full lyghtly L 4881 es] es called R 4882 Ire] hym W dose] gerres L, mas W him] it R 4883 braunche . . . es] ys pruesce as I gesce R Pruesce] prowest L 4885 of] in S

þat Glotony may doun drawe.
þe seuent es Largesce so fre
þat mas Auaryce away to fle.
  þise er þe seuen vertus to tast
þat þe Seuen Dedely Synnes may wast.
þis seuen vertus ful wyde spredes,
For þe Gift of Knawyng þam ledes,
Ilka vertu after his degre
By þe right way of Equyte.
þat shewes it when men wele dose
In alle þe werkes of othir vertus,
For withouten Euenhed to hald
Na vertu may be vertu called,
Bot it tynes of vertu þe name
And bicomes vyce to mykell blame.
Bot whaso wil his defautes se
In þise seuen poyntes of Equyte,

De virtute Equitatis

Iniquite sal he oft fynde fo. 31ra
þare, [þ]ar Equite es left byhynde.
þat es to say he may fynde amange
Oftner wyckednes and wrange
þan he may fynde Euenhede,
Outhir in worde or in dede.
þan sal he wepe and make murnynge
Thurgh þe haly Gift of Knawynge.
þan es he blissed, als God gun telle
Til his disciples in þe godspelle,
For he called þam blissed þat gretes fast
For þai sal be comforted at þe last.
For he þat here has receyued right
þe Gift of Knawynge þat es of myght
May haue in þis werlde na dwellynge

4888 may] wyll L 4897 þat] þan L 4901 of] of þe W 4905 Iniquite] Inequite EPSW, In quyte L, Equyte R 4906 *þar] ar AW, *om.* L, ? os P, whar R byhynde] of byhynde W 4907 to] at L 4908 Oftner] Ofte E, Ofter LPS, Wele after R wyckednes] wycked W 4911 þan] þar R 4912 Gift] gost W 4913 es he] be R God] *int.* P, he S God gun] *trs.* E 4915 called] calles S gretes] gret R 4916 þe] *om.* L 4917–18 *couplet trs.* P 4917 here has] *trs.* LPS 4919 þis] þe P

Withouten sorow and gretynge.
 Bot sex maners of gretynges sere
Parfyte men has in þis werlde here,
þat thurgh þe Gift of Knawyng springes
In a mans hert for sex thinges.
Ane es forþi þat he feles euen
þat he has wretthed God of heuen;
Anothir es for þe drede to telle
þat he has of þe payne of helle;
þe thridde es for þe angres sere
þat he sees gode men suffre here;
þe ferthe es for synnes and folys
þat foles haunt[es] þat er noght wys.
þe fift es for þis wreched lyf
þat we fele here with angers and strif,
And for þe tothir lyf þat es commande
þat es fra vs so lange taryande.
þe sext comes of deuocioun
And of mynde of Crystes passyoun
And of þe grete plente of blisse
þat God has graunted til alle his,
And of þe felynge þat men may tast
Of þe grace of þe Haly Gast.
He þat þus gretes als I haf talde,
Men may hym right blissed halde,
For gretly comforted sal he be,
Als clerkes in Haly Writte may se.

De dono Fortitudinis De peccato Accidie Panem nostrum etc.

fo. 31rb For Godde says þus thurgh wordes swete,
Beati qui lugent, quoniam ipsi consolabuntur 'Blissed be þai alle þat grete,
For þai sal be comforted wele
Thurgh ioy and blisse in heuen to fele'.

4921 gretynges] gretyng LSRW 4924 for] of S 4925 forþi] for he thy E 4928 of[1]] for P 4930 gode] goddes W 4932 *hauntes] haunt A þat] and L 4934 angers] anger PSRW 4935 And] For and S for] *om.* L þe tothir] þat L 4936 so] *om.* P 4942 Of] And of L þe] *om.* P 4943 þus gretes] *trs.* L, þusgates S gretes] getes W 4944 hym right] right wele hym R 4947 thurgh] wyth L wordes] worde E 4948 þai alle] þase L grete] lufes to grete L *sidenote*: at 4918 ES, repeated here S, Beati qui lugent E ipsi] ipse P

Vnto þat siker blissedhede
þe vertu of Euenhede may vs lede,
þat comes of þe Gift of Knawynge,
þe whilk we wynne thurgh þe fift askynge
þat in þe haly Pater Noster es, *Et dimitte etc.*
Als þe boke beres wyttenes.
þusgates shewes þis gift his myght;
Godde graunt it in our hertes to light.
Amen

De dono Fortitudinis

After þat gift, als clerkes wate wele,
þe Gift of Strengthe we may fele.
þat gift amange alle othir thynge
We aske thurgh þe ferthe askynge
Of þe Pater Noster when we pray,
If we þat bede bouxsomly say.
þat gift may make a mans hert
Stalwarde and hardy and smert
And balde to vndirtake and proue
A grete thynge here for Goddis luf.
For it may arme þe hert so wele
þat it na hurt of angre fele.
þat gift out of þe hert drawes
þe synne of Accyde, als clerkes knawes.

De peccato Accidie

Accyde es sleuthe in Goddis seruyse,
In whilke I fynde many a vice.
For when þat synne in þe hert es knytte
Aghtene vices may sprynge of itte,
Of whilk aghtene sex er ful ryf
þat lettes bigynnynge of gode lyf,

4953 gift] vertew S 4954 þe[1]] *om.* S 4955 þe] *om.* W haly] *om.* LR *sidenote om.* PW etc.] nobis ES, nobis debita L 4957 þis gift] the gost W 4958 graunt] graunted R hertes] hert P 4958a *om.* LPSR 4958b Donum fortitudinis L 4959 als] þat R 4962 *sidenote*: Panem nostrum cotidianum E 4968 here] *om.* L 4970 it] it may P fele] may fele L 4972a *rubric om.* W, De accidia P(*marg.*)R 4973 es] es a P 4975 þe] *om.* EL 4976 Aghtene] Aght R vices] synnes L *sidenote*: xviij. vices ES 4977 aghtene] aghtene vices P 4978 lettes] *adds* þe W gode] godes W

And sex fordose gode amendement
And puttes a man til appayrement,
And othir sex may sone brynge
A man til a wicked endynge.
First er sex mikell in vse
þat gode bigynnynge of lyf fordose.
Ane es Dasednes of hert anely,
Anothir es Tendernes of body,

Donum Fortitudinis De peccato Accidie Panem nostrum etc.

fo. 31va þe thridde Idelnes of man in quert;
þe ferthe es Heuynes of hert,
þe fift Lithernes of hert wythinne,
þe sext es Arghnes gode to bigynne.
Tepeditas Dasednes of hert, als clerkes proues,
Es when a man Godde dasedly loues
And slawly his luf in Godde settes;
Swilk luf gode bigynnyng of lyf lettes.
Bot whaso wil gode lyf bigynne
And kepe him here clene fra synne,
He suld luf Godde with al his myght,
Brennandely bathe day and nyght,
And parfytely in hert and thoght
Ouer alle thinge þat euer was wroght.
And þat luf mas a ground lastande
On whilk clene lyf may fast stande.
Teneritas Tendernes of flesshe, als I fynde,
Haldes a man mykell byhynde,
þat may here na penaunce bere
Ne thole nathinge his body to dere.
Forwhy he may na harde thing touche,
He may be called þe fendes couche

4980 ap-] en- ELPSR 4981 sex] sext R 4982 a] *om.* L *in-column heading:* Sex vicia impediunt incepcionem beate vite R 4983 er sex] *trs.* LPS 4985 anely] namely P 4987 Idelnes] ys idilnes R *sidenote:* Ociositas E 4988 hert] man in hert L 4989 fift] fyft ys R lithernes] lichernes L, licherus P 4990 gode] *om.* L, of good R 4991 Dasednes] Dasenes P *sidenote om.* L 4994 of lyf] *om.* L 4995 -so] *om.* P lyf] luf R 4996 And] *om.* P here clene] wele ay R, *trs.* W fra] fra de`d´ly P 4997 with] of LS 5002 fast] *om.* S 5003 *sidenote om.* W 5005 may] wil R bere] here W 5006 to] may L, *om.* PSRW 5007 may] will R harde] *om.* W 5008 couche] couthe S

þat to þe fende es ful soft,
On whilk he sittes and lenes him oft
And says til hym on þis manere
With a fals flaterand chere,
'þou hast bene norisshed tenderly;
þarefore tent wele to þi body,
And putte þe til na penaunce, I rede,
For parchaunce it myght be þi dede.
Forwhy þou may na penaunce bere
Als othir þat er stalwardere.
þou ert of a wayke conpleccioun;
Penaunce myght sone brynge þe doun.
It war to þe a foul meschaunce
To fordo þiself thurgh penaunce'.
þus can þe fende a man shryue
And lette his bigynnynge of gode lyf.
  Idelnes, als þise clerkes says, *Ociositas*
Es a synne þat þe fende pays.

Donum Fortitudinis De peccato Accidie Panem nostrum etc.

For when þe fende fyndes a man fo. 31vb
Idell, he comes to hym þan
And occupyes hym in his nedes
And puttes hym to synful dedes.
For he dose hym thinke þan on foly,
On Pryde and on Litchery,
On Glotony and othir folys,
On whilk thurgh þe fende he studys.
After þat he has na drede
To fulfille þam alle in dede.
þus þe fende thurgh Idelnes can

5009 fende] fendes L es] es made PR 5010 whilk] þe whylk L him] full L, *om.* R 5012 flaterand] flakerande P 5014 to] *om.* L 5015 þe] it L 5016 myght] may LS 5018 stalwardere] stalwarde here ESW, stalwortere L 5019 þou ert] In hert W a] *om.* W 5020 myght] may L sone] full sone R, so W 5024 his] *om.* P, *after* gode R 5025 *sidenote*: Ocietas ES, Ocium L 5026 fende] deuell P pays] wele pays L 5030 to] to do L, vnto R 5031 dose] garres L, makes S thinke] to thynke ES þan] *om.* P on] of W 5032 On] Of W and] envye and R on] *om.* R, of W licchery] þe syn of lychery S 5033 and] and on LS 5034 whilk] swylk L he] hym P 5036 To] For to R

Lette þe gode lyf of a man.
Grauitas Heuynes of þe hert es to drede
Þat fordose sauour of gode dede.
For when a man in hert es heuy,
Hym list noght do bot sitte or ly
Or slepe, outhir naked or cledde,
And lathe to ryse out of his bedde;
Ne hym list noght go to kirke,
Ne na haly werkes to wirke.
He wald are tyne four messes or ma,
Ar he a slepe walde forga
Or a swete in a mornynge,
For þarto has he oft likynge.
He vneses hym noght, nyght ne day,
Bot tas al þe esement þat he may.
Bot somtyme he es ful wakande
And ful bisily trauayllande
Obout þe werldes nedes to wende
And to serue his flesshe and þe fende.
Bot when he suld God worshepe,
Þan list hym best ly and slepe;
Al hys tyme þan he tynes
And alle his gode dedes away dwynes.
Lythernes of hert withinne
Es when a man ligges in synne
And feles þe fondynge of þe fende
And of his flesshe þat wil him shende,
And thurgh lythernes and þe fendes rede,
Wil noght anes lift vp his hede
Vnto Godde, ne haf repentaunce
Ne shryue hym ne do penaunce.

5039 þe] *om.* P to] for to S *sidenote*: *add* cordis ELS, *om.* W 5040 sauour] þe sauoure LS 5041 man in] mans S 5043 slepe outhir] elles slepe L 5044 his] *om.* L 5045 noght] *om.* LS go] come R to] to þe ELPS, at þe R 5046 to] *om.* LW 5048 a slepe walde] walde a slepe LPS slepe] morn sleip R 5049 Or] Or ȝit R 5050 For] *om.* L has] *repeats* P has he] *trs.* E 5051 vneses] vses L, vn(n)ese PS (= '*unethe*'), noyes W hym] *om.* L noght] nouther ELS, *om.* R 5052 al] *om.* L esement] ese PRW 5054 bisily] besy L 5056 his] þe L 5060 dedes] werkes L dwynes] swynes W 5061 Lythernes] Licherus P, Lychernes R *sidenote*: Falsitas cordis E, Luxuria cordis P 5062 ligges] lyfs R 5065 lythernes] lichernes PR and] of R þe] *om.* W rede] frende S 5066 anes] enes P 5067 ne] and E 5068 Ne] Ne to S hym] hym wele R ne do] and take P

De peccato Accidie

He wil noght his synne forsake fo. 32ra
Ne nane amendes wil he make.
Men may him licken, als men can,
Vntill a lyther forworthen man
þat had leuer ly rotande
In a prisoun þat es stynkande
þan hym war any penaunce thole
Of clymynge out of þat hole.
Methinke here es grete lithernes
Whare na bigynnynge of gode lyf es.
Arghnes also methink es harde, *Pusillanimitas*
For þat mas a man a cowarde;
þat may be called Littelhede
Of Trayst of helpe in gode dede.
For he þat falles in þat synne,
He dar na gode werke bygynne
þat suld til saul-hele auaylle,
For he dredes þat Godde wil him faylle.
He has mykell trauaylle in thoght,
For he has grete drede of noght.
He may `be´ lickened, als we rede,
Til a man þat of his dreem has drede
And til a man þat es so ferde
þat dar noght entre þe kirke-yherde
For þe snaylle þat crepes about
þat agayne him puttes his hornes out.
Bot als a chylde he es herteles
þat dar noght, so arghe he es
Passe by þe way at his ese,
For he sees þe goos at hym whese.

5069 He] Ne W noght] na wyse R 5071 men[2]] þay P 5073 had] *om.* P leuer] wele leuer R ly] ly `has´ P; ly in a dyke S 5074 In] Or in S 5075 þan] þat L war] has P 5076 Of] Or L clymynge] clymbbe L, clymbyng vp R, clybyng W 5077 here] he P grete] a grete PR lith-] lich- PR 5078 na] na gode L 5079 also] *om.* S also methink] *trs.* LR *sidenote om.* W 5082 helpe] helth W 5084 werke] dede R 5085 til] vnto L saul-hele] þe saule L 5088 grete] full grete R 5089 be] *later* A 5090 his] *om.* P 5091 til] *om.* L 5092 þe] into þe P 5093 snaylle] sneynell L, snele S 5095 he] þat L 5096 noght] noght do LW, noght go P, noȝt wele R so] *om.* W arghe] rad R 5097 way] way wele R 5098 at] on ES, apon L

þise er sex vyces knawen ryf
þat lettes bigynnynge of gode lyf.
Othir sex er here on rawe sette
þat amendement of lyf may lette,
Als Taryinge and Reckelesnes,
Forgetynge and Slawenes,
Latches also and Fayllynge;
þise sex mas a grete lettynge.
Dilacio þe first es Taryinge þat es ille,
Als when Godde sendes a man wille
To amende his lyf and wele to do
And he hym spede noght tyte þarto.

De peccato Accidie

fo. 32rb þan comes þe fende to hym þat tyde
And biddes hym yhete a whyle habyde
And says, 'Al bytyme yhete þou may
Amende þe and serue Godde vntil pay.
For þou ert yhunge and hale of hert
And þou semes stalward and smert,
Bathe to ryde yhete and to gange,
And be þou siker þou sal lyf lange.
Sen þou of lyf has lange space,
Whyle þou ert yhunge take þi solace;
For when þou ert ane alde man,
Of alle þou may amende þe þan.
For when þou bicomes a papillarde,
Of þe sal na man take rewarde'.
þis es þe fendes compasment
þat lettes a mans amendement.
Necligencia After þat comes Reckelesnes;
þat vyce amange many man es.

5099 er] *om.* W sex] þe sexe ES ryf] full ryfe L 5100 lettes] *add* þe LR *adds in-column heading* Sex impediunt correccionem vite R 5101 er here] *trs.* W here] *om.* L 5103 reckelesnes] reckelnes PR 5104 and] also and P 5105 Latches] Latchenes L, Lathtnes S 5107 þat] and þat LS *sidenote om.* W 5108 man] mans S wille] þat es ille L 5111 þan] þat R 5113 yhete] *om.* L 5114 þe] *om.* P vntil] to LPRW 5115 ert] es L 5116 stalward] stalward man R 5117 yhete] *om.* LS yhete and] *trs.* E gange] range W 5118 þou[1]] *om.* L 5123 papillarde] bapillard R 5125 fendes] fende ER 5126 amende-] mende- L 5127 Reckelesnes] reckylnes R 5128 man] men LP, a mon W

For he þat taryes gode dede,
He es a reckeles man in nede.
He es reckeles and vnredy
þat list noght in hert be bisy
To amende hym and fle al ille
And to do þat þat es Goddis wille.
For Reckelesnes oft sythe dose skathe
To body and saul and shendes þam bathe.
After þat comes Forgetynge, *Obliuio*
To whilk Reckelesnes a man may bringe.
For whaso es reckeles and gifs na tale,
Forgetes bathe grete synnes and smale,
þat to shewe in shrift nedeful ware
On whilk he may think na mare.
Bot Reckelesnes and Forgetynge
Mas til a man a grete lettynge
Hys synnes and his defautes to fele;
þarefore he can noght shryue him wele.
And þat es a grete perill to drede,
When a man forgetes his mysdede,
Of whilk to prest he suld him shryue
While he had space and war on lyue.
For if he think noght what his syn es,
Whareof sal he aske forgifnes?

Donum Fortitudinis De peccato Accidie Panem nostrum etc.

And bot he graunt what he has wroght, fo. 32va
Forgifnes of þat ne getes he noght.
For it es nane þat synne can fele,
If he grape his conscience wele,
þat ne he may fynde inoghe ilk day

5129 gode] a gode LP 5130 a] *om.* S 5131 vnredy] vnde redy W 5132 þat] And S 5133 fle] to fle S 5134 þat²] *om.* L 5135 Reckelesnes] reckylnes R sythe] sythes PR, *om.* W 5136 body] dody S þam] *om.* LP 5138 Reckelesnes] rekylnes R may] wille ELS 5139 na] neuer LSR 5141 nedeful] full nedeful R, nedfyl W 5143 Bot] For L Reckelesnes] reckylnes R 5144 Mas] Es S a¹] *om.* P a²] *om.* ELPS grete] full L 5145 defautes] fautes E 5149 whilk] þe whylk L to] to þe ELS 5151 noght] *om.* R 5152 sal] sulde PRW 5154 Forgifnes] Forgynes W ne] *om.* ELPSW he] *om.* S 5155 For] Bot L 5156 If] And L grape] wyll grape L 5157 ne] *om.* LSW ilk] ike E

Of his defautes in shrift to say.
Bot Reckelesnes, als clerkes fyndes,
And Forgetyng þe synful blyndes
So þat he may nathinge se
þat in his conscience suld be.
Pigricia Slawenes es a perillous vyce,
To whilk þe flesche a man wil tyce.
þat vyce comes of a faynt hert
þat feble es and noght in quert
And of a wicked coustom
þat to þe saul es vnhaalsom.
For whaso wones him to be slawe,
þat wone fra alle gode wil him drawe
And his wille so bynde and lede
þat vnnethes hym list do a gode dede.
Bot somtyme he wil thurgh foly
Swilk hardnes do til his body,
Thurgh grete fastynge ouer myght
And thurgh wakynge, day and night,
And othir penaunce ouer mesure
þat he falles in grete langure
And þarto in a grete sekenes,
And þan es he made so myghtles
þat he ne may on nane wyse
Trauaylle in Goddis seruyse,
Ne hym loue ne hym honour
Ne of deuocioun haue sauour,
Ne of matyns, houres, ne orysounes,
Ne of messes, ne of sarmounes.
þus men may fynde Slawenes
Redy þar a faynt hert es.
Remissio After þat comes Latchesce

5158 to] for to L 5159 Reckelesnes] reckylnes R 5161 So] *om.* P 5163 Slawenes] Slothnes W *sidenote*: Accidia E, *om.* L 5164 þe . . . man] a man þe fende S 5167 a] *om.* E 5167–8 *couplet trs.* R 5168 vnhaalsom] vnboxsom S 5169 For] Bot R 5171 so] to ELS bynde] blynde L 5172 hym list] *trs.* L, he wil W 5174 hardnes] hardynes PW 5176 wak-] wayk- P day and] days or R 5177 othir] þurgh L 5178 in] in a L 5179 a] *om.* P 5180 es he] *trs.* PW 5181 ne] *om.* LS nane] nanekynne L 5183 hym[2]] *om.* PS 5185 ne[2]] and P 5187 men] mon W men may] *trs.* ELW fynde] fynd ay R 5188 þar] whare L 5189 latchesce] lacchnes L, latthnes S

And puttes a man to swilk febillesce
þat ilk day after othir þat dawes,
His wille fra Godde somwhat drawes.
So es he ilk day apayrande
Til he be made al recreande.

Donum Fortitudinis De peccato Accidie Panem nostrum etc.

Fayllyng þe sext vyce may be, fo. 32vb
Als men may oft in seruauntes se. *Defectio*
For first to serue þai er bouxsom
And sithen fraward, ar þair terme com.
Bot he es worthy to be hyreles
þat serues noght als þe couenaunt es.
So serues men Godde þat we to calle,
For we suld be his seruauntes alle.
Som bigynnes wele Godde to pay
And faylles lange ar þair terme day,
Bot he es vnworthy to haf mede
þat wele bigynnes and faylles in nede.
þise sex vyces lettes amendement
And mas a mans saull + to be shent.
Othir sex yhete fynde I can
þat til ille endynge bringes a man.
þise er þa sex þat er noght gode,
Vnbouxsomnes and Vntholemode,
Grochynge also and Drerynes,
Langure and Wanhope þat werst es.
Vnbouxsomnes first puttes obacke *Inobediencia*
A man þat wil noght blethely take
Penaunce þat þe preste him bedes
In shrift anely for his misdedes.

5190 And] þat PSRW febillesce] febellnes LPSR 5191 day] day þat W dawes] drawes ES 5192 Godde] godward R drawes] thrawes E, wanes S 5193 es he] þat he ys R apayrande] prayand L 5194 be] haue W 5195 Fayllyng] Fallyng L sext] sex R *sidenote om.* W 5197 first] frist P 5200 þe] his R 5201 serues] serue S men] we S, *om.* W to] *om.* L, so P 5203 wele] *om.* P 5204 þair] *om.* L, þe S 5205 vnworthy] worthi LS mede] na mede L 5206 faylles] `noght' fayles S in] at R 5208 *to] for to AS, *om.* PRW *adds in-column heading* Sex vicia ducunt hominem ad malum finem R 5209 yhete] vices S 5211 þa] the PW 5214 and] *om.* L þat . . . es] and wrecchednes W 5215 *sidenote om.* A 5217 þe] *om.* L

þis vice mas a mans hert harde
And vnbouxsom and frawarde
Vnto Godde and to Halykirke
þair commaundementes for to wirke,
Or to hym þat es his souerayne
To do aftir þat he wil ordayne.
Vntholemodenes wrange wil lere
Inpaciencia A man þat wil noght blethely here
What he es worthy for his synne
And þe perille þat he es inne.
þis vyce puttes a man fra skille
To thole þat þat es agayne his wille.
Murmuracio Grochynge comes þan þat es þis:
When men says a man þat he dose mysse,
He groches þarewith and greues him tyte
And thinkes men dose it for dispyte.
þareafter comes a Drerynes,
Tristicia In þe whilk som men fallen es.
Swilk men we may oft se

De peccato Accidie

fo. 33ra þat ful gretly greued wild be
Of allekyn thinge þat men þam says,
Or men þam dose þat þam noght pays.
Langor After þat may com Langure,
þat es murnynge ouer mesure.
þat comes in a mans hert sone
For som dedes þat he has done,
For so mykell sorow may he tast
þat hym irkes with his lyf mast
And yhernes oft his awen dede,
And þat comes of þe fendes rede.
Desperacio Wanhope comes þan alderlast,
In whilk þe fende haldes a man fast.
For when a man in Wanhope es broght,

5221 to] *om.* LPS 5230 þat[2]] *om.* LP 5232 men] a mane ES a man] *om.* ELS mysse] omysse L 5233 groches] grotthes S 5234 And thinkes] Als L, thenk W dose] dyd L it] hym W 5235 a] *om.* P 5236 þe] *om.* PW 5237 Swilk] Whilk RW we may] *trs.* R oft] of R 5238 gretly] gret W wild] will PW 5239 allekyn] allskynes W 5240 þam[1]] þat S þat] *repeats* S 5241 may] *om.* P 5242 es] *om.* P ouer mesure] efter mesourese S 5249 comes þan] *trs.* P alder-] allert S, all þe R, a lyer W *sidenote om.* L

In Goddis mercy ne traystes he noght,
For hym thinke so mykell his mysse
þat he may neuer haf heuen-blisse.
And in þat he may parchaunce
Sla hymself thurgh þe fendes combraunce.
þus may þise sex vyces brynge
A man vntil ane ille endynge.
 þise er þe aghtene vyces to knawe,
In whilk men falles þat er slawe;
Alle þai sprynge on ilka syde
Out of þe synne of Accyde.
þis synne þe Gift of Strengthe out drawes
Of þe hert, als þis clerkes knawes,
And in þat stede euen to gesce
Settes þe vertu of Pruesce.

De virtute Probitatis

 Pruesce es a vertu of prys *De virtute Probitatis*
þat mas a man hardy and wys,
Thurgh whilk he may ouercom thurgh grace
Alle vyces and vertus purchace.
Seuen degrees has þat vertu
And seuen braunches of grete valu.
 þise er þe degrees first to knawe,
Als þai er sette here on rawe:
Nobillesce of Hert in ilka chaunce;
Traystynge, Sikernes, and Suffraunce;
Stedfastnes þat mykell may vaylle;
And Lastandnes withouten faylle;

De virtute Probitatis

Hunger and Threst of Rightwisnes; fo. 33rb
And ilkane of þise a vertu es.

5252 ne] AE, *om.* LPSRW 5253 thinke] thynkes SW, thynk þan R 5254 may] ne may W 5256 combraunce] -branche P, encumb- R 5258 vntil] to P ille] euel W 5261 sprynge] sprynges S 5263 strengthe] trowth W 5264 Of] Oute of LW þe] mannes L þis] *om.* P 5265 þat stede] stede of þat L 5266 Settes] He settes L 5266a *om.* ELPSW 5267 a] þe W of] *om.* W *sidenote om.* EL 5269 whilk] þe whylk L ouercom] euer come E thurgh[2]] by P 5270 and] *adds* all L 5272 of] of þat W 5273 þe] *om.* L 5274 er] are þai E 5275 Nobillesce] nobylnes R 5276 sikernes] sobernesse ES 5277 vaylle] avayle LSR 5278 -nes] -les R faylle] any fayle L 5279 of] and L 5280 ilkane] in vchen W

Magnanimitas Nobillesce of Hert þar gode wille lyse
Shewes it wele in twa partyse,
On þe ta syde to dispyse and fle
þe werlde þat es noght bot vanyte.
Augustinus For Saynt Austyn says, als I gesce,
þat þis es verray Pruesce:
When a mans hert dispyses here
Thinge þat es noght in his powere,
þat es thinge þat hym bihoues mysse
And tyne foreuer, mawgre hisse.
Whaso has þat vertu right
Dispyses þe werlde, bathe day and nyght,
And al þe welth þat þareinne es;
Hym think it noght bot wrechednes.
Nobillesce on þe tothir syde
Mas a man balde to habyde
And a grete thynge to vndertake
And to chese for Goddis sake.
Als þe wys philosofre says,
þat Nobillesce of Hert þat God pays
Es a skilfull vndertakynge
Of a right heghe dredeful thynge.
For he þat es at lyf parfyte,
Bot he be war, he may falle tyte,
Bot þe vertu þat I bifore talde
Mas a man hardy and balde
To vndirtake with hert boun
þe right way of Perfeccioun
And to chese with stable hert
þe lyf þat semes here sharp and smert.
Fiducia Traystyng settes a mans hert fast
And mase it stable and strange to last.
For he þat wil vndirtake

5281 Nobillesce] nobylnes R *sidenote*: Magnitas L, Nobilitas S, *om.* W 5283 On] And on L syde] *om.* W 5284 noght] *om.* P 5285 *sidenote om.* LW 5286 es] is a P 5291 þat] þis W 5292 þe] þis W bathe] *om.* W 5294 wrechednes] wrytthednes S, wyckydnes R 5295 Nobillesce] nobylnes R *sidenote*: Nobilitas E, Magnanimitas W 5297 a] *om.* S 5298 chese] *adds* hardynes R 5300 Nobillesce] nobylnes R þat[2]] *om.* L 5301 Es] þat es L, Als P 5303 at] at þe L 5304 falle] fayle E, *adds* full L 5306 Mas] May mak R 5307 with hert] swythe L 5310 here] *om.* L sharp] harde LPSR smert] sharp R 5311 *sidenote*: Fidencia E, *om.* S 5312 strange] lang L

A gode way for Goddis sake,
So fast he suld his hert sette
On his purpose þat noght it lette
And of nathinge be abayst,
Bot sikerly in Godde ay trayst
To fulfille with al his myght
þat þat he has bigunnen right.

Donum Fortitudinis De virtute Probitatis Panem n.c.d.n.h.

Sykernes a mans hert ledes — fo. 33va
So þat he na perille dredes, — *Securitas*
Ne na wickednes ne na payne
þat men may here ordayne.
For þe Gift of Strength mas him smert
And gifs hym a noble hert
To vndirtake a grete thinge
Withouten any fayllynge.
Aftirward it gyues hym luf
And wille þat thing for to proue,
And to folwe it a yhernynge,
And trouthe to þe ende it to brynge.
After þat it gyues hym myght
And mas him siker als a gode knyght
þat he dredes noght perill ne payne
Ne yhete þe dede þat es certayne,
Bot yhernes angres and to þam tentes
Als þe gode knyght dose turnamentes,
And als þe haly martirs did
þair turmentes, þat felle war kidde.
Suffraunce helpes a man in case — *Paciencia*
To ouercom his mast faas.
þa er his flesshe, þe werld, þe fende

5315 he . . . sette] hys hert þan sall he sett L 5316 purpose] spouse L 5317 of] on LS be] þan be R 5319 To] For to R myght] wille and myght E 5322 he na perille] perill he none P perille] perills S 5324 may] may for hym R here] *adds* or canne L 5326 noble] full nobyll R 5327 grete] nobell L 5328 any] any kyn R 5330 wille] wele PR 5331 to] *om.* S to folwe] *trs.* E it] ay L a] with a ES, *om.* P, to a R, ay W 5332 trouthe] trowe ELW, *om.* P þe] *om.* LP 5334 a] *om.* W 5335 þat] And P he] *om.* L noght] nouther LPS 5336 Ne] And L 5338 þe] a P dose] þat dos E 5339 als] *om.* S 5340 þair] þe R turmentes] turnementes LSR (extra minim R) 5341 *sidenote om.* L 5343 þa] þat LW

þat nyght and day waytes him to shende.
For Suffraunce may be right tolde
Til a man a shelde of golde
þat for Goddis luf noy dar byde;
þat shelde him couers on ilka syde
So þat na strake of tribulacioun
May him sare hurt ne stryke doun.
For na man may haue victory
Withouten Suffraunce, ne maystry,
Ne nane may com to Perfeccioun
Bot he suffre tribulacioun.
Constancia Stedfastnes es profitable
þat festes þe hert and mas it stable,
Als a toure þat ground has tane
Opon a harde roche of stane,
And als a tre in erthe rotefast
þat na wynde ne stormes may doun cast.
So suld a man þat has wytte

Donum Fortitudinis De virtute Probitatis Panem n.c.d.n.h.

fo. 33vb Stedfastly his hert knytte
So þat na chaunce, gode ne ille,
It may remu ne turne his wille,
For na man may haue victory
Withouten Stedfastnes namely.
Perseuerancia Lastandnes es ay ilyke newe;
þat vertu comes of hert trewe,
Thurgh whilk a man suld ay be boun
To take þe way of Perfeccioun,
And in þat way to be ay-lastande
And neuer for wele ne wa faylland

5345 tolde] calde L 5346 Til] Vntill R 5347 dar] *after* þat E, *after* luf L byde] abyde ELSR 5348 shelde] schuld W him couers] *trs.* LS 5349 na] *om.* E strake] strakes S 5350 stryke] *adds* hym L 5352 ne] ne þe P, and S 5353 nane] he L *sidenote*: Nota E 5354 Bot he] Bot if he her R 5356 festes] festens LPR stable] able P 5357 Als grounde of a toure þat is well tane P þat] þat þe E 5359 rote] roted L, rode S 5360 wynde] wyndes L 5361 has] hade W 5362 Stedfastly] So s. R knytte] ay knyte R 5363 na] *om.* E 5365 haue] *adds* na S 5367 ay] *om.* LS ay . . . newe] comande nowe E ilyke] in lyke LR, like P 5368 of] oute of E 5369 ay be] *trs.* P 5372 And] þat L ne] na for L

Vntil he com til his lyues ende
When he sal out of þis werlde wende.
  Hungre and Thrist of Rightwisnes *Esuries et sitis iusticie*
Ane hertly yhernynge of gode þat es,
For a man suld yherne, day and nyght,
To yhelde and do þat at es right,
Bathe to Godde and to ilka man
After þat he may do and can,
And on hym his luf vouchesaue
þat for hym his awen lyf gaue.
And if he be somtyme myghtles
þat he may noght do þat right es
Bot puttes his myght to Goddis wille,
þan wil Godde þat faylles fulfille.
For Godde sayd noght þus, als I wene,
'Blissed be þa þat rightwys bene'.
Bot he sayde þus, mare curtaysly,
Als he þat es ful of mercy,
'Blissed be alle þa, mare and lesse, *Beati qui esuriunt et siciunt iusticiam*
þat yhernes to do ay Rightwisnes'.
þise er called þe seuen degrees
Of Pruesce þat a man suld chese,
þat may hym lede þe right way
To þe heghe lyf þat lastes ay.
  Bot seuen braunches er þare yhitte
þat men calles and haldes thurgh wytte
Seuen victorys þat here auaylles
Of seuen manere of bataylles,
Thurgh whilk a man may noght mysse
Of þe seuen corounnes of blisse.
þe first bataylle to bygynne
Es þe bataylle of Dedely Synne;

5375 *sidenote*: Esuries EPSW, *om.* L 5376 Ane] And ELW hertly] erthly ELS 5378 do] do all R, to do W at] *om.* LPRW es right] *trs.* S 5379 ilka] *om.* L 5380 and] or L 5385 to] to do L, in PRW 5386 þan] þat E 5387 sayd] says PW noght] *om.* E 5388 be þa] þai be E 5389 sayde] says W 5390 þat] *om.* W 5391 þa] þat W *sidenote om.* EL 5392 ay] *before* to LS, *om.* RW 5393 seuen] seuend L 5394 a] *om.* LS man] men S 5395 þe] to þe L 5396 To] Vnto R þe] *om.* L lyf] way P 5400 manere] maners ELSRW of] of vij. R 5401 may] ne may R 5402 þe] *om.* P

De virtute Probitatis

fo. 34ra Anothir es of Penaunce harde;
þe thridde es of Flesse so frawarde;
þe ferthe and þe fift of þe Werld er twa,
þe tane of welthe, þe tothir of wa;
þe sext of wicked men and felle;
And þe seuent of þe fende of helle.
Prelium peccati mortalis Dedely Synne es þe first bataylle
þat bigynnes a man to assaylle.
Agayne þat bataylle bihoues him fight
Or flee it fast with al his myght.
Bot he þat flees may noght al leese,
For he fightes wele þat wele fleese.
For whaso assentes noght to synne,
He ouercomes withouten dynne,
Bot whaso es felled in þat stour
May noght ryse withouten sokour.
He has mare nede with help to mete
þan he þat standes opon his fete,
Bot Godde thurgh grace most take his hand,
Ar he may ryse agayne and stande,
And arme hym agayne þat chaunce
With þe stronge armure of Penaunce,
þe whilk þe Haly Gast hym brynges
And þat byhoues be of thre thinges.
Ane es Repentaunce called of Hert;
Anothir es Shrift of Mouth appert;
þe thridde Amendes thurgh wille fre—
He suld be armed with þise thre.
Contricio cordis Repentaunce of Hert es þis:
When a man wil knawe his mysse
And has sorow for þat labour

5405 Anothir] And aneother L 5406 flesse] þe flesche LR, his flessh W so] *om.* E 5407 of] es L er] *om.* L 5409 of] es E felle] felthe L 5410 And] *om.* L fende] deuell L helle] hele R 5411 *sidenote*: *as in-column heading* R, *om.* W 5413 bihoues] behoued W 5416 wele[2]] faste S 5418 He] He it PSR dynne] blynne dyn P 5419 Bot] For L 5422 opon] on W 5425 hym] *adds* wele R 5426 þe] *om.* PW 5428 of] on R 5429 repentaunce called] *trs.* ES repentaunce] penaunce L 5431 thridde] *adds* es L thurgh] with W 5433 *sidenote*: *as in-column heading* R, *om.* W 5434 When] When þat L 5435 þat] his SW

þat he has wrethed his creatour;
And þe mare þat he has wroght als fole,
þe mare in hert suld be his dole.
For whaso es synnefull and ille,
þise thre names beres thurgh skille:
'Goddis theef and theues fere',
'Murthere[r] of his doghter dere',
And 'Goddis traytour'—þus men calles
þe synnefull man þat in synne falles.
First 'Goddis thief' he may be knawen,
For he wastes þat es noght his awen,
þat Godde hym toke to kepe and welde,

De virtute Probitatis

Of whilk hym bihoues acount yhelde. fo. 34rb
'Murtherer' he hymseluen mas
þat thurgh synne his saul slaas,
þe whilk Godde made to his lickenes,
þat thurgh grace his doghter es.
'Goddis traytour' he es bi resoun,
For he dose Godde a grete tresoun
When he yheldes to þe fende haally,
þat es Goddis mast enmy,
þe castell of his hert so queme,
þe whilk Godde toke hym for to yheme.
þe secund thynge es Shrift of Mouthe; *Confessio oris*
þat mas a man to Godde ful couthe.
þe whilk has sex condiciouns,
Als men has herde in sere sarmouns.
First shrift suld be wysely done,
And also hastyly and sone,
Appertly and bisily ay,
Haally and mekely and oft to assay.
First suld shrift be made wysely, *Confessio discreta*

5437 þat] *om.* ES als] als a LPS 5440 beres] he beres LP, beres he R thurgh] wyth L *5442 Murtherer] Murthere A, And m. R 5443 þus men] men hym L 5444 synnefull] *om.* W 5448 acount] acountus? E 5451 to] of W 5454 a] *om.* P, full R grete] mekill P 5456 mast enmy] aldermast envye R 5457 so] to P 5458 for] *om.* S *adds in-column heading* Confessio oris habet sex condiciones R 5459 thynge] *om.* L 5462 sere] diuers W 5463 First] For EL wysely] wyterly W 5464 also hastyly] *trs.* R hastyly] hastly W 5467 suld] *om.* P wysely] dyscretely E *sidenote*: Confessio sapiens P

For a man suld make him bifore redy
And of allekyn synne bithynk him wele,
Bathe of dedely and of venyele,
þat he has wroght als vnbouxsom
Ar þat he bifore þe prest com.
Yhete suld he loke, ar he hym shryue,
What he es þat sal here his lyue:
If he be conande his shrift to here
And to assoylle hym has powere.
Confessio festina Shrift suld be done hastyly
For many skilles to telle why.
For taryinge of shrift in þis lyue
Es perillous for skilles fyue:
Ane es for þe condicioun
Of synne, þat es a confusyoun.
For synne es, als telles þis clerkes,
A brynnande fyre þat wastes gode werkes
þat may on nane wyse sleckened be
Withouten teres in shrift pryue.
Anothir es for þe sekenes of synne,
To whilk shrift es þe medecyn.
For he þat sekes noght to be hale,
Of his hele he gifs neuer tale.

Donum Fortitudinis De virtute Probitatis Panem n.c.d.n.h.

fo. 34va þe thridde skille es for þe dede
þat waytes a man in ilka stede.
Forwhy þe dede es so sodayne
þat na man may be certayne
Of þe tyme þat may noght faylle
When þe dede sal hym assaylle.
þe ferthe es for godes þat es done
þat a man thurgh synne may tyne sone.

5469 And] *om.* L allekyn] ilk P, all hys R synne] synnes R 5470 of[2]] *om.* R 5473 loke] *om.* L 5474 What] Wytt what L 5476 has] haue LS 5477 hastyly] hastly W 5482 Of] þat L þat] *om.* LP 5483 telles] says E þis] þe P 5484 þat wastes] wastande P gode] godes L 5485 sleckened] sloknede ELSR 5486 in] of P 5488 To] þe W þe] *om.* E 5490 he gifs] *trs.* R 5493 þe] *om.* S es so] þat es L 5494 man] man here R be] *adds* of L 5495 may] *om.* E 5497 godes] gude P 5498 tyne] *adds* þaim L

þat es al þat he has done wele,
Wharethurgh he suld heuen-blisse fele,
And al his tyme þat myght auaylle
Thurgh his synne sal hym faylle.
Bot al may he recouer agayne
Thurgh verray shrift—þat es certayne.
  þe fift skille and þe last es þis,
For forgetynge of his mysse.
For whaso late his shryft bigynnes,
He may forgete many of his synnes,
Of whilk he may neuermare mene;
How suld he þan shryue hym clene?
  þe thridde condicioun of shrift es, *Confessio aperta*
Als þe boke here beres wyttenes,
þat a man suld shryue hym appertly
And for his synne in hert be sory.
þat es to say, he suld shewe sone
Certayne synnes þat he has done
And al þe entencioun and þe wille
þat he had to do þat ille.
  þe ferthe es a man suld be redy *Confessio diligens*
To shryue him wele and bisily.
þat es to say, a man suld sone
Telle his synne als it es done
And when and whare and þe cause why
And how oft he did þat foly
And þe manere how he did þat synne
And how lange he has lyen þarinne.
  þe fift condicioun es þat a man *Confessio integra*
Suld shryue him haally als he can
Til a prest þat has powere
Al his lyf haally to here,
And noght depart his shrift in twa,
To com fra ane and til anothir ga.

5500 -thurgh] -fore P 5501 his tyme] *om.* L myght] *adds* hym L 5502 his] *om.* S 5506 For] *om.* LS 5509 mene] on mene E 5511 es] is þis P *sidenote om.* L 5512 here] *om.* P here beres] *trs.* ES 5514 his] *om.* E synne] synnes LW, *om.* R hert] hys hert L 5516 has] hade P 5517 entencioun] entencons R þe[2]] all þe LW 5518 to] for to R 5519 es] es þat E *sidenote: partly in gutter* P, *om.* W 5520 bisily] besy L 5525 how] and how L 5526 lyen] lyfed SR 5528 haally] hale L 5529 Til] Vnto R 5532 and] *om.* P

For if he at ane his shrift bigynne
And telle til anothir anothir synne
Or any synne in shrift layne,

Donum Fortitudinis De virtute Probitatis Panem n.c.d.n.h.

fo. 34vb I telle þat shrift done in vayne.
Bot he þat wil make his shrift haale
Suld telle alle his synnes, grete and smale,
Til ane þat hym may gif penaunce
And telle hym alle þe circumstaunce
Circumstancia peccati þat ekes þe synne, als I talde are.
þat es how he did, when and whare,
How oft and why and þe dwellyng þarinne
And what he es þat didde þe synne,
Whethir he lered or lawed be
And what state he has and what degre
And of what state he es kydde,
With wham he or sho þe synne didde.
For a synne in a persone may be
Mare þan in othir twa or thre;
And in som stede mare and in som stede lesse,
After men sees þat þe stede es;
And mare may a synne in a heghe tyme der
þan in anothir þat es lawer;
And mare es a synne done on som wyse
þan on anothir manere thryse;
And þe oftner þat he dose a synne
And þe lengar þat he dwelles þarinne,
þe mare penaunce he es worthy
þat suld weghe agayne þat foly.

5533 at ane] anes P 5535 shrift] schrynfte E, his schryft R 5536 in] all in R 5537 he] *om.* E 5538 Suld] And S 5539 hym] *after* gif ELPS 5541 talde] sayd R *sidenote om.* W 5542 how . . . when] when . . . how R did] *adds* it R when and] and L, and when he W 5543 How] And how W 5543–4 *couplet trs.* W 5544 he] *om.* W þat] *repeats* P þe] þat LP 5545 be] es (*cancelled?*) be E 5547 of] *om.* LR what] whatkynne L he es] þai er R, *trs.* W es] *add* of LS 5548 þe] þai þat L, þat R P *adds couplet*: Bot noȝt tell þe persone name | If he do he is to blame 5550 othir] another L 5551 and[2]] *om.* RW in[2]] *om.* L stede[2]] *om.* PS 5552 After] Efter þat S þat] *om.* ESR 5553 may] is PW 5555 es] *om.* R on] in R 5556 anothir] oþer P 5557 þe] *om.* P oftner] ofter ELPSRW þat] *om.* ELS a] þe W 5558 þat] *om.* ELS 5559 he es] *trs.* P 5560 weghe] weehe W

And þe wers þat þe cause es,
Wharethurgh he dose a wickednes,
þe mare penaunce bihoues hym do
For þat synne, als falles þarto.
  þarefore ilk man, lered and lewed,
Suld shryue him þus als I haf shewed
And shewe haally withouten dyn
Al þe circumstaunce of þe synne.
Bot whaso wele wil shryuen be,
Hym byhoues parte himself + in thre.
First at þe hert he sal bigynne
And sithen at þe mouth and þe tunge withinne
And aftirwarde at al þe body
Til he haf ransaked ilka party.
For ilkane mas his cours euen
Thurgh alle þe dedely synnes seuen.
  First suld he telle his thoghtes ouerthwert

De virtute Probitatis

And þe wicked yhernynges of his hert fo. 35ra
And þareafter his wordes ilkane
þat out of his mouth wrange has gane
And afterward he suld telle sone
Alle þe ille werkes þat he has done.
And so may he, if he be wys,
Putte out in shrift alle his folys.
  For alle synnes þat on conscience hynges
Comes specially of þise thre thinges,
Of hert, of mouthe, and of werke.
By þise thre may we take our merke
To shewe in shrift what we haf thoght,
What we has sayde, what we haf wroght.
And ouer þat, may we knawe sone

5562 a] þat P 5564 þat] swylk a R als] þat EL 5566 him] *om.* E shewed] talde LS 5569 wele wil] *trs.* ELS 5570 parte] *om.* W him-] þaime L *in] hin A 5571–6 *repeated in the lower margins of this and the facing leaf* W 5571 he sal] hym behoues L 5572 at] with W þe[1]] *om.* RW þe[2]] *om.* ELPSRW 5573 al] *om.* P 5577 his] all hys LS thoghtes] thoght P 5578 yhernynges] yernnyng PSR his] þe LPW 5579 ilkane] euer ilkane L 5580 out] *om.* P 5581 And] *om.* P -ward] that R suld] shull R 5582 þe] *om.* P þat] *om.* L 5583 if] and L 5584 in] of W 5585 *sidenote*: Nota E 5586 þise] *om.* P 5587 of[2]] and of L 5589 thoght] wroght L 5590 *line om.* L sayde] done P 5591 may we] *trs.* E we] *om.* W sone] full sone R

þe synnes of leuynge of gode vndone.
Bot first I wil telle yhow som
Of þe synnes þat of þe hert may com.

Peccata cordis

þe synnes of þe hert er þise bi skille:
Thoght, delyte, consentynge, and wille,
Yhernynge and vnfaythfulnes,
Slewth, dulhede, and vndeuoutenes,
Wrangehope, ouerhope, and wrange wenyng;
Wanhope þat werst es and vntraystyng;
Fole luf þat es ille brynnande;
Drede þat es ay ille lawande;
Assotynge and fole affeccioun,
Vayne gessynge and suspecioun,
Wrethe, hatrede, and lytherhede,
Rancour, envye, and carles drede;
Ioye of othir mens angre and care,
Sorow of othir mens welefare;
Dedeyne, murnynge þat þe hert shendes,
And flesshely affeccioun of frendes;
Trechery and vnconable gladnes,
Vnsuffraunce and werldely drerynes,
Vayne dole, perplexte, and pryde,
Irkynge of gode and accyde,
Couatyse and auaryce,
Hardnes of hert and maly[c]e,

De virtute Probitatis

fo. 35[rb] Vnstedfastnes and forgetynge,
Forthinkynge of penaunce doynge,
Studyinge of ille to bigynne,

5592 leuynge] 'ille' (*later*) leuyng S, lykyng W of[2]] þe ELS 5593 I wil] will I now R 5594 þe[1]] *om.* R þat] *om.* L 5594a *marg.* EPSW, *om.* L, *as in-column heading* R 5595 þe[2]] *om.* E 5597 Yhernynge] Garnnenyng L 5599 Wrange-] Wan- W 5600 werst] wars RW -trayst-] -strayst- EL 5601 Fole] Foule L, Foly W ille] alle L 5602 lawande] hawand L 5603 Assotynge] Assentyng W 5604 suspecioun] ille s. S, wrang conspeccioun W 5605 hatrede] hatereden LP lyther-] lecher- P, lycher- R 5606 Rancour] Rancorn and W carles] carle L 5608 Sorow] And sorow LR 5609 Dedeyne] Dedeyenynge P murnynge] mornnenyng L, and m. W 5610 affeccioun] affeccious L 5612 drery-] drere- E 5614 Irkynge] Irked L 5616 Hard-] Hardy- P *malyce] malye A (*in a crease*)

Ioye þat a man has of his synne
And sorow þat he na mare ille did;
Ipocrysy þar þe synne es hidde;
Luf to plese a man agayne skille;
Drede to displese hym þat dose ille;
Shame to do any gode dede
In sight of men when it war nede;
Hardynes and baldenes in synne;
Argnes of godedede to bigynne;
Singulere witte and luf pryue;
Yhernynge of state or of dignyte;
Vayneglory and vayne likynge,
þat of thre maners of gode may springe—
Of godes of kynde, of happe, of grace,
þat Godde vs gyues for our solace;
Laynynge of sothe in hert hidde;
Shame of frendes þat pouer er kidde;
Despyte of bidynge of souerayne;
Vnrewith of þam þat feles payne;
Misbileue in hert to halde.
Alle þise er synnes of þe hert called.

Peccata oris

þe synnes of þe mouth er vayne spekyng
And oft swerynge and forswerynge;
Sclaunderynge of Godde almyghty,
Takynge of his name vnreuerently,
Threpying agayne rightwisnes;
To telle oght þat errour es;
Houres vnreuerently to say,
Withouten deuocioun to pray;
Backebytyng, leghes, and losenger⟨y⟩,

5621 ille] *om.* ES 5622 þar] *om.* W hidde] kyd W 5625 any] ay R 5627 Hardy-] Harde- L 5629 luf] full R 5630 or] and LP of[2]] *om.* P dignyte] degre W 5632 thre maners] þar manere R of[2]] *om.* W gode] godes SR 5633 godes] gode W of[2,3]] or S 5635 Laynynge of] Laynenyng of þe L 5636 pouer] prowd W 5638 feles] suffers L 5639 Misbileue] And mysbeleue R 5640 er] are þe ES of] in W called] talde P 5640a *marg.* EPSW, *om.* L, *in-column heading* De peccatis oris R 5643 Sclaunderynge] Skladryng R 5644 name] *om.* W 5646 To] For to R oght] oghe R 5647 Houres] *adds* oure L 5649 losengery] *leaf torn* A (as also 5651, 5662, 5653, 5654)

And reprouynge of vylany;
Stryfs, missayinge, and banny⟨n⟩ge;
Sclaundre, vpbraydynge, and t⟨h⟩retynge;
Lackynge and louynge agayne conscience;
Agaynesayinge of obedyen⟨c⟩e;
Pynchynge at luf and at ch⟨a⟩ryte
And lettynge of luf þar luf suld be;
Fals pleynynge of men þat er giltles

Donum Fortitudinis De virtute
Probitatis Panem n.c.d.n.h.

fo. 35va And fole berynge of fals wyttenes;
False flateryng to mayster or to lorde;
Wreghynge and sawynge of discorde;
Tellynge of vayne trewfles with tung;
Skornynge outhir of alde or yhunge;
Eggynge and counsayllyng agayn skille;
Misturnynge of gode vnto ille;
Discurynge of mens priuyte
Þat thurgh right layned suld be;
In kirke to plede þat halwed has bene;
To stir a man to ire and tene;
To threpe on men þat þai noght did;
To agaynesay þat sothe es kidde;
To reproue a man of a thinge felly
Of whilk þe reprouer es gilty;
Mikell speche and oft iangelynge,
Fole speche and vayne vauntynge;
Excusynge and defendynge of syn;
Skrykyng, cryinge, and vayne dyn;
Grochynge agayne Godde and man;
Blawynge of bost þat som men can;

5651 Stryfs] Stryfe LR 5652 Sclaundre] Sklawder W vp-] vm- PW -braydynge] -brayde L thretynge] threpyng LPR 5654 of] and R 5655 at[2]] *om.* P 5656 þar] whar R 5657 pleynynge] pleyng L, plenyg S 5658 And] A R fole] foule W 5659 or] and R 5660 Wreghynge] Wrething LP, Wynwynge W 5661 trewfles] trolles W 5662 Skornynge] Scornnenyng L or] or of LPW 5663 counsayllyng] counsayle L 5664 vnto] into ES 5667 to plede] to plete S, or place W has] had W 5668 and] or ES 5669 on] of L men] mane ES, *adds* thing L þai] he S 5670 þat] thing þat L 5672 Of] Of þe LP whilk] *adds* thing L reprouer] reproue W 5673 oft] *om.* W 5674 vauntynge] avauntyng L 5676 cryinge] and crying LSR 5677 *written into gutter on same line as 5676* P

To snybbe and sette men to resoun
Agayne skille withouten enchesoun;
To mote in causes vnrightwys;
To lere a man to greue his enmys;
Fals demynge of othir mens dedes;
Fals endytynge þat men dredes;
Laghinge, grynnynge, and vayn likenyng,
Dispytous blerynge, and mowe-makyng;
To synge sanges of iolyte;
To rede on bokes of vanyte;
To shewe wordes of herlotry,
To speke foul wordes of vilany;
To study mare in voice-brekyng
In kyrke þan in deuoute syngyng;
To dispute and argu in vayne,
To shew fallaces vncertayne;
To aske on hethyng or wrange to answer
To þam þat men suld forbere;

Donum Fortitudinis De virtute Probitatis Panem n.c.d.n.h.

To spire how a thinge may be fo. 35vb
þat es Goddis awen priuite.
þise er þe synnes of þe mouthe;
Yhete er þare ma, whaso þam couthe.

Peccata operis

þe synnes þat comes of werk and dede
Of þe body er þise to rede:
Drunkennes and glotony
And manslaghter and litchery;
Sacrylege, theft, and rauyn
And symony þat I hald grete syn;

5679 and] and to W to] fro P, vnto R 5680 skille withouten] swylk ar verray R enchesoun] chesone PRW 5681 causes] cause W vnrightwys] of vnryghtwysnes L 5684 þat] þat other LR, þat o P 5685 likenyng] lykyng ELS 5686 *line om.* E Dispytous] Dyspotes L mowe-] mowes LPW 5687 To] For to R synge] synges P 5688 on] of PS 5690 vilany] vanyte E 5691 in] of P 5694 fallaces] falces R 5695 to[2]] *om.* LP 5696 To] Vnto R 5697 a] any R 5699 þe[2]] *om.* R 5700 þare] þai W þam] may R 5700a *marg.* EW, *om.* LS, Peccata corporis (*marg.*) P, *in-column heading* De peccatis operis R 5701 synnes] synne E dede] *in gutter* A (as also 5714) 5703 -nes] -hede P 5704 man-] mannes L 5706 I hald] is L, *trs.* W grete] a grete LP

Oker þat gretly Godde myspayse;
Brekynge of dere haly dayse;
Brekynge of vowes þat men maas;
Forsakynge of order þat men taas;
Takynge of housil vnworthily,
Vnreuerence vnto Goddis body;
Bisynes obout vayne reuerys;
Faylyng thurgh fayntys in Goddis seruy⟨s⟩;
Ille ensaumple in dede to gif
To othir men þat suld wele lyf,
Or any werke to haunt or wirke
þat may be sclaundre to Halykirke;
To hurt a man in his persoun,
In his godes, or in his renoun;
Tresoun, falshede, and gilry
And wichecraft and tregetry;
Extorsyouns þat er laweles;
Sellynge of lawe and \`of´ rightwisnes;
Fals marchandyse and fole sleghtes,
Hauntyng of fals mesures and weghtes;
Plays, iapes, als men oft sees
þat er noght bot vanytees;
Hauntyng of carols and of daunce;
Feynynge of fole continaunce;
To gif ioglours and mynstrales
Giftes for iapes and for vayn tales;
T⟨o⟩ drawe fra a mans awen body
His n⟨e⟩deful fode þat he suld lif by,

De virtute Probitatis

fo. 36ra Or ouermykell to take and vse
In outrage, als som men dose;

5707 gretly Godde] *trs.* W 5708 Brekynge] And brekeyng L 5709–10 *couplet trs.* ERW 5709 Brekynge] And brekyng E 5712 Vnreuerence] *adds* do S vnto] vndo L 5713 reuerys] reuerense W 5714 Faylyng] Fallyng LSR fayntys] faytyng W 5716 suld wele] *trs.* LPSR 5718 be] *om.* W 5719 persoun] presoun W 5720 in[2]] *om.* R 5721 falshede] falles W 5722 tregetry] trechery ES, tregery P 5723 Extorsyouns] Extorcioun W 5724 of[2]] *int. later* A 5725 and] *om.* P sleghtes] weghtes L 5726 weghtes] weyghes L 5727 iapes] and iapes E sees] seses W 5728 þat] þe whilk R vanytees] vaniteses W 5730 fole] gude P continaunce] councynances R 5732 for[2]] *om.* LPR 5733 To] *leaf torn* A (as also 5734) drawe] withdrawe R 5734 His] þe R þat] *om.* L 5736 outrage] outragnes R

To vndirtake with a grete wille
To do mare þan men may fulfille;
Offyce to halde and to haunt
To whilk a man es noght sufficiaunt,
Or offyce or craft to bigynne
þat may noght be withouten synne;
Agayne to turne and to haunt eft
þe synne þat a man has left;
Custom to synne þat es harde to breke;
Bataylle to mayntene or conteke,
To smyte or to assayle on som wyse;
To fynde and to vse nouayllleryse;
Sturdynes of men—þat I hate—
Agayne othir men of mare state;
Hardnes þat som dose þat may
To men þat er meyner þan þai;
To trespas in vnderstandynge,
In sight, in heryng, or in felynge,
In smellynge, in tastynge with mouthe,
In kyssynge—þat es a taken couthe—,
In halsynge or in vndertakyng,
In beckenyng and in signes makyng,
In wrestelynge þat es play of strengthe,
In ekynge and lessynge of brede and lengthe;
In gifinge or takynge of giftes,
After þat men þair handes skiftes;
In any of Goddis commandementes,
Or in Haly Writte þat men to tentes;
þe circumstaunce of synne to take
þat þe synne ful greef may make,
Als tyme, stede, manere, and tale,

5737–8 *couplet trs.* L 5738–9 *lines trs.* P 5738 þan] þat L men] he P 5739 halde] haue L and to] or for to R 5741 to] for to R 5744 a] *om.* E a man has] þu has anes R 5745 to[1]] of LR 5746 or] es E, and to L, and PS 5747 assayle] sayl W on] in R 5749 þat] þat mykell L 5750 men] *om.* R mare] hegh S 5751 Hard-] Hardy- PW som] some mene EP þat[2]] þat men L 5752 men . . . meyner] menere men S 5753 -standynge] -takying S 5754 heryng . . . felynge] *trs. sbs.* P or] and W 5755 with] *adds* þe R 5756 a] *om.* E taken] takenyng L 5757 halsynge] askyng `in h'alsyng (*int. later*) E 5758 and] or R 5759 es] es a LP 5760 ekynge] eggyng W and[1]] or PW of] in W and[2]] or P 5761 or] or in L, and R 5764 haly] any L 5765 of] of þe L 5766 ful] of W greef] grefull R

Person, dwellyng, elde, and witte haale—
þe whilk er declared in þis boke
A lytell bifore, þar men may loke;
And when a man him puttes to synne
Bifore ar fondynges bigynne,
Or paynes hym to synne mare
With his body þan myster ware.

De virtute Probitatis

fo. 36rb þise er þe synnes to telle shortly
þat comes of werk and dede of body.

Peccata omissionis boni

þe synnes of leuyng of gode vnwroght
Es to haue noght Godde in thoght,
To luf him noght, ne to drede;
To thank him noght of al gode dede;
To halde noght done thurgh Goddis myght
þe dedes þat a man dose right;
For synnes here na sorow to make,
Als a man suld do for Goddis sake;
To make him noght ay redy and able
Grace to resayue þat es profitable;
To vse noght grace, ne to kepe wele
þat men has getyn and may fele;
To turne him noght ne hym hast
To þe enspyrynge of þe Haly Gast;
To confourme noght his wille haally
Vnto þe wille of Godde almyghty;
To ga noght to þe kirk, ne to pray,
Ne þe houres of þe day to say;
To leue thing vndone thurgh neclygence
To whilk he es halden of obedyence;

5768 dwellyng elde] eldyng dwellyng P 5770 þar] þat W 5771 him puttes] *trs.* LS to] in R 5772 ar] er he W fondynges] fandyng L, \`he' fandes to S 5773 to] for to R 5776 of[2]] and LSR 5776a *marg.* EP, *om.* LS, *as in-column heading* R, De virtute probitatis (*marg.*) W 5777 synnes] syne R of[2]] *om.* LR gode] *om.* L, dede S 5778 to] *om.* P 5779 noght] *adds* god R to] hym to L 5780 al] hys L 5782 dedes] deyd R a] *om.* S 5783 synnes] synnyng L to] wyll L, for to S 5785 ay] *om.* ELPSRW 5787 ne to] and L, \`ne' to P kepe] kepe it L 5788 may] may it L 5789 noght] *om.* L hym[2]] *om.* S, *add* to LSR 5790 þe[1]] *om.* LP 5793 ne] and L 5794 Ne] Ne no\`ne' S þe[1]] na R 5796 To] To þe E To . . . halden] þat he es halden to L

To do noght his offyce ne to hald vowe;
To fader or moder noght to bowe;
To resayue noght anes in þe yhere
Housill and shrift with conscience clere;
To knaw noght himself ne his state;
To reproue noght his synnes ne hate;
His conscience noght right to lede,
Nouthir in worde ne in dede;
To tary and to do noght sone
Thinge þat felle be tyte done;
To haf na ioy ne solace
Of othir mens welefare and grace,
Or to haue na sorow ne care
Of othir mens angre and illefare;
To relese noght ne to forgieue
Wranges, al-if þai might gretly greue;

Donum Fortitudinis De virtute Probitatis Panem n.c.d.n.h.

To kepe noght trouth ne leaute fo. 36va
To othir men, als falles to be;
To answer noght to þe gode dede
þat othir men has done in nede.
Also to do noght blethely
Als falles þe Werkes of Mercy:
To chasty noght þam þat mysdose;
To snybbe þam noght þat syn wil vse;
To make noght pees als falles bi skille
þare þar stryf es and ille wille;
To teche noght vnconande men,
þe whilk men er halden to kenne;
To comfort þam noght saddely

5797 to[2]] *om.* LP vowe] his vow P 5798 or] and ES, and to L, ne R noght to] *om.* L 5799 anes] enes W 5800 and] ne W 5801 ne] ne þaim E, and S 5802 synnes] syn P 5804 ne] *int.* P, ne ȝit R 5806 felle be tyte] tyt fell to be R be tyte] tyte to be LS, to be tyte PW 5807 na] *om.* E ne] ne na R 5809 Or] Or ȝit R to] for to L na] nouther L ne] and S 5810 ille-] wele- L 5811 to[2]] *om.* SW 5812 al-if] if all L might] noȝt R 5813 ne] and P 5815 to[2]] vnto P þe] þi R 5816 in] in in P 5817 Also] Als P 5818 falles] *add* to ELPS, to W 5819 noght þam] *trs.* ES 5820 snybbe] snob W wil] *om.* P 5821 pees] *om.* L 5822 þar[2]] *om.* LS, als PW, whar R 5824 þe whilk] þat L men] we S to] for to L

þat has angre and er sary.
To do noght after gode mens rede;
To be noght deuout in haly bede.
Here men may se and knawe
Many synnes wryten on rawe;
He þat lokes þam ouer graythely
May wyte of what syn he es gilty;
Swa may he ransake al his lyf
And knawe of what he sal him shryue.
Confessio humilis þe sext condicioun es þareby
þat a man suld shryue him mekely.
For he þat in shrift his hert lawes
Spekes to Godde þat it wele knawes,
For þe preste þat es of shrift herer
In shrift he es tolde Goddis a[wne] ere,
And al þat es shewed hym þan
He heres als Godde, and noght als man.
þarefore þe synful suld thurgh right
In shrift him meke with al his myght,
Als he war bifore Godde of heuen
And with dole and drede his synnes neuen.
Confessio frequens þe seuent condycioun es þis to se,
þat a man suld oft shryuen be
Of wicked dedes and thoghtes and willes,
And þat war nedeful for sex skilles.
Ane es for mare grace to wynne
And to be made mare clene withinne.

Donum Fortitudinis De virtute Probitatis Panem n.c.d.n.h.

fo. 36vb Anothir es for synnes venyele
þat men may ilk day newe fele,
For þat at oft fyled es sene,

5826 has angre] angers haue R 5829 men may] *trs.* ELPR se] bathe se R 5830 Many] Full many R on] on a W 5832 wyte] se LP es] es of L 5834 of what] wharof R what] what synne L 5835 sext condicioun] sex condicions R *sidenote om.* W 5836 suld] sall P 5838 it wele] *trs.* E 5839 es] *after* shrift P 5840 tolde] calde LSR *awne ere] avener AELS, ane ere P 5841 And] In P hym] to hym R 5845 of] in L 5846 synnes] *adds* to L 5847 seuent] secound W þis] *om.* PRW 5849 and[1]] *om.* R 5850 nedeful] nede L 5852 clene] clere LPS 5854 newe] `nere' P

Oft bihoues be wasshed clene,
And thinge þat oft comes þat dere may
Men bihoues oft do it away,
Als dose þe shipman þat þe shippe kepes
Ay when þe water withinne crepes:
Als oft als it comes in fast,
Als oft bihoues hym out it cast;
And bot he do, þe shippe sal synke
Thurgh weght of þe water, als methynk.
So fares a mans saul withinne,
In wham comes ilk day newe synne
þat him bihoues in shrift roun,
And elles it suld his saul weghe doun.
For als many smale cornes may make
A grete charge til ane hors backe,
Right so may many synnes smale
Make a grete dedely synne hale.

De minimis granis fit maxima sarcina caballi

þe thridde skille es to chace þe fende
Fra him away, þat wald hym shende.
þe ferthe skille es for to lere
To shryue him wele while he es here.
þe fift skille es to telle forþi
þat he ne wate neuer certaynely
If he war euer shryuen clene
Of alle his synnes þat he may mene.
þe sext es to be þe mare meke
And for þe mare mede to seke.

Bot fyue thinges shrift mast lettes
þat þe fende in mans hert settes.
Ane es shame in hert ful euen
þat a man has his synnes to neuen;
Anothir es wicked drede þarto
þat a man has penaunce to do.

5856 clene] and made clene P 5857 And] A W þat[2]] and L 5858 do it] *trs.* W 5859 dose] *after* shipman P 5860 withinne] *adds* it E 5861 als[2]] at E it] þe water P 5862 hym] men P out it] *trs.* PW 5863 And] *om.* L 5864 weght] þe weght PW þe] *om.* S als] *om.* P 5866 newe] 'nere' (*corr. later*) P 5867 him bihoues] *trs.* R shrift] schryt L 5869 *sidenote*: *largely in gutter* A, *om.* ELPS 5872 Make] May make L 5873 skille] *om.* L, synne S 5877 forþi] forwhy L 5878 ne] *om.* S neuer] *om.* P 5879 If] If þat L shryuen] *om.* L 5880 his] *om.* E mene] of mene L 5881 þe[2]] *om.* LSR 5883 Bot] For R 5884 þat] And E 5886 synnes] synne W neuen] nemen W

þe thridde es wicked luf to telle
þat a man has in syn to dwelle;
þe ferthe es wrangehope of hert
þat a man has of lange lyf in quert.
þe fift es wanhope, werst of alle,
In whilk þe fende mas a man falle.

De virtute Probitatis

fo. 37ra þe thridde thynge es Amendes to make
Satisfaccio operis þat man suld to þe armure take.
For a man suld be ay redy
To make amendes of his foly
And penaunce do þat þe saul auaylles,
Als his shrift-fader him counsaylles,
þat Amendes in shryft demes
After þe perille of his synne semes.
Bellum penitencie þe secund bataylle es of Penaunce
þat puttes a man oft fra Suffraunce,
For when a man hym sal repent
Of his synne þat hym has shent,
þan at first comes ouerthwert
A new stryf vntill his hert
þat mas a man so vnstedefast
So þat his purpose may noght last.
Ful chaungeable es his thoght;
Forwhy certayne of wille es he noght
To what penaunce he suld him spede
And what lyf he myght here lede.
For som bigynnes Penaunce to haunt
þat in þat bataylle er recreaunt,
Bot aftir þe wedircocke lyf þai
þat with alle wyndes turnes ay;
So lightly chaunges a mans thoght:

5892 in] and R 5894 In] In þe L falle] to falle ELPS 5895 thridde] fyrste L *sidenote: as in-column heading* R operis] *om.* L 5896 man] mene ELSRW 5897 be ay] *trs.* S 5898 of] for L 5899 do] to do P 5902 synne semes] synnes R 5903 of] *om.* L *sidenote: om.* L, *as in-column heading* De bello penitencie R 5904 puttes . . . oft] a man oft puttis P 5905 hym sal] *trs.* LP 5906 synne] synnes P hym has] haues hym LSRW 5907 first] arst P 5908 stryf] schryft R vntill] intil W 5909 vnstedefast] vnstabell stedfaste L 5911 es] þan ys R 5912 he] it R 5914 what] watkyn R 5916 recreaunt] creaunt W 5917–18 *couplet trs.* L 5917 Bot] *om.* L 5918 turnes] turne will P

Now he wille, and now he wil noght.
Bot when a man þat God wald pay
Settes his hert in swilk a way
To do penaunce and it fulfille
So þat nathynge chaunge his wille,
Ne in his penaunce wil noght faylle,
þan ouercomes he þat bataylle.
  þe thridde bataylle es ay fresshe; *Bellum carnis*
þat es þe bataylle of his Flesshe.
þat bataylle es bathe kene and felle
And langest with a man wil dwelle.
For when þe Flesshe penaunce beres
Or any hardnes þat it deres,
It groches þarewith and pleynes it oft,
For it lufs wele alle thing þat es soft,
And alle eses and + delyces

De virtute Probitatis

þat ledes a man to many vices. fo. 37rb
And if þe Flesshe haf al þe wille,
It ouercomes a man thurgh skille.
  Bot I wil licken after I can
þe Flesshe vntill ane ille womman,
Of wham þe maners er noght to prayse,
Als Salamon þe wyse man says.
For euer þe mare men folwes hir wille,
þe mare fraward sho es and ille,
And þe mare felle and þe mare kene,
Als was in Sampson þe forte sene
þat of a womman ouercommen was;
For hir wyles his strengthe gun passe.
For in his hare was al his strengthe,
þat semely was of brede and lengthe;
Al þat was haally fra hym reft

5920 Now] þat now L and] *om.* L 5924 chaunge] chaunges W 5927 *sidenote*: *om.* L, *as in-column heading* De bello carnis R 5928 his] þe ELR 5933 it[2]] *om.* EP 5934 wele] *om.* L alle] a P 5935 alle] *om.* P, allkyns R eses] eyse PW *and[2]] and alle AELS, and þe P 5939 after] als LR 5942 *sidenote*: Salamon ES 5943 euer] ay L folwes] fylghes E, dose L 5945 þe[2]] *om.* LPS mare[2]] *om.* L 5946 þe forte] force L, þe force S 5951 was . . . him] haly fra hym wasse L, was fra hym haaly R

So þat na strengthe was with him left;
þan felle he in þe handes of his enmys—
Al was thurgh a wommans quayntys.
  Forsothe right so oft it fares
Of a mans Flesshe, whaso it spares;
If he lat it hym ouercom,
It castes hym intill a thralledom,
For it maas him to synne ful boun,
When it bicomes wylde and wantoun.
Bot it war gode for þe saul bote
To halde þe Flesshe ay vndirfote
And lat it haue na delyte;
þan may [he] lightly it skomfyte.
For whaso ouercomes þat bataylle
Godde him hetes withouten faylle
þe whyte robe of his lyuere;
þat es þe robe of Chastyte.

Bellum mundi et fortune

  þe ferth and þe fift bataylle þan
þe Werlde brynges to assaylle a man
And Dame Fortune with hir whele
þat turnes obout, als men may fele.
þe Werlde a man here assaylles
On aythir syde with twa bataylles;
þe tane es þe ferthe to neuen
And þe tothir þe fift of þe seuen.
  þe ta bataylle es, als I gesce,
Of honours, delices, and ritchesce,

Donum Fortitudinis De virtute Probitatis Panem n.co.da no.h.

fo. 37va

þe whilk þe Werld profirs in sight;
þat assaylles a man on þe syde right.
þe tothir bataylle es ful smert;

5952 with] in L, *om.* PW 5953 þe] *om.* E handes] hand R 5954 Al] Al þat P, And all R 5955 oft] *om.* L, full oft R oft it] *trs.* S 5957 lat] will lat R 5958 a] *om.* L, a depe P 5961 Bot] Bot gyf R þe] *om.* P 5963 haue] haue right R 5964 *he] *om.* A it] *after* he P skomfyte] dyscomfyte E 5966 him hetes] *trs.* R 5969 fift] *om.* S *sidenote*: *om.* SW, *as in-column heading* De duobus bellis mundi R et fortune] *om.* P 5970 brynges] bygynnes W to assayle] and assailes P 5973 here] *after* werlde P 5976 þe[2]] is þe P þe[3]] þase L 5978 delices] delites W 5979 werld profirs] *trs.* E 5980 a man] *after* þat P

þat es angre, iuel, and pouert
þat Godde sendes for þe saul bihoue,
Som to chasty and som to proue;
þat assaylles fast on þe left syde.
þat bataylle suld a man habyde
And stand stalwardely in þat stour,
For Godde wil helpe him and sokour.
Bot whaso flees Werldes likynge
And bides angres withouten grochyng,
He ouercomes þe bataylles bathe
And passes away withouten skathe.
For þe first bataylle God hetes him þis,
Worshepe and lykinge in heuen-blisse;
For Godde sal sette him with him right
In his trone so richely dight,
Als Saynt Iohan beres wittenes *Nota*
In þe *Apocalips*, als wryten es.
And for þe tothir, Godde rightwys
Hetes hym þe delyces of Paradys,
þe whilk he grauntes alle þa at þe last
þat in þat bataylle standes fast
And ouercomes with gode chere
þe angres of þis Werlde here.
þe sext bataylle þat I wil telle *Bellum praue gentis*
Es of wicked men and felle,
þe whilk er lyms of Antecryst
þat þe fende of helle has noryst.
þai noy þa þat gode men er kidde
Als wicked tyrauntes martirs didde,
And als Antecryst sal do to som
In þe ende of þe werld þat sal com.

5982 angre iuel] angers well (*corr. from* iwell) S iuel] and ille L 5983 þe] *om.* W 5984 *sidenote*: Nota E 5985 þat] þen W 5988 For] *om.* L Godde] `he' P helpe] hegh W 5989–90 *couplet trs.* L 5989 Bot whaso] And L werldes] þe werldes L, wardly PSR 5990 And] For he þat L bides] abides LS 5991 þe] þase L, þai R 5993 God] *om.* P him] *om.* L 5996 trone] riche trone R 5997 *sidenote*: *om.* EP, Iohannes euangelista L, Iohannes S, Iohannes Apocalipsis W 5999 Godde] *adds* þat es L 6000 Hetes] Hete S delyces] ioy L 6001 þa] *om.* P þe[2]] *om.* L 6002 þat[2]] þe W fast] fastes S 6004 þis] þe W 6005 þat I wil] þan wyll I L telle] þe tell W *sidenote: as in-column heading* De bello praue gentis R 6006 Es] þat es L of] of þe P men] folk R 6007 þe] *om.* L lyms] þe lymmes L 6009 noy] neyȝe W þa] þaim ESR gode men] men þat L 6010 martirs] god martyrs E 6011 And] *om.* L

For þai þat wil noght to hym assent
Sal be done to swilke tourment
þat vnnethes sal any lif þan
þat dar hym clayme for Cristen man.
Bot he þat in þis werlde leues
þe whilk wicked men oft greues,
If he take alle his greuaunce
Als Iob did with gode suffraunce
And trayst in Godde, mast of myght,
He ouercomes þat bataylle right.

Donum Fortitudinis De virtute Probitatis Panem n.co.da no.h.

fo. 37vb Til hym þat dose opon þis wyse
Godde hetes power ouer his enmyse.
Bellum diaboli þe seuent bataylle and þe last
Aftirward assaylles vs fast.
þat es þe bataylle of þe fende
þat assaylles a man ay at þe last ende.
Forwhy þe fende es so wyly
And til a man he has swilke enuy
þat when he has ouercommen thurgh myght
þe sex bataylles þat I touched right,
And es clommen vp on þe mountayne
Of parfytenes of lyf certayne,
þan comes þe fende vnto þat man
With sleghtes to ouercom hym þan
And assaylles hym to stryke him doun
Thurgh Vayneglory and Presumpcioun.
For when he has wele ouercommen
þe sex bataylles and es heghe clomen,

6014 to] into R tourment] turnament R 6017 þis] *om.* E, þe S 6018 whilk] *adds* þat L 6019 If] And L take] will tak R 6021 trayst] *om.* W 6022 He ouercomes] þan ouercomes he LR 6023 dose] duse ay R opon] on PRW 6024 hetes] *add* hym LPS ouer] of R 6025 seuent] second W *sidenote*: *om.* W Bellum] Prelium P, De bello (*as in-column heading*) R 6028 þat] þat is þe P assaylles] sayles W a man] men L ay] *om.* ELPW 6029 es] ys ay R 6030 a] *om.* L he] *om.* LRW 6031 ouercommen] *adds* hym R 6032 sex] sext L bataylles] batayle LR I] I haue L touched] tolde P 6033 es] *om.* P clommen] commen L 6034 of] of þe L 6035 vnto] to W *sidenote*: Deceptio diaboli R 6036 *line om.* L sleghtes] sleghtnes R 6037 hym[1]] *om.* R stryke] smyte L doun] dome R 6040 sex bataylles] sext batayle L es . . . clomen] ouercommen L

Hym think hym þan mare worthy
þan othir er and mare haly
And with Godde of heuen mare priue
þan any othir man suld be,
For him think þai haf noght so wele done.
So mas þe fende hym falle sone
And als lawe to þe sight of eghe
Als him thoght bifore he was heghe,
Als Lucifer did in a short tyde
þat felle fra heuen til helle for pryde.
þarefore methink it war grete nede
Til hym þat wil parfyte lyf lede
þat of þa bataylles has victory
To defende hym fra Vayneglory
And fra Presumpcioun alswa.
For þe fende about ledes þise twa,
Als þe rerewarde þat comes bihynde
To assayle gode men þat he may fynde
And to ouercom þam and doun cast
þat clymmes heghe and standes noght fast;
For thurgh þat rerewarde parchaunce
A man may falle oft in combraunce.
Als a shippe may tittar perisshed be
Nere þe hauen þan inmyddes þe see,
Right so a man, als clerkes knawes,
þat to þe hauen of hele drawes
Thurgh þe fende es tempted mare
þan he fer fra þe hauen ware.

De virtute Probitatis De dono Consilij

For þe fende a man mast waytes fo. 38ra
þat parfyte lyf and saul-hele laytes,
Bot a man suld sette his hert haally

6041 hym þan] *trs.* E þan] þe P, þat wele R 6043 of heuen] *om.* L 6044 man] men S 6045 think] think þat L 6046 So] þare L falle] to falle EL 6047 þe] *om.* E 6048 he] þat he L, *om.* R 6049 a] *om.* P 6052 wil] walde L 6053 þa] þe W 6057 rerewarde] reward RW 6059 ouercom] euer come E doun] to doune ES 6061 For] Bot L þat] þe P rerewarde] reward RW 6062 falle] fayle E, *om.* P 6063 perisshed] peryss S 6064 þe[2]] *om.* E 6066 hele] helle ELSRW 6067 tempted] tempede P 6068 fer] ferrer S 6070 and] in L saul] *om.* W 6071 *sidenote*: Nota (*later*?) P

And his luf in Godde almyghty
And hungre after rightwisnes
And yherne to do þat Goddis wille es
And to defende hym be ay redy
Fra Presumpcion and Vayneglory.
So may he þat bataylle skomfyte
And do þe fende a grete dispyte.
  And he þat ouercommes þat bataylle
Sal haue þe mede þat neuer sal faylle.
For Saynt Ione says, als þis clerkes sees,
In þe *Boke of Priuytees*
þar Godde says þus, mast of myght,
Til hym þat ouercommes right,
'I sal þe gif at ete, withouten strif,
Of þe fruyte of þe tre of lyf
þat es in midward Paradyse'—
þat fruyt passes al fruyt of pryse.
Whaso wille þe fende ouercom,
Of þat fruyt þan getes he som.
  þise seuen bataylles er seuen degrees
Of Pruesce þat gode men suld chees,
þe whilk vertu a man may lede
Euen vnto þe blissedhede
Of Hungre and Thrist of Rightwisnes
And to þe mede þat þarefore es,
þat es þe blissefull Fillynge
Of ioy and gastly lykynge.

Beati qui esuriunt et siciunt iusticiam, quoniam ipsi sat⟨ura⟩buntur

  Als Godde says þat es ful of myght,
'Blissed be þay þat hungre right
And thrist[es] after rightwisnes,
For þai sal be filled' of ioy endeles,
To whilk Pruesce—þat anely springes

6072 his] all hys L 6073 after] *adds* his W 6074 yherne] *om.* S Goddis] god L 6078 do] to L, to do P a] be L 6081 þis] *om.* LP *sidenote*: Iohannes ES 6082 þe] þe nobell L 6083 þar] þat L says þus] þat es L 6084 Til] þus says to L, Vnto R 6085 þe] *om.* PRW gif] *adds* him W at] to EW at ete] *om.* S strif] schryft W *sidenote*: Dabo tibi edere de ligno vite quod est in medio paradisi ES 6087 midward] *adds* of R 6088 al . . . pryse] of all fruytes þe prise L 6090 he] *om.* R 6092 Pruesce] prowest L 6094 vnto] to L 6095 of[2]] and PW 6099 Als] And als L *sidenote*: *om.* LW quoniam . . .] etc. P 6100 hungre] hungres ESRW *6101 thristes] thrist AR 6102 of] wyth L, of þe P 6103 To] To þe E

Of þe Gift of Strengthe—a man bringes.
þan may men wyte þat tentes þarto
What þe Gift of Strengthe may do
þat þe ferth askynge þat we say
In þe Pater Noster wynne vs may,
In whilk namely þis gift we craue;
Godde graunt vs þat we may it haue.
Amen

Panem nostrum cotidianum da nobis hodie

De virtute Probitatis De dono Consilij

De dono Consilij

fo. 38rb

Anothir gift may mykill auaylle
þat es þe Gift of Counsaylle,
þat teches vs wele Goddis wille
And mas our wille acorde þartille.
þat gift amange alle othir thynge
We aske in þe thridde askynge
Of þe Pater Noster þat we bidde,
þat mast haly prayere es kydde.
þat gift out puttes of þe hert a vice
þat þise clerkes calles Auaryce.

Fiat voluntas etc.

De peccato Auaricie

Auaryce shewes it in thinges thre:
Bisy Wynnynge ane may be;
Strayt Haldynge anothir es;
þe thridde es Spendynge of Skarsnes.
For Auaryce es swilk a synne
þat mas a man be bisy to wynne
Werldely godes þat bihoues faylle,
And in þat has he grete trauaylle.

De Auaricia

6104 a] þat a L 6105–6 *couplet om.* W 6105 men] man L 6107 þat] *om.* L þe] `in' þe (*later*) P þat] *om.* P *sidenote*: *as in-column heading, with* etc. *at end* W nostrum] *ends* ES cotidianum] *ends* L 6108 wynne vs] when we W 6109 namely] anely P 6110a *om.* LPSR 6110b Donum consilij ELS, *as in-column heading* R, *as running title* W 6111 may] may vs L 6114 acorde] to acorde L 6116 in] *om.* P *sidenote*: *om.* W etc.] *om.* E, tua PS 6117 þat] `when' P 6118 þat] þe R mast] þe maste L 6119 gift] gyftes S out puttes] *trs.* S, cf. fra þe hert puttes L, out puttes out W 6120a *om.* ELPSW, *as in-column heading* R 6121 shewes] it schewes L it] *om.* SR *sidenote*: *om.* L, Auaricia P 6122 wynnynge] -nges P 6124 of] in ELS skarsnes] skarnes S 6126 þat] þat it LR be] *om.* ELPS 6127 faylle] to fayll R

Auaryce a mans hert settes
To halde straytly þat he gettes,
And in þat has he grete drede
For he wenes ay he sal haf nede.
Auaryce makes a man so skarse
þat he noght spendes, bot ay spars;
And mas hym haue at þe departynge
Of þa godes dole and myslykynge
And parchaunce payne withouten ende
For þam when he sal hethen wende.
þus has a man in þe wynnynge
Trauaylle, and drede in þe haldynge,
And [in] þe departynge sorow and wo,
And parchaunce endeles payne also.
Auaryce may be tolde bi skille
Bigynnynge and rote of alle ille;
þat es a craft þat þe fende leres
To þam þat wil be his skolers.
Auaryce men may bi skille calle
A tre þat growes and spredes ouer alle,

Donum Consilij De peccato Auaricie
Fiat voluntas . . .

fo. 38va Of whilk springes braunches ten
þat spredes amange alle maner of men.
Ane es Oker first to bygynne;
Anothir es Theft, þe thridde Rauynne;
þe ferth es Chalenge in falshede;
þe fift es Sacrilege to drede;
þe sext braunche Symony es;
þe seuent braunche es Wickednes;
þe aghtned es Fals Marchaundyse
þat som men hauntes on many wyse;

6129 a] in a W 6130 straytly] st`r´angly (*corr. int. later*) P, ay straytly R 6131 grete] ay grete R 6132 he] þat he L 6136 þa] þe W dole] dele W 6137 payne] do payne L ende] endyng L 6138 he] þai E hethen] hyns R 6139 þus] þis W þe] *om.* L wynnynge] begynyng P 6140 drede] *om.* L 6141 *in] *om.* AL, ate ES departynge] passyng of þaime es wyth L 6143 tolde] calde EL 6148 growes] grofes P 6149 Of] Of þe L 6150 spredes] sprynges L 6153–4 *couplet trs.* L 6153 ferth es] fyft L chalenge] chalangyng L 6154 fift] ferthe L 6156 braunche] *om.* RW 6157 aghtned] aghted W

þe neghent es Craft of Foly
And also Offyce of Vylany;
þe tende may be called Fole Play
þat foles vses and nane bot þai.
Okir thurgh sleght of okereres *De Vsura*
Shewes it on many maneres.
þe first es when men frestes a thing *j.*
And takes oght for þe frestynge
Thurgh couenaunt bifore þat men mas;
Alle es Oker þat men swa tase.
þis may be halden commonly
Okir withouten curtaysy
And þat bihoues him yhelde agayne,
Or elles he sal haue helle payne.
Anothir manere of Okir es *ij.*
þat es þis, bot it es lesse:
Als when a man of his wille fre
Lenes siluer or gold in mone
And takes oght for þe frestynge
Of curtaysy withouten hetynge.
Yhete es þat Okir als men says,
Bot he þat tase it es curtays.
þat bihoues hym stoppe in þe dette,
Or elles wreth of Godde sal he gette.
For ilk man suld for Goddis sake
Til othir frest and noght þarefore take;
þan wil Godde for þat dede
Specially graunt him his mede.
þe thridde maner of Okir kidde *iij.*
Es þis þat es here mykell hidde:
Als when a man weldes a thinge
þat his frendes wan with okeryng,
And þai be passed out of þis lyf,

6159 craft] trayste L 6160 also] als of S offyce] offycye E 6161 fole] fulle fuyle E, foly SW 6162 vses] hauntes L 6163 *sidenote*: *om.* L, *as in-column heading* R De] *om.* W 6164 on] in P 6165 þe] *om.* P men] we L men] mens E, a man S *sidenote*: j^{us}. ramus E 6167 men] mens E 6169 þis] þase L halden] called L 6173 es] es þis S *sidenote*: ij^{us}. ramus ES 6178 Of] Or L hetynge] hethyng W 6180 he] *om.* W es] is noȝt P 6181 þat . . . stoppe] Or elles stopp sumwhat L hym] *om.* S 6182 wreth] wreke P, werthe R sal he] *trs.* LP 6187 *sidenote*: iij^{us}. ramus ES 6188 here] *om.* LP es . . . mykell] mekill is P 6189 weldes] her weldes R

Be it fader, moder, or wyf.

Donum Consilij De peccato Auaricie
Fiat voluntas . . .

fo. 38vb He suld noght halde it in store
Bot he wald make assethe þarfore,
þat es to say if he may witt
How his frendes had wonnen it.
And if he do, he es gilty
Als he þat first didde þat foly.
iiij. þe ferthe manere es chargeand;
þat es þis to vndirstande,
Als when a man a seruaunt has
þat Okir til his vse tase.
If he þareof payde hym halde,
He may be mayster okerer cald.
v. þe fift manere of Okir es þis
þat som men vses þat lifs mysse.
Als when a man for Okir lens
þe siluer þat es othir mens
þat he in kepyng has to saue—
With þat þus wil he Okir haue.
Or if he borow in priuite
For Okir siluer or othir mone
To lene to othir for to haue
Mare Okir þan he þarefor gaue.
He þat es disciple okerere;
þat manere sal he bye ful dere,
Bot he þarefore amendes make
Ar þe dede hym hethen take.
vj. þe sext es þis: when a man selles
Corne or beste or oght elles

6193 noght] no wyse R 6194 wald] sulde P 6195 if] and L 6196 *line om.* L How] Howgates R 6197 And if] Bot L do] ne do E, noght do S, restore it L 6198 first didde] *trs.* R 6199 ferthe] ferther S *sidenote*: iiij^{us}. ramus ES 6201 a^{2}] his P 6202 his] *om.* R 6203 If] And L 6204 okerer] of okerer W cald] talde L 6205 okir] okerer L *sidenote*: v^{us} ramus ES, *om.* L 6206 vses] lufes L lifs] lenys? P mysse] omysse LS, of mysse P 6208 þe] *om.* LS siluer] syluer or golde S 6210 he] he þe P 6211 if he borow] it be borowed L he] a man P 6212 okir] *adds* of L othir] any L 6213 for] to for E haue] *repeats* R 6214 þarefor] to oþer P 6217 amendes] mendes P 6218 hethen] hyns R 6219 þis] *om.* L *sidenote*: vj^{us}. ramus ES, *om.* L

And frestes it til a terme day
And selles derrer for frest of þe pay.
In þe dette if he do wele,
He suld allowe it ilka dele,
þat he has mare, als I vnderstande,
þan he wald first haf tane in hande.
And bot he do, he mon be shent
When he es of þis werlde went.
þe seuent maner of Okir soght *vij.*
Es þis þat som men charges noght:
Als when a man selles a thing namely
Til him þat nede has it to bye,
For he sees wele and can wit
þat he þat byes may noght tharne it.
þan selles he it for double prys;
He takes ouermykell on þat wyse.
Na mare he suld take of hym þan

De peccato Auaricie

þan it war worth til anothir man, fo. 39ra
For al þat he þat tyme tas mare
þan þe worth him sal rewe sare.
For on þa[t] wyse dose he noght
Als he wald til hym war wroght;
þarefore sal he aresouned be,
For he dose agayne charyte.
þe aghned manere es þis to drede, *viij.*
When a man sees anothir haf nede
To selle corne, catell, or fee
Bifore þe tyme þat fell to be.
þan byes he it for a light prys
Til his auauntage on þis wyse,
So þat he make bifore þe pay

6222 derrer] der W þe] þat R 6223 if] and L 6224 suld] sall L, bus R 6225 has] had W 6226 þan] þat E 6229 *sidenote*: vij^{us}. ramus ES 6230 som men charges] *trs. phrs.* P 6231 namely] anely P 6232 nede . . . it] it has nede R it] *om.* ELS to] for to L 6233 can wit] knawes it L 6234 he þat byes] þe byer L tharne] thary R 6235 for] *om.* P 6237 he suld] *trs.* ELS, shuld be R hym] þam E 6239 þat^{1} . . . tyme] *trs. phrs.* P þat tyme] *om.* L 6240 him] he L 6241 *þat] þan A dose] ne duse R 6242 til] vnto R 6245 *sidenote*: viij. ramus E, *om.* LS 6246 a man] he L haf] has P 6247 To] For to R 6249 a] *om.* E

And þe corne habide til a day,
'For he has na dout + ne þe corn sal be
At þe day mar worth þan þat payed he'.
[þusgates es þe bargane wroght]
So þat þe byer has half for noght,
For at þe day may falle swa
þat þe corne es worth swilke twa.
þarefore he suld when he it tase
Pay hym mare als þe corne þan gase,
And if he rewarde hym with na mare,
þan tase he Oker als I sayde are.
ix. þe neghent maner of Okir I fynde
þat mas som mens conscience blynde
þat es, when a man for auauntage
Lenes siluer for rent in morgage
And tase þe profete of þe rent
Ouer þe siluer þat es lent
Of al þe tyme vntill þe day
þat es sette to take þe pay.
Bot he þe profyte to prys sette
And allowe it in þe dette,
His saul sal be in grete daungere
Als he þat es ane okerere.
x. þe tende manere of Oker may be
In þis case þat men may oft se:
Als when a man withhaldes for ay
A wedde þat layde es til a day
For he has noght þe pay of þe dette,
Namely at þe day þat es sette.
Al-if þe couenaunt swilke ware,

6252 habide] byde ELS til] vntille E a] anoþer P *6253–4 *om.*, *added vertically in the margin later* A; *om.* EPS *6253 ne þe] þat ne þe A, þat þe LRW 6254 At . . . worth] *trs. phrs.* RW þat] *om.* L, furst R payed] gaf RW *6255 *as* ELPS, þus may þe corne be sald and boght *over erasure later* A, And (*om.* R) so may þe corn be sald and boght RW 6256 So] *om.* RW has] has þe P, sall haue RW 6257 at] *om.* P 6258 þat] *om.* P worth] wor⟨g⟩ht (g *erased*) P 6260 þe] *om.* RW þan] *om.* L 6261 And] For R 6263 *sidenote*: ix. ramus ES, *om.* L 6264 conscience] ociens W 6266 morgage] morage LS 6267 of] for W 6268 es] it P 6269 vntill] to PW 6270 þat] þe whilk R take] make ELSR 6271 to] to þe L 6275 *sidenote*: x. ramus ES, *om.* L 6276 oft] *om.* P 6277–8 *couplet trs.* L 6277 with-] for- L for] *om.* W 6279 þe[1]] *om.* L þe[2]] *om.* S 6280 es] wasse L, he has W 6281 Al-] And L

Yhete [i]f þe wedde war worth mare

De peccato Auaricie

þan þe dette amount myght, fo. 39rb
Hym bihoued yhelde agayne thurgh right,
Or elles he sal haue ane harde fitte
When he sal out of þis werlde flitte.
Or if a man a wedde þat es layde
Were vntill þe dette be payde,
If it be appayred, als I trowe,
In þe pay hym bihoues allowe
And stoppe als mykell and na lesse
Als þe wedde appayred þan es.
And bot he do, I warne him wele
He mon þarefore harde payne fele.
  þe elleuent manere fynde I now *xj.*
þat es þis þat dar I avowe:
When a man tase til a marchande
Siluer or gold bi þis couenande,
þat he haf half þat wynnynge es
And his awen siluer neuer þe lesse.
If he take half wynnynge fre
Withouten Oker may þat noght be,
For he wil haue ay half wynnyng
And noght allowe, al-if þare be tynyng.
Bot if he make first swilk couenand
þat he to perille of losse wil stande,
And alowe, als falles, alle costage,
þan may he take half auauntage
Leeffully als þe couenand wille
Withouten Okir, and þat es skille.
  And þe same maner in catell lys

*6282 if] of AES 6283 þan] *om.* P dette] wedde L 6286 sal] *after* werlde R out] *om.* L þis] þe W 6287 a[2]] *om.* P 6288 Were] *adds* it L vntill] ay to PW 6289 ap-] en- LR, *om.* P 6290 allowe] it alow L 6292 ap-] en- LR þan] *om.* L, *before* appayred R 6294 -fore] *om.* E 6295 *sidenote*: xj. ramus E, *om.* L, xj[us]. S 6296 þat[2]] *om.* L dar I] *trs.* LSW 6298 bi þis] of þe L 6301 take] so tak R 6302 þat] *om.* E, *after* noght LS, *after* oker P 6303 ay] *om.* LP 6304 al-] *om.* ELPSRW if] it R tynyng] tuynnyng E, tynenyng L, lessynge W 6305 first] *om.* LP swilk] *add* a ELP 6306 to] to þe L of] of þe L losse] lesse W wil] *om.* L 6307 alle] all þe L, to all P 6308 half] *adds* þe L 6309 wille] es P 6310 es skille] *trs.* P

þat to half es laten on þis wyse:
When a man lates catelle or fee
To half, if swilk þe couenaunt be,
þat he half þe auauntage haue
þat þareof comes and his awen saue,
So þat if þat catelle be lost,
He wil haue haally þat it cost
Ne yhete allowe na costage,
þan hald I Okir al his auauntage.
xij. þe twelft manere of Okir es ille
þat es þis þat som men vse wille:
Als when a man wil frest or len
Siluer or corne til symple men

Donum Consilij De peccato Auaricie
Fiat voluntas tua etc.

fo. 39va Or othir thinge þat myght þam auaylle.
þan puttes he þam vnto trauaylle
In his werkes þat he wald war wroght,
And elles wald he frest þam noght.
Or if þai may noght þe dette pay
Als þai er halden at þe day,
þan mas he with þam couenand
To wirke his werkes with fote or hand
For þat dette þat þai hym awe
And þarto he byndes þam with þe lawe.
He wil for ilk peny of þe dette
Thre penyworth of werke sette.
þis es a synfull bargayne
þarefore he mon haf mykell payne.
Now haf I shewed yhou on sere wyse
þe cases in whilk Okir lyse.

6313 a man] *om.* W 6314 if] if þat W 6315 þat] If R þat he] `he´ þat P þe] *om.* LS 6316 þareof] þer L 6317 þat[1]] *om.* LW þat[2]] þat þe W 6319 yhete] nathing L, hit W yhete allowe] alow will P na] þe L 6320 auauntage] vauntage P 6321 twelft] twelfe L *sidenote*: xij. ramus E, *om.* L, xij^{us}. S 6322 þis] *om.* L men] *om.* PR 6323 or] and PS 6325 auaylle] vaile P 6326 vnto] to LPW 6328 wald he] he wald ne R 6329 þai] he L 6330 þe] a LP 6331 mas he] he `makes´ (*later*) P þam] hym E 6332 or] and ELSR 6334 And] Or L, *om.* P þareto] elles L þam] him E þe] *om.* E 6335 þe] *om.* LW 6336 sette] gette S 6337 a] a full R 6339 yhou] *om.* LP

þe secund braunche of Auaryce *ij. De Latrocinio*
Es Theft þat es a wicked vyce.
Bot fyue maners of Theft I fynde,
In whilk Couatys mas men blynde.
For if þai þat men here theues calles
Couthe se what dome to theues falles
Thurgh lawe of lande and Goddis lawe,
To stele oght þai suld haf awe.
A maner of Theft es Theft Appert,
Anothir Pryue, þe thridde Couert;
þe ferthe es Lytell Theft to knawe;
þe fift es Theft of Theef Felawe.
Appert Theft dose he þat man *De Latrocino Manifesto*
þat thurgh sleght appertly stele can
And hauntes oft þat foly
To sustayne him and his þarby.
He war worthy, als I vndirstande,
Be tane and hanged thurgh law of lande.
A Pryue Theft dose he þis *De Latrocinio Occulto*
þat takes oght þat es noght his
And haldes it priuyly als his awen
And yhete es he for trewe man knawen.
B⟨ot⟩ whethir he take mare or lesse
A priue theef he þat es.
Bot al-if he be here for trewe kidde,
Fra Godde may noght þat theft be hidde;
And þoghe he skape here þe lawe of land,

Donum Consilij De peccato Auaricie
Fiat voluntas tua etc.

To Goddis lawe hym bihoues stande. fo. 39vb
For when his saul es hethen flemed,
Thurgh Goddis lawe he sal be demed

6341 *sidenote*: *as in-column heading* R ij.] *om*. ELPSRW 6345 here theues] *trs*. ES 6346 Couthe . . . to] Knew þe dome þat to L 6352 es] als L of] or S theef] thefes LP 6353 *sidenote om*. W 6354 appertly] a party E, aperly W appertly stele] *trs*. P 6355 oft] oftsithes R 6358 thurgh] be LP 6359 theft] theffe E, theft as R *sidenote om*. S 6361 priuyly] pryue LS 6362 man] *om*. L 6363 whethir] *om*. L 6365 al-if] if L be] be all L 6366 noght þat theft] it noght L 6367 And] For L þoghe] alle ELS, if R he skape] eschape (ehtchape E) he ELS þe] fra L 6368 hym bihoues] *trs*. LR 6369 hethen] hyns R

And parchaunce to endeles payne,
Bot he yhelde it here agayne.

De Latrocinio Palliato

A Couert Theft dose he in case
þat kepynge of his lordes godes hase,
Als bayllif, seriaunt, othir grayue
þat falles his lordes rentes resayue,
And in his acount reckenes lesse
þe receytes þan þe spens es.
So sleghely he can his acount sette
þat his lorde rynnes in his dette,
And puttes hymself vntill auauntage
þare he suld be in arerage.
So sleghely steles he his lordes rent
Methink he war worthy be shent.
Yhete thurgh colour of his offyce
He hauntes couertly þis vyce,
Auauntage of othir men to take
With fals sleghtes þat he can make.
þus can he couertly stele
And yhete he semes als he war lele.
Bot if he wist what he war worthy,
For swilk dedes hym aght be sory.
Also a wyf suld vnderstande
þat takes þe godes of hir husbande
Agayne his leue or his wille,
Sho steles þa godes and dose ful ille.
Or he þat es man religious
þat takes þe godes of his hous
Withouten leue of his souerayne,
He steles þa godes for certayne.
For wyf ne man of religyoun
Of þe godes þat es comoun

6372 Bot] Bot if LR 6373 *sidenote*: *om.* E palliato] pallato L, occulto S 6375 bayllif] bayles L seriaunt] sergauntes L othir] or other L, or yitt S, or els R 6376 resayue] to receyue LPSR 6377 his] *om.* L acount] cou(en?)ntes L, count P 6379 sleghely] lyghtly E acount] accountes PW 6380 þat] So þat R 6381 -self] *om.* L vntill] till ELPSR, intil W 6382 þare] And L, Whar R he] hys lorde L arerage] a reuerage (*with expunction* A) AR 6383 he] *om.* E 6384 be] to be LR 6385 Yhete] And yitt L 6386 vyce] wyse R 6391 if] and LR, *om.* P 6392 hym aght] he walde L 6393 Also] As W 6394 of] fro R 6395 or] and S 6396 þa godes] þat gode L 6397 man] a mane EP, a man of LS 6399 his] þe L 6400 *line om.* (*at page-bound*) W þa] þes P 6401 ne] and S

Has na manere of proprete;
þe lawe wil þat it so be.
þarefore þai may noght selle ne gif
Withouten þair soueraynes leef.
  Also þat wyf dose grete foly
þat has a chylde in auoutery.
If it be to hir lorde vnknawen
And he wenes þe chylde es his awen,
þe whilk als heyre beres herytage

De Auaricia

Agayne þe lawe of maryage, fo. 40ra
And his awen þat heyr suld be
Es disherite—þat es pyte.
Thurgh hir foly þat es so hidde
A couert theef sho may be kidde.
þat sal sho somtyme bye ful dere,
Bot if sho may make amendes here.
  þe Litell Theft es mykell in vse *De Paruo Latrocinio*
þat oft a mans seruaunt dose;
þat steles oft when hym best thinke
Withinne house, bathe mete and drinke,
Hennes, chikens, and swilk smale store,
And no mare thinkes to pay þarfore.
Yhete þe seruaunt gyues neuer tale
To stele othir thinges þat er smale;
Hym think it a common custom
Of his mayster godes to stele som.
  Yhete he has lytell drede in thoght
To take his hyre and serue it noght.
For if he serue noght leelly
To haue hyre he es noght worthy,
And al þat he oght takes mare

6406 leef] wyll L 6407 þat] þe L, a W dose] duse a R 6408 þat] þas E auoutery] voutry R 6410 wenes] wene LW chylde] chyde E es] be LS 6413 awen . . . be] awn chyld þat borne es fre R, awen þat is his (*om.* W) muliere PW 6414 þat] and þat ELS 6415 es so hidde] swa dyd L 6418 may] *om.* LPR 6419 þe] *om.* LS *sidenote om.* ELP 6421 hym best] þat hym P 6422 house] houses E 6423 Hennes] Henne P smale] mare L 6424 no mare] neuer P, neuermore W 6425 Yhete] And yitt L neuer] no W 6427 it] *om.* P a] bot a R 6428 godes] good R 6429 he has] haue þai L, *trs.* R 6430 his] grete L 6431 he] þai L 6432 he es] er þai L es] nys W 6433 he oght] euer he R oght] *om.* LP oght takes] *trs.* E

þan he has serued or worthy ware,
He suld yhelde agayne in þis case
For al he steles þat he mare tase.
And bot he do, I warne hym wele
Ful harde payne sal he fele
þat lastes parchaunce withouten ende,
When he out of þis werld sal wende.
  Yhete a chylde at frendes fyndynge
þat tas of þairs anythinge
Withouten leue, agayne þair wille,
He steles it—he dose right ille.
Or if his frendes him fynde to skole,
And he haunt ryots als a fole,
And spendes his tyme on ille manere
And his frendes gode, and wil noght lere,
Be he neuer his frendes so leef,
Onence Godde he es a theef,
And þat he sal ful dere habye,
Bot he amende here þat foly,
þat es to say if he haf skille

De Auaricia

fo. 40rb And witte to knawe bathe gode and ille.
  Yhete he þat fyndes a thing of cost
In any stede þat som has lost
And wil noght be þe thing oknawen,
Bot haldes it stille als his awen
And fra him þat awe it þe thing seles,
Certaynely he þat it steles.
De Participacione Latrocinij Theft of hym þat es Theef[es] Felawe
Es when a man a theef may knawe
And wil take of him of gift or bye

6434 or] and ELS 6435 þis] þat L 6436 tase] has P 6437 And] *om.* L bot] bot if W 6438 payne] paynes P sal] þan sall R 6441 at] þat es at hys LW, þat P 6444 it he] it and P, þa gooddys and R right] full LPR 6445 him fynde] *trs.* LR to] at R 6446 haunt] hauntes P 6447 spendes] spende L tyme] tyme so W on] in RW ille] ane ille L 6448 gode] gudes ELPSRW wil] *om.* L 6450 Onence] Als enence R 6451 he sal] *trs.* RW habye] by W 6455 of] on light P 6457 be] of E, be of P oknawen] onknawen LS 6458 it stille] ay styll it R his] for hys L 6459 þe] þat L seles] feyles E, eles L, feles PW 6460 he . . . it] þat thing he L 6461 *theefes] theef ARW *sidenote*: latrocinij] *om.* L 6463 of him] *om.* E of[2]] *om.* PS, for R

þat he wate es stolne theefly;
Or wytandely a theef recettes,
Or oght þat he thurgh theft gettes.
Whaso dose on þis manere,
He may be called Theues Fere,
For he es þan als wele gilty
Als he þat did þe felony.
For swilk a common worde men has,
'Als gode es he þat haldes als flaas';
And þe same dome may he drede
þat him falles haue þat dose þe dede.
Also a bayllyf þat attachen may
A theef and lates him skape away,
Or iustyse þat þe lawe suld lede
þat saues a theef for gift or mede,
Or quest þat thurgh gift anely
þat says a theef es noght gilty,
Or he þat procures a theef to saue
For any auauntage þat he may haue,
Or he þat mase hym right bisy
To bye a theef fra þe withy.
þise manere of men, als I vnderstande,
Vnto þair theft er assentande.
For swilk men, als I haf here talde,
Mayntenes theues and maas þam balde;
And warne þai ware, als I wene,
Swa many theues suld noght be sene
Als now er, þat som men knawes.
þarefore þai er als Theues Felawes
And onence Godde þai er als gilty
Als theues þat dose þe felony.
For þai make þat theues er balde
And er noght chastyde als þe lawe walde.

6464 þat] Thynge þat R wate] wele wate L theefly] thefedly LW 6468 theues] a theefes ELS 6469 es] *om.* P 6470 Als] Als wele as E þe] þat P 6472 gode] gylte S he] *om.* L 6474 þat . . . haue] Als he L dose] didd L 6475 Also] Als E 6480 þat] *om.* R sayes] saues L es noght] þat es L 6485–6 *couplet trs.* L 6485 als] *om.* L 6486 þair] þe P er] er þai L 6487 haf here] haue of L, haf ere P, *trs.* S 6489 And] A R warne] nere W þai] þat R 6492 als theues] *trs.* E, all L 6493 als] all LS 6494 þe] þat P 6495 For] Forwhy R make] it make L 6496 er] *om.* RW chastyde] chastiede P

Donum Consilij De Auaricia Fiat voluntas tua etc.

fo. 40va þarefore harde payne sal þai fele,
Bot þai here amende þam wele.
iij[us]. De Rapina þe thridde braunche es Rauyn
þat es tolde a grete synne,
Bot sex manere of Rauyn to kenne
Er þat vses sex maner of men:
A maner of men er Comon Robbours;
Anothir es Fals Executours;
þe thridde es Fals Dettours sene;
þe ferthe, Lordes þat Couatous bene;
þe fift es Prelates of Halykirke
þat thurgh couatyse wrang wil wirke;
þe sext es, als þe boke telles,
Officials, denes, and bedelles,
And also baylifs and shirreues
þat many men falsely greues.
De communibus predonibus Common Robbours may þai be called
þat men sees comoun paase halde
þat robbes and reues bi wode and strete
Alle manere of men þat þai with mete.
Som robbes on watir and som on lande,
And nouthir spars pilgrym ne marchand.
þai sal bye swilk dedes ful dere
Outhir in þe tothir werlde or here.
De falsis executoribus Fals Executours may bi skille
Be called Robbours for þai do ille;
þai suld thurgh Halykirke rede
Mynistre leelly þe godes of þe dede,
For thurgh athe þai er bunden þarto

6497 harde] a harde E, full hard R 6498 Bot] Bot if R 6499 es] þan es L, ys called R, of W *sidenote*: *om.* L, *as in-column heading* R, iij. W iij[us].] *om.* EPSR 6500 þat] þe whilk R tolde] calde LW a] *om.* P 6501 manere] maners LPW to] er to L 6502 Er . . . vses] þat haunted er wyth L 6505 sene] *om.* E 6506 lordes] `þe lorde´ (*later*) es E, lauerdynges L, er lordys RW *adds line* þat in many a countre are sene E 6507 -kirke] wyrke E 6508 couatyse] couatous R wrang] *om.* L 6509 es] *om.* ES 6512 men] *om.* E falsely] ful falsly R 6513 *sidenote om.* L 6514 paase] places R 6515 wode] way R and] or S 6517 som[2]] *om.* W on[2]] of R, *om.* W 6520 or] or elles EP 6521 *sidenote*: falsis] *om.* LS 6524 godes] wyll L

And with þe dede godes leelly to do.
If þai þa godes to þamself take
And wil noght leel mynystracion make
Bot spendes þam in þair awen vse,
þai robbe þe dede þat so dose.
Bot þai agayne yhelde þat tresor,
þai sal haf harde payne þarfore.
Fals Detours er mykell to wyte *De falsis debitoribus*
þat mykill borwes and noght wil quyte,
Or fra seruauntes þat serued has lange
Withhaldes þair hire and dose þam wrange.
þai er Robbours thurgh Goddis lawe
þat wrange withhaldes þat þai awe.

Donum Consilij De Auaricia Fiat voluntas tua etc.

þarefore harde payne mon þai gette, fo. 40vb
Bot þai here quyte leelly þair dette.
Lordes þat ay bene Couaytous *De cupidis dominis*
Ledes a lyf þat es perillous,
For þai rayme pouer men and pille
And takes þair godes agayne þair wille;
Fra þam þat er þair bondemen knawen
þai take þair godes als þair awen,
And alle þair tenauntes dose outrage
Thurgh taxinge and thurgh tallyage,
And ta[s]e thurgh lordeschip and maystry
þair godes þat þai suld lyf by.
þai er als Robbours, and so þai seme;
He mon þam quyte þat al sal deme.
Prelates of Halykirke [so fre], *De cupidis prelatis*
Thurgh myght of þair auctoryte,
Dose þair sogettes grete outrage

6526 And] *om.* P þe] *om.* W 6527 þa] þe PR to] *om.* L þam-] þaire- S 6528 leel] lely LSW 6530 so] sogates R 6531 Bot] bot if L 6534 noght wil] myght wele W 6535 serued has] *trs.* LS 6536 hire] hyres S 6540 here quyte] *trs.* SW (cf. lely qwyte L) 6541 Lordes] Louerdynges L þat] þai R ay] *om.* L 6542 Ledes] þai lede R þat es] full L 6544 godes] god W 6545 bondemen] bonde P, bondene SR 6547 tenauntes] tenaunde LS 6548 tallyage] tolage? P *6549 tase] take A, takes ELPRW, *om.* S and] and þurgh L 6550 þair] þe L 6551 and] for L 6552 al] þaim P 6553 *so fre] to se AELPS *sidenote*: cupidis prelatis] *trs.* E cupidis] *om.* L 6554 of] and R

And puttes þam to grete costage,
When þai þam visyte þat make maystryes
And rayses of þam grete procuracyes;
And what þai aske þam bihoues pay,
For þai dar noght agayne þam say.
þa þat dose þus out of course
þai may be called als Robbours.
De officialibus et decanis Officyals and denes bathe
Som dose lytell gode bot skathe.
Oft þair chapiters þai wil sette
To gadir al þat þai may gette;
þai take bathe of grete and smale.
þohe þai do wrange, þai gif neuer tale,
For þai haf mare affeccioun
To siluer þan to correccyoun.
And yhete þai do noght so grete reddure
To riche men als þai do to pouer,
For riche men for mede þai forbere,
And pouer men wrangwisly þai dere.
Til saul-hele ne tent þai noght,
Bot in wynnynge es al þair thoght.
Alle with maystry oft þai wirke
Thurgh cursynge and doinge out of kirke.
With swilk manere of ordinaunce
þai chace men vnto penaunce,
Ay til þai make redempcioun.
þat may be called extorsyoun,
And al þat þai on þis wyse wynne

De Auaricia

fo. 41ra Semes a manere of Rauyn.
De apparitoribus et bedellis Yhete somonours and bedelles
þat vndir þam in office dwelles
Wil for na conscience lette

6556 to] oft to R 6557 þam] *repeats* P þat] þai PS þat make] wyth þaire L 6558 -cyes] -tise PR 6560 agayne þam] *trs.* P 6562 als] as R 6565 wil] *om.* P 6567 bathe] ay L and] and of E 6568 þohe] If ESR, To L þai] *om.* L 6572 þai do] *om.* PS to[2]] to þe P 6574 þai] to P 6575 ne] *om.* ESW 6576 in] on LW, to S 6577 Alle] And L 6579 swilk] skilke E 6580 þai] To P vnto] oft vnto R 6582 þat] þai R 6585 somonours] somondours S *sidenote*: et bedellis] *om.* E

þat þai ne take al þat þai may gette.
Shirrefs and baylifs yhete dose duresce;
De vicicomitibus et balliuis
þai put men oft to grete distresce
þat leel bene, withouten blame,
þai prisone þam and dose þam shame
And fettres þam and dose þam pyne
Til þai haf made to þam a fyne.
Na sewet gete þai of prisoun
Til þai gif a grete raunsoun.
Bot pouer men þat may noght gif
Sal haf na mare eise þan a theef;
þogh þai be leel men and trewe,
þai wil neuer þe mare on þam rewe,
Swilk hardnes do þai and malyce
Thurgh colour of þair offyce.
Alle þat þai take þus wrangwisly
Semes a manere of Robbery.
þe ferthe braunche Chalenge men calles
iiij^{us}. De calumpnia
þat in aght maner of men falles,
þat of Godde here standes nane awe
And falshede vses agayne þe lawe.
Ane es Fals Playntif motande;
Anothir es Fals Defendande;
þe thridde, Fals Wittenes and Sisour;
þe ferth, Fals Auoket and Pledour;
þe fift, fals Procuratour and Attourne;
þe sext, Fals Notere and Clerk of fee;
þe seuent, False Iuge and Iustyse;
þe aghtned es Assesour Wrangwyse.
Fals Playntif, als methink, es he,
De falsis querentibus et agentibus
Lered or lawed whethir he be,

6588 ne] wyll L, *om.* S 6589 duresce] doxysche L, dorys S *sidenote*: -tibus] -toribus P 6590 þai put] þat puttes W grete] *om.* S 6593 and dose] to P 6595 Na . . . þai] þai may nog`ht´ gett þaim S of] none of P 6596 gif] haue gyfen L, þam gyf R 6599 þogh] If alle ES, If þat all L, If R leel . . . and] neuer so lele ne R 6600 þe] *om.* E þe mare] titter P 6601 hard-] hardy- P do þai] *trs.* S 6602 Thurgh] All thurgh R of] and R 6605 braunche] *om.* P chalenge] *om.* L *sidenote*: *om.* P, *as in-column heading* R, iiij. Calmpnia W iiij^{us}.] *om.* ELSR 6606 maner] maners LS of men] *om.* L 6609 playntif] playntyng P, playntyd R 6611 thridde] *adds* es E 6612 auoket] uocete PW 6614 clerk] clerkes R 6615 iuge] domessman L 6616 assesour] assysoure E, a sysoure LPSRW wrangwyse] wrangwysly R 6617 als] *om.* EL *sidenote*: quer-] conquer- ELPS 6618 or] and R

þat sekes a false enchesoun
To mote a man agayne resoun,
And a fals accioun feynes
And thurgh a fals colour him pleynes
To putte a man, thurgh ille conscience,
To trauaylle and til grete [di]spens;
Ne of þat wrange wil noght seese

De Auaricia

fo. 41rb Til he be fayne to make his peese.
þus he dose for he wald wynne,
Bot he mon by ful dere þat synne.
De falsis defendentibus þe Fals Defendand, als men says,
Es he þat sekes fals delays.
When a man him motes thurgh right,
He him defendes with al his myght
Thurgh delays and fals cauteles,
Forþi þat he him gilty feles.
Bot he þat motes, be wele war
þe defendand wil him forbarre
Of þat þat he askes hym bi lawe
þat he wil nouthir graunt ne knawe.
For he wil ay þe lawe fle—
At þe lawe wil he noght be—
Bot he þat flees here rightwisnes
Of Goddis mercy sal be partlesse.
De falsis testibus Fals Wittenes I hald a legher
þat on þe boke wil him forswer,
þat in causes beres fals wittenes
And namly þare þar matrimoyne es.
For þat es a bande for terme of lyf
þat byndes a man vnto his wyf;
Quid deus coniunxit homo non separet þar þat band thurgh God es knytte

6619 a] any R *6624 dispens] spens AL 6627 þus] þusgates R 6629 *sidenote om.* (*torn leaf*) E 6631 When] When þat L him motes] sekes hym L 6635 wele] *om.* L, right wele R 6636 forbarre] forbere R 6637 þat þat] þat LW askes] aske L bi] by þe L 6638 he wil] *trs.* EL nouthir] noght E, *om.* P 6639 wil ay] *trs.* P ay] euer L 6640 At] And at S 6641 flees here] here euer flese L, *trs.* S 6642 Of . . . sal] He sall of goddes mercy L sal] salle he EP, he sall S 6644 wil him] *trs.* ES 6646 þar²] whare LR, als PW 6647 for²] of LRW 6648 vnto] to W 6649 þar] Whar R *sidenote*: *om.* W Quid] Quos ES, Quod P separet] separabit P

It falles to na man to louse itte,
And whaso dose þar, it es certayne
He beres Fals Wittenes þaragayne
And wrethes God and dose grete skathe
To his awen saul and to othirs bathe.
Also þe Fals Sissour es prest *De falsis assisoribus*
To gange opon a fals enquest
þat puttes a man fra his right tyte
Thurgh schewyng of a fals verdyte.
Als Fals Witnes, fals tales þai telle;
Bot þai þam mend, þai sal haf helle.
A Fals Auoket es he bi skille *De falsis aduocatis*
þat a fals cause mayntene wille,
For al-if he allege lawes amange,
He can turne right into wrange
Thurgh sutell cauteles þat he can.
þarefore som haldes hym a wyse man,
Bot he es a fole and a Fals Auokett

Donum Consilij De Auaricia Fiat Voluntas t.s. in c. et in t.

þat in causes þe right can lette. fo. 41va
A Fals Pledour wil noght forsake
A fals plee to vndirtake,
For he can shape a wrange delay
And fourme an enquest wrange to say.
He charges noght his conscience
To shewe a fals euydence.
His falshed may men noght wele knawe,
For he can couer it with þe lawe.
þarefore in wrange he es mare balde;
A False [Auoket] he may be talde.

6650 to[1]] *om.* R to louse] for to losse R 6651 þar] whare S 6652 He] þat L 6654 othirs] other LR 6655 Also] As W *sidenote*: assisoribus] -sorijs EW, assorijs LS 6656 gange] gon W 6658 Thurgh] *adds* a L, To W 6659 Als] And E, Alsswa L 6660 mend] amende L 6661 A] *om.* E, Als (*canc.*?) a P auoket] uoket P 6663 al-if] if L allege] legge LS lawes] þe laughe L, law W 6664 right] þe ryght L into] vnto LS, to R 6666 som] some mene E 6667 auokett] vokete EP 6668 þe] *om.* P 6669 A] *om.* E *sidenote*: De falsis placitatoribus L 6671 a] and R 6672 fourme] enfourme L 6675 His] For `his' (*later*) P men noght] *trs.* PR 6678 *auoket] *canc.*, `pledour' *later* A, avokete ELSW, voket P, pledour R talde] calde LR

De falsis procuratoribus

A Fals Procuratour noght dredes
To folow and procur a fals nedes,
Ne he lettes noght to do falshede
Ay til he may þat nedes spede.
He studyes after wrenkes and wiles;
Many a man þus he bygyles.

De falsis attornatis

Þe same manere yhete dose he
Þat es a Fals Attourne,
For he folwes with al his myght
Als wele a wrang ple als a right,
And yhete he wil be of þe assent
To thole his mayster nedes be shent.
He þat dose so he es a traytour,
Be he attourne or be he procuratour.

De falsis notarijs

A Fals Notere hym men telles
Þat mas fals lettres or libelles
Or fals actes or instrumentes
In any nedes þat he to tentes.
He war worthy, als I vndirstande,
For þat falshede to lese þe hande,
Bot if he attaynt war of þat vyce
He suld be suspende of his offyce.

De falsis clericis curie

Or he þat Clerke es of þe coroun,
Of kynges court, or of court baroun
Þat mas any fals recorde
Or dose falshede to his lorde—
Shewes his counsaylle or falses his seele—
Or his lordes auauntage stele,
Methink he war worthy be drawen
Als a traytour if it war knawen
And sithen ⟨be⟩ hinged bi þe hals

6679 noght] nathing L *sidenote*: falsis procuratoribus] *trs.* P 6680 a] *om.* W 6681 noght] *om.* L 6682 þat] þase LP 6684 Many] Full many R þus he] he PW, he so R 6685 yhete] *om.* L *sidenote*: f.a.] *trs.* P 6687 For] *om.* L 6689–90 *trs. couplet* P 6689 And] He (*canc.*?) P 6690 thole] latt L be] to be S 6691 dose so] dose als L, *trs.* R a] a fals L, *om.* S 6692 attourne] tornne L or] *om.* L be he[2]] *trs.* E 6695 actes] accesse R 6698 lese] los E, tyne L þe] hys LPSR 6699 Bot if] Warr L attaynt war] taynted L 6701 þe] *om.* EW *sidenote*: *om.* P falsis] *om.* L clericis curie] *trs.* E, clericis a cur' L 6702 Of[1]] Ouer W of[2]] *om.* LW court[2]] *om.* E 6704 dose falshede] *trs.* R -hede] -nes L to] vnto LSR 6706 Or] Or vnto L, Or ȝit R stele] es noght lele L 6708 if] and L it] he W 6709 be] *torn* A, *om.* EP

Donum Consilij De Auaricia Fiat voluntas t.s. in c. et in t.

If he war attaynt so fals. fo. 41vb
Bot al-if he skape þe payne here,
His saul mon by þat falsed dere.
A Fals Domesman es to drede *De falsis iudicibus*
þat dose mare wrange þan Euenhede,
For when he sittes in iugement
Til his auauntage wil he tent,
And to þat party þat greses his hande
He wil thurgh fauour be heldande.
And yhete may it so bityde
þat he wil take on aythir syde;
Bot he þat on hym mast vouches saue
Mast fauour of hym sal haue
And a dome giuen in þat case
For him þat na right hase.
þus dose Fals Iuge of Halikirke, *De falsis iusticiis*
And right so wil Fals Iustys wirke.
Also yhete þe Fals Ass[e]sour— *De falsis asseisoribus*
þat es þe domesman consayllour
And als his felawe syttes him by—
Yhete heldes he to þe ta party
For gift þat he taas amange;
He counsaylles him to do wrange,
Parchaunce to gif a fals iugement
Or tary þe right bi his assent.
þarefore somtyme þam sal sare rewe

6710 If] If þat LR attaynt] taynted L, attenyd R 6711 al-if] all L al-if he] *trs.* E he skape] eschape he L þe] þat L 6714 þan] þat R 6716 his] þe L wil he] he takes all L tent] hent W 6717 to] *om.* R 6718 fauour] gyft L 6719 yhete] *om.* L, ȝit parchance R it] *om.* R 6721 þat] *om.* P 6722 sal] sal he R 6724 him] his byhoue R na right] noȝt R 6725 þus] Als L iuge] iuges ELR *sidenote*: *om.* W iusticiis] iusticiaribus et ES, iusticiarijs L, iustificatoribus P 6726 fals] *om.* E 6727 Also yhete] And swa L þe] þat L *assesour] assisour AEPSRW, assysours L *sidenote*: *om.* L De] *om.* E De falsis] *om.* S asseisoribus] assisorijs E, assesic' S, assis- PW 6728 þe] þe fals R domesman] domessmen L consayllour] counsolours L 6729 als] *om.* LS his felawe] þaire felaughes L syttes] þat sittes LS him] þaime L 6730 heldes he] helde þai L, haldes W þe ta] þat L 6731 he] þe iustice L taas] haues tane L, will tak R 6732 He] And L him] hym oft R 6734 right] *adds* party L his] *om.* L 6735 somtyme . . . sal] þai sall sometyme R þam] þai S sare] *om.* S

þat euer þai any lawe knewe.
  Bot vndirstandes, als I yhow ken,
þat I speke anely of fals men
þat in falsede er sleghe and balde,
Als I haf shewed bifore and talde;
And noght of þam þat trewely dose
þat gode conscience and trewith wil vse,
Als gode faythe and þe lawe wille;
And til ilk man do resoun and skille,
Als þai wald men to þam didde,
Of what state so þai er kidde—
What craft so þai haunt or faculte,
Or what offyce þai haue or dignyte.
If þai þair conscience right lede
After þe lyne of Euenhede
And Rightwisnes do to ilka man,
Grete mede er þai worthy þan,

De Auaricia

fo. 42ra For þai may þan be als parfyte
Als any frere es or hermyte.
vus. De sacrilegio   Sacrilege þe fift braunche es
þat mas a man ay graceles.
þat synne, als I sal shewe sone,
On many maners may be done:
First a man may Sacrilege wirke
þat brekes or brynnes Halykirke,
Outhir wyndous, dores, or walles
Or houses þat to Halykirk falles,
Or boke or chalyce or vestyment
Or any outhir ournament;
Or vilany in any place dose
þat es apropred to Halykirk vse;
Or entres with`in with´outen leue

6736 þai euer] *trs.* S any] þe P 6738 I] *om.* W 6740 shewed] *adds* ȝhow W
6742 þat] And L gode] trew L trewith] trewe ER, trewly L, rew W wil vse] vses L
6743 and] as R 6747 so] *om.* L haunt] vse W 6748 or] of P offyce] offycye E
6750 lyne] lyfe ELPSRW 6751 do to] *trs.* LW 6753 For] *om.* L 6754 es] *om.* L or] or any EL 6755 *sidenote: as in-column heading* R vus.] *om.* ELPRS, v. W
6756 graceles] gracyles LS 6757 shewe] *add* yow RW 6763 boke] bokes P
6765 any] haly L, *after* Or P 6767 within] in P -in with-] *later corr.* A

Any harme to do or greue.
Of grete cursynge he es noght quyte
For Halykirk he dose dispyte.
Sacrilege also he wirkes
þat steles oght of Halykirkes
Or oght withouten wyse mens rede
Beres out of any halwed stede
Or out of vnhalwed (þat es lesse)
Beres anythinge þat halwed es—
Vestyment, boke, or chalyce—
If he do it thurgh malyce.
He þat dose swilk foly
To be cursed he es worthy.
Sacrilege yhete may þis be called
When a man wil withhalde
Agayne right with maystry
Thynge þat falles to sayntwary,
Outhir lande or tenement
Or oght þat falles be payde als rent
Or teendes þat men right dette telles
Or offerandes or anythinge elles.
Whaso wrange withhaldes swilk thinge
Rynnes in þe sentence of cursynge.
Sacrilege agayne conscience
Dose he þat dose þat vyolence
In halwed stede, or sheddes blode
Or litchery dose—hym hald I wode.
For when halwed stede es so fyled,
þan bihoues it be recounciled.
Sacrylege may þis be neste

6769 he es] *trs.* P 6770 he dose] *trs.* R 6772 of] oute of L -kirkes] -kyrk L 6774 out] oght oute L any halwed] any þat haloghde E, haly L 6775 out] oght out S 6777 boke] or boke W 6779 swilk] *add* a LP 6780 be] be to E 6781 yhete] *om.* L may þis] *trs.* W be] *om.* E 6782 When] When þat L 6783 right] þe ryght L with] or with R 6786 oght] *om.* RW be] to be L 6787 Or] As R teendes] tethynges W right . . . telles] haldes as dettes W 6788 Or] *om.* L -randes] -rande PW 6789 Whaso] *adds* with P wrange withhaldes] with wrang haldes L, haldes with wrang S with-] *om.* R thinge] thinges L 6790 cursynge] cursynges L 6791 conscience] sentence (*expunged?*) c. P 6792 þat[2]] *om.* W 6793 or] *om.* L, þat R 6794 dose] *om.* P hym . . . I] I hald hym RW 6795 when] *adds* a L 6796 þan] þe W 6797 þis] ȝhet W

De Auaricia

fo. 42rb Als when a man smytes a prest
Or any clerke þat has tane croun
Or man or womman of religyoun,
Or a womman þat es religyous
Drawes with force out of hire hous
Agayne hir wille—if it so be,
Appert Sacrilege þan dose he,
For swilk er lyms of Halykirke
And Goddes seruauntes his werkes to wirke.
He þat dose þus him aght haf drede
For he es cursed of þat dede.
  Yhete dose he Sacrylege and dose ille
þat drawes a man agayne his wille
Out of kirke or halwed stede
To whilke he flees for drede of dede,
Halikirkes grith for sokour to haue,
Als lange als þe law vouches saue.
And he þat dose hym þat greuaunce,
Withdrawes fra hym his sustinaunce,
Or dose any payne þarewith
To do hym forsake his grith,
Or lettes hym þe way gangande
þat has forsworne þe kinges lande,
Or puttes him out on any wyse,
He brekes Halykirkes fraunchyse.
Cursed es he þat so wil do
And alle þat assentes þarto.
  Sacrilege also dose he
þat has godes of Halykirke fre,
Als prelate, persoun, or vykere,
þat spendes þa godes on ille manere.

6799 tane] *om.* L 6800 man, womman] mene, wymmen ELS 6801 a] *om.* L 6802 out] *om.* S hire] þaire L 6803 if it so] þat if it L 6804 Appert] Apertly þan] *om.* L 6806 Goddes] god S Goddes . . . his] seruaundys of goddys R werkes] werke E 6807 aght] aughe L haf] to haue L, to R 6809 ille] full ille LP 6811 of] of þe L or] or of L 6812 flees] drawes P 6813 for . . . to] socoure for to LS 6816 fra hym] *trs.* W 6817 dose] *add* hym LR 6818 To] þat may L do] gerre L, lette S, *om.* W hym] *add* for to ESR, þaim W his] þe L 6819 þe] o L gangande] goand W 6820 forsworne] forsaken P 6821 on] *om.* W 6824 þat] þat euer L 6827 or] and W 6828 þa] þat L, þaire W godes] gode LW

Of þat he mon be accused
Als he þat sacrylege has vsed.
  Sacrilege yhete clerkes calles
Spousebreke þat oft falles.
For sposaylle es a sacrament
Of Halykirk þat men suld tent,
þat here es mast nedefull to neuen
Of alle þe sacramentes seuen.
He þat thurgh any counsaylle
Dose any dispyte vnto sposaylle
Or brekes þe vowe of chastyte
þat es solempne or yhete priue
Of religious or seculere
þat haly order beres here,
He dose dispyte to Halykirke,
And þus he may Sacrilege wirke.

Donum Consilij De Auaricia Fiat voluntas tua etc.

  Sacrilege he dose, men says, fo. 42va
þat kepes noght þe halydays
þat Halykirke commandes haly.
He þat þam brekes dose vylany
To Halykirke þat vs forbedes
To do oght þan bot haly dedes;
þat tyme suld men haunte þe kirke
And werkes of halynes þan wirke,
For haly tyme has his fraunchyse
Als haly stede has on þe same wyse.
  þe sext braunche es Simony *vj^{us}. De Simonia*
þat es vsed ouer-comonly,
And namely amange lered men
þat þe perille mast suld ken.
Thurgh Symony lered men wil wirke

6829 be] be hard R   6832 oft] ofttym R   falles] befalles L   6837 any] haly L   6838 vnto] to LPW   6839 Or] Or dos or E   6841 Of] Or L   religious] religioune E   or] or ȝhyte EL, or of R   6843 to] vnto S   6844 sacrilege] sarylege S   6845 men] as men W   6846 þe] his P   6847 haly] to haly L   6849 Halykirke] halyk S   -kirke] *repeats* E   6850 þan] *om.* P   6852 þan] *om.* P   wirke] to wyrk LP   6854 has] ys R   6855 *sidenote*: *om.* LP, *as in-column heading* R   vj^{us}.] *om.* ESR, vj. W   6858 mast] best L

þat es made stiwarde of Halykirke,
For þai þat wil haue benefyce
Bihoues com in thurgh his offyce.
þarefore men of sere nacioun
Sekes to hym for warysoun,
And alle þat him sekes spede may
þat siluer or gold has for to pay.
  Symony, als som clerkes says,
Openly shewes him by sex ways:
Ane es in Order, als I wene,
þare Symony es oft sene,
For when a man wald ordayned be
Of bisshop hande in any degre,
Parchaunce vnnethes sal he spede
Withouten grete prayere or mede.
  Anothir es þar I fynde a vyce
þat es in gift of benefyce.
For he þat may a benefyce gieue
On whilk a clerke may godely lieue—
Kirke, prouendre, or vikery,
Fre chapell or chauntery—
He thinkes noght gif it in wast;
He gyues it him þat gyues him mast
Or to hym to wham he dette awe
Or for frendship of som felawe
Or for othir cause þat may be,
And noght anely for charyte.
  In chaunge of benefyce þe thridde es,
To chaunge a mare for a lesse.

6860 made] maste L 6862 his] þis E, *om.* P 6863 sere] dyuers W 6864 to] vnto L 6865 alle] þai R him] *om.* R may] þai may L 6866 or] and R for to] to LRW pay] spen pay P 6869 *sidenote*: j^{us}. E 6872 Of] *adds* þe L 6873 sal he] *trs.* W 6875 es þar] whare L, is þat W *sidenote*: ij^{us}. E 6876 in] *om.* R, in a W of] or in L 6877–8 *couplet trs.* L 6877 þat es if he wyll thryfe L 6878 On] On þe E 6879 prouendre] prouande ES, parauntore L, prebende R 6680 chauntery] chauncery R 6881 gif] gyfte of E, to gyf L in] noght in L 6882 gyues] `will' (*later*) gif P 6883 to^{1}] vnto L to^{2}] *om.* L 6885 othir] som other L 6886 for] par L 6887 chaunge] chaungeing LP *sidenote*: iij^{us}. E 6888 for] ay for R

Donum Consilij De Auaricia Fiat voluntas tua etc.

For when twa auaunced men assentes fo. 42vb
To chaunge þair auauncementes,
He þat þe leste has sal bote take
Forthy þat he þe chaunge sal make.
Swilk manere of chaunge es oft done,
Bot rightwys chaunge makes ful fone.

þe ferth may in eleccioun be
Of prelacy or of dignyte.
For when a college or a couent
Sal chese a prelate thurgh assent
To dignyte or prelacy,
þai chese ane þat es vnworthy.
In swilk eleccioun þai acorde
Thurgh prayere or procurment of lorde.
þus er chosen thurgh swilk fauour
Bisshop, abbot, and pryour.
þarefore thurgh swilke eleccioun
Halykirk gase nere doun.

þe fift way es in-comynge
Of religioun thurgh procurynge,
For fone for þair condicioun
Er resayued intil religyoun—
Amange possessioners namely
þat has rentes to lyf by—
Withouten prayere or procurment
Or a pitance vnto þe couent.

Yhete freres þat has nathinge
To lif by bot of begynge,
þai vse oft swilk a manere:

6891 þe] *om.* E leste] lesse ELSRW bote] þe bote L 6892 þe] *om.* L 6894 fone] sone S 6895 *sidenote*: iiijus. E 6896 prelacy] prelate P 6897 a[2]] *om.* W 6899 or] or to ESR, of W 6901 swilk] whylke EP, *om.* R 6902 prayere] procuryng L, praying S procurment] procuryng ES, prayer L of] of a P 6903 er] are þai ELS, is W swilk] *om.* L 6904 Bisshop] Bath bishopp R 6906 Halykirk gase] Ys halykyrk R gase nere] *trs.* W nere] nerehand LPRW doun] broght done 6907 *sidenote*: vus. E 6908 Of] Vnto L, Into R 6909 For] Full L fone] few RW 6910 intil] vnto LR 6911 possessioners] possessours R 6912 þat] þe whilk R to] for to R 6914 vnto] to ELSW 6916 of] on W 6917 vse] haunte L oft] mykell L, *int.* P, full oft R

þai wil resayue nane to frere
Bot he can do þam auauntage
Or for hope of helpe of his lynage.
þus do þai for þair awen prow.
þis cause methink es noght at allow,
Bot þis suld þair entent be:
þai suld anely for charyte
Resayue a man for his awen mede
þat religyous lyf wald lede.
  þe sext es shewynge of Goddis worde
And mynysterynge of Goddis borde.
For he þat falles to preche or telle
Haly Writte and þe godspelle
And wil noght blethely sarmon make
Bot he oght for his trauaylle take,
I hald þat prechour nerehande wode

De Auaricia

fo. 43ra þat selles Goddis worde for erthly gode.
Or he þat preste es and wil noght
Synge a messe, bot it be boght;
Or wil noght here a mans shrift
Ne housill hym, bot he haf gift,
Or oght takes bi þat entent
For any othir sacrament—
Na better may he be talde
þan Iudas was þat Cryst salde.
With clerkes es Symony mast vsed
Bot lewed men bees noght excused
Of þat vyce þat assentes þarto
Or helpes in þat þai may do.
vijus. De Malignitate þe seuent braunche Wickednes we calle
þat in sex thinges oft may falle:

6918 þai] þat þai LR nane to] na L 6919 Bot] Bot if LR þam] *adds* som L 6920 for] of P 6921 do þai] *trs.* P 6922 cause] case L at] to LPRW allow] lowe ESW 6923 *sidenote*: vjus. E 6924 for] par L 6926 religyous] relygyone E wald] sulde P 6928 of] at L 6929 to] at L 6930 Haly] Or haly L 6931 sarmon] sermouns L 6934 erthly] werldly PRW 6937 Or] Nor S noght] *om.* S 6938 bot] bot if L bot he haf] withouten P 6940 For] Or for L 6941 be] þan be R talde] cald R 6942 was] *om.* L 6945 assentes] consentes L 6946 þat] þat at LPRW 6947 we calle] is P *sidenote*: *om.* LSW, *as in-column heading* R vijus.] *om.* EPR 6948 oft] *om.* W falle] *adds* iwis (*later?*) P, befalle W

Ane es Renaying of Crystes lawe;
Anothir es Wichecraft to knawe;
þe thridde es Procuryng of Mans Dede;
þe ferthe Distroying of Toun or stede;
þe fift es Raysynge of Discorde;
þe sext es Wrange Wrying to lorde.
  Renaying es, als men says,
When a man Godde renays
And his lawe, and waxes vntrewe
And bicomes Sarzyne or Iewe,
And so es made þe fendes man
Forthy þat he suld be ryche þan.
For couatys of werldes ritchesce
þis may be called a grete wickednes.
  Wichecraft suld na man vse
Ne charmes, for whoso it dose
Or to Wichecraft assentes
Or to vnleeffull experimentes
Or mas wrange coniurysounes
Or rayses þe fende to wyte resounes,
Mawmetry þan þai wirke
Agayne þe trouthe of Halykirke.
  Procurynge of Mans Dede es ille
Whethir it be done loude or stille.
For he þat manslaghter wil do
Or procures or assentes þarto
Or hyres men to do þat dede,
Helle þarefore mon be his mede.

De Auaricia

For he semes withouten pyte fo. 43rb
A grete wickednes may þis be.
  Distroyinge of Toun or of manere

6951 of] to R 6952 ferthe] *adds* es E toun] toure W or] or of L 6953 es] *om.* P 6955 es] *om.* E *sidenote*: j^{us}. E 6956 When] When þat L a] any R 6957 lawe] laughes L and^{2}] *om.* P 6958 Sarzyne, Iewe] a sarryzene, a iewe E 6959–60 *couplet trs.* L 6960 Forthy] For L be ryche] by right W 6961 of] or W werldes] werldly SR 6963 *sidenote*: ij^{us}. E 6964 charmes] charme L 6965 wiche-] wyth- L 6966 to] vnto LR -leef-] -leue- LS, -lel- W 6968 Or] And E to wyte] for L 6971 *sidenote*: iij^{us}. E 6972 be done] *trs.* S 6973 man-] mans LR 6976 his] þaire LR, þair, *corr. to* his (*later*) P 6978 þis] þat W 6979 *sidenote*: iiij^{us}. E

Es a grete wickednes to here.
For he þat distroys or brynnes
Toun or stede wickedly he synnes
Or procurs othir to do þat ille,
Bot he be excused thurgh skille.
Parchaunce he mon haf þarefore helle
For it es a grete wickednes to telle.
  Makynge of Discorde also es
Bitwene men a grete wickednes.
For he þat obout wendes
To make discorde bitwene frendes,
Or bitwene man and his wyf
Mas any debate or stryf,
Or rayses wreth þar luf suld be,
A grete wickednes dose he.
  Fals Wreghyinge, als I halde,
A wickedenes it may be called
þat baylifs and bedels oft vses
And pouer men falsely accuses
To þair lordes and þair soueraynes
þat þam in offyces ordaynes
To do þam lesen þair werldes gode
þat þai haf wonnen to þair lyues fode.
Yhete er som men þat wil assent
To make a fals endytement
To endyte a man vngilty
Outhir of trespase or felony.
Whaso it dose or procures þarto
He wald fayne þat man fordo,
In als mykell als in hym es.
þis may be tolde a grete wickednes,

6980 to] of to L 6981 he þat] whasoeuer R 6982 Toun] Tounes L stede] stedes L, streyt R wickedly] full ille L 6984 Bot] Bot if R 6985 haf þarefore] *trs.* ELS 6988 a] es a L 6989 obout] ay about R *sidenote*: v^{us}. E 6991 man] a man P and] or S 6992 Mas] þat makes S 6993 wreth] wyrth R þar] whare LR 6994 grete] ful grete R 6995 wreghyinge] wyckednes L, wrethynge PW *sidenote*: vj^{us}. E 6996 A] A gret W A . . . may] May wreyghing wele L it] *om.* LRW, þat P 6997 þat] Als P oft] mykell L 6998 And] þat LR 6999 To] Vnto R þair^{2}] to þair W 7000 þam] in þaime S ordaynes] ordayne S 7001 do] gerre L do . . . lesen] þaime þat loses S lesen] lose EL gode] gudes ES, godes (-s *expunged*) P 7002 fode] fudes ES 7003 men] *om.* L 7006 of] for L or] or of ESR 7008 fayne] full fayn R 7010 þis] þees W tolde] called LR

And swilk wickednes, als men may se,
Mas many men dampned to be.
  þe aghtned braunche of Couatyse *viij^{us}. De falsis mercatoribus*
May be called Fals Marchaundyse
þat es vsed amange marchaundes
þe whilk þise fyue maners hauntes:
A manere es in Lither Bargaynynge;
Anothir es Leghyng and Forswerynge;
þe thridde es Hauntynge of Weghtes vntrewe
Or fals mesures, olde or newe;

Donum Consilij De Auaricia Fiat voluntas tua etc.

þe ferthe es Fals Shewyng to sight; fo. 43va
þe fift es Laynynge of þe sothe right.
  First es Lyther Barganynge,
Vnskilfulle byinge and sellynge.
For som men þat sal oght by
Bargaynes with men vnskilfully
þat thurgh myschief has nede to selle
Corne or beste or othir catelle.
He sees þe sellar es noght wys;
He byes þe thinge at a vyle prys
So þat when it es salde and boght,
He has þe thinge nere half for noght.
Also to selle þus es hym leef
Til hym þat byes at meschief.
þus wynnes he mykell lightly,
Whethir he selle or he by.
  Leghes and fals athes amange
In marchandyse dose mykell wrange.
For som man, when he sal selle oght,

7012 many] a P men] ane L to] *om.* LRW 7013 of] es L *sidenote: as in-column heading* R, *om.* W viij^{us}.] *om.* ELPSR 7015 *line om.* S vsed] haunted L 7016 fyue maners] four maner R 7017 in] a R 7018 es] *om.* LR leghyng] lesyng S 7019 hauntyng] haunted L 7020 Or] O L, Or of R 7021 to] in R 7022 þe sothe] sothe and L 7023 First] In furst R *sidenote*: j^{us}. E 7024 -fulle] -wyse S 7025 men] *om.* W sall oght] *trs.* LP 7028 or^{1}] *om.* L 7029 wys] full wyse L 7030 þe] þat L a] *om.* E vyle] litill P, veyl W 7032 þe] þat L nere] *om.* LS 7033 Also] And swa L þus] *om.* LP es hym] he es full L 7034 byes] es L 7035 mykell] *adds* gode full L, *adds* good R 7036 Whethir] Wheþerso R 7039 man] mene ES sal selle] selles E

Leghes and athes spares he noght.
He says þe thinge es better þan it es;
So leghes he agayne sothfastnes.
He sweres þat he has þareon lost
And þat it cost mare þan it cost.
þan bihoues hym forsworne be;
þusgates his marchandyse mas he.
And als he selles, so can he bye
Thurgh leghes and athes and gilry,
For þat thinge þat he bye wille
He lackes it gretely agayne skille
And telles defautes þar nane er sene
And sweres it es noght gode ne clene.
He lakkes it falsly on þis wyse
þat he myght haf it for lytell pryse.
Hauntyng of Fals Mesures and weghtes
Es oft in marchandyse thurgh sleghtes.
For som hauntes, bath riche and pore,
Double weght and double mesure
And vses bathe thurgh lithernes,
Byes with þe mare and selles with þe lesse.
Or if þe weght or mesure be leele
And seled with þe kynges seele,
Yhete he can in a short whyle
In weghyng or metyng do gyle.
In sellyng he can þe mette scarse sette

Donum Consilij De Auaricia Fiat voluntas tua etc.

fo. 43vb And in byinge haf mare þan þe mette.
þis manere of marchandyse es ille,
For it es agayne lawe and skille.

7040 and athes] ne athes ne R 7043 has þareon] *trs.* LS þareon] þar oft R 7044 And . . . þan] More þen euer yit P 7045 þan] And L hym] *om.* L 7047 *line om.* R 7050 it gretely] *trs.* P 7051 And] He L þar] whare LR 7052 noght] noþer W 7053 falsly] falsy R 7054 for] of L, on S lytell] lyght ES, lesse L 7055 mesures, weghtes] *trs.* S weghtes] of weghtes L 7056 thurgh] and L 7057 som] som men W 7060 Byes] To bye L þe[1]] *om.* L selles] selle L lesse] lesses P 7061 Or[1]] *om.* L or[2]] or þe L 7062 seled] selled E, merkede P 7063 Yhete] *after* can P he can] *trs.* R a] *om.* ELS 7064 do] do a L, to P 7065 he can] *trs.* RW

Fals Shewynge, als I wene,
In som marchandyse es sene.
For som man his ware can dight
To make it seme plesand in sight
Or shewe it in stede of dymnes
þar it semes bettir þan it es.
So dose som draper þat es lathe
In mykell light to shew his clathe.
þis manere semes na lewte;
Fals Marchaundyse may þis be.
Laynynge of sothe þat es hidde
Mas fals marchaundyse be kidde.
For som can selle a thinge to wynne
þat has priue defaute withinne
þat withouten may noght be sene;
Yhete semes it to sight gode and clene.
Als þis fals cosours dose
þat can þair horse falsely rose;
Alle þair defautes knaw þai wele,
Bot þai layne þam ilka dele.
þai wille noght þe sothe telle
For þai suld þam þe derrer selle.
Whaso selles on þis wyse
Methink he mas Fals Marchaundyse.
þe nyeghent braunche, als vndirstand I,
Es Offyce or Craft of Foly
þat hauntes seuen manere of men;
Whilk þai er I sal yhow kenne.
Common Wymmen hald I ane
þat to þe bordell has þam tane.
Anothir es called Iogelours;

ixus. De Temerario Officio et Artificio

7069 shewynge] weghyng W 7071 man] men L 7072 seme] *om.* L in] to mans L 7073 shewe it] shewyd R stede] place LS 7074 þar] þat W 7075 draper] drapers L es] er L 7077 semes] schewes L 7078 be] wele be L 7079 of] of þe L 7080 be] to be ELR, *om.* W 7081 som] sum men L 7082 defaute] defautes W 7083–4 *couplet trs.* W 7083 may noght] *trs.* ES 7084 it] *om.* E to] to þe L 7085 cosours] skosers L 7087–8 *couplet trs.* L 7087 defautes] fautes L knaw þai] þat þai knaw L 7088 Bot] Bot ȝit R ilka] euere R 7090 For] Bot S suld] may L 7091 Whaso] *adds* oght R on] vpon R 7092 fals] a fals E 7093 als] es als L *sidenote: as in-column heading* R ixus.] *om.* ELPSRW Officio] et officio L 7094 Es] *om.* L or] of LR, of or S of] or of L 7096 Whilk] *adds* þat L, þe whilk P

þe thridde may be called Faytours;
þe ferthe men calles Sneckedrawers,
þat er halden als ille or wers.
þe fift er Herlotes with þair gaudes,
And þe sext men calles Haraudes;
þe seuent also er Champiouns;
þe aghned er Tollers of market touns;
þe neghent er Hyngemen of offyce.
þis craftes er alle ful of vyce.
In swilk craftes na man may wynne
þair sustinaunce withouten synne.

De Auaricia

fo. 44ra Common Wymmen þair bodys selles;
For þair lyflade þai do noght elles.
þai werne na man with þam to rage
Of wham þai may haue auauntage.
With synne þai wynne þair sustinaunce;
þai do nane othir cheuissaunce.
A synnefull craft methinke es þis
þat dose þam tyne heuen-blisse.
Iogelours grete auauntage gettes
Thurgh fals iapes and tregettes
And leges þat þai make amange;
Whaso hauntes swilk craft lyues wrange.
Faytours wynnes mete and mone
Of þam þat has mercy and pyte,
For lithir wyles can þai fynde
To make þam seme crokid or blynde
Or seke or mysays to mens sight.
So can þai þair lyms dight
For men suld þam mysays deme,

7100 may] may wele R 7101 snecke-] lacche- W 7104 And] *om.* L men calles] er calde P 7105 er] mene calles ELS 7106 er] *om.* L 7107 hynge-] hyg S 7109 swilk] whilke ER, þir L may] *before* na LPR 7110 þair] Hys L 7111 bodys] bodye ES *sidenote*: j^{us}. E 7113 Wyth ilka man wyll þai rage L 7114 Of wham] þat L may] hope of to L, *om.* W 7115 þai wynne] *trs.* R þair] þaim P 7118 dose] gerres L, makes S tyne] lese W 7119 *sidenote*: ij^{us}. E 7121 make] cane mak R 7122 Whaso] þat L swilk] skille E, þat R craft] craftes LPS lyues] dos ES, þai lyf L 7123 *sidenote*: iij^{us}. E 7125 can þai] þat þai canne L 7126 or] and ELPSRW 7127 mysays] mesyll R mens] mannes L 7129 mysays] for mysseys L, myssai and (*later corr.*) P, for mesyll R

Bot þai er noght swilk als þai seme.
Mikell gode wynne þai þus;
Methink þis manere es perillus.
  Sneckedrawers men may kenne;
Som men calles þam 'robertmen'.
At many a dore þai drawe þe snecke
And opens bathe þe dore and þe hecke.
If þai þe husband at hame fynde,
þai say alle þair godes er brynde
Or þat þai war amange theues stadde
And er robbed of al þat þai hadde.
Riche men þai say þai ware
And now þai er pouer and bare.
Som also telles and says
þat þai haf lost hors and hernays
And þair armour and othir gere
Thurgh myschief in lande of were.
Som says þair rentes and þair landes
Er alle in othir mens handes
And er wedde-sette til a day,
And alle er leghes þat þai say.
Yhete þai say þai er of gentill blode
For þat men suld do þam mare gode.
When þai haf leghed, þan þai craue
Bot þai ga noght til þai haue.
  And if þai fynde þe husband out,

De Auaricia

þan þai cast þair sight about fo. 44rb
And sees þe wyf has na socour;
Parchaunce þai folow hir into þe bour.
Al þat þai aske sho wil þam take
For drede of þam—swilk boste þai make.

7130 swilk] *om.* L 7133 may] *adds* hethe L *sidenote*: iiij[us]. E 7134 men] *om.* R 7135 a] *om.* PR 7136 þe[1]] *om.* LW þe[2]] *om.* W 7137–8 *trs. couplet* P 7137 þe . . . hame] *trs. phrs.* S 7138 say] say hym þat L þair . . . er] hys gode es L 7139 theues] chefes L 7140 er] *om.* L þai] euer þai L 7144 lost] lest W 7145 armour] harmours RW othir] þair othir R 7149 And er] *om.* L til] vnto LPR 7150 þat] þat euer L 7151 Yhete] *om.* L 7152 For þat] To gyf L, For R suld] talent to L mare] *om.* L, þe mare R 7154 Bot] For L ga noght til] wyll noght gang or L 7155 And] Bot R 7156 sight] eghen L 7159 take] it take E

þe grace of Godde methink þam wantes
þat ledes þair lyf with swilk trantes.
Herlotes walkes thurgh many tounes
With specked mantels and burdouns,
And at ilk mans hous ga þai in
þare þai hope oght for to wynne.
Bot herlotes men calles comonly
Alle þat hauntes herlotry.
Herlotes falles to stand on þe flore
And play somtyme at þe spore,
At þe bene and at þe catte;
A foul play hald I þat,
And þareagayne may þai noght be
When men biddes þam for þaire fee,
For þe rewell of þair religyoun
Es swilk thurgh þair professyoun.
þis es a poynt of þair rewell ilk tyme
To licken men þare þai com in ryme.
Yhete haunt þai oft othir iapes;
Som ledes beres, and som ledes apes
þat mas sautes and solaces þat sese.
Alle þise er folyes and nycetese.
Haroudes of armes oft er sene
In stede þar grete lordynges bene.
Bot at dede of armes wil þai be
To deme to wham suld falle þe gre;
Be it in iustynge or turnament,
þai wil take ful gode entent
To wyte wham falles haue a prys,
For þan sal þair auauntage ryse.
þai halwe his name thurgh grete cry;

7162 ledes] wynnes L lyf] lyues E, lyfelade L 7163 *sidenote*: v^{us}. E 7164 specked] specled R 7165 at] *om.* L ga] gang L 7166 þare] Where W for to] to PSW 7168 Alle] All þas R *sidenote*: Harlotes W 7170 And] And to R 7171 At] And at R 7172 hald I] þen hald I P, þan I hald R 7175 For þe] Bot W þair] *om.* P 7177 þis] It L 7178 þare] whare LR in ryme] in tyme E, rynne R 7180 beres] ? heres P ledes^2] *om.* LP 7181 solaces] solace ELPW *þat^2] *expunged*, als men *int. later* A, als men L 7182 Alle] And all L folyes] bote foly E folyes and] bot L 7183 *sidenote*: vj^{us}. E, Herraudes W 7184 stede] stedes LPS þar] whare L lordynges] lordes LPR 7185 Bot] For L 7186 suld] sall L gre] degre L 7187 in] *om.* LW iustynge] iustis P or] or in S 7188 entent] tente EL 7189 wham] wha LW haue] to haue LR a] þe LPR 7191 thurgh] with R

þarefore þai haue giftes of curtaysy,
Riche robes or othir ritchesce,
Bot þam bihoues crye a largesce.
þus wynne þai pompe to mayntene;
þis manere of wynnynge es noght clene.
Champions with lordes dwelles
To fight for þam in þair querelles
For thing þat es in debate
þat may be termyned nane othir gate.
And wha`so´ may othir ouercome

Donum Consilij De Auaricia Fiat voluntas tua etc.

Wynnes þe right thurgh coustome. fo. 44va
þarefore þai wille take grete wage
Or bouche of court with auauntage.
Methink swilk men lifs noght wele,
And þat mon þai hereafter fele.
Tollers office yhete es ille,
For þai tak tolle oft agayne skille
Of diuers men þat falles nane gieue,
And many man ful oft þai greue.
For mykell tolle þat þai take
Es thurgh es[t]resce þat þai make,
For it was neuer tolle-gaderere
þat he ne wald greue men and dere.
Swilk offyce I rede he flee
þat wil out of perille be,
Forwhy we fynde wryten in boke
þat Cryst Mathew þarefra toke
For þe perille þat es þareinne,
For men vses it noght withouten synne.

7193 or] and ER 7194 þam bihoues] þan behoues þaime L 7195 wynne] wene W to] for to LR 7196 þis] Swylk L 7197 *sidenote*: vijus. E, Campiouns W 7203 wage] wages W 7204 Or] And R auauntage] auauntages W 7205 Methink] *adds* þat R 7206 And] *om.* R 7207 *sidenote*: viijus. E, Tolleres W 7208 tak tolle] tolle `take´ W 7209 þat] þat þat W gieue] to gyf L 7210 man] mene ES, a man LR ful] *om.* PW 7211 tolle] *om.* S 7212 Es] Is þus W *estresce] W, escresce AEP, dystresche LSR 7213 neuer . . . gaderere] yitt neuer na toller L 7214 he ne] *trs.* R ne] *om.* ELS and] do þaim L 7215 he] hym L 7217–18 *trs. couplet* P 7219 es þareinne] þare wasse in L 7220 vses] hauntes L noght] *om.* E

Hynger of men prayse I leste,
For þat offyce es mast vnhoneste.
For þai er fayne withouten pite
Hynge many men for þair fee,
Þai recke neuer how many þai hinge,
If þai may haue gode wynnynge,
Ne how many heueds þai of smyte,
If men wil þam þair trauaylle quyte.
Al haf þai leue thurgh lawe of lande,
Þai synne yhete, als I vnderstande,
Þat of offyce bihoues nedely be
Withouten reuthe and pyte.
Þam war bettir thigge þair mete
Þan any gode on þat wyse gete.
Þis es an offyce of grete wrechednes
Als ilkane of þe tothir es.

x^{us}. De Ludo Temerario

Þe tende braunche may men calle
Fole Play, þat es last of alle.
Þat es play of tables or of dyce
Of whilk comes neghen manere of vyce.
Ane es Couatyse þat wyde es spredde;
Anothir es Rauyn, and Okir þe thridde;
Þe ferth es Multiplying of Leghes
And idell speche þat fra þe mouth fleghes;
Þe fift es Sclaundre of Godde of heuen
And of his halwes þat we oft neuen;

Donum Consilij De Auaricia Fiat voluntas tua etc.

fo. 44vb

Þe sext es Ille Ensaumple to tast;
Þe seuent Spendynge of Tyme in wast;

7221 Hynger] Hangers R men] *adds* þat L leste] best R *sidenote*: ix^{us}. E, Heynger W 7224 Hynge] To hynge ELPRW 7225 recke] rake R 7226 If þai may] Elles at þai L gode] grete L, any R 7227 heueds] handes R þai of] *trs.* EP 7228 trauaylle] seruice L 7229 Al] Of all L thurgh] o L 7230 þai . . . als] Yitt synne þai gretely L 7231 þat of] For þat LPRW nedely] nedelynges L 7233 þam] þai R thigge] begge LSR 7234 on] in R 7235 þis] It PRW 7236 þe] þase L, þat W tothir] other LW 7237 may men] *trs.* P *sidenote*: *om.* S, *as in-column heading* R x^{us}.] *om.* LPRW 7239 or of] or L, and P dyce] dyces ES *sidenote*: Nota mala de talibus W 7241 Ane] þat S es spredde] spredes L 7242 es] *om.* L and . . . thridde] þe thryd oker es L 7244 speche] wordes P 7248 of] oft E, *om.* L

þe aghtned es Corrupcioun called
In þam þat vses swilk plays to bihald;
þe neghent es Vnbouxsomnes to wirke
Agayne þe defense of Halykirke.
Couatyse I fynde þareinne,
For he þat plays couaytes to wynne;
Sen he of wynnyng settes his thoght,
Withouten Couatyse ne es he noght.
Rauyne þare es, als men may knawe,
For he þat playes spoylles his felawe.
To take of hym he wil noght lette
Al þat euer he may gette,
And þat he getes withhaldes stille.
þis may be called Rauyn bi skille.
Okir also men may þare kenne,
For he tas for neghen shillynges ten,
Noght for a moneth to pay
Bot for an houre anely of þe day.
Sen he tas so mykell fre,
Appert Oker may þis be.
Multiplyinge of Wordes in vayne
And athes and leghes vncertayne
Er mykell vsed at þat gammen,
When twa or thre playes sammen.
Bot alle `þa' wordes vndirstande I
Er noght withouten synne and foly.
Yhete sclaundre þai Godde, als I wene,
And his halowes þat with him bene.
For when þair chaunce comes noght tyte,
þai flyte with Godde and al hym wyte,
And his halowes þai myssprayse
And says þai er alle vncurtayse.
þai say Godde and his halowes bathe

7250 plays] play PRW bihald] halde P 7251 vn-] *om.* E 7252 þe] *om.* ES defense] defend R 7253 I fynde] *trs.* R 7254 þat] *om.* E 7255 he] *om.* E of] on ELSR wynnyng] couaytese L 7256 ne] *om.* ELPRW 7257 þare] *om.* P es] es in L 7258 he] *om.* P spoylles] wyth L, sp`o'les P, spoles R 7261 withhaldes] he haldys it R 7262 rauyn] rayn R bi] þurgh 7263 þare] þarein S 7264 neghen] noght ELS 7266 anely] *om.* PRW of] on ES þe] a LP 7267 tas] so takys R 7269 of] in L 7271 vsed] haunted L þat] þat þe E 7272 playes] er playand R 7273 þa] *int. later* A wordes] *adds* als L 7274 and] of R 7276–8 *lines om.* S 7278 al] *om.* E, all þai L 7279–80 *trs. couplet* P

Helpes þam noght bot dose þam skathe.
A grete Sclaundre to Godde es þis
And til his halwes with him in blisse.
  Ille Ensaumple methink þai gyf
Til othir men þat suld wele lyf,
For som þan gifs þair willes þarto
To do right als þai se þam do.
Thurgh Ille Ensaumple men may make
Foles þat wille aftir it take.
  Yhete spende þai þair tyme noght wele,

De Misericordia

fo. 45ra Bot þai lese it ilka dele
And þe gode þat þai suld do to-whyles,
And vses folyes þat þair saulles fyles.
Swilk Spendynge of Tyme in vayne
Mon putte þair saulles to mykell payne.
  Corrupcion to þam may be
þat vses of custom it to se.
For many lufs, nyght and day,
To stande or sitte to se þat play.
Methink þat manere es vnhaalsom
To þam þat vses it of custom.
  Yhete methink vnbouxsom er þai
Til Halykirke þat vses þat play.
For Halykirke defendes swilk werkes
And namely to prestes and to clerkes.
Alle þa þat dose þareagayne
Suld be chastyde thurgh þair souerayne.
  Bot whaso any wynnyng hentes
In play of dyce or in turnamentes,
Be it in town or be it in felde,
þam bihoues it agayne yhelde

7286 suld wele] *trs.* LPR 7287 willes] will LRW 7289 ille] *om.* L 7290 wille] *after* it S aftir it] þare-efter L it] þam E 7291 þai] *add* noght ELS noght] ryght ELS 7292 Bot] Forwhy R lese] lose L 7293 And] Fore E to-] *om.* LSRW, þe P 7294 vses] hauntes L saulles] saule L 7298 to] for to E 7301 es] *om.* L vn-] noght S 7302 vses] hauntes L 7304 vses] hauntes L 7305–6 *trs. couplet* W 7305 swilk] þase L 7306 And] *om.* L to[1]] fra L to[2]] fra L, *om.* SRW 7309 hentes] entes L 7310 in[2]] of LS, *om.* W turna-] tour- P 7311 or] *om.* ELS be it[2]] ȝit P 7312 þam] Hym L, þai W

Or to pouer men it alle dele,
For þat wynnynge es noght leele.
Here haf I shewed on sere wyse
þe ten braunches of Couatyse
þat þe Gift of Counsaylle drawes
Out of þe hert þat it lawes,
And settes þareinne instede of þat
A vertu þat Mercy hatt.

De uirtute Misericordie

Mercy may wele lickened be *De Misericordia*
By gode skille vntill a tre
þat men sees bathe growe and sprede,
Bathe on heght and also on brede.
Seuen degrees of þat tree er sene, *vij^{tem}. sunt gradus misericordie, videlicet natura, gracia, preceptum Sacre Scripture, honor Dei, largitas Dei, timor iudicij extremi, fructus Misericordie*
And out of it springes braunches fourtene,
Of whilk bene seuen, to telle þam eft,
On þe right syde and seuen on þe left.
þe first degree es kynde right;
Anothir es grace for vs dight;
þe thridde es þat rewels our witte,
þe commaundement of Haly Writte.
þe ferthe es honour to Godde of heuen,
þe fift largesce of Godde to neuen;

De Misericordia

þe sext es drede of þe dome namely; fo. 45rb
þe seuent es þe fruyt of Mercy.
þise seuen degrees er seuen skilles
þat our hertes to Mercy tilles.
First kynde suld vs to Mercy lede *j[^{us}]. gradus est*
To helpe our euencrysten in nede, *natura*

7313 to] vnto L alle] haally R 7317 drawes] oute drawes L 7318 Out of] Fra L 7319 þareinne] þare L 7320a *om.* ELPSRW 7321 *sidenote: as in-column heading* R, *om.* LP 7322 vntill] till S 7323 growe] grofe? P sprede] sperde R 7324 heght] lenght EL also] *om.* L brede] drede E 7325 of] on W *sidenote: om.* W (*numbers the seven marginally*), *last numbered member at* 7337 P videlicet . . . f.m.] *om.* S videlicet] vt EL honor] amor E 7327 Of] *om.* W whilk] þe whylk LW bene] *om.* L 7330 for vs] vs for to L dight] in syght P 7332 þe] To þe LS -ment] -mentes ELSW writte] kyrk L 7333 to] of PR 7337 *sidenote*: Fructus misericordie P 7338 hertes] hert L to] vnto R 7339 to] vnto R *sidenote*: Natura W, *om.* L *j^{us}.] j. A

Forþi þat we er alle, mare and lesse,
Of a kynde and a lickenes.
In kynde of bestes may we fynde
Ensaumple þat vs to Mercy suld bynde:
þat som foulle thurgh kynde wil lette
Of flesshe of þe same kynde to ette;
And yhete a meer thurgh kynde wil thole
Souke hir anothir meeres fole;
And wolfes, als we fynde in iestes,
Has keped childer fra othir bestes.
Wele mare suld we be mercyable
þan bestes þat er vnresonable,
Thurgh kynde to helpe othir and saue
þat we se our lickenes haue.

ij[us]. gradus est gracia Grace suld vs to Mercy drawe
To help þat nede has for Goddis awe.
For we er alle lyms thurgh grace to wirke
Of a bodi þat es Halykirke,
And thurgh grace Godde rightwyse
Boght vs alle with a pryse.
þat was his awen precious blode
þat he shedde for vs on þe rode.
For Mercy he had of mans kynde
þat aght vs ay to haue in mynde,
And forthy we er alle brethir fre,
And a fader and a moder haf we.
Our fader es Godde þat sendes solace
And Halykirk our moder thurgh grace.
Sen ilkane of vs es othir brothir
Ilkane suld we haf Mercy on othir.

iijus. gradus est preceptum Sacre Scripture þe commandement of Haly Writte
Suld our hertes to Mercy knytte,

7341 Forþi] Forwhi S alle] *om.* LS 7342 and] *add* of LPSR 7345 þat] *om.* L kynde] *om.* P 7346 Of1] Of þe LR 7348 Souke hir] Be sucken of L 7349 And] A R in] in þe W 7352 þan] þat þan E 7353 Thurgh] Other þurgh L 7354 our] *adds* awn R 7355 *sidenote*: Gracia W, *om.* L *ijus.] ij. A est] *om.* P 7356 help] *adds* þaime S þat] at L has] *om.* L 7359 grace] *adds* of E Godde] *adds* þat es all L 7360 Boght] Bot L with a] þurgh hys L a] a grete P 7363 had] has W of] on LP 7364 to] *om.* LSW mynde] hande mynde P 7366 And] *om.* W 7367 sendes] *adds* vs L 7370 Ilkane] *adds* of vs W we] *om.* LPSRW on] of W 7371 -ment] -mentes R *sidenote*: *om.* LW 7372 to] *om.* E, in P, vnto R

For Haly Writte vs biddes be bisy
To do þe Werkes of Mercy.
þa werkes passes alle othir vertus;
þai kyndell þe luf of Godde in vs.
For als oyle þat þe laump has withinne

Donum Consilij De Misericordia
Fiat voluntas tua etc.

Passes oboun al lykour thynne, fo. 45va
So passes Mercy þat es clene
Oboun alle othir vertus þat bene.
And als þe oylle in a laumpe bright
Maas þe fyre þareinne to brynne light,
So þe oylle of Mercy to proue
Norisshes in hert þe fyre of luf.
And als þe fyre out wil ga
When þe oylle withdrawes þarfra
And to þe light noght auaylles
When þe oylle in þe laump faylles,
So faylles luf of Godde first knawen
When Mercy faylles and es withdrawen.
Mercy, als þise clerkes says,
Es þe vertu þat mast Godde pays
And þe fende of helle mast deres,
For it es þe armes þat mast him feres.
þarfore þai þat wil wele spede
Haue Mercy of þam þat has nede
And help þam in þair mischief
So þat þai may þe better lief.
For þat þai gif es halden als store,
þai mon haf heuen-blisse þarfore.
And þa þat þe pouer help wil warne
In þair mast nede help mon þai tharne.

7377 als] *adds* þe R has] *adds* hym L 7378 Passes] Fletes L al] *adds* þe W lykour] lycours L 7379 passes] ouerpasses L 7380 Oboun] *om.* L 7381 And] *om.* L a] *om.* L 7382 light] ryght L 7384 Norisshes in] *trs.* L in] in þe E 7385 out wil] *trs.* W 7386 When] *adds* men L 7387 þe] *om.* L 7389 faylles] *add* þe LSW 7390 faylles] falles P 7392 mast Godde] *trs.* LSRW 7394 armes] armoure L mast him] *trs.* ELS feres] weres L 7395 -fore] *om.* L 7396 of] on RW 7399 þai] *om.* R als] in P 7400 heuen-] þe L 7401 þe . . . wil] wyll þe pore men L pouer help] pore *later in blank* P 7402 help] *om.* P þai] *om.* EPS

iij[us]. gradus est honor Dei
Honour to Godde almyghty
Suld stir vs sone vnto Mercy.
For þai do Godde grete honour
þat þe pouer wil help and sokour.
For þat men dose to þe pouer þat es nedy
Men dose it vnto Godde almyghty,
Als Godde himseluen beres wyttenes
In þe godspelle þat sothe es.
He says, 'Yhe þat haf done to myne,
Yhe did it to me; þat sal yhe noght tyne'.
þe pouer men þat here er sene
Goddis awen menyhe bene.
Whaso thurgh Mercy þam sokours
Or worshepes, he Godde honours,
For he þat worshepes þe menyhe
Honour to þe lorde dose he,

Donum Consilij De Misericordia
Fiat voluntas tua etc.

fo. 45vb
And he þat to þe menyhe dose shame
Vnto þe lorde he dose þe same.
A fayre ensaumple of þat we haue
Of Saynt Martyne þat vouched saue
For Goddis luf to parte his mantell
And to þe pouer man gaf a cantell.
And sone þareafter his sight was ledde
þar he sagh Godde þarewith cledde
And herdde him to his aungelles say,
'Lo, how Martyn cledde me today'.

v[[us]]. gradus est largitas Dei
Largesce of Godde þat es large of gift
Suld our hertes to Mercy lift,
For Godde gyues to ilk man largely

7403 to] vnto R *sidenote*: *om*. W, Honor Dei L 7404 sone] *om*. L vnto] to W 7405 do] to S, *om*. R Godde] *add* full LR 7408 it] *om*. W vnto] vt vnto E, to PRW 7410 *sidenote*: In euangelio Amen dico vobis quamdiu (*adds* vni S) ex hijs fratribus meis fecistis michi fecistis ES 7412 it] *om*. RW 7414 menyhe] mene þai ELS bene] þai bene P 7415 -so] þat L, þaa *corr. to* saa S 7416 honours] honor dose L 7417 þe] in (*expunged?*) þe S *sidenote*: Nota E 7418 þe] '*later*' E, our R 7420 Vnto] To W 7421 *sidenote*: Exemplum R, Martin W 7424 þe] a W man] *adds* he W 7427 him] god L 7428 how] *adds* saynt R to-] þis LS 7429 *sidenote*: Largitas Dei LW *v[us].] v. A 7430 Suld] Schal W to] vnto R 7431 For] And L to] vntyll L

After he es of his curtaysy.
Sen Godde giues largely, we suld gief
Largely to þam þat has myschief,
For Godde biddes vs mercyable be
Als þe Fader es, þat es ful of pyte.
Goddis sones, als þe boke þam leres,
Suld folow þe gode Faders maneres.
þarefore þe wyse man biddes vs,
'Be merciable to do almus
And helpe þa þat nede has here';
So may we be Goddis sones dere.
  Drede of þe dome at þe last day
Suld stir our hertes to Mercy ay,
For alle þat here has na pyte
Withouten mercy demed sal be,
Als says þe haly man appertly:
'Iugement withouten Mercy
Sal be gyuen agayne ilka wight
þat þe Werkes of Mercy dose noght right',
And þai þat þe Werkes of Mercy has done
þat day þai sal haf mercy sone.
Bot alle þat Mercy here wil warne
Mercy of Godde þai sal þan tharne,
For Godde turnes þam þe deef ere þan
þat turnes þe deef ere to þe pouer man.
  Of þat we may ensaumple telle
þat Godde shewes in þe godspelle
Of þe riche man, and es wryten þus,
þat warned þe lazar his almus.

vj[us]. gradus est timor extremi iudicij

De Misericordia

þarefore Godde warned him þareagayne

fo. 46ra

7432 After] *adds* þat L 7433 suld] sall P 7434 þam] þase LS 7435 vs] *om.* E mercyable] mercyfull L 7437 sones] sone W þam leres] þan beres L 7440 to] and L 7441 þa] þaim EPSR, *om.* W nede has] *trs.* P here] nere E 7442 sones] sonne P 7443 þe[1]] *om.* P *sidenote*: Timor extremi iudicij W, *om.* L *vj[us].] vj. A 7445–6 *trs. couplet* L 7445 For] *om.* L 7448 mercy] any m. R *sidenote*: Nota E 7449 agayne] withouten to P 7451 þe] *om.* R 7452 þai] *om.* LS þai sal] *trs.* R (cf. sal *at head of the line*) L 7453 alle] *adds* þai R 7454 þai . . . þan] þen sall þai PR 7455 þam] to þaime L, *om.* S 7456 þe[1]] now þe L, here þe P 7457 þat] all L may] haue L telle] to t. L 7458 Godde] *om.* W shewes] says S *sidenote*: In euangelio E, Euangelium S 7459 and] þat L 7460 lazar] lazarar S

A drope of water to slocken his payne
When he in þe fyre of helle was
And brinned hate for his trespas.
And þe fole maydens, how þai war stadde
þat in þair laumpes nane oylle hadde.
þarefore Godde þat al synne hates
At þe bridale sperred þe yhates
Agayne þam, for þai nane oylle broght,
And sayde to þam, 'I knaw yhow noght'.
Right so þe yhates of Paradyse
Sal be sperred on þe same wyse
Agayne alle þa men namely
þat has in hert here na Mercy,
And withouten Mercy be þan
In helle als was þe riche man.

vij[us]. gradus est fructus Misericordie

þe fruyt of þe tree þat Mercy es called
Suld make vs Mercy in hert halde,
For Mercy, als þe boke vs leres,
Shewes his fruyt on many maners.
First Mercy thurgh grace to vs wynnes
Forgifnes of alle our synnes.
Mercy saues vs fra alle mischaunce
And wynnes vs here our sustinaunce.
Mercy vs may fra þe fende saue
And multiplyes þe gode þat we haue,
Als we may fynde and proue itte
By many ensaumples in Haly Writte.
Mercy es þe gode marchande
þat ay wynnes and neuer es tynande.

Paulus

Als says Saynt Paul thurgh short shewyng,
'Mercy es worthe to alle thynge'.
For þat stane es ful precious
þat to alle + thing es vertuous;

7464 brinned] brynande EP 7465 þe] *om.* P 7468 bridale] bryde all R sperred] sp`e'rede⟨s⟩ P, spred W 7469 þai] þai hadd L 7473 þa] þe W 7475 And] *om.* W be] sall be L, be þai P 7477 þe^{2}] þat R *sidenote*: Fructus misericordie W, *om.* L vij^{us}.] vij. A misericordie] penitencie S 7478 hert] *add* to ELPSW 7480 on] of E 7481 mercy] *om.* W to] *om.* E 7482 of alle] haly of R 7483 alle] *adds* maner of L 7484 vs] *om.* P 7486 gode] godes W 7491 says] *om.* ELR *sidenote om.* L 7492 worthe] worthy W to] vntill R alle] alkyn L *7494 thing] thinges A

þat es Mercy þat wynne vs may
Alle manere of gode, þat es to say
Bathe werldely gode and gastly to neuen
And endeles gode, þat es þe blisse of heuen.
Of werldely godes þat Godde lenes vs
Salamon spekes and says þus, *Salamon*
'With þi ritches þou Godde honour
And with þi gode þe pouer sokour,

De Misericordia

And Godde sal ful fille þi gerners fo. 46rb
Of corne and with wyne þi celers'.
Bot vndirstande with al þi witte
þis worde als Salamon says itte:
He says, 'Of þi gode and þi ritchesce',
And noght of þat þat othir mens es,
Als som þat wil þair almus make
Of othir mens gode þat þai take
Thurgh okir or theft or rauyn
Or thurgh gilry. If þai it so wynne,
For swilk almus gete þai na mede;
þai do mare synne þan almusdede.
Swilk almus es made in vayne,
For Godde wil þat þai it yhelde agayne
And almus do thurgh Mercy
Of þat þat þai haf wonnen leelly.
Mercy may be to our pru
Lickened to sede of grete vertu
þat growes after þe kynde of þat
Better in lene erthe þan in fatte.
For Mercy shewes his frute sone
When it es to þe nedefull done.
Mercy fordose þe fendes rede
And saues vs fra alle manere of dede:
Fra dede of helle þat es endeles,

7496 manere] maneres ES to] for to L 7499 godes] gode LPR 7500 *sidenote om.* LR 7502 gode] gudes ELS þe] þu R pouer] *adds* þou L 7504 with] *om.* L 7506 worde] wordes L 7507 *sidenote*: Salamon E 7508 And] A R þat^{2}] *om.* ES 7510 gode] godes L 7511 or^{1}] *om.* L 7517 do] dede L 7518 þai] men L 7519 to] vnto R 7524 to] in ELS þe] *om.* L 7526 vs] *om.* R

Fra dede of synne þat gastly es,
Fra bodily dede þat alle bihoues fele,
Bathe gode and ille, als clerkes wate wele.
  For men may fynde ensaumples in boke
Of haly mens lyfs, whaso wil loke,
þat men fra dede has bene raysed
Thurgh Werkes of Mercy þat mast es praysed.
þarefore Mercy mykell auaylles;
It es þe tresour þat neuer faylles.
Thurgh Mercy grace here wynne we may
And aftir þis lyf blisse for ay.
  þise er þe degrees of Mercy seuen,
And now I wil þe braunches neuen.
þe braunches bene Werkes of Mercy
þat bene bath bodyly and gastly.
Out of Mercy, als says þis clerkes,
On aythir side growes seuen werkes.

Donum Consilij De Misericordia
Fiat voluntas tua etc.

fo. 46va On þe right syde seuen gastly springes,
And on þe left syde seuen bodily hinges.
De vijtem. Operibus Misericordie Spiritualibus
  þe Gastly Werkes bene þise to knawe,
þe whilk I wil recken here on rawe:
þe first of þe Gastly Werkes þis es
To counsaylle þam þat bene redeles.
Anothir es, als I vndirstande,
To teche þam þat bene vnconande.
þe thridde Werk also es þis
To chasty þam þat done amisse.
þe ferthe es þis in ilka case
To comfort þam þat angre has.
þe fift also [es] to forgif

7528 gastly] gylty R 7531–2 *couplet trs.* P 7531 -ples] -pelle EPSRW 7533 þat] Fra S 7536 neuer] *adds* mare L 7538 lyf] *adds* þe R 7540 I wil] *trs.* LR 7541–2 *couplet trs.* L 7541 bene werkes] þat er L 7542 þat] þai L 7545 On] Oute of L 7546 And] *om.* LS 7547–8 *couplet trs.* L 7547 þe] þir L *sidenote*: *om.* P, *as in-column heading* R misericordie] *om.* SW 7548 here] *om.* P 7549 of þe] *om.* L, 'of' P werkes] werk L, *adds* is P þis] *om.* L 7550] bene] ys R 7553 also] als P 7554 a-] of L, *om.* W *adds* 7486, *a blank line,* 7487–93, 7554 *repeated (no variants within the lines)* E 7555 in ilka case] to do solace L 7556 To] And L 7557 also] is for L *es] *om.* AES

Alle wranges and trespas þat may greue.
þe sext es to haue in hert pyte
Of þam þat we in angre se.
þe seuent es withouten fayntyse
To pray ilk day for our enemyse.
 þe first Werk es counsaylle to bede
To þam þat has of counsaylle nede,
For Goddis luf when þai it craue
And noght for werldely wynnyng to haue,
Als pledours dose and auokettes
þat þair hertes on wynnyng settes.
Bot som of þam, als men vndirstandes,
Wynnes and takes on bathe handes:
þai gif na counsaylle bot for mede
Or for fauour`e´ or for drede.
For Goddis luf wil þai nane gieue,
For þat trauaylle wald þam greue.
 Bot þair counsaylle mast auaylles
þat bisily and wele counsaylles
Synfull men to leue þair synne
And men of gode lyf to dwelle þarinne,
Als dose prelates and confessours
And othir gode counsayllours;
þai wirk right þat werke gastly.
þis es þe first braunche of Mercy.
 þe secund Werk es to kenne
And to teche vnconande men.
And þat suld þai namely do
þat er halden and bunden þarto,
Als prelates þair suggettes to preche;
Als maysters þair disciples to teche;
Als fader and moder to chasty

Primum opus est consulere consilio indigentibus

ij^{m}. opus est instruere ignorantes

7558 *line om.* L wranges] wrange PW 7560 we] *om.* W se] be W 7563 *sidenote*: *om.* L, *as in-column heading* R, j. opus W Primum . . . est] *om.* R est] *om.* S consilio] *om.* P 7566 werldely] werldes L 7568 hertes] hert L on] in P 7570 on] of P bathe] *add* þe EP 7572 fauoure] -e *later over eras.* A 7574 For þat] Forwhy þar R wald] wyll L 7575 Bot] *adds* ay R counsaylle] couatys R 7576 wele] maste L 7577 Synfull men to] To gerre þe s. L leue] lese? P 7580 gode] nobyll R 7582 þis] þat P bruanche] werk LR 7583 *sidenote*: *om.* L, *as in-column heading* R, ij. opus W ij^{m} . . . . est] *om.* R opus] *om.* S est] misericordie P ignorantes] indigentibus P, ignoscentes R 7584 And] For P 7586 bunden] bone P 7588 Als] And P to] *om.* W 7589 fader, moder] faders, moders LR

And to teche þair childer curtaysy.
  Prelates suld þair suggettes wisse

Donum Consilij De Misericordia
Fiat voluntas tua etc.

fo. 46vb And teche þam þe way to blisse,
And kenne þam how þai sal forsake
Synne and to gode lyf þam take,
And teche þam whilk es Goddis lawe
And how þai sal his wille knawe
Thurgh gode ensaumples of Haly Writte
To make þair hertes fra synne flitte;
And how þai suld luf Godde and drede
And gif þam gode ensaumple in dede.
For ilka prelate es ensaumplere
Til his suggettes þat he suld lere,
For al say he wele and dose noght so,
He gifs þam ensaumple ille to do;
And als many paynes he worthy es
Als he gifs ensaumple of wickednes.
  Maysters to teche suld bisy be
Þair discyples in som faculte
Of science, craft, or mistere
Þat þai er halden þam to lere,
So þat na tyme of lerynge faylle
In defaute of þe maysters trauaylle.
For if þai spende þair tyme in waste,
Þair maysters, þat er to wyte maste,
Of al þat tyme þat wrange es vsed
Sal bifore Godde be accused,
When alle dedes sal be shewed,
Bathe of lered men and of lewed.

7590 curtaysy] curtaysly EP 7591 *sidenote*: Nota prelates sulde teche E 7592 to] to þe L 7593 kenne] teche W sal] sulde PSR 7594 to] *om.* R þam] to R 7595 es] þe R Goddis] due E 7596 sal] sulde L his wille] hit wele W 7597 -ples] -ple ELPSR 7598 synne] *add* to LP 7602 he] þai L 7603 al] of-all L, if-all P say he] *trs.* P he] we W dose] do LS 7604 ensaumple ille] *trs.* S 7605 he] *om.* LS 7606 of] to W 7607 *sidenote*: Maysters sulde teche E 7609 science] *adds* of L or] or of L 7611 na] *after* lerynge E 7612 þe] *om.* LS 7613 in] *om.* P 7614 maysters] mayster L þat] *om.* EPS, þai R 7615 Of] For W 7616 Sal] *adds* þai L be] *adds* hard R 7617 alle] *adds* be (*canc.*?) P 7618 men] *om.* LR

Fader and moder suld teche right
þair childer with al þair myght
And norisshe þam in gode thewes,
And kepe þam fra company of shrewes
And fra swerynge of grete athe
And fra leghynge þat oft dose skathe.
And chasty þam when þai do wrange
And spare þam noght þarefra ouerlange.
For als we se men settes a shoo
On a last þat es mete þarto;
þe shappe it tase when it sittes fast
Shal halde whyles þe sho may last.
And als a colt a tetche ay hauntes
þat he tase first when men him dauntes,
So haldes a chylde thurgh hande and tunge
þe tetche for ay þat he takes yhunge.
þarefore men suld, when þai leste couthe,
Kenne þam gode thewes in þair yhouthe.
For þe fader and þe moder sal be

De Misericordia

Accused bifor Godde, so wil He, fo. 47ra
Of alle ille tetches in worde and dede
þat þair childer takes in barnhede,
Thurgh þe defaute at þe bigynnynge
Of þair faders and moders techynge.
þe thridde Werk of Mercy es þis, *iij^{m}. opus est castigare malefactores*
To chasty þam þat dose amysse.
þat falles til prelates specially
And til kynges and lordes þat bene myghty.
þai suld chasty with al þair myght

7619 Fader, moder] Faders, moders R *sidenote*: Fader and moder sulde teche E, Nota R 7620 þair] *adds* awn R 7621 in] with P 7623 Fra foule spech and sweryng bathe R athe] athez LS 7624 leghynge] leyghynges S dose skathe] skathez L, dose skathes S 7626 þarefra] *om.* LS 7627–30 *lines om.* R 7627 se] *om.* L 7630 Shal halde] And haldes þat schappe L þe sho] it L 7631 And] For R 7634 tetche] teches L 7635 men] þai E leste] best R 7636 Kenne] Tech W 7637 fader, moder] faders, moders R þe^{2}] *om.* W 7638 *line over eras.* P 7639 tetches] thewes ELS 7640 childer] barnes L takes] has R in] in þer R barn-] yout- L 7641 þe^{1}] *om.* LS at] of W 7643 *sidenote*: *om.* L, *as in-column heading* R, iij. opus W iij^{m} . . . . est] *om.* R 7644 a-] of PS, *om.* W 7646 and] and to P

þair suggettes þat dose noght right,
For if þai suffir thurgh reckelesnes
Or thurgh fauour, any wickednes
þat þai thurgh lawe may amende here,
Of þat synne er þai partenere.
  þarefore nouthir prince ne prelate
Suld suffre na synne þat þai wate
Bot þai þareinne amendement sette
And nouthir for luf ne fauour lette.
For if so falle þat þare be
With a lorde wicked menyhe
And þe lorde þair wickednes knawe
And wil noght sette þam in awe,
A grete taken may men se þan
þat þe lorde es na gode man.
For swilk a worde es in ilka cuntre
þat men says, 'Swilk lorde, swilk menyhe'.
Bot thurgh ille menyhe, als es sene,
Lordes with wrange oft sclaundred bene.
  þarefore þise lordes suld take kepe
And nouthir for luf lette ne frendshepe
To chasty þair menyhe or suggettes
Of þair folys þat gode lyf lettes.
For þai suld drede Godde mare þan man
And luf Hym mare after þai can.
Men suld luf wele mens persounes
And hate þair fole condicioungs.
þarefore prelates and princes of þe lande
And othir lordes suld vnderstande
þat vnknawyng þam noght excuses
Of folys þat þair suggettes vses.
For þai er halden thurgh þe lawe
To enquere þe defautes and knawe

7648 suggettes] suggett? L 7649 reckeles-] reckyl- R 7652 er þai] *trs.* W part-] parc- LPS 7653 þare-] þat L 7655 þare-] þaires P amendement] amendes L 7656 fauour] fauours S 7657 if] if it P 7658 a] any R lorde] *add* a LS 7661 taken] takenyng L 7662 þe] þat L es na] ne es a P, nys no W 7663 worde] lorde E ilka] *om.* L, sere R 7664 þat men says] *om.* L 7667 þise] *om.* E 7668 ne] ne for EL 7669 or] and þaire L 7670 Of] Or P folys] foly W 7671 Godde] *adds* ay R 7674 fole] folye EP, foule RW 7675 *line om.* L 7677 þam noght] *trs.* EL 7680 enquere] eqwer R and knawe] if þai may L

Thurgh men þat bene gode and leele
þat þe sothe wil noght concele.

De Misericordia

For wyte þai wele at domesday *fo.* 47rb
þai be noght excused for to say,
'Lorde, swilk defautes knewe we noght';
þare sal þai se what þai haf wroght.
  þe ferthe Werke es of Mercy *iiij^{m}. opus est consolare desolatos*
To comfort þam þat er sary,
Als seke men þat bedde-red lyse
Or þa þat er in othir anguyse.
Men suld þam comfort in alle þair bales
Thurgh gode ensaumples and fayre tales
To brynge þam out of wrange thoght
So þat þair hertes faylle þam noght,
Als Saynt Paul says, 'Yhe þat has quert, *Paulus*
Comforte þam þat er feble of hert'.
And Salamon says and beres wyttenes *Salamon*
þat he þat at malese of hert es
Suld haue comforte and wax light
Thurgh gode wordes þat men says him right.
For als þe hert þat has grete lykynge
In gode sawors thurgh smellynge,
So feles þe saul swetnes þat vaylles
In gode wordes and gode counsaylles,
If a sothfast frende him counsaylle swa
þat lufs hym bathe in wele and wa.
For a man may fele and se in dede
Wha es his frende when he has nede.

7681 bene] *adds* bath R 7683 at] on LS 7684 to] þat W 7685 knewe] knaw P 7687 es] *om.* L *sidenote*: *as in-column heading* R, iiij^{us}. opus W iiij^{m} . . . est] *om.* R 7688 To] Es to L 7689 Als] And L 7690 þa] þam R anguyse] angers R 7692 -ples] -ple ELSRW 7694 þair] *om.* E þam] *om.* L 7695 Als] And W yhe] we P, ȝhet W *sidenote om.* P 7698 at] *om.* LS 7699 haue] *om.* P wax] way R 7700 gode wordes] goddes worde L him] *om.* L 7701 þat] *om.* LPRW 7702 sawors] w *and* r *later over eras.* A, sarmouns ES, sauore L 7703 feles] smelles P swetnes] *om.* L vaylles] auayles EL 7704 gode wordes] goddes worde L 7705 him counsaylle] *trs.* LS 7706 lufs] lyues W hym] *om.* LW and] and in L 7707 For] For if S fele, se] *trs. infs.* LW

Quatuor sunt specialiter cogitanda in omnibus tribulacionibus: pena inferni, gaudium Paradisy, passio Cristi, vtilitas tribulacionis

Four thinges may men shewe þat can
þat in alle angres comfortes a man;
If he his thoght on þa four sette,
Alle his angres he sal forgette.
Ane es to think on þe paynes of helle
þat er mare þan tunge may telle;
Anothir to think withouten fayntyse
On þe grete ioye of Paradyse.
þe thridde es with gode deuocioun
To think on Crystes passyoun;
þe ferthe to think what godes and grace
Angres and noyes may purchace
To þam þat tholes it with gode wille,
Als men may shewe bi sere skille.

j. de peni⟨s⟩ inferni

First suld he think þat in angre es
On þe payne of helle þat es endeles,
þat synful men þat dwelles þareinne
Sal thole eueremare for þair synne.

Donum Consilij De Misericordia
Fiat voluntas tua etc.

fo. 47va

þe paynes er so hidous to here
þat alle þe clerkes, fer and nere,
þat euer was or þat lyues yhete,
Couthe noght imagyne a payne thurgh witte.
þa paynes bene so sharp and felle
þat alle þe angres þat men may telle,
Or persecucions or anguys
þat men tholes here on any wyse
Er noght bot als ane oyntyng ware
To regarde of þe paynes þare.

7709 may] *om.* W þat] *om.* W *sidenote*: De quatuor rebus confortantibus hominem in omnibus angustijs (*as in-column heading*) R, 4. W specialiter] spiritualiter P in] et in P pena] videlicet pena P, de penis S gaudium] gaudia S Cristi] Ihesu Cristi ES vtilitas] vtilia L tribulacionis] -cionum S 7710 a] *om.* P 7712 angres] anger L 7713 to think] thynkynge R paynes] payn W 7714 mare] *adds* hard R may] can L 7715 Anothir] *add* es EPR withouten] *add* any LS 7716 On] Of L 7719 and] of P 7720 Angres, noyes] *trs. sbs.* R 7721 it] þam R 7722 sere] seres P, gode LS 7723 angre] angers LS *sidenote*: *om.* W j.] *om.* PS 7724 On] Of L payne] paynes LP 7726 -mare] payne L 7727 þe] Tha EPS er] er of L 7728 þe] *om.* E clerkes] *adds* þat er L 7729 þat[2]] *om.* L 7732 men] man PR 7733 -cions] -cioun L 7734 on] in L any] many R 7735 noght] *om.* LS

Whaso thinkes what þa paynes ere,
Angres him sal here lytell dere
þat he tholes in his lyf-dayse.
Als Saynt Austyne to Godde þus says, *Augustinus*
'Lorde, lat britten me here and broylle me
þat I to helle noght dampned be'.
Methink it es ane eesy thinge
To suffre þe wande of chastyinge
To skape þe glayue þat strikes sare
And þat slaas þe saull for euermare.
þat es þe sharp dede of helle
þat neuer has ende, als clerkes can telle.
Godde shewes a man grete semblant of luf
When he sendes angre him here to proue,
Als Godde says þat es ful of Mercy,
'þam þat I luf I wille chasty'. *Quem diligo castigo*
þe ox þat men wil slaa in sesoun
Men fedes fatte for þat enchesoun.
Bot þe ox þat sal noght be slayne
Men puttes to yhock in plogh or wayne.
Swa it es a signe of dampnacyoun
Til hym þat here has na tribulacioun
Bot allekyn welthes and delyces has here
To wax fatte to þe fendes lardere.
Als says Saynt Austyne, and may wele be, *Augustinus Rerum habundancia et sanitas continua sunt eterne dampnacionis indicia*
þat whaso has of welthe plente
And continuele hele, a token it es
Of dampnacioun þat es endeles.
Bot he þat Godde haldes to his store
Him most thole here angres þarefore.
A token of luf shewes þe emperour

7736 To] As to þe R 7738 him sal] *trs.* S (cf. him *after* lytell L) here] *om.* LS 7739 tholes] *adds* here R his] þis R 7741 me] *om.* W here] *om.* P broylle] boyle LS 7745 skape] eschape L strikes] smytes L 7749 semblant] takenyng L, sample P 7750 angre] angres LS him] *om.* E here] *om.* L 7752 þam] þan R I wille] *trs.* R wille] *om.* P *sidenote*: *om.* L Quem] Quos W 7754 fedes] makes it L, fedys hym R for] to L 7756 to] it to L, to þe W in plogh] *om.* L or] and PSW 7757 *sidenote*: Nota E 7759 delyces] delytes EP 7760 to wax] And waxes L to] vnto R þe] *om.* L 7761 says . . . Austyne] *trs. phrs.* ELR and] þat S *sidenote*: Augustinus W Augustinus] *om.* ELS sunt] *repeated* P 7762 of welthe] welthes and P 7763 token] takenyng L 7766 Him] He W most] behoues LS 7767 token] takennyng L

To þat man and dose him grete honour
To wham he sendes, als him gode think,
His awen coppe þareof to drynk.

Donum Consilij De Misericordia Fiat voluntas tua etc.

fo. 47vb þe coppe es angre þat here es ryf
And persecucioun of þis lyf.
þat es þe first saus to sette
With whilk men suld swilk mete ette,
þat es angre of bitter tast;
þat bitternes may sour saus wast.
þat saus I calle of mynde a mees
Of þe payne of helle þat neuer sal sees.
þat calle I vynegre þat es soure,
þat dose away al þe sauour
Of þe wyne of worldely delitz
þat mas men falle in many a vyce,
Als þe vynegre dose men tyne
þe sauour and þe tast of gode wyne.
ij. De gaudijs Paradysy þe secund thinge to thynk es þis
Of þe grete ioye and þe grete blisse
Of Paradyse þat lastes ay,
Als men has herde haly men say.
So mykell ioye þare es to telle
þat alle þe delitz here þar we dwelle
Es noght bot sorow—trowe ilk man þis—
To regarde of þat grete blisse.
þat blisse sal þai haue at þe last
þat here tholes angre with hert stedfast;
Bot na man getes þat warysoun
Bot he thole here tribulacioun.

7768 To] *om.* L and] þat R grete] *om.* W 7770 -of] oft R 7771 þe] þat L es[1]] of W 7772 And] *adds* many L -cioun] -ciouns LS, *adds* and angers S of] in L þis] his R 7773 saus] sand? W 7775 bitter] *adds* to P 7777 I calle] *trs.* R 7780 al] *om.* LW 7781 delitz] delycez E, delice L, delite S 7782 men] men to L a] *om.* RW 7783 þe] *om.* L dose] garres L 7784 and] of P þe[2]] *om.* RW of] of þe P 7785 thinge] es L to thynk] *om.* P es] on L *sidenote*: *om.* LPW ij.] *om.* S 7786 Of] *om.* PW and] of P 7790 delitz] delycez ELSR, delite W þar] whar R 7791 sorow] sour W 7792 To] Vnto R 7793 þe] *om.* L 7794 angre] angres L 7796 here] grete E

þarefore ne suld na man stryue
With þe angres of þis lyue
Bot yherne oft with þam to mete
For al seme þai bittir, þai er swete.
For thinge þat bitter to þe body es
To þe saul es grete swetenes.
þarefore he suld nane angre drede
þat wald þarefore haf blisse to mede,
For angre suld litell dere him þan,
Als Saynt Gregor says þe haly man: *Gregorius*
'Trayst of mede þat may noght faylle
Alleges mykell a mans trauaylle'.
þe thridde thinge es in tribulacioun *iij. De passione Cristi*
To think ay on Crystes passioun
þat he tholed for mans trespase.
Whaso thinkes how harde it was—
First how he had many sare buffet,
And sithen naked with scourges bette

De Misericordia

þat his body ran al on blode, fo. 48ra
And sithen naylled was on þe rode,
And þareon he dyed and yhelde þe gast,
And al tholed he for our luf mast—
So harde payne had neuer man
Als Cryst for vs suffred þan,
Ne harder payne myght neuer be,
For he spake þis worde of grete pyte
Thurgh Ieremye þe prophete: *Ieremias*
'Yhe men', he sayde, 'þat passes bi þe strete
Habyde a whyle ar þat yhe ga
And bihalde my payne and my wa,

7797 ne] *om.* ELPS 7798 þis] his W 7799 oft] *after* þam P 7800 bittir] *adds* bote E, *adds* þ`o´f P er] er full L 7801 bitter] *after* body S þe] *om.* L 7802 To] Vnto L 7806 Gregor] gegor S þe] þat L *sidenote om.* PS 7809 thinge] *om.* SW *sidenote*: iijus. W iij.] *om.* LS, iijus. P Cristi] domini nostri Ihesu Cristi E, Ihesu Cristi S 7814 sithen] *adds* was R 7815 þat] And PS on] of ELW 7816 on] apon L 7818 tholed he] *trs.* P 7819 man] nane S 7821 neuer] *adds* nane L 7822 worde] wordes L grete] *om.* P 7823 þe] *int.* P, his awn R *sidenote*: *om.* L, Ieronimus PS 7824 men] all R he sayde] *om.* L sayde] says W þe] *om.* W 7825 Habyde] Haabehaldes L þat] *om.* LRW yhe] ȝe hyns R

If euer was any sorow or pyne
So harde and bittir als es myne.'
Mynde of þis suld do vs grete
And make our angres to vs swete.
  Nathinge to vs here may be better,
Na noght may make our angres swetter,
Als I fynde wryten in Haly Writte
Ensaumple þar men may rede it,
How þe childer of Iraell
þat Moyses ledde, Goddis profyte leele,
Come til a water þat þai soght,
Bot drynk þareof ne myght þai noght,
For þe water was bitter to fele.
Bot aftirward God payed þam wele;
He bad Moyses lay þareinne a tre,
And al þe water suld swete be.
Moyses did als Godde hym sayde,
And it was swete þar þe tre was layde.
þe bitter water, als I halde,
þe angres of þis werlde es called;
þe tree þat made it swete sone
Es þe croyce on whilk Godd was done.
  Wharefore whaso in hert has mynde
What payne þat Cryst had for mankynde
On þe croyce, als was his wille,
Hym suld think here nane angre ille.
For it ne es payne, ne aduersyte,
Ne angre þat in þis werlde may be
þat ne þe mynde of Goddis passyoun
Suld make it swete thurgh deuocioun.

7827 was] war LW, *after* sorow P   sorow] sour W   7829 Mynde] þe mynde L do] gerr L, make S   7830 angres to] anger vnto L   7831 to . . . be] *trs. phrs.* R here] *om.* L   7832 noght] *om.* PW, þat R   angres] anger L   7834 men may] *trs.* R rede] fynde L   7836 *sidenote*: Moyses exemplum E, Moyses W   7838 ne] *om.* PRW 7842 suld swete] *trs.* LP   7843 hym] *om.* L   7844 þar] whare L, þer as W 7845 water] wasse L   7846 þe] *om.* E   angres] anger L   7848 whilk] *om.* L 7849 Whare-] þare- LW   whaso] he þat L   in] in hys L   7850 payne] paynes ES þat] *om.* LS   7851 On] Opon R   7853 ne es] es L, es na S   payne] anger L 7855 ne] *om.* LS   þe] *om.* P   Goddis] cristes P

De Misericordia

þe ferthe thinge es to think in thoght fo. 48rb
When we er in anger broght
What godes þat angre wynne may iiij. *De vtilitate*
Til him þat mekely suffirs it ay. *tribulacionum*
First angre proues Goddis knyght
To loke how hardy he es and wight;
A knyght may noght his strength fele
Til he in stoure be proued wele.
For Saynt Paul says, als I fynde can, *Paulus*
þat Pacience mast proues a man.
And als þe aungell spak þarby
And sayde þis worde vnto Thoby:
'For þou paied Godde, it bihoued
þat þi fondynge had þe proued.'
Angre, þogh it be greef to sight,
It clenses þe saul and mase it bright—
Right als fyre mas golde fyne,
And als þe fyle dose þe iren to shyne,
And als þe flaylle þe corne dinges
Out of þe caffe þat on it hynges,
Als Saynt Gregor telles and says *Gregorius*
In a boke þat es mykell to prayse
þat angres bene medycynes leele
þe grete sekenes of synnes to hele.
For als þe boke openly shewes vs
þare we may fynde wryten þus,
þat 'Sekenes þe saul sobre maas'
þat synne oftsythe couerd haas.
þarefore says þus Saynt Gregor, *Gregorius*
'þou suld noght think hard þarfore
þat þou feles here malady

7859 angre] angers R *sidenote*: iiij^{us}. W iiij.] *om.* LS, iiij`us´. (later) P -cionum] -cionis EP 7860 him] þam R mekely] mekill P it] *om.* LP, þam R 7861 angre] wyth a. L, angres R proues Goddis] God p. hys L 7864 in stoure] iuster R be proued] *trs.* P 7869 it] þe S 7870 had] at had R 7871 Angre] And L þogh] yf ELS greef to] grevous vnto L 7872 bright] lyght E 7873 als] als þe E 7874 dose] gerres L, makes S to] *om.* L 7875 als] *om.* W 7876 on it] *trs.* E 7877 Gregor] gegore R 7879 -cynes] -cyne P 7880 þe] To PW synnes] synne ELS 7882 may fynde] *trs.* W wryten] openly P 7884 couerd haas] coueryng takes W 7885 þus] *om.* L *sidenote om.* LW 7886 suld] sall S

Withouten þe on þi body,
If þou be heled clene withinne
Of allekyn sekenes of synne'.
  Also thurgh tribulacioun
Men wynnes of blisse þe coroun,
Iacobus For Saynt Iame says þat blissed es he
þat tholes fandynge and aduersyte,
Als þe gode knyght þat in stour takes
And endures many harde strakes.
Forthy þe heghe coroun of blisse,
When he es proued, sal be hisse.

Donum Consilij De Misericordia
Fiat voluntas tua etc.

fo. 48va þise four thinges þat I haf talde
We suld in our hertes falde
And think on þam nyght and day
In alle angres þat greue vs may,
For nathinge vs may comfort mare
þan mynde of þam when we er in care.
v[^{m}]. opus est remittere iniuriam þe fift braunche es of þe tree of Mercy
To forgif alle wranges hally.
Gregorius Forwhy Saynt Gregor says þus,
þat he þat gyues his almus
To nedefull men þat pouerly lifs
And wranges done him noght forgifs,
Bot haldes rancour in his thoght,
His almusdede auaylles him noght.
For Godde payse noght þe gift of þe hande,
While rancour es in þe hert dwelland;
Godde weghes þe gift on [þ]is manere
Aftir þe wille es of þe gifere,

7891 thurgh] of L 7893 þat] *om.* L *sidenote om.* W 7894 fandynge] fandynges ?LW 7895 knyght] *om.* W in] in þe P 7896 harde] sare R 7897 Forthy] Forwhy R 7899 þat] als P 7900 suld] *adds* þam R falde] halde EPS 7901 on] vpon R 7902 greue vs] grevous L vs] *om.* P 7903 vs may] *trs.* P, may S (cf. vs *after* comfort L) 7904 of] on P 7905 es] *om.* LSRW *sidenote*: *om.* L, *as in-column heading* R, v^{us}. opus W v^{m} . . . . est] *om.* R *v^{m}.] v. A iniuriam] iniurias R 7906 To] Es to LSRW 7907 Forwhy] *om.* L *sidenote om.* LW 7910 done] *adds* to R 7911 haldes] *adds* ay R 7912 -dede] -dedes L 7915 weghes] whethes W þe] hys L *þis] his A 7916 es] *om.* LW

Als Godde says in þe godspelle
On þis wyse, als I sal yhow telle:
'If þat yhe wil noght forgif
Ilkane othir whyle yhe here lif,
þe Fader of heuen ne wil noght
Forgif yhow þat yhe wrange haf wroght.'
Forthy methink he dose ful ille
þat othir here forgif noght wille,
For agayne himself als oft he prays
Als he þe Pater Noster says.
þar we pray 'Godde, forgif vs sone,
Als we do þam þat vs has mys done'.
If we forgif noght, þan say we þus
And biddes þat Godde noght forgif vs.
  þe sext braunche es to haf compassioun *vj[^{m}]. opus est compati hijs qui sunt in tribulacionibus*
Of þam þat er in tribulacioun,
Or in any angre of hert,
Or in synne þat þe saul may smert.
For we er als lyms of a body,
Ilkane suld fele othir malady
And alle othir angres and waa,
And haf rewthe in hert, whareso þai ga.
Thurgh kynde a lym suld fele and bere

Donum Consilij De Misericordia
Fiat voluntas tua etc.

þe + 'sekenes' þat anothir may dere, fo. 48vb
Als says Saynt Paul, 'Wha has sekenes, *Paulus*
And I noght seke als he es'?
And Saynt Gregor also says *Gregorius*
In a boke he made in his days
þat euer þe mare a man es parfyte
þe mare he suffres angre and dispyte.

7917 *sidenote*: Euangelium S 7919 yhe] we S 7920 Ilkane] *adds* till R yhe] we S here] *om.* L 7921 ne] *om.* L, þe P, he S 7923 Forthy] þerfore P, For R 7924 here] *om.* L noght] ne PRW 7926 þe] hys LS 7928 vs has] *trs.* EL, vs S mys done] *trs.* P 7931 *sidenote*: vj^{us}. W *vj^{m}.] vj. A tribulacionibus] tribulacione P 7932 er] er here R 7935 als] all LP 7938 þai] we L, þe P 7940 þe] þat W *sekenes] angre 'sekenes' A, angre RW anothir may] *trs.* S, myght anothir R 7941 Paul] Austyn L *sidenote*: Augustinus L, *om.* W 7943 also] al'so' he P *sidenote om.* W 7944 boke] *add* þat LSRW, 'þat' P 7946 angre] angers LPSW

vij[^{m}]. opus est orare pro inimicis et peccatoribus

þe seuent braunche es to pray
For our enemys nyght and day
And for men þat in synne lyse
þat God gif þam grace to ryse,
Als Godde himself commandes vs
In þe godspell þare he says þus:
'Prayes for þam with gode wille
þat yhow harme dose, loude or stille.
þan sal yhe be Goddis sones right
And his heyres in heuen bright.'
Whaso dose noght þus I halde
Goddis sone sal noght be called,
And þai þat er noght Goddis sonnes
Getes na parte þar Godde wonnes
Of his herytage þat falles
Till þam þat he his sones calles.
þise er þe braunches of Mercy
þat bene þe seuen Werkes Gastly
þat springes fra Mercy on þe right syde
And amange gode men spredes wyde.

De vij^{tem}. Operibus Misericordie Corporalibus

On þe left syde springe othir seuen
þat er þe Bodily Werkes to neuen.
Ane es hungry and thristy to fede
With mete and drynk þat has nede.
Anothir es ay, when nede ware,
To clethe þam þat er naked and bare.
þe thridde es to frest þam for Goddis sake
þat has grete nede of frest to take
And of þe dette to gif respyte
And þam forgif þat may noght quyte.
þe ferthe es, als men vndirstandes,
To visyte þat liggen in Goddis bandes.

7947 to] for to R *sidenote*: *om.* P, vij. W vij^{m} . . . est] *om.* R *vij^{m}.] vij. A et] et pro L, *om.* R 7948 For] For all R 7949–50 *trs. couplet* P 7952 þare] whare L 7953 with] *adds* a L 7954 dose] *add* outhir RW 7955 sones] sonn L 7956 his] *om.* L 7957 þus] þis L 7958 sone] sons R sal] sal he E 7962 sones] sonne L 7966 spredes] sprynges P 7967 On] In P othir] *om.* R *sidenote*: *om.* L, *as in-column heading* R corporalibus] spiritualibus E 7968 þe] þir L neuen] heuen W 7969 hungry] hunger PR thristy] thrist P 7972 and bare] ere P 7973 to] *om.* P 7974 grete] *om.* L 7977 es] *om.* R 7978 visyte] *add* þam EP þat liggen] þe lyggand L

þe fift es pouer men to herber
And pouer pilgrimes þat walkes fer.
þe sext es, als in boke es funden,
To visite þam þat er in prisoun bunden.

De Misericordia

þe seuent es to biry þe dede. fo. 49ra
þise seuen Werkes stand mykell in stede.
þe sex of þam er of þe gospell,
Als men may here þis clerkes telle;
Bot þe seuent Werke of Mercy
Ordayned þe haly man Thoby.
First we suld fede þe hungry *j.[m]. opus est pascere esurientes et potare scitientes*
And gif a drynk vnto þe thrysty.
So biddes Haly Writte vs do
In many stedes þat accordes þarto.
First gifs Thoby swilk a rede *Toby*
And says, 'þou sal ete þi brede
With þe nedefull þat pouerly gase
þat defaut of mete and drynk has'.
And þus says Salamon þe wyse: *Salamon*
'If þou se any of þine enmyse
Haf defaute and hungre grete,
For Goddes luf gif þou þam mete;
If him thrist, lette for na swynke
For Goddis luf to gif hym drynke'.
Also in þe gospelle men may lere
How Godde says on þis manere: *Dominus in euangelio*
'When þou mas feste þus saltou do:
Calle feble and blynde and croked þarto;
þan saltow be talde blissed tyte,
For þai may noght it þe quyte.

7981 es] *om.* S in] in þe W 7982 bunden] funden L 7985 þe[1]] *om.* L sex] sext S er of] ordande E 7987 werke] werkes P 7989 we suld] suld men L *sidenote*: j. opus W j[m] . . . est] *om.* R esurientes] esurientem EL scitientes] sicientem E 7990 vnto] to ELPRW 7991 vs] vs to P 7993 *sidenote*: Tobias S, *om.* W 7995 nedefull] pore L pouerly] nedefull L 7996 *line om.* S 7997 *sidenote*: *om.* W E *adds* Si esurierit inimicus tuus ciba eum 8000 gif þou] *trs.* R þou þam] hym PW, þou hym R 8001–2 *couplet om.* L 8001 lette] *adds* noght E *sidenote*: Si inimicus scitierit potum da illi E 8002 to] *om.* PR hym] *add* a PSR 8003 lere] here R 8004 *sidenote*: Euangelium ES, *om.* LPW 8005 feste] festes L 8006 croked] halte L 8007 be talde] *adds* for L, in blis be P, be called R 8008 þe] *om.* S

Bot Godde sal yhelde þe on his wyse
When alle men sal at domesday ryse.'
Þis es agayne þe riche men right
Þat mas grete outrage in sight
For pompe and pryde of þe werlde to se
And of þe pouer has na pyte.
Bot þam aght haue grete drede alle
Þat it suld swa with þam bifalle
Als with þe riche glotoun bifelle
Of whilk Godde spekes in þe godspelle,
Þat alle his lyf in delyces ledde
And with delicious metes hym fedde
And lete þe lazer of pouer state
For hungre perisshe at his yhate.
Bot when þai bathe thurgh dede gun passe,

De Misericordia

fol. 49rb Þe chaunce of þe dyce chaunged was.
For þe lazer was borne vp euen
With aungels to þe blisse of heuen,
And þe riche man was biryed in helle,
Als wryten es in þe godspelle,
Þat nede had of a drope of watir
Þar he brynned, neuer thinge hatter.
For if al þe water of þe see myght rynne
Opon his tunge oboun his chynne,
Al þat water myght noght him kele;
So grete hete gan he þare fele
Of brynnand fyre þat lastes ay
Þat nanekyns thinge slecken may.

8009 Godde] he L yhelde] quyte L his] þis LPS 8010 at] on L 8011 þis] þat L þe] *om.* LS men] men full L 8015 þam] *om.* S, þen W aght] *adds* to L, *adds* hom W *sidenote*: Euangelio (-gelium LS, *ends* L) Homo quidam erat diues qui induebatur purpura et bysso (*adds* etc. *and ends* S) et epulabat splendide cotidie Et erat quidam mendicus nomine Lazarus qui iacebat ad ianuam diuitis vlceribus plenus cupiens saturari de micis que cadebant de mensa diuitis et nemo illi dabat ES, de diuite ⟨.⟩'gone W 8016 with] in P bi-] *om.* EPS 8017 bi-] *om.* PW 8018 whilk] wham R þe] his R 8019 delyces] delytes EP, delite W 8020 metes] mete RW 8022 perisshe] perrisede be P 8024 chaunce] chaunge E, chaunche LR 8030 he] *om.* LS 8031 water] wate E of] in ELS 8032 oboun] opon R 8033 noght him] *trs.* ELR 8035 Of] For L 8036 nanekyns] na LS slecken] sloken ELPSR

þarefore it es gode, als methink,
To fede þe pouer with mete and drynk,
For þat may men fra helle lette
And make þam þe blisse of heuen gette,
Als men in þe gospelle here may
How Godde sal þus at þe grete dome say,
'Comes, yhe blissed, alle bidene,
þat my fader childer has bene
Into his kyngedome with me
þar ioye and blisse sal euermare be.
For when I hunger and threst hadde,
With mete and drynk yhe made me gladde.
Wharefore þe pouer er my menyhe;
þat yhe þam didde yhe didde to me'.
Anothir Bodily Werk es tolde, *ij[^{m}]. opus est vestire nudos*
þat es to couer þe naked fra colde.
For we suld of our clathes gieue
To þam þat colde mast may greue,
And also gif þam þat nede has
Hose and shone þat barfote gas.
So fynde we wryten of Thoby *Toby*
þat taght his sone þus specially;
'þe naked', he sayde, 'þou honour
With þi robes and þam sokour'.
And Isaye says, 'þou sal take kepe *Isaye*
Of þe naked and þam worshepe'.
Saynt Petir þat was and es so haly
Thurgh swilk a noble Werke of Mercy
Raysed a womman þat ight Dorcas
Fra dede to lyue, þat dede was.
For sho helped pouer þat was helpeles,

8040 heuen] *add* to ELS 8041 here] may (*over eras.*) here P 8042 þus] vs (*canc.* ?) þus E, *om.* LSW 8047 and] or L 8049 Wharefore] -fore *int. later* P, Forwhy R Wharefore . . . pouer] For all pore men L 8050 þam didde] dydd to þaime L 8051 es] is þis P tolde] cald R *sidenote*: Vestire nudos (*as in-column heading*) R, ij^{us}. opus W *ij^{m}.] ij. A vestire] vestigare? L 8052 to] *om.* LS fra] for LPR 8055 þat] *adds* maste L 8056 and] or R shone] sone L 8057 *sidenote*: Toby] Thobyas exemplum E, Tobias PS 8058 þus] so P 8061 *sidenote*: Ysaye] Ys' A, Isayas exemplum E, Isaias LPW 8062 Of] On LP 8063 and es] *om.* L es] lys? R *sidenote*: Petrus exemplum E, Petrus SW 8064 swilk] whilk W noble] *om.* ES 8066 Fra dede to] Vnto L 8067 helped] *add* þe LP

Donum Consilij De Misericordia
Fiat voluntas tua etc.

fol. 49va Als Haly Writte beres wittenes.
Anothir ensaumple fynde I can
Of Martyne þat cledde þe pouer man,
Of whase werke Godde was payed,
Als I tolde bifore and sayde.
Bot þe clath þat gyuen es
To þe pouer man þat es clatheles
A grete menynge to hym may be,
Ay when þe pouer þareon may se,
To pray for hym, þat he mede haue
þat þe clathe on hym vouched saue.
iij[m]. opus est mutuare indigentibus et remittere debitum soluere non valentibus
þe thridde braunche es to frest and len
To þam þat nede has þat er trew men,
And if þai may noght þe dette pay,
To forgif it þam, whaso may.
For almus es noght anely to deele,
Bot it es almus to frest þe leele
Sympilly for Goddis sake,
Withouten any oker to take;
And for Goddis luf þe dette forgieue
To þam þat er at grete myschief;
And to wham þat þai er in dette broght
To pay for þam þar þai may noght,
Als Godde commanded in þe Alde Lawe.
þar he sayd þus, whoso wil knawe,
'If þi brothir in pouert be broght,
Agayne hym þou ne sal noght
Make þine herte harde to stande,
Ne fra hym withdrawe þi hande;

8070 Martyne] Saynt Martyn L *sidenote*: Martinus exemplum (*om.* S) ES 8071 whase] þat W was] *add* wele LS 8072 I] I haue LR 8074 man, es] men, er P 8075 A grete] Ay-lastand L hym] þaim W 8077 he] he þe E 8078 clathe] clathes E 8079 braunche] werk W *sidenote*: *om.* L, iij. opus W *iij.[m]] iij. A iij . . . est] *om.* R (*as in-column heading*) est] *om.* S 8080 þat[2]] and L þat . . . men] and trewe men bene ES 8082 it] *om.* LR 8088 grete] *om.* LR, any P 8089 wham] þaim EL þai] *om.* LS 8090 þar] whare L 8091 -manded] -mandes LW 8092 þar] Whare S 8093 pouert] dett L 8094 ne] *om.* PS 8095 þine] þe W

Bot þou sal worshepe pouer men
And whatso þam nedes þam len'.
For Godde in þe godspell þat we rede
Biddes yhow frest þam þat has nede,
Withouten hope of werldely wynnyng
To haue ouer þe dette for þe frestyng.
And Godde þat yheldes al gode dede
Sal yhelde yhow þarefore yhour mede.
þis es agayne þis okerers
þat pouer men oft greues and deres;
When þai þam frest, þai do outrage
For þai take for þe frest auauntage
In siluer or seruys or trauaylle
Or in othir thinge þat may auaylle.
Bot Godde biddes yhou for þe pouer bihoue

Donum Consilij De Misericordia
Fiat voluntas tua etc.

Frest þam þat nede has for his luf, fol. 49vb
And Godde sal yhelde yhou with vsure
For al þat yhe do to þe pouer.
And if yhe may persayue or knawe
þat þe pouer þat yhou dette awe
May noght þe paye of þe dette make,
Yhe sal forgif it for Goddes sake.
For þus says Godde, ful of myght,
In þe godspell, als wryten es right:
'If yhe forgif noght ilkane othir,
Sen ilkane es othir brothir,
Godde yhou forgif wil noght
þat yhe haf agayne him wroght.'
Of þis ensaumple es to vndirstand *Exemplum Euangelium*
þat Godde shewed of þe ille seruand,
To wham his lorde forgyuen hadde

8098 þam[2]] *om.* S 8099 þat] als P *sidenote*: Euangelium ES 8101 -outen hope] *trs.* E werldely] any L 8103 dede] dedes L 8104 yhelde yhow] *trs.* P mede] medes L 8105 þis[1]] þat L þis[2]] þe P okerers] okernes R 8106 oft] *om.* L 8108 þe] *om.* P 8111 Bot] For L 8114 For] *om.* S to] vnto ES, for W 8115 or] and W 8116 yhou] þe L 8117 þe[1]] *om.* L 8118 it] *om.* W 8119 For] Forwhy R 8120 *sidenote*: Euangelium ES 8125 *sidenote*: *om.* PW 8126 þat] *corr. from* þe A Godde] *om.* W of] to LS *sidenote*: *om.* LPSW

Alle his dette and made hym gladde.
Bot for þat seruaunt wald noght lette
To greue anothir þat aght hym dette
And wald noght forgif hym sone,
Als his lorde to hym had done,
He come bifore his lorde agayne
And was done to distresce and payne,
Als his lorde commanded and badde
Til he al his dette yholden hadde.
So sal Godde do to þam thurgh skille
Þat wil noght forgif with gode wille.

iiij[m]. opus est visitare infirm⟨os⟩

 Þe ferthe braunche es to visite þe seke;
Þis Werke our mede mast may eke,
For þis es a werke þat Godde may plese,
To comfort þam þat er at malese,
And wele mare to our mede auaylles
Þan dose fastyng or othir trauaylles.
For men may fynde yhete in a boke,
In *Vitis patrum*, whaso wil loke,
Þat an hermyte of grete deuocioun
Asked swilk a manere of questyoun
At ane of þe haly faders fre
Þat war wyse and with Godde priue,
Whethir his lyf war mare to prayse
Þat ilk woke fasted sex dayse
And þarewith trauaylled with al his myght,
Or his lyf þat seke men serues right,
And whethir ware of bettir lifynge;

De Misericordia

fol. 50ra Þis was þe hermetes askynge.
Þe gode man answerd and sayd þus,
Als þe boke openly shewes vs,

8127 for-] *om.* P 8128 Alle] All haall R 8129 for] *om.* E 8132 to hym had] hadd hym L, had to hym P 8136 he] *after* dette P al] *after* dette L, *om.* P 8139 braunche] werk W *sidenote*: iiij. opus W iiij[m].] iiij. A iiij[m] . . . est] *om.* R (*as in-column heading*) 8140 þis] þat W 8141 þis] hit W þis es] þat P may] *adds* maste L 8143 to] *om.* P 8144 or] and W 8145 fynde yhete] *trs.* R yhete] it L *sidenote*: In Vitas Patrum ES 8146 Vitis] Vitas EL 8147 *sidenote*: Exemplum E 8152 fasted sex] fastes foure E 8153–4 *couplet trs.* P 8153 -with[1]] -to P -lled] -lles P, -land W 8154 serues] serued LRW 8157 þe] þis P sayd] says E 8158 þe boke] bokes L shewes] *adds* tyll L 8160 men] *om.* W

þat he suld haue mare mede bi skille
þat serues seke men with gode wille
And helpes þam; he mare Godde payse
þan he þat fastes so many dayse.
  Swilk Werk of Mercy to bigynne
Es mykill worth to fordo synne,
For swilk a Werke es þareagayne
A grete remedy; þat es certayne.
For Iob says þus, 'þou þat hale es, *Iob*
þou sal vysyte þine awen lickenes',
þat es hym þat þou vnderstandes
Es seke and ligges in Goddis bandes.
He es like þe als þi brothir,
For he es a man als þou ert anothir.
So saltow lightly synne flee
Thurgh swilk a werke of Charyte,
For Godde sal þe fra synne kepe
For swilk a werke of Frenshepe.
And Saynt Iame says þus, als I wene, *Iacobus*
þat it es a religyoun clene
Byfore Godde to vysyte blethely
Seke men þat has grete malady.
  And to þat I wil telle als I can *Narracio*
A tale of a synnefull man
þat putted him a seruaunt to be
In a spitell biyhonde þe see
þe seke men to serue and tent
Thurgh grace þat Godde had him sent.
Opon a day wasshe hym felle
A seke mans fete þat was meselle.
Als he þam wesshe vppe and doun,
He had grete abhominacioun.
þarefore he had himself in despyte
And toke and drank þat water als-tyte;

8167 says] sayd R es] has E 8173 lightly synne] *trs.* LS 8177 And] Als ES *sidenote*: *om.* W 8178 religyoun] religiouse L 8181 I wil] *trs.* W *sidenote*: *om.* W 8183 him] *om.* P 8185 men] *adds* þair R 8186 grace] *om.* S sent] lente EP 8187 wasshe hym] *trs.* L, he wasche S, to wassh R felle] tofelle L, als hym felle S 8188 fete] *perhaps* fote? A 8189 þam wesshe] *trs.* S þam] hym W wesshe] wasshe R and] had E 8190 had] had a ELSR 8191 -self] *om.* ES 8192 þat] þe P als-] *om.* L

Agayne his hert he drank fast,
Bot he feled it at þe last
So swete likour, and sauory
Als it war ful of spycery.
þat was a token þat his trespase
And al his synne forgyuen was
Thurgh þat werke þat he wroght

De Misericordia

fol. 50rb For he hadde Mercy þat he had soght.
Also swilk Werke may men brynge
To parfytenes of haly lifynge.
For þe wyse man says, 'If þou be meke,
Groche noght to visyte þe seke,
For thurgh þat werk þou sal at þe last
In þe luf of Godde be rotefast'.
Thurgh þat werke men bydes grete mede
þat þai sal haue for þat gode dede;
þat es ioye and blisse endeles,
Als þe godspelle beres wittenes.
Narracio Men telles of a lauedy þat hight
Mary Torgan, þat lyued right
And was ane haly womman and wyf;
Scho turned hir lorde vnto gode lyf.
þai bathe left al þat þai hadde,
Als scho counsaylled hir lorde and badde,
And putted þam bathe, als men telles,
To serue seke men þat war meselles,
Thurgh whilk seruyse þat þai had soght
To parfyte lyf þai war bathe broght.
þare come a voyce til hir on þe nyght
And sayde to hir þise wordes right:
'þi lorde, þat has bene felaw with þe
To serue seke men, so meke wald be,

8193 Agayne] And agayne P fast] it faste LR 8198 forgyuen] forgeten P, *adds* hym R 8199 Thurgh] For W he] he had R 8200 had] *om.* L 8203 þe] *om.* W 8205 þe] *om.* L 8206 rote-] rotede P 8207 bydes] begges L 8208 þat[2]] þaire LW 8211 hight] lyght W *sidenote*: Torgayn W, *om.* S 8212 Togan] Torkan ELS, Torgayne PRW 8214 vnto] to LPRW 8219 seruyse] seruicez L þat] *om.* W 8220 war bathe] *trs.* LPR bathe] *om.* S 8221 on þe] opon a L 8222 þise] *om.* S

Sal be with þe þi felawe euen
In þe heghe kyngdom of heuen.'
Yhete grete ensaumple Godde gifs vs
In þe godspelle þat witteneses þus,
þat Cryst þe meselles touched bare
And of þair sekenes heled þai ware.
þarefore þe seruaunt ne suld noght
Think dedeyne ne shame in thoght
To visite and serue þe seke at hame
When þe Lorde of heuen did þe same.
He come fra heuen doun right
Into erthe thurgh his myght
In his awen seruaunt lickenes,
Als Saynt Paul beres wittenes,
To serue vs and vs hele withinne
þat war in grete sekenes of synne.
þe fift braunche of Mercy es
To herber pouer þat er herberles

v[m]. opus est hospitare pauperes

Donum Consilij De Misericordia
Fiat voluntas tua etc.

fol. 50va

And pouer pilgrymes þat about wendes
þat in þis werlde has fone frendes.
þis es a Werke þat Godde wele payse,
Als Haly Wrytte proues and says,
And many ensaumples may we fynde
þat suld our hertes to þat Werke bynde.
First of Abraham þat vouched saue
To herber alle þat herber wald haue.
In lickenes of pilgryms come aungels
þat he herbard, als þe boke telles.
þarefore þai hight him for certayne
þat Sarre his wyf þat was barayne

8225 be] *om.* S 8226 kyng-] kyn- W 8227 Godde gifs] gifs he P 8228 witteneses] witenes ELPSRW 8229 meselles] messell RW 8230 þai ware] þaim þare E 8231 ne] *om.* LP 8232 dedeyne] deyne P 8236 erthe] þe erthe L, erthde S 8237 In] And 'in' (*later?*) P awen] *om.* E 8238 Als] And E *sidenote*: Paulus PW 8239 vs[2]] *adds* to L 8241 braunche] werk W *sidenote*: Hospitare pauperes (*as in-column heading*) R, v. opus W *v[m].] v. A est] *om.* L, *add* misericordie ELS 8242 pouer] *adds* mene E, þe pore L, *om.* P 8244 fone] few RW 8247 -ples] -pele EPS we] men L, wele W 8250 To herber] þat harbard P

Suld conceyf a childe sone
For þat þat he hadde þam done.
  And Loth þat helde hospitalite
Herber þe pouer blethely wald he.
þare come in lickenes of pouer men
Aungels þat he myght noght kenne.
þarefore þe aungels þat to him come
Hym saued fra perille of Sodome.
For when þe cyte suld synk for synne,
þai badde he suld noght dwelle þarinne.
Paulus þarefore Saynt Paul says, 'I bidde þe
þat þou leue noght Hospytalyte,
Thurgh whilk men has God oft plesed
And aungels in stede of pouer men eesed'.
And þat es na ferly if swilk men
Resayf aungels þat þai noght ken,
For Godde þai herber þat mare es,
Als þe godspelle beres wittenes.
For Godde says þus til his menyhe,
'Whaso resayues yhow, resayues me';
Alle þat men dose to þe pouer sone,
Als Godde says, til hym es done.
[Gregorius] Exemplum   Of Saynt Gregor ensaumple we se,
þat was a man of grete pyte;
He resayued ay of coustom
Alle þe pouer men þat wald com
And himself, when he suld þam fede,
Wald þam watir to þair handes bede.
On a day he did his almus,
Resayued pouer men in his hous,
And when he wende haf gyuen right

8255 childe sone] sonne L 8260 he myght] myght þai L 8261 þe] þase L, *om.* S 8262 perille] þe p. EL, perills S 8263 þe] þat P 8264 þai] He L 8265 Saynt . . . says] *trs.* P *sidenote*: *om.* L 8267 men, God] *trs.* R God] *om.* L God oft] *trs.* SW 8268 eesed] sesede ELS 8270 Resayf] Resayued L aungels] *om.* P 8273 til] vnto L 8274 resayues[1,2]] resaued R yhow] you he L 8275 þat] *om.* E 8276 hym] hymself R 8276–7 *sidenote*: *om.* L *Gregorius] *om.* A, Exemplum Gregorius E Exemplum] Narracio S, *om.* W 8279 of] cost of E 8282 þair handes] handes and feet (*partly erased later*) R 8285 haf] he hadd L haf gyuen] to gif P

Donum Consilij De Misericordia
Fiat voluntas tua etc.

Water to wasshe til a pouer wight fol. 50vb
þat he sawe þare þat day,
Whyle he hym turned, he was away.
þe gode man þan awondred was
How he suld so away passe.
þe nyght after our Lorde Iesus
Appered to hym and sayde him þus,
'þou has oft resayued me wele
In my lyms, als I myght fele;
And þis day hastow after þi myght
In my persone resayued me right'.
 Swilk Werke thurgh right conscience
Halde I better þan Abstinence,
And mare mede þareof may cum;
Als I fynde in *Vitis Patrum*
A tale þat men suld noght ouerhippe
Of ane haly man in Egipt,
þat herberd ay in alle tymes
Passand men and pouer pilgrymes
In his hous and made þam gladde
And gaf þam swilk gode als he hadde.
On a day come a pouer pilgryme
þat he hadde herberd with hym
þat was of grete abstinence
And satte at þe mete in his presence.
He wald noght ete na drynke þat day
For noght þat þe gode man myght say.
þan sayde þe gode man to hym þus,
'Brothir, go we bathe to proue vs

8288 Whyle] When W hym turned] *trs.* P 8290 How] How þat L so] *om.* L 8291 þe] Ne R 8292 him[2]] *om.* LPR 8293 oft] full oft R 8294 my] alle my ELS als] þat LP myght] maght P 8299 mare] well mare R -of] *om.* W 8300 Vitis] vitas LS 8301 *sidenote*: Narracio E, Vitis patrum W 8302 man] woman W in] þat dwelled in S 8303 herberd] harber L alle] all hys L 8304 and pouer] þat were P 8305 þam] hym R 8306 And gaf þam] Of L gode] godes L 8307 pouer pilgryme] *trs.* P 8308 hadde] *adds* bene P herberd] *adds* before L hym] *adds* before P 8310 þe] *om.* LS 8314 proue] rone P

In þe yherde vnder yhone tre
þat growes fayre, als þou may se,
And pray we Godde þat þe tre in hast
Bowe to hym þat payes Godde mast'.
þai went forth and þat prayere made,
And als þai stode a whyle and bade,
þe tree boghed doun til hym þan
þat hadde resayued þe pouer man,
Bot it boghed noght to himward
þat thurgh abstynence lyfd harde.
So semes it þat Hospitalyte
Es mare þan Abstinence may be.
Many ma ensaumples has bene
Of Hospitalyte ful oft sene,

De Misericordia

fol. 51ra Bot I may noght so lang dwelle
Alle þa ensaumples now to telle.

vj[m.] opus est visitare incarceratos et eos consolari ac ipsos redimere

þe sext braunche es þat we `be´ boun
To visite þam þat er in prisoun
And to comfort þam nyght and day
And helpe þam out if þat we may.
For alle er we halden to do þus,
Petrus Als Saynt Petir commandes vs
þat says, 'Think ay on þam and mene
þat in prisoun bunden er sene,
Als þou war bunden with þam þarinne'
And wald be out, if þou myght wynne.
þat es to say, þou þam visyte
And þam comforte with grete delyte
þat lys in prisoun nyght and day
Bunden and may noght wynne away,

8315 yherde] garthe R vnder] vndernethe S yhone] ȝonde P, þe ȝhender W 8317 we] to R 8318 Bowe] Might bow R 8319 þat] þaire LSW prayere] prayers P 8321 til] vnto L 8322 hadde] he R 8323 to] vnto R 8324 thurgh] thughe R 8325 it] *int. later* P, *om.* S 8326 may be] to se L 8328 ful oft] þat oft haues bene L, full ofte es S 8330 þa] þe W -mples] -mpell S now] for LP, *om.* S 8331 braunche] werk W es] *om.* R be] *int. later* A *sidenote*: *om.* LS, *as in-column heading beginning* Visitare R, vj. opus W vj[m.]] vj. A 8334 þat] *om.* PRW we] þai E 8335 to] for to LR 8336 Als] And L commandes] biddes P *sidenote*: *om.* ELW 8337 ay] *om.* S 8340 if] and LS 8341 þam] may W 8343 lys] er L, es S 8344 wynne] wynd W

Als þou wald, if þou lay þare,
Men + comforte þe in þi care.
So dyd Thoby þat ay was boun [*Toby*]
To visite alle þat war in prisoun
And comforted þam als he couthe
With gode wordes of his mouthe.
Als Salamon says þus in a stede, *Salamon*
'Delyuer þam þat men ledes to dede',
Als Danyell somtyme right didde
þat was a gode prophete kidde
þat fra dede delyuerd Sussan;
And als Godde delyuerd þe womman
þat staned suld haf bene, forthy
þat sho was tane in avoutry,
Als þe lawe wald þat þan was,
Bot Godde made hir harmeles passe.
  Bot Godde did noght swa bi þat skille
þat men suld noght þe lawe fulfille
Of mysdoars þat hauntes synne
þat er funden gilty þareinne.
Bot thurgh þat dede he wald kenne
What þai suld be þat er domesmen,
And how þai suld þe lawe yheme
And how þai suld othir men deme.
  Wharefore Godde teches vs four thinges
þat on þat ensaumple hynges
þat ilka domesman suld wele tent
And kepe þat sittes in iugement.
  Ane es þat mykell may auaylle

De Misericordia

Gode auysement and gode counsaylle. fol. 51rb
For Iob says, 'In causes þat I noght knawe *Iob*

8345 if] and L *8346 comforte] comforted A, *over eras.* S *8347 *sidenote*: *om.* AS, Thobyas ELPW 8349 comforted] comforthe LSRW 8350 gode] godes L wordes] word W 8351 Als] And L þus] *om.* W *sidenote*: *om.* W 8352 men ledes] *trs.* W to] to þe P 8353 *sidenote*: Danyell ELS 8354 gode] nobyll R 8355 fra] fra þe LR delyuerd] liuerede P 8356 delyuerd] lyferde P 8360 passe] to passe LR 8361–2 *couplet trs.* R 8362 noght] *om.* L 8363 hauntes] hauntede P 8366 What] þat L 8367–8 *couplet trs.* E 8367 suld] sall PW lawe] laughes LS 8368 suld] sall PW suld . . . men] *trs. phrs.* R 8369 Whare-] þare- S 8370 þat] þe whilk R 8375 noght] moght L *sidenote*: *om.* LS

I sal mare bisily seke þe lawe';
þis may we vndirstand þareinne
þar sho was accused of synne.
Our Lorde þat al wist and wate
With his fynger in þe erthe wrate.
In þat wrytynge with fynger of hande,
Discrescion we sal vnderstande
And þarewith grete avysement,
For Godde gaf noght als-tyte iugement.
  þe secund es right entencioun
þat men suld haue with discrescioun,
For þai suld noght be fletchand
For na prayer ne gift in hande,
Ne for luf of man ne drede namely.
þat vndirstande we hereby
þat our Lorde Godde, mast of myght,
When he had wryten, stode vpright.
  þe thridde thing es gode lyf and clene
þat in þe domesman suld be sene.
For he þat demes and gifs sentence
Suld be man of gode conscience;
Elles may he in grete drede dwelle
Thurgh þe sentence of þe godspelle
þat says, 'Als yhe deme othir now
Swilk dome sal be gyuen to yhow'.
Paulus And Saynt Paul says on þis manere
Vnto þe wicked domesman here,
'In þat þat þou demes othir wrange,
þou dampnes þiself to paynes strange;
For þou dose þe thinge þat wrange semes,
Wharefore þou othir men oft demes'.
þarefore Godde sayde when he vp stode,
'He þat es clene of synne and gode
Cast at hir þe first stane

8376 mare] *om.* L bisily] besy PR 8378 þar] þat R of] of hir P 8380 erthe] ertde S 8382 sal] sulde LS 8383 þare-] all R 8385 *sidenote*: ij. E 8387 þai] þat ELS noght be] be neuer P fletchand] fletthand LS, flittande PW 8388 in] of P 8389 of man] *om.* L 8390 þat] For þat R 8391 mast of] *trs.* W 8393 thing] *om.* L lyf] *om.* R 8394 þe] *om.* L 8399 als . . . deme] \`als´ (*later*) þat þou demes P 8401 *sidenote*: *om.* LP 8402 þe] *om.* R -man] -men R 8406 Wharefore] Whare (*over eras.*) L 8407 þarefore] þare L

þat þus es in avoutry tane'.
And when þe Iewes him herd þus say,
For shame þai skulked alle away
Ilkane after othir sone,
For þai saw wryten þat þai had done.
þai thoght þam ar þai away gun passe
Mare synnefull þan þe womman was.
þe ferthe thinge suld in hert be.
þat es compassyoun and pyte

Donum Consilij De Misericordia
Fiat voluntas tua etc.

þat þe domesman þat deme can fol. 51va
Suld haue when he demes a man.
For he suld be mare merciable,
And thurgh Mercy mare fauorable
And haf pyte of mankynde amange
(So þat he do þe lawe na wrange),
þan be ouer-felle and fauourlesse
Thurgh reddure of Rightwysnes.
For Rightwysnes withouten Mercy
Es cruelte þat greues gretely,
And Mercy withouten Rightwisnes
Es halden foly and latches.
þarefore þai er togider ay,
And nouthir es fra othir away.
Bot somtyme, als proues Haly Wrytte,
þe tane es hidde, þe tothir shewes it.
Bot Mercy es oftner sene
þan Rightwisnes es, als I wene.
Saynt Iohan says with þe gilden mouth, *Iohannes cum ore aureo*
þat mykell of Haly Wrytte couthe,
þat better it es resounes to yhelde
At domesday, of yhouthe and elde,

8411 him herd] *trs.* LPS þus] *after* Iewes P 8412 skulked] schulkede P 8414 þat] whate ELPS 8415 þam] þan L, þanne (*over eras.*) S gun] con W 8416 Mare] þai warr mare L þe] þat L 8417 thinge] *adds* þat L 8419 þat²] þan (*?over eras.*) E 8424 he] *om.* E 8430 latches] latthenes L, lathli es P, latchnes S 8432 And nouthir] Another W away] way W 8434 it] tite E 8435 oftner] ofter LPSR 8436 es] *om.* LP 8437 *sidenote*: Ion W 8439 it] *om.* LS 8440 and] þan of L

To do Mercy þat sikerest es
þan to do reddure of Rightwysnes.
Iacobus And Saynt Iame says yhete openly
þat iugement withouten Mercy
Sal on hym þat day be gyuen sone
þat na Mercy here has done.
  þarefore our Lorde, God al-weldande,
When he had dresced him vp to stande,
He bowed eft to þe ertheward þan
And sone after delyuerd þe womman.
For þe domesman suld heldand be
Thurgh compassyoun and pyte
To þe man þat he suld deme,
With a grete drede to seme;
And als it war agaynes his wille,
He suld hym deme and þe lawe fulfille.
Forwhy if he deme and do wrange,
He sal be demed to paynes strange
At þe day of tremblynge and drede
When ilk man sal se his awen dede.
  Now se we it es a grete almus
To visite prisounes, als Godde biddes vs.
Forwhi hymself went to helle doun

Donum Consilij De Misericordia
Fiat voluntas tua etc.

fol. 51vb To delyuer out of þat prisoune
þe haly men þat hym lufd best
And broght þam vnto ioye and rest.
vij[m]. opus est sepelire mortuos þe seuent braunche and þe last namely
Es þe dede in erthe to biry.
For swilk werke, als says Haly Writte,
Was Thoby loued þat oft did it;

8441 þat] and R 8443 says yhete] *trs.* R openly] apertly W *sidenote*: *om.* LW 8445 be] *after* sal E 8447 our Lorde] *om.* L 8448 had] has W vp to] *trs.* E 8449 -ward] *om.* L 8450 þe] he þe ES 8451 suld heldand] *trs.* S 8453 To] Vnto LR þe man] þam R 8459 At] And R and] and of L 8460 awen] *om.* P 8461 we] ȝhe E es] *om.* S a] *om.* PR 8462 prisounes] prisoners R 8465 þe] þase L 8466 vnto] to EPW 8467 braunche] werk W *sidenote*: Sepelire mortuos *as in-column heading* R, *om.* LW *vij[m].] vij. A est] *om.* E 8468 to] for to R 8470 oft] *om.* L *sidenote*: Thoby E

He left his mete oft for þat dede,
To biry þe dede, when it was nede.
  And Godde loued þe Magdelayne
For þe oynement sho did ordayne
þat sho somtyme on hym had layde.
Godde wyst what þat tokened and sayde
þat sho did it in right mesure
In tokenynge of his sepulture.
And Ioseph asked Crystes body
And when it was graunted him frely,
He toke it of þe croyce doun
And biryed it with deuocioun.
  Men in olde tyme amange þam straue
For þaire sepulture þat þai wald haue,
For þai had rewarde, als wryten es,
To þair fadirs halynes.
þarefore þai wald after þair dede
Be biryed in þe same stede,
By þair faders þar þai lay;
þis maner in olde tyme vsed þai.
Wharefore Iacob sayde þus right *Iacob*
Til his sone þat Ioseph hight,
'In Egipt ne biry noght me
Bot by my fader; þare wald I be'.
  þarefore war gode when a man es dede
To lygge in a religious stede,
Amange gode men of relygioun
þat lifs in contemplacioun,
To haf parte of þair prayers
And of þair gode dedes als parteners.
Thurgh kynd ilk man in honest stede
Suld biry othir þat er dede.
We fynde in þe see a maner of fisshes

8473 Godde] *add* oft RW 8474 þe] *om.* L did] gerte ELP 8475 on hym] *om.* S 8476 þat] *om.* L tokened] betokened LR, takenyng was W 8478 tokenynge] tokyng R, taken W 8482 with] *adds* grete L 8485 es] it es L 8486 To] Vnto LR 8489 þar] whare LS 8490 vsed] haunted L 8491–4 *lines om.* W 8491 *sidenote*: *om.* LW, Iacob dixit filio suo Ioseph ELS, Iacobus P 8492 Til] Vntill R 8493 ne] *om.* P biry] bery þou LR, ber þer S 8495 es] wer P 8496 lygge] bery R in] hym in LSR 8499 prayers] preyere W 8500 gode] *om.* E als] *om.* E, be S -teners] -ceners LPS, -tenere W 8501 Thurgh] Thughe R 8503 þe] *om.* P

þat þe water thurgh kynde norisshes;
When a fisshe es dede and fordone,
þe tothir þam gaders togider sone
And beres it to þe ground of þe se,
Als in *Boke of Kynde of Bestes* fynde we.
And in þe erth of þe ⟨groun⟩d lays itte;

De Misericordia

fol. 52ra þair kynde kennes þam swilk a witte.
Yhete Iewes and Sarzynes wil so do,
For kynde and pite þam stirs þarto.
Wele mare suld kynde and pyte þam ken
þat thurgh right trouthe er Cristen men
To biry here þe dede bodys
þat with þe saulles vp sal ryse
At domesday and togider wende
To ioy and blisse withouten ende.
And þarefore whaso lufs leelly
His neghpur saull, he lufs his body;
þan suld he do hym at his dede-day
Alle þe kyndenes þat he may.
Now haf yhe herd þe Werkes of Mercy,
Bathe Bodily Werkes and Gastly;
Alle er þai werkes of grete almus
þat to grete mede may brynge vs.
De elimosina Bot forthy þat many er sene
Tyne þair almus, als I wene,
And many gode dedes þarto,
For þai do noght als þai suld do.
þarefore I wil shew yhou þe manere
How yhe suld do yhour almus here
þat mast suld pay Godde almyghty,
And þat I sal yhow shewe shortly.

8505 When] þat when L 8506 þe] þase L þam] þan SR togider] sammen P 8508 in] in a ERW boke of] *om.* L 8509 þe¹] *om.* W 8510 kennes] kend P 8511 so do] *trs.* R 8512 and] of P 8513 þam] þan W 8516 þe] *om.* E saulles] saule LPW 8517 wende] sal wende W 8523 þe] þe seuen L 8525 grete] *om.* L 8526 þat] And L 8527 þat . . . er] þer er many P *sidenote: om.* L, *as in-column heading* R 8528 Tyne] To tyne L þair] þan P 8530 For] Forthy L 8531 yhou] *om.* L 8534 I sal] *trs.* R yhow] *om.* L yhow shewe] *trs.* SW

Tria sunt consideranda in elimosina facienda: de quo, cui, et qualiter fieri debet

Whaso almusfull here wil be,
He sal take kepe of thinges thre:
Ane es, als þe boke shewes vs,
Of what he sal make his almus.
Anothir es to wham he sal it take;
þe thridde how he sal his almus make.

De quo debet fieri elimosina

First suld ilk man take kepe and se
Of what his almus here suld be.
For he suld make it of his awen
And noght of othir men⟨s⟩ gode knawen,
Bot of þat þat he myght leelly wynne
And noght of þat þat he wan with synne.
For þe almus þat es done here
Of þat þat es geten on ille manere,
Als of theft, rauyn, or othir wrang taking,
Okir, gilry, or wrange withhaldyng,
Noght auaylles ne to God pays
Bot wele mare greues him, als clerkes says.
For Haly Writte, als clerkes tas kepe,

De Misericordia

fol. 52rb

Says, 'þou sal noght of ox ne shepe
Vnto Godde make sacrafyce,
If þare be any wemme of vyce'.
For swilk offerand es vnconable
And vnto Godde abhomynable.
Yhete ouer þat says Haly Writte,
Als þis clerkes vndirstandes it,
þat he þat any sacrafyse mas
Of godes þat he fra pouer men tas
Dose als he þat with maystry and myght
Slaas þe sone in þe fader sight.

8535 *sidenote*: *om.* LW, Nota bene R consideranda in elimosina] *trs. phrs.* P facienda] *om.* P de . . . debet] *om.* S et] *om.* P 8536 of] to L, on RW 8537 als] howe ELS shewes] sais P 8538 he] we L (*and similarly to* 8540) 8539 es] *om.* L 8540 how] of what L, is how P his almus] it P 8541 *sidenote*: *om.* LSW debet fieri] *trs.* P 8543 suld] sall L it] *om.* E 8544 mens] *possibly* mene A? gode] godes L, *om.* RW 8545–6 *couplet om.* W 8545 myght] may L 8546 þat^{2}] *om.* EP 8547 þe] *om.* L, þat P 8548 þat^{2}] *om.* W 8549 of] *om.* P or] and P 8550 or] or other L 8551 ne to] nor noght L 8552 him] *om.* EL als] als þis L 8556 be any] *trs.* E wemme] venem S, wone R of] or ELS 8557 -and es] -andes er L vnconable] vnsemable W 8558 vnto] to EP 8560 it] tite E

Augustinus And Saynt Austyn þus spekes and says,
'Whatkyn gift es þis to prayse
Of þat þat ane taas with gladde sembland
þar anothir it tharnes gretande?'
Tharefore ilk man suld gode kepe take
Whareof he suld his almus make.
Cui debet fieri elimosina Anothir þat he suld take kepe to:
To wham he suld his almus do.
For Haly Writte says on þis manere,
'Loke to wham þou sal do gode here;
Do gode to gode'. þat suld be he
þat þou wenes wele þat gode be,
And noght to wicked þat wyckednes can
And take na kepe to þe synful man.
þat es to say, þou sal noght gif
To þam þat þou sees with syn lif,
For resoun of þair synne anely
þat þai vse, als herlotry.
Als som men dose þat oft dotes,
þat gifs to iogelours and herlotes
And to othir mynystrales
þat vses lesynges and vayne tales.
To þam men gifs for iapes makynge
(And elles men wald gif þam nathing),
And þat es synne þat worthy es payne
And spendynge of þe tyme in vayne.
Bot whaso haues pyte in hert
And compassion of þair pouert,
Or of þair wyues or of þair barnes
Or of fader or moder þat fode tharnes
And gifs þam oght for þat skille
Or to withdrawe þam fra ille,

8565 þus] *om.* L *sidenote*: *om.* LSW 8567 taas] says R 8568 tharnes] ȝhernes E 8571 þat] *om.* E *sidenote*: *om.* LW debet fieri] *trs.* P fieri] firi S 8574 *line om.* E sal do] dose P gode] almous L 8576 wele] *om.* L be] sulde be L 8577 to] to þe L 8580 þat] *om.* P with] in S 8581 anely] namely P 8582 þat . . . vse] For þai vse it L 8583 men] *om.* EL 8584 and] and to EPW 8586 vses] hauntes L 8588 men wald] walde 'þai' (*later*) P 8589 þat[2]] and P 8590 spendynge] spekyng R 8591 haues] hauntes L 8593 or[2]] and P 8594 Or] *om.* P of] of þair R or[2]] or of E, and R þat] þat þe L tharnes] ȝhernes E 8595 gifs] gif S 8596 fra] fra þe L

Donum Consilij De Misericordia
Fiat voluntas tua etc.

And noght by resoun of þair foly, fol. 52va
He dose wele, a[s] he þat es witty.
  Wharefore men suld almus bede
Vnto þe pouer man þat has nede,
And mare to þe verray pouer by skille—
þat er ay pouer of hert and wille;
þat has left al þat þai hadde
For þe luf of Godde, als he badde—
þan to þam þat er in pouert
Agayne þair wille and agayn þair hert.
  Bot always suld men blethely gif
To alle þat men sees pouerly lif;
And namely to pouer þat shameful bene
And to þam þat feble and alde er sene
And to alle þat nede has men suld do
Almus þat er of myght þarto.
And if þat men be halden þus
To do to strange pouer þair almus,
Men er halden to fader and moder
To helpe þam here bifore alle othir
And sustayne þam and þair lyf saue,
þat es to say if þai nede haue.
And swa teches kynde in alle landes
And Godde in þe godspell so commandes.
  Men redes, als es wryten right, *Exemplum*
Of a manere of foull of flight
þat fader and moder wil noght faylle
When þai for elde may noght trauaylle,
Bot fyndes þam þair sustinaunce
Of þat þai gete thurgh cheuissaunce;

*8598 as] and AEW 8600 Vnto] To W man] mene ES 8602 of] in ELS 8603 left] lost R 8604 *line om.* L als] all R 8605 er in] in hert haues L *repeats line* R 8606 Agayne[1]] And ageyne P agayn[2]] *om.* LR 8607 always] allwyse ER blethely] gladly L 8609 to] to þe L shame-] synne- E 8612 þat] men þat L 8614 strange pouer] *trs.* S pouer] pore men L 8615 Men er] Mare er þai L *sidenote*: Nota E 8616 here] *om.* LR 8620 so] so ⟨.⟩ei P, þus S 8621 *sidenote*: Exemplum parentum E, *om.* W 8622 of[2]] of a E foull] fowghe L, folegh S 8626 þai] þat þat LW thurgh] with W

þus do þai als þai thurgh kynde can.
Right so thurgh kynde suld ilka man
Helpe þair fader and moder in nede,
With + gode wille þam cleth and fede;
And whaso dose noght, hym I halde
Vnkynde. So may he right be called,
For he synnes agayne kynde euen
And agayne our Lorde Godde of heuen,
þat commaundes vs here to honoure
Fader and moder and þam sokour.
þarefore methink it es grete skille
þat he þat vnkyndely dose and ille
To fader and moder haf myschaunce

Donum Consilij De Misericordia
Fiat voluntas tua etc.

fol. 52vb Thurgh synne and þe fendes combraunce,
Als has oft fallen, bathe mare and lesse,
For swilk manere of vnkyndenes.
Qualiter debet fieri elimosina þe thridde men suld for saul-hele
Knaw hou men suld almus dele,
And þe manere of gifyng of it
Men þat gifs almus suld wit.
Four condicions men may rede
þat falles namely to almusdede.
Ane es þat he þat gifs almus here
Suld gif it with gode wille and gode chere.
Anothir es þat almus suld be done
To þe pouer hastyly and sone.
þe thridde: it suld be done largely
After þe gifar es myghty;
And þe ferth condicion es

*8630 gode] a gode AES 8631 hym] *om.* W 8632 right] *om.* L be] *om.* E 8633 For] And L synnes] semes L euen] full euen L 8634 our Lorde] *om.* L 8635 þat commaundes] þan comaundes he P commaundes] command R here] *om.* LR 8637 grete] gude P 8639 and] or EW haf] haue a L, sal ha W 8640 combraunce] encombrance R 8641 oft] *om.* E fallen bathe] *trs.* E bathe] *om.* LR 8643 *sidenote*: *om.* PW 8645–6 *couplet trs.* L 8645 And] *om.* L of[1]] and þe L 8646 suld] sall L 8647 men may] *trs.* R 8648 falles] *om.* E namely] a`ne´ly (*later*) P, anely S to] vnto L 8649 *sidenote*: iiij^{or}. sunt condiciones in elemosina facienda ELS 8650 gode[2]] *om.* PRW 8653 it] es itt E largely] hastily (*canc.*?) largely P

þat it suld be done with mekenes.
  First men suld do þair almus
With gladde chere, þe boke says þus.
For Godde tas kepe, als I vnderstande,
Mare to þe hert þan to þe hande.
Forwhy Saynt Gregor says openly *Gregorius*
þat our Lorde Godde almyghty
Taas na kepe how grete thinge
Men wil to þair offerand bringe,
Bot to þe hert he tase mast kepe
Of hym þat dose hym any worshepe.
  Of þat ensaumple telle I can *Exemplum Euangelium*
In þe godspell of þe pouer womman
þat of hir awen na mare had fre
Bot twa mytes of þat mone.
þat sho offred with gode wille
Vnto þe temple, als hir thoght skille.
Wharefore our Lorde þan sayd sone
þat þat pouer womman had mare done
Of þat offerand þat sho made þare
þan alle þe tothir þat had done mare.
For mare pays Godde somtyme here
Ane halpeny on þis manere
þat a pouer man gifs gladdely
For þe luf of Godde almyghty
þan a riche man gaf with hande

De Misericordia

Ane hundreth mark with hert grochand. fol. 53ra
  And þarefore says þe wyse man þus
In Haly Wrytte, als þe boke shewes vs:
'Make gode chiere', he says, 'while þou lifs
In alle þi giftes þat þou gifs.'

8656 suld] sall L 8657 do] gif P 8661 *sidenote*: *om.* W 8663 grete] grete a L 8664 to] vnto R 8667–8 *sidenote*: *om.* W Exemplum] *om.* S Euangelium] *om.* L, in euangelio S 8668 þe[2]] a R 8670 mytes] mynntes E 8672 Vnto] To PRW hir] scho L 8673 þan] *om.* S þan sayd] syade full L 8674 þat[2]] þe L 8675 þat[2]] *om.* LR 8676 þe tothir] þase other L, þe other W done] gyuen W 8678 on] done on E, of L 8681 þan] þan if L 8683 And] *om.* E 8684 shewes] says L, schewe S 8685 he says] *om.* LR 8686 þi] þe ELS þou] ȝe L

Paulus Hillarem datorem diligit Deus

For Godde lufs, als Saynt Paul says,
A blithe gifar and a curtays.
Bot it er som þat faylles nurture
þat er oft vilaynes vnto þe pouer,
For when þai any almus craue,
þai by it dere ar þai oght haue.
For vilaynesly þai þam reproue
Ar þai gif oght for Goddis luf;
þai calle þam faytours and trowans,
Theues, mychars, and lurdans,
So þat when þai sal haf oght
þair almus sal be ouerdere boght.
Swilk almusdedes with reproues
Our Lorde hates mare þan lufs.
þarefore þe wyse man of grete wytte
þusgates says in Haly Wrytte:
'To þe pouer helde þine ere
And to hym debonerly answere.'
  þe secund condicioun to rede
þat falles vnto almusdede
Es þat a man þat es myghty
Suld do his almus hastily.
For Salamon teches and says þus,
Als þe *Boke of Wisdom* shewes vs:
Salamon 'þou sal noght, if þou be of powere,
Say to þi frende on þis manere:
"Ga and com tomorne agayne,
And I sal gif þe for certayne",
When þou als-tyte gif hym may
Withouten any lengar delay.'
Salamon   In anothir stede þus says he:
'Lat noght þi gift taryed be
Fra pouer þat þou sees nede haue,

8687 lufs] *at head of 8688* L als] *om.* E *sidenote*: *om.* W 8688 blithe] blyther S 8689 it] ȝit PR faylles] wantes L 8690 oft] *om.* L vnto] to L þe] *om.* W 8692 oght] it S 8693 For] Full RW 8698 ouer-] *om.* L 8699 with] and P 8700 mare] wele mare R þan] þan he LS 8702 -gates] *om.* L 8703 To] Vnto LR pouer] *adds* man þou L, *adds* þou R ere] eyre E 8704 to] *om.* L debonerly] *add* þou LS, bonerly P 8705 *sidenote*: ij^{a}. condicio W 8707 Es þat] *trs.* L, *om.* R 8711 if] and LS of] on R *sidenote*: *om.* W 8712 þi] þe R 8716 lengar] large P 8717 anothir] a nouthir R *sidenote*: *om.* LSW 8719 Fra] Fra þe L

If þou þair lyues here wil saue.'
þat es to say, lat þam noght hone,
When þou may gif þam als sone.
þis es agayne riche men namely
þat lates pouer men ay on þam crye
þat of þair helpe has grete nede
And taryes þam lange ar þai spede.

De Misericordia

For so lange bihoues þam pray and craue, fol. 53rb
Ar þai may spede or oght haue,
So þat wen þai do þam oght
þan es þat dede ful dere boght.
  For Senek says on þis manere, *Seneca*
'Nathinge here es boght so dere
Als þat thinge þat men of gift tas
Thurgh grete prayere þat men mas'.
For men says commonly þis worde soght,
'He byes ouerdere þat askes oght'.
  þarefore suld ilk man here gode do
Als-tyte while he es of myght þarto.
Forwhy þus says þe wyse man
In Haly Writte þat þis clerkes can:
'Tyte do þiself gode for Goddis sake, *Sapiens*
If þou haue whareof to take,
And offir with þine awen handes
Vnto Godde worthy offerandes
Whyle þou lifs and may wele gange,
For þe dede sal noght tary lange.'
  And in anothir stede says he
On þis manere, als men may se:
'Do gode', he says, 'vnto þi frende
Byfore þi dede and þi lyues ende.'
þat es to þe saul, als I halde,

8720 lyues] lyfe R 8721 hone] hofe hone P, *corr. from* haue W 8723 namely] anely P 8724 lates] *adds* þe L ay] *om.* W 8731 *sidenote*: Seneke L 8732 here es] *trs.* PR 8735 worde] world R 8736 oght] oft LS 8738 Als-tyte] Sone L of] *om.* E 8740 þis] *om.* P can] fynde canne L 8741 þi-] þe- E gode] *om.* L *sidenote*: *om.* LW 8742 If] If þat R 8743 with] it wyth L 8744 Vnto] Vnto þi R 8745 wele] *om.* L 8746 sal] ne sall R 8749 he says] *om.* L vnto] to W 8751 þe] þi PR

þat bi skille þi frende es called,
To wham þou suld thurgh gode rede
Do ay gode bifore þi dede;
Or to þi frende þat es best to neuen,
þat es our Lorde Godde of heuen,
To wham þou suld do gode ay
Bifore þi dede here whyle þou may.
And almusdede do for his luf
To pouer men for þair byhoue,
For þat men dose to pouer mens vse
To Godde almyghty þat men dose.
  Wharefor almus þat a man gifs
Whyle he here in þis werld lifs
Sal mykell mare stand him in stede
þan þat þat gifn es aftir his dede,
Als þe lanterne þat borne es
Bifore a man in grete myrkenes
Wisses him bettir þe way to take

Donum Consilij De Misericordia
Fiat voluntas tua etc.

fol. 53va þan þe light borne bihynde his backe.
Paulus þarefore Saynt Paul biddes vs ay
Do gode in þis lyf whyle we may,
And while we haue þe tyme to tent
þat our Lorde Godde here has vs lent.
  When a riche man mas him boun
To com to a cyte or to a toun,
His forayers bifore sendes he
To take his inne þare he suld be.
Forayeres þat taas on þis wyse
Innes to riche men in Paradyse
Er þe almous þat þai gif
Whyle þai in þis werlde lif.

8753 thurgh] be L 8755 to[1]] vnto L 8758 þi] þe R 8764 In þis werlde whyles þat he lyfes L 8765 stand him] now stande P 8767 borne es] burnes R 8771 ay] say P *sidenote om.* LW 8772 þis] þi P we] þou P 8773 þe] *om.* L 8774 here] *om.* E here has vs] vs here has P has vs] *trs.* L lent] sente E 8775 When] When þat L 8776 to a[1]] a gode P 8777 forayers] messangers E bifore] *after* he P; *om.* W *sidenote*: Nota E 8778 inne] innes R þare] whare L he] *om.* E 8779 Forayeres] *adds* or messangers E 8780 in] of L 8782 þai] þai may L

For almus þat after a man es dede
For hym es done, hym standes in stede
Als dose þe seruaunt þat bifore gaas
þat ouerlate his lordes innes taas,
So þat his lorde somtyme es
Ille herberd thurgh his latchesce.
  þe thridde condicioun þat suld be
In almusdede es þis to se:
To gif to pouer þat pouerly gaas
Largely aftir a man haas.
For þe wyse man says þus in a boke,
Als clerkes may se þat wil it loke:
'Gif God', he says, 'with hert fre *Sapiens*
After þat he has gyuen þe.'
And Thoby says þus: 'Aftir þi myght *Toby*
Be mercyable til ilka wight;
If þou haf mykell and es myghty,
Gif of þi godes here largely.
If þou haf lytell and knawes skille,
Gif curtaysely and with gode wille.'
Forwhy ilk man, als clerkes wate,
Suld gif blethely aftir þair state
And after þat Godde has vouched saue
To gif to ilk man þat þai haue.
  We rede of a ryche kynge þarby
þat a pouer man asked a peny.
þe kynge answerd þat so littell thinge
Ne felle noght be gift of a kynge.
And of Kynge Alisaundre rede we
þat gaf his seruaunt a cyte,

Donum Consilij De Misericordia
Fiat voluntas tua etc.

And þe seruaunt gun it forsake, fol. 53vb

8784 For . . . standes] Es done for hym sall stand L hym] itt E 8785 þe] a E 8788 Ille] Ful ill R latchesce] latnes P, lathenes S 8789 *sidenote*: iij. condicio W 8791 to[2]] þe ELPR 8792 a] þat a LR 8793 a] *om.* PW 8794 Als] þat L clerkes] *om.* W it] *om.* LR 8795 he says] *om.* L *sidenote om.* W 8796 þat] *om.* W þe] to þe L 8797 *sidenote*: *om.* P 8800 of] *repeats* W 8802 and] *om.* P gode] a gode L 8804 þair] his P 8807 *sidenote*: Exemplum S 8808 asked] *add* hym ES, hym asked L 8809 littell] *add* a EL 8810 gift] gyuene ES, þe gyft LRW 8812 his] a L 8813 gun] con W

For him thoght þe gift ouergrete to take.
þan sayde þe kynge, 'I take na kepe
What falles to þe, bot to my worshepe'.
  þe ferthe condycion þat we rede
Es to do here almousdede
With grete Mekenes and Deuocioun
And with a gode entencioun.
For whaso dose it suld be meke
So þat he na Vayneglory seke,
Ne to þe pouer be dispitous
To wham he suld gif his almous,
Ne haf presumpcioun þarby,
If he be in synne dedely,
þat he es worthy for þat dede
To haue of Godde special mede.
  It er some men þat almus dose
Appertly for men suld þam rose.
Sapiens Bot þe wyse man says on þis manere,
þat men suld with a gode chere
Putte þair almous, aftir þai can,
In þe bosom of þe pouer man.
Gregorius For Saynt Gregor says þarto,
'It es inoghe to þe to do
Almus, so þat he se þat dede
Of wham þou thinkes to haf mede'.
In euangelio þarefore Godde says in þe godspell þus,
'When þou sal do þine almus,
Lat noght þi left hand wyte na fele
What þ[i] right hand dose; þan dose þow wele
So þat þine almusdede done be
In hidels þar na man may it se.
And þe Fader of heuen heghe

8814 -grete] -mykell L 8816 What] þat L 8817 *sidenote*: iiij^{us}. E 8823 be] *adds* noȝt P dispitous] to spytus W 8824 suld] sall L gif] do (*over eras.*) P 8826 If] If þat LR 8828 of Godde] þe good R special] specyalye E, a speciall P 8829 It] ȝit R men] *om.* L 8831 man] *om.* W *sidenote om.* LPW 8835 For] Fore þe E, Foryi R *sidenote om.* W 8836 inoghe] noght L 8838 haf] *add* þi EPR, *adds* of L 8839 *sidenote om.* W; Euangelium ES, Dominus in euangelio L *add* Tu autem facientem (-te S) elemosinam nesciat sinistra (*adds* tua S) quid faciat dextera tua (*the rest om.* S) vt sit elemosina tua in abscondito et pater tuus qui videt in abscondito reddit tibi ES *8842 þi] þe AL 8844 þar] þat P it] *om.* L, *int.* P

þat al þat hidde es sees with eghe
Sal yhelde it þe, als þou sal fele'.
þus sayd Godde, als clerkes wate wele.
  þat es, when þou sal almus do,
Loke Vayneglory be noght þarto.
For Vayneglory þat es fayllande
Es vnderstanded bi þe left hande.
Bot when þou gifs almus in sight,

De Misericordia

Loke þat þine entencioun be right; fol. 54ra
þat es, to vndirstande shortly,
By þe right hande of þe body.
Bot I say noght þat ne men may
Do gode dedes, bath nyght and day,
Appertly in ilk mans sight
Gode ensaumple to gif right,
Wharethurgh Godde, als he es worthy,
May be þe mare loued þarby.
  For Godde says þus in þe godspelle *In euangelio*
þat we suld do our werkes smelle
Amange men þat þai þam fele,
Forþi þat Godde suld be loued wele.
And noght for loos of þe werlde þat wytes,
Als dose þis fals ipocrytes.
  þe gode seruaunt suld na shame haue
To serue his lorde, his menske to saue
Bifore men wharesoeuer he com
And in his seruyse to be ay bousom.
Forwhy God says þis worde þat byndes,
Als clerkes in þe godspell fyndes: *In euangelio*

8846 sees] may se LW 8847 it] *om.* RW als] þat L 8848 þus] þis W 8849–82 *lines om.* W 8850 Loke] *adds* þat L noght þar-] *trs.* E 8852 vnderstanded] -standene ER, -stand LPS 8854 þat] *om.* LS 8856 þe[2]] þi ELP 8857 ne] *om.* LS, no P ne men] *trs.* E 8858 bath] *om.* L, boȝe P 8860 to] for to R 8861 worthy] myghty R 8862 þe] *om.* L 8863 *sidenote*: *om.* LW, Euangelium ES 8864 suld] sall L do] gerre LS smelle] snelle P 8865 þat . . . þam] þai in þaim P þai] *adds* may L 8866 þat] *om.* P 8867 loos of þe] *om.* E þe] þis R þat] þe þat E 8868 þis] þe P 8869 *sidenote*: Cum ieiunatis nolite fieri sicut ypocrite tristes (Matt. 6: 16) E 8871 men whare-] whayme L wharesoeuer] euer whareso P 8872 in] to P to] *om.* EP 8873 worde] wordes PS 8874 *sidenote*: *om.* LW, Euangelium ES

'He þat shames', he says, 'with me
Bifore þe men þat may him se,
Me sal shame with him in his nede
Bifore aungels at þe day of drede.'
þis worde es agayne þam right
þat leues to do gode in sight
For drede þat men suld þam halde
Ipocrytes, and so be called.
Gregorius þarefore says Saynt Gregor right
þat he þat sal do gode in sight,
He sal his werkes so bigynne
þat his entent be right withinne.
  Ouer þat whaso wil almus do
To pouer men, þis falles þarto:
þat it be done wele on þat wyse
So þat þe pouer he noght dispyse,
Als þe prophete says on þis manere:
'Dispyse þou noght þine awen flesshe here.'
þat es þe pouer þat þou may se
þat thurgh shappe es like to þe;

De Misericordia

fol. 54rb And of þe same kynde, als þou sees now,
Of flesshe and blode of whilk ertow;
And of þe same matere and lickenes
Of whilk þou ert þe pouer man es.
  It bene som men þat er myghty
þat settes bi þe pouer ouerlightly.
How ille þai fare þay noght recke
And deynes noght with þam to speke;
And if þai speke, þai speke ouerthwert
Dispitously thurgh pryde of hert.
Of swilk men Godde es noght payde,
Bot Iobe did noght þus þat sayde

8876 þe] *om.* L may him] *trs.* P 8878 þe] *om.* S 8879 worde es] wordes er L 8880 leues] lufes R 8883 *sidenote om.* W 8885 werkes] werk? L 8888 þis] þat R 8890 þe] *om.* E he] be R 8891 *sidenote*: Propheta ELS 8892 þou] *om.* L 8894 es] *after* þat W to] vnto L, *om.* P 8895 als] þat ES 8896 and] of S of[2]] *om.* L, of þe P whilk] swilke ELR 8897 matere and] matere of R 8899 It] þit LR men] *om.* L 8902 noght] *om.* W 8905 swilk] whilk LP 8906 *sidenote*: Iob EP

He neuer dispysed, arely ne late,
Men þat war in pouer state,
Forþi þat he somtyme had nede.
Bot he wald þaim bathe clathe and fede.
Ane haly man of clene lyfyng,
Al-if he war grete lorde and kyng,
Of þe pouer him thoght na shame,
Als som lordes dose þat beres grete name—
þat grete almusdedes dose
On þair manere þat þai vse.
Bot always for þair pouert,
þai haf þaim in despyte of hert.
And if þai ware rightly meke
And na losengery wald seke,
þai suld luf mare þe company
Of gode men þat lifs here pouerly,
For þe luf of God þat þam couthe
Edyfye thurgh gode wordes of mouthe,
þan of many riche men of myght
þat er about þam day and nyght.
þar men may noght bot flateryng se
And couatyse and vanyte
þat mas þis lordes oft do wrange
Thurgh þair wicked counsaylles amange,
And mykell gode gers þam leue sone
þat warne þai ware, suld be done.
Also it er som men lifande
þat gifs oft almus with þair hande,
Bot to synne dedely es ay þair thoght;
þat almusdede sal saue þam noght.

Donum Consilij De Misericordia
Fiat voluntas tua etc.

For if þai dyed in þat state, fol. 54va

8908 in] ate E 8909 had] at had R 8913 him] he S 8914 lordes] *om.* L 8916 On] Of L, Opon R 8919 rightly] ryghtwysly L, riȝt P 8923 þam] þai ne L 8924 Edyfye] Myght edify L gode wordes] goddes worde L 8925 þan . . . men] Bitter þan þurgh any riche man L 8926 and] or L 8927 þar] Mare L 8928 and[2]] and grete S 8929 do] to do LR 8930 -saylles] -sayll LPRW 8931 gers] mas W þam] *om.* P 8932 þat . . . þai] And þai na L, þat nere þai W 8933 Also] Als P it] ȝit SR 8935 ay] all L 8936 saue] gayne P

þair almusdedes, als clerkes wate,
Might noght þam saue fra payne of helle
For þair synne þat þai in dwelle.
Swilk men may right lickened be
Til hym þat bigges an hous of tre,
þat on þe ta syde to bigge es boun
And ay on þe tothir syde drawes doun.
  þarefore Haly Wrytte þus says right,
'If þou wil paye Godde, mast of myght,
Haf first pyte and mercy
Of þine awen saulle principally'.
For he þat to hymself dose ille,
Til wham suld he be gode thurgh skille?
He may noght leelle to othir be
þat to hymseluen dose na lewete.
Augustinus And þarefore says Saynt Austyn þus,
'Whoso ordaynely dose almus,
He sal first withouten dyn
At his awen saul bygynne.
For he suld luf mare his saul in body
þan any othir man, saue Godde anely'.
  By skille may na man say þat he
Es ful of mercy and of pyte
Whase hert pyte may noght meke
To his moder þat es pouer and seke,
War he neuer so ful of mercy
þat he had done til othir many.
On þe same wyse, I ne hald him noght
Pitefull in hert and thoght
þat has na pite ne na mercy
Of his awen saul in his body,
When he wate what state it es inne,

8938 -dedes] -dede LP 8939 noght þam] *trs.* R saue] gayne P payne] þe payns EL, paynes S, þe payn R 8941 men] *om.* P right] wele L 8943 þat] And LP þe ta] a L to bigge] bygged L 8944 ay] *om.* P on] *om.* L drawes] es drawen L 8945 þus] *om.* L *sidenote*: Sacra scriptura ES 8946 mast of] all L 8948 Of] On RW principally] specialy L 8949 hym-] his P 8950 be] do ELS thurgh] be W 8953 *sidenote*: Agustinus P, *om.* W 8957 his] his aughen L, þe R in] of his R 8958 man] mans L, *om.* P saue] sa L anely] almyghty P 8960 of[2]] *om.* PSW 8961 may] ne may R meke] make meke L 8964 War] Whare ES 8965 ne] *om.* LPS 8966 in] in his P and] ne in R 8967 ne na] *trs.* E, ne RW 8968 awen] *om.* PW 8969 *sidenote*: Miserere anime tue placens Deo E

þat es seke thurgh dedely synne.
  Now haf I shewed yhou openly
þe vertu of þe tree of Mercy,
And specially þe degrees seuen,
And þe fourtene braunches þat spredes euen,
And þe fruyt þat comes of it,
Als es funden in Haly Wrytte.
  Of þe fruyt of þis tre to fele
Spekes Dauid in þe sauter wele,

Dauid

Donum Consilij De Misericordia
Fiat voluntas tua etc.

fol. 54vb

þar he þus says, 'Blissed es he
þat to þe pouer wil tent and se'.

Beatus qui intelligit super egenum et pauperem etc.

þat es to say, þat he byde noght
Til þat þe pouer wil aske him oght,
Bot gif hym tyte withouten askynge
First, ar he aske hym anythynge.
For þus says a prouerbe þat we haue,
'He byes ouerdere þat bihoues craue'.
For gode hert to gif has noght he
þat gifs noght ar ane askynge be.
  Bot he dose wele and noght ille
þat gifs þe pouer þat aske him wille.
Bot he dose bettir, to Goddis lykynge,
þat gifs þe pouer withouten askynge.
And by hym Dauyd þis worde toke,
Als es wryten in þe sauter boke
þat says, 'Blissed es he for þat dede
þat tentes to þe pouer þat has nede.
For him sal delyuer Godde rightwys
At þe ille day of his enemyse'.
þat es þe day of dome þat bi skille

Dauid Beatus qui intelligit super egenum et pauperem in die mala; liberabit eum Dominus

8972 þe[2]] *om.* R 8975 þe] þat P of] *om.* E 8978 in þe sauter] wounder L *sidenote*: *om.* W 8979 þus says] *trs.* R es] be W 8980 þe] *om.* P *sidenote*: Beatus] *adds* vir W pauperum] in gutter L etc.] *om.* ESW 8982 Til] When L wil] *om.* S 8983 tyte] *om.* W 8986 bihoues] oft behoues (*trs.* S) LS, bus oght P *sidenote*: Nota E 8987 has] ne has R 8988 ane] any PW 8990 aske him] *trs.* P 8992 withouten] *adds* any L 8993 *sidenote*: *om.* LP Dauid] *om.* W 8995 says] sayde LS es] be P 8997 him] he R 8998 þe] þat E

Til wicked men sal be ful ille,
þat dampned sal be, for þai had noght
þe Werkes of Mercy here right wroght.
  Wharefore þe domesman sal say
Ane hidous worde to þam þat day:
Ite maledicti in ignem eternum
'Yhe weryed wightes, fra me wende
Into þe fyre of helle þat has nane ende
To dwelle þareinne for euermare
With alle þe fendes þat sal dwelle þare.
Forwhy when I had hunger grete,
Yhe vouched saue on me na mete;
When me thristed, na drynk yhe me bedde;
When I was naked, yhe me noght cledde;
When I was seke, ye visite me noght;
To me in prisoun noght yhe soght;
And also when I herberles was,
Withouten herber yhe lete me passe.'
þan sal he reproue þam straytely
þat has noght done þe Werkes of Mercy,
And þarefore þai sal delyuerd be
To þair enemys þat þai sal se,
þat es to þe deuelles of helle

De Misericordia Donum Intellectus
De Luxuria

fol. 55ra Euermare with þam to dwelle.
  Fra wham þai þat pitefull bene
And þat tentes to þam þat pouer er sene
Sal be delyuerd þat day euen
And be broght to þe kyngdom of heuen,
Als our Lorde Godde almyghty
In þe godspell says appertly.
For he sal say þan to þam sone

9000 ful] *om.* W 9001 þat] þai L 9004 hidous] hodous R 9005 me] me ȝhe EL *sidenote om.* W Ite maledicti *only* L *add* qui preparatus est (*ends* S) dyabolo et angelis eius ES 9006 Into] To PRW þat has nane] wythouten L 9008 alle] *om.* L þe] *om.* E 9011 me] I LW yhe me] *trs.* E 9013 visite] vesed R *sidenote*: men (*in rubric, later*) P 9014 noght yhe] ȝe ne hafe P, *trs.* R, ȝhe ne W 9015 And] *om.* L when] *adds* þat L 9016 herber] *om.* L 9017 he] ȝe L 9018 þe] of E, þer P 9021 to] vnto LR deuelles] -uell L 9024 er] *om.* E, *int.* P 9025 þat] ate þat E day] *add* full LR

þat þe Werkes of Mercy here has done:
'Comes to me, yhe þat bene here
Mi Fader blissed childer dere,
And resayues þe kyngedome right
Of heuen þat to yhow es dight
Fra first tyme þat þe werld bigan,
When heuen and erthe was made and man.
For þat yhe did in my name
To þe pouere, to me yhe did þe same.'
  Godde sal þan do grete worshepe
Til al þat blissed felawshepe
And thank þam þan ful swetely
For þat þai didde þe Werkes of Mercy,
And he sal gif þam for þair godedede
þe lyf þat ay sal last to mede.
  þarefore says Godde þus, als I wene,
'Blissed er þai þat mercyfull bene,
For þai sal fully Mercy haue',
For þai helped pouer mens lyues to saue
Whiles þai lifd thurgh þair almus.
Blissed er alle þat haues done þus;
It es gode right þat Godde þam gif
þe lyf withouten ende to lif.
  And forþi þat þai had pyte
Of þam þat Goddis lyms suld be
And þam had comforted and sustend wele
In grete myschief þat þai gun fele,
It es skille, sen þai war stedfast,
þat he do þam mercy at þe last
And þat he delyuer þam of meschiefs
And of alle angres þat þam greues.
And so sal he do for þai er hisse,
For he sal gif þam þe coroun of blisse

Venite benedicti patris mei etc.

9030 þat] He þat S 9031 to] vnto L *sidenote*: *om.* SW patris mei etc.] *om.* L etc.] percipite regnum quod vos paratum est ab origine mundi E 9034 to] vnto R 9035 Fra] *add* þe ELSW tyme] *om.* L 9037 þat] þat þat L, -why þat R 9039 þan do] *trs.* S, *adds* full L 9043 gif þam] *om.* L þair] þat L 9044 þe] Haue þe L 9046 er] be P *sidenote*: Beati misericordes (L *ends*) quoniam (S *ends*) misericordiam consequentur ELS (Matt. 5: 7) 9050 alle] þaa L, all þaa S 9051 right] *om.* E 9053 And] *om.* R 9055 had] haues L 9056 gun] con W 9059 meschiefs] myschefe P

Printed and bound by CPI Group (UK) Ltd, Croydon, CR0 4YY